Virtual Traumascapes and Exploring the Roots of Dark Tourism

Maximiliano Korstanje
University of Palermo, Argentina

Babu George
Fort Hays State University, USA

A volume in the Advances in Hospitality, Tourism, and the Services Industry (AHTSI) Book Series

IGI Global
DISSEMINATOR OF KNOWLEDGE

Published in the United States of America by
IGI Global
Business Science Reference (an imprint of IGI Global)
701 E. Chocolate Avenue
Hershey PA, USA 17033
Tel: 717-533-8845
Fax: 717-533-8661
E-mail: cust@igi-global.com
Web site: http://www.igi-global.com

Library of Congress Cataloging-in-Publication Data

Names: Korstanje, Maximiliano, editors. | George, Babu, editors.
Title: Virtual traumascapes and exploring the roots of dark tourism / Maximiliano Korstanje and Babu George, editors.
Description: Hershey PA : Business Science Reference, [2018]
Identifiers: LCCN 2017009419| ISBN 9781522527503 (hardcover) | ISBN 9781522527510 (ebook)
Subjects: LCSH: Dark tourism.
Classification: LCC G155.A1 V55 2018 | DDC 306.4/819--dc23 LC record available at https://lccn.loc.gov/2017009419

This book is published in the IGI Global book series Advances in Hospitality, Tourism, and the Services Industry (AHTSI) (ISSN: 2475-6547; eISSN: 2475-6555)

British Cataloguing in Publication Data
A Cataloguing in Publication record for this book is available from the British Library.

Advances in Hospitality, Tourism, and the Services Industry (AHTSI) Book Series

ISSN:2475-6547
EISSN:2475-6555

MISSION

Globally, the hospitality, travel, tourism, and services industries generate a significant percentage of revenue and represent a large portion of the business world. Even in tough economic times, these industries thrive as individuals continue to spend on leisure and recreation activities as well as services.

The Advances in Hospitality, Tourism, and the Services Industry (AHTSI) book series offers diverse publications relating to the management, promotion, and profitability of the leisure, recreation, and services industries. Highlighting current research pertaining to various topics within the realm of hospitality, travel, tourism, and services management, the titles found within the AHTSI book series are pertinent to the research and professional needs of managers, business practitioners, researchers, and upper-level students studying in the field.

COVERAGE

- Casino Management
- Customer Service Issues
- Service Training
- Service Management
- Food and Beverage Management
- Service Design
- Tourism and the Environment
- Travel Agency Management
- Hotel Management
- Destination Marketing and Management

IGI Global is currently accepting manuscripts for publication within this series. To submit a proposal for a volume in this series, please contact our Acquisition Editors at Acquisitions@igi-global.com or visit: http://www.igi-global.com/publish/.

The Advances in Hospitality, Tourism, and the Services Industry (AHTSI) Book Series (ISSN 2475-6547) is published by IGI Global, 701 E. Chocolate Avenue, Hershey, PA 17033-1240, USA, www.igi-global.com. This series is composed of titles available for purchase individually; each title is edited to be contextually exclusive from any other title within the series. For pricing and ordering information please visit http://www.igi-global.com/book-series/advances-hospitality-tourism-services-industry/121014. Postmaster: Send all address changes to above address.

Titles in this Series

For a list of additional titles in this series, please visit:
http://www.igi-global.com/book-series/advances-hospitality-tourism-services-industry/121014

Tourism and Opportunities for Economic Development in Asia
Patricia Ordóñez de Pablos (University of Oviedo, Spain) and Zeyar Myo Aung (Ministry of Hotels and Tourism Myanmar)
Business Science Reference • ©2017 • 389pp • H/C (ISBN: 9781522520788) • US $205.00

Handbook of Research on Strategic Alliances and Value Co-Creation in the Service Industry
Shai Rozenes (Afeka Tel-Aviv Academic College of Engineering, Israel) and Yuval Cohen (Afeka Tel-Aviv Academic College of Engineerin, Israel)
Business Science Reference • ©2017 • 507pp • H/C (ISBN: 9781522520849) • US $235.00

Driving Tourism through Creative Destinations and Activities
Alžbeta Király'ová (University College of Business in Prague, Czech Republic)
Business Science Reference • ©2017 • 375pp • H/C (ISBN: 9781522520160) • US $200.00

Handbook of Research on Holistic Optimization Techniques in the Hospitality, Tourism, and Travel Industry
Pandian Vasant (Universiti Teknologi PETRONAS, Malaysia) and Kalaivanthan M. (Rasa Sayang Resort and Spa, Malaysia & Golden Sands Resort, Malaysia)
Business Science Reference • ©2017 • 515pp • H/C (ISBN: 9781522510543) • US $235.00

Opportunities and Challenges for Tourism and Hospitality in the BRIC Nations
Mohinder Chand Dhiman (Kurukshetra University, India)
Business Science Reference • ©2017 • 426pp • H/C (ISBN: 9781522507086) • US $205.00

Strategic Place Branding Methodologies and Theory for Tourist Attraction
Ahmet Bayraktar (Bozok University, Turkey) and Can Uslay (Rutgers University, USA)
Business Science Reference • ©2017 • 394pp • H/C (ISBN: 9781522505792) • US $205.00

Global Place Branding Campaigns across Cities, Regions, and Nations
Ahmet Bayraktar (Bozok University, Turkey) and Can Uslay (Rutgers University, USA)
Business Science Reference • ©2017 • 368pp • H/C (ISBN: 9781522505761) • US $205.00

For an enitre list of titles in this series, please visit:
http://www.igi-global.com/book-series/advances-hospitality-tourism-services-industry/121014

IGI Global
DISSEMINATOR OF KNOWLEDGE

701 East Chocolate Avenue, Hershey, PA 17033, USA
Tel: 717-533-8845 x100 • Fax: 717-533-8661
E-Mail: cust@igi-global.com • www.igi-global.com

Table of Contents

Detailed Table of Contents

The present chapter questions to what extent visitors in dark sites are really interested for heritage issues or understanding the roots of moral disasters as the specialized literature suggests or simply are in quest of pleasure-maximization. This text is based on a criticism of the book Heritage that hurts authored by Joy Sather-Wagstaff. Far from any emotionality, dark tourism represents an ideological mechanism to reinforce the supremacy of liberal cultural values which are enrooted in late-capitalism. As the previous backdrop, to what extent tourists visiting these sites emulate (living as victims) or produce a genuine empathy with suffering is the main question goes unnoticed for sociologists and anthropologists. This essay review, which explores the roots of emotions not only continues our previous research in regards to the rise of Thana-Capitalism.

The present chapter focuses on the role of museums as producer of dark myths, which means the cultural background that leads visitors to consume “other´s death”. Anthropologically speaking, museums are symbolic instrument that helps understanding traumatic events. For this reason, it is important to deepen the connection between tourism consumption and disasters. Over centuries, positivism trivialized mythology as a fictional story, or rumors proper of primitive cultures; rather, not only myths play a leading role in configuring culture, but also the borders between life and death. Here we propose an alternative fresh methodology to study dark tourism issues in the decades to come.

This chapter discusses construction of niche tourism in postmodernism. It aims to give a flavour on how the arguments are presented. Utilising death sites and Voluntourism, coupled with proliferation of Information and Communications Technology (ICT) as backdrop, this chapter sets to the layer of dark tourism as the revelation and contemplation, it bridges the nexus between visiting the death sites and extreme poverty areas, and hospitality features as core essence attributed to authentic experience. This chapter thus is an agreement of the previous studies which suggest authentic experience derived from cool authenticity and existential authenticity. It would emerge as not only the answer for searching authentic experiences but also most importantly it could extend the niche tourism formation and deepen Voluntourism conceptualisation. Findings of this study provide practitioners in the tourism and hospitality industries with clues to position death sites and Voluntourism as premium market offerings. Eventually, some directions for future study are discussed.

As Haiti lacks visitor attractions, the development of an authentic event programme is going to be an essential part of the on-going tourism strategy. Culturally rich events are part of the appeal of a destination and can be cost efficient to organise. Furthermore it is well documented that planned events have the ability to improve national pride in small developing countries. From our findings we have highlighted the fact that Voodoo has helped the Haitian people to maintain its true nature and culture and now offer economic development options to the destination. The development of voodoo events will enhance Haiti's tourism and provide opportunities for locals to embrace their cultural heritage and come to terms with their past. That said, unless the 'blind spots' of the destination are removed, there is no empirical evidence to confirm that tourism will bring prosperity to Haiti nor that voodoo can play a significant role in the country's tourism sector.

The current chapter delves into the methodologies as well as limitations of used method in dark tourism fields. As fieldworkers are familiar, sometimes interviewees not only are incognizant of their inner-world, but in other occasion, they simply do not say the truth to protect their own interests. Though in tourism and dark tourism fields, researchers are prone to administer questionnaires or interviews as the main methodological option, no less true is that results are far from being clear or have very problems to be organized in an all-encompassing model.

This paper argues the popular black spots of Turkey, which are really few, initially serve as a political instrument to construct and deepen the national identity. Gallipoli, Anıtkabir, National Park for Commander-in-chief, the deathbed of Ataturk, Ulucanlar Prison, and Sakarya Earthquake Museum are well-known black spots in Turkey which could be addressed to improve this argument. The discourse of sterile interior designs, introductory brochures, official web pages, digital presentation and the quantitative gap between domestic and foreign visitors are some proofs, supporting the claim. On the other side of the coin, however, the construction of realms of memory, belonging to the "others" is continuously is suspended and included in official ideology through normalization processes. Diyarbakır Prison, Madımak Hotel Aşkale are the discursive given "darker sites," exemplifying the counter-discursive black spots in this sense. So, it can be concluded that the initial function of few samples of dark tourism sites in Turkey is mainly political rather than being economic or cultural.

Although dark tourism attracts many scholars from different backgrounds, there is no consensus about its definition. Yet still, it is possible to classify the discussions revolving around the definition issue: The first group focuses on the descriptive side of dark tourism in terms of "sudden death and disaster," while a second group gives priority to the existential dimension of the dark touristic interest in terms of "never-ending death and disaster." However, fear appears as a surrounding component of both approaches. At that point, this study questions the relationship between the rise of dark touristic interest since the 1990s and the notion of governmentality of fear.

In this respect, the study attempts to make bridge between the existential context of dark tourism and its political dimension with the Foucauldian terms, especially by shedding light on dark tourism in terms of "biopower technology."

Taking cues from the surging popularity of thana-tourism, this paper argues that its prevalence echoes the end days of capitalism. The predominant forms of tourism in a society reflect the ethos of that society. What we once called 'mass tourism' reflected the spirit of classical capitalism; later, ecotourism and various other alternative forms of tourism reflected a critical turn in capitalism, often called the 'sympathetic capitalism'. These were incremental alternations, however. Thana-tourism is a qualitatively discontinuous form of tourism and its surge should thus correspond with a similarly discontinuous, radical, shift in capitalism. The authors present scholarly perspectives to bring home the view that thana-tourism might indeed be symptomatic of the end of capitalism

Simply put, tourism is about travel and its associated services. Yet, beyond its glittery appearance, at least sometimes, these services contain elements of domination and control of fellow humans, nature, and culture. Even innocent animals are not spared in the pursuit to making money. The extant literature on "dark tourism" barely addresses the darkness of tourist behavior derived from the nexus between human avarice and animal suffering. Sexual relations with animals has been documented for many centuries; yet, this exploitation as a touristic pursuit is relatively new. In this paper, conditions for the growth of this phenomenon and international regulatory responses are described and the structure and dynamics of the underground animal sex tourism industry are explored.

Preface

MACABRE DAYS OF THE DEATH: THE ONTOLOGY OF DARK TOURISM IN A VIRTUALIZED WORLD

It is tempting to say that dark tourism captivated the attention of scholars and academicians over the recent years (Lennon & Foley, 1999; Hartmann, 2014; Korstanje 2016). As Stone (2011) puts it, though the fascination for death seems not to be new, dark tourism certainly challenges the classic patterns of leisure consumption, inasmuch as we need to discuss furtherly new methodologies and epistemological borders for this complex issue. The interrogations behind the intentions of visitors to visit these types of sites are manifold, but two contrasting waves converge. While some voices emphasize on dark tourism as an anthropological attempt to domesticate death, in secularized societies, others more radical studies alert on the morbid nature of dark consumption. Though such a debate remains open to date, no less true is that the introduction of technology, allowed consumers to reach spaces or sites otherwise would be inexpugnable for them. As a result of this, virtual dark tourism, which turns a trend where visitors enter in macabre places that are inaccessible by the majority of tourists. In this respect, the present book gathers 10 chapters which are oriented not only to provide with a theoretical understanding of virtuality and dark tourism but also the intersection with applied-research. The content was organized into four distinguishable sections. The first signals to the conceptual notions of dark tourism whereas the second is reserved to a much deeper methodological approaches that would be of importance for fieldworkers and policy makers. The third section encompasses two pungent chapters where author deciphers the political nature of dark tourism. Ultimately, last section centers on the power of globalization and modern hyper consumption not only in molding culture but also virtualizing individual behaviour.

As the previous backdrop, the first chapter explores to what extent the phenomenon is previously determined by rationality or emotionality. In sharp contrast with the book *Heritage that hurts*, which was authored by Sather Wagstaff, this chapter offers a new alternative diagnosis that helps reconstructing a new epistemological borders for dark heritage.

The second chapter discusses the morbid element in the formation of museums. There is a *dark mythology* which is enrooted at museums to be learned by the generations to come. The main thesis here is that the theatralization of death corresponds with traditional dispositiffs to hold memory in community.

In the third chapter, it is hypothesized on the needs of constructing a niche tourism in view of the rise of new ICT as fertile background. Dark tourism should be comprehended as a contemplation and as a revelation, which mediates between the figure of death and the quest for authenticity. Complementarily, the chapter fourth introduces the use of qualitative methods in order for giving fresh evidence how dark tourism offers a fertile ground to improve the daily lifestyles of locals. Though polemically blamed of commoditizing culture, dark tourism, instead, accelerates the post disaster recovery process. One of the main interesting points seems to be the rise of a neologism: *post-disaster destination* which merits to be discussed.

The fifth chapter highlights the main strengths and limitations of dark tourism research as well as the next challenges the discipline will face in the years to come. One of the main problems found in dark tourism research seems to be an exaggerated confidence in what tourists say. Such a methodological position leads to many conceptual problems to understand sometimes interviewees lie or simply are unaware of their real reasons to visit dark tourism sites.

The sixth chapter, rather, contemplates the political nature of Dark tourism in Turkey. Unlike earlier mentioned chapters, these reflections on the role played by politicians in fulfilling the allegory or the memory to remind. In consonance with this, seventh chapter painstakingly complements how the sociological dimension of fear resonates in public opinion through the articulation and thematization of dark-destinations. There is evidently a clear connection between the ontology of death consumption and the socio political environment of fear, which paradoxically explains why others` death becomes so attractive for us.

The eighth chapter succinctly describes the rise of a new stage of capitalism, where others` suffering has situated as the main commodity to exchange. If the postmodern sociologists claimed of risk society, the 9/11 inaugurated not only a new cosmology, but also a new version of capitalism, which combines the narcissism of consumption with the spectacle of disasters.

The ninth chapter, which is not limited to dark tourism in the strict sense of the word, devotes attention and efforts to discuss a problem that goes unnoticed for tourism industry, the darkness of animal sexual tourism. This raises a more than interesting question, what is the connection of sexual tourism and dark tourism? The chapter conceives convincingly like dark tourism where the others suffering is instrumentalised to maximize tourists` pleasure, in animal sexual tourism the same applies. What this reminds is that in the global capitalism, the alterity is commoditized to obtain individual gratifications. To sum up, this pungent chapter will lead reader to reconsider the concept of bestiality as well as opening the doors towards the understanding of sadism.

More intriguing, tenth chapter revisits the definition of Thana Capitalism through the articulation of slumming and poverty. Authors who take part in this discussion understand that dark tourism and slumming are homologous terms associated by the rise of a new class -named as death seekers- where the suffering of others leads to maximize the pleasure of global audience which is not limited to tourists to a broader spectorship.

We, the editors, wish to express our particular gratitude not only to IGI Global, a leading world publisher that accepted our proposition, and to all contributors as well as the involving reviewers who devoted their time in discussing critically the selected chapters.

Maximiliano Korstanje
University of Palermo, Argentina

Babu George
Fort Hays State University, USA

REFERENCES

Hartmann, R. (2014). Dark tourism, Thana-tourism, and dissonance in heritage tourism management: New directions in contemporary tourism research. *Journal of Heritage Tourism*, *9*(2), 166–182. doi:10.1080/1743873X.2013.807266

Korstanje, M. E. (2016). *The Rise of Thana-Capitalism and Tourism*. Abingdon, UK: Routledge.

Lennon, J. J., & Foley, M. (1999). Interpretation of the unimaginable: The US Holocaust Memorial Museum, Washington, DC, and dark tourism. *Journal of Travel Research*, *38*(1), 46–50. doi:10.1177/004728759903800110

Sather-Wagstaff, J. (2016). *Heritage that hurts: Tourists in the memoryscapes of September 11*. Abingdon, UK: Routledge.

Stone, P. R. (2011). Dark tourism: Towards a new post-disciplinary research agenda. *International Journal of Tourism Anthropology*, *1*(3-4), 318–332. doi:10.1504/IJTA.2011.043713

Chapter 1
Emotionality, Reason, and Dark Tourism:
Discussions Around the Sense of Death

Maximiliano Emanuel Korstanje
University of Palermo, Argentina

Babu P. George
Fort Hays State University, USA

ABSTRACT

The present chapter questions to what extent visitors in dark sites are really interested for heritage issues or understanding the roots of moral disasters as the specialized literature suggests or simply are in quest of pleasure-maximization. This text is based on a criticism of the book Heritage that hurts authored by Joy Sather-Wagstaff. Far from any emotionality, dark tourism represents an ideological mechanism to reinforce the supremacy of liberal cultural values which are enrooted in late-capitalism. As the previous backdrop, to what extent tourists visiting these sites emulate (living as victims) or produce a genuine empathy with suffering is the main question goes unnoticed for sociologists and anthropologists. This essay review, which explores the roots of emotions not only continues our previous research in regards to the rise of Thana-Capitalism.

INTRODUCTION

Not surprisingly, in recent years dark tourism has captivated the attention of the greater part of academy as well as scholars interested in these new emergent segments worldwide. This activity includes visits to cemeteries, abandoned prisons,

DOI: 10.4018/978-1-5225-2750-3.ch001

museums, or spaces hit by natural disasters or terrorism. In the wide spectrum of these products, death is the common-place (Stone & Sharpley, 2008; Stone, 2011; Cohen, 2011; Biran, Poria & Oren, 2011; Podoshen, 2013; Korstanje & George, 2015). Though originally dark tourism research permeated in United Kingdom, sooner this expanded to others nations which have suffered a traumatic past as slavery, genocides, or natural disasters (Hartmann, 2014). Following Phillip Stone (2012), dark tourism serves for visitors to prefigure their own death, gazing through the others' death. The potentiality of dark tourism not only accelerating recovery processes in post disaster context, in which case community reinforces its resiliency to adversity, but by recycling obliterated cities into a more profitable spectacle has been widely studied by specialists from different angles (Seaton 1996, 1999; Foley & Lennon, 2000; Strange & Kempa, 2003; Korstanje & Ivanov, 2012). The polemic is given by the controversy it wakes up. While some voices claim that dark tourism commoditizes human's suffering to levels which may very well lead towards sadism (Howie, 2010; Verma & Jain, 2013; Heuermann & Chhabra, 2014; Korstanje, 2016), others, rather, emphasizes on the quest of more real experiences to interpret the own life or being-in-this-world is one of the main interests of these tourists (Miles, 2002; Ryan & Kohli, 2006; Wilson, 2008; Stone, 2013; White & Frew, 2013).

As the previous backdrop, to what extent tourists visiting these sites emulate (living as victims) or produce a genuine empathy with suffering is the main question goes unnoticed for sociologists and anthropologists. This essay review, which explores the roots of emotions not only continues our previous research in regards to the rise of Thana-Capitalism (see further Korstanje 2016), but discusses the chief argument of Sather Wagstaff (2011) who considered Dark Tourism as an instrument to forge an universal solidarity across cultures and nations. In her book *Heritage that hurts* she holds the thesis that visitors are receptive building empathy with victims, which leads to engage emotionally their biographies with tragedy. In sharp opposition to this belief, we argue that dark tourism reinforces the sacred- aura of first world consumers commoditizing others' pain as a reminder of their own supremacy. Far from being an instrument of mutual understanding, dark tourism disciplines emotions to impose an atmosphere of social Darwinism where winners take all.

The following questions were drawing our reflection: what are looking visitors of these site for? is death consuming the end of emotions? to what extent, may emotions be rechanneled through heritage or consumption as specialized literature suggests? are emotions conducive to altruism or individualism? are people aware of their inner emotions?

Preliminary Comments

At a first look, for some reason, fieldworks in tourism appeal to open and ended questionnaires as the main instrument to gather information. The same applies, in many cases, to dark tourism research. To our end, this represents a serious limitation in order for academicians to expand their current understanding of dark tourists' motivations. Let's explain the following anecdote happened, in one of my ethnographies. During my fieldwork in Republica de Cromañòn (a night Club situated in Buenos Aires Argentina) a young person called my attention saying he has vital information about what happened that tragic night where 194 died in a fire. Though his interview, which was recorded by more than 3 hours, rested on shaky foundations, it served me to guide my conceptual framework to adjust my original hypothesis. This suggests not only sometimes people lie to feel more important than they really are, or even to impress "the other" but also the validity of true should be reconsidered (Korstanje, 2016). As Ernest Sosa puts it, each person, as long as its biography, draws not only its own interpretation of the World, but also a cthird group of theorists dognitive structure to judge what is an ethical behaviour. In this respect, he cites some examples that validate the idea that two types of knowledges coexist, *judgmental and functional*. While the former is based on an individual or collective affirmation which is aimed at undermining dissonance, the latter escapes to the control of human desire (Sosa, 2015).

What are Emotions?

Emotions should be understood as a derivative conscious experience defined by a mental activity and disposition between the poles of pleasure and displeasure (Cabanac, 2002). Though modern science has devoted considerable attention to dualism, where emotions precede cognition or beliefs, both are inextricably intertwined. While organisms are in danger a derived arousal activate bodily tension to determine an experience. This is the reason why specialists agree that emotions are associated to behaviour (Barret & Russell, 2015). Eva Illouz (2008) has called attention to the rise of therapy as the symbolic space where Self confronts its emotional world, in so far, culture and politics cede to the advance of a Narcissist personality. However, less radical as Lasch or Thrilling, she considers the rise and consolidation of therapy situates as a sign of ego confirmation, which is a symbol of individualism. By the introduction of psychoanalytic therapy, the scholar adds, introspection is embraced as a necessary closure with external world (forging a narcissist spirit). As an inevitable result of this, the self abandons to the public sphere to conform "a private agency", indifferent to "the other". This begs a more than interesting point, are emotions be disciplined to create a specific personality?

Though specialized literature suggests that emotions are very hard to grasp, no less true is that under some conditions, emotions revitalizes the tendons of motivation which may be externally manipulated. Despite the current fragmentation respecting to outcomes and advance, in view of the curiosity of many different disciplines, three key elements have been found:

1. Feelings are subjective internationalization or representational figures each people make of their inner-emotions.
2. Moods, signal to state of affect which takes much time than emotions, and can be determine the life of a person.
3. Affect, refers to the disposition to describe a situational experience processed by a specific organism.

In the same vein, psychology and neuro-psychiatry envisaged that emotions are functionally adaptive instrument developed by evolution, to protect organism from external hazards. Basic emotions, which were widely studied and classified by Paul Ekman, consists in anger, disgust, fear, happiness, sadness, and surprise (Ekman, 1992; Ekman & Davidson, 1994). Some sociologists declared that emotions can be contextually drawn by the combination of sanctions and awards. J. Turner (2007) argues that people often face situations with expectation how the event should happen. Depending on stimuli or sanctions, the self evaluates some or other course of actions. Turner develops a conceptual model based on four types of action-reaction, as assertive-anger, aversion-fear, satisfaction-happiness and disappointment-sadness (or depression).

Interesting research suggests the biological nature of emotions, but taking into consideration reactions can be culturally formatted. Let us setting the case of fear, which corresponds with a basic emotion but remains subject to cultural background. First and foremost, while some ethnicities are afraid of Gods others as secularized societies developed a great aversion to death. Even, at the time, men are educated to repress their emotions, transforming fear in anger, woman are socialized to express overtly their concerns. The concept of risk, as well as the manipulations of fear, are sometimes constructed by cultural factors, which are conducive to human organization (Douglas & Wildavsky, 1983; Dake 1992; Zinn 2008; Skoll & Korstanje 2013). This raises a more than pungent question, are emotions politically used or manipulated to gain further legitimacy?

The specialized literature suggests that though feelings or moods can be intentionally influenced by external environment, emotions are not. As adaptive dispositions which vary to situation and person (for example, before a Lyon all we feel an extreme fear but while some of us confront the danger, others are paralyzed or even escape towards a safer place), emotions cannot be externally designed simply because they follow situational nature. What would be more than interesting to discuss is why fears (as well as other emotions) can be selected according to a cultural matrix. In fact, this evinces how developed-societies have fleshed out similar dispositions and reactions in regards to the same threat, for example, terrorism, while in other underdeveloped nations terrorism does not worry to authorities.

However, not all voices go in the same direction. Faucher and Tappolet (2006) hold conveniently while some emotions as Fear, seems to be a biological nature, others as shame are entwined to cognition serving to evaluate future horizons in order for the better decision to be made. In this token, Karen Jones (2006) suggests that emotions, beyond what a whole portion of philosophers preclude, contribute substantially to rationality in three salient ways,

- Improving access to our reasons which is used for potential deliberations.
- Facilitating planning action.
- Improving efficiency to take the appropriate action.

In their book, *Valuing Emotions,* M. Stocker and E Hegeman question whether emotions are significant for the lives of peoples and the reasons behind philosophy glosses over emotionality as the touchstone of live. Authors understand that there is a syndrome of Mr. Spook from Vulcan, one of the protagonist of *Star Trek* and assistant of Commander who were emotionless. His strongholds rested not only in the incapacity to feel like humans, but he belongs to a hyper-rational race that escaped from human's vices. Undoubtedly, as Stocker and Hegeman said, a discourse of this caliber resonated in the whole portion of social imaginary in western societies, but what should be discussed is that far from being real, humans need from emotions to get a healthy life. Quite aside from this, while we agree rationality does not work without an emotional background, no less true is that lay-people are not familiar with their inner-life, which means they often are unable to explain their basic emotions as love, fear, or hate.

So too, one can be angry about something without recognizing what one is angry about. I might recognize that I am angry but fail to see that I am angry at you, or at you for insulting me. I might be angry without realizing it. It might, instead, misidentify my emotional state at anxiety or boredom. Or I might mistakenly think that I am in no emotional or affective state at all (Stocker & Hageman 1996: 22)

Although a lot of studies focused on Cartesian dualism as the epicenter for the division between rationality and emotions, following the above noted discussion, it is tempting to remind this dualism comes from Plato's *Republic*, where Socrates introduces readers into his "Principle of the opposites". At a first glance, human soul divides into two different parts. On one hand, the reason which not only regulates "desires" but also is responsible for making reasonable judgments. On another, the part of appetite marks the needs of fulfilling the desire regardless the consequences. The paradox lies in the fact that any soul shares conflicting desires respecting to the same object. He cites the story of Leontius who had developed a strange sexual desire for pale young boys. One day while walking by the wall, he met with a lot of corpses which were just executed. His appetite to look these corpses was strong but at the same time it turned disgusting for him. Leontius struggled with his crave between watching or not watching, to he opened his eyes saying "look for yourselves, you evil wretches, take your fill of the beautiful sight! (Cooper, 1984; Roochnik, 2008).

With the benefits of hindsight, a dilemma of this caliber seems to be emulated in dark tourism practices, insofar it represents one of the most polemic forms of emotions. The same object can share two contrasting appetites: pleasure and displeasure. This explains how at the time, visitors manifest their concern, shock or dismay by the unfortunate victims faced, they are obsessed to witness. In the following sections, we will give further description to this phenomena, enunciated by Plato and ancient philosophy.

DARK TOURISM: THE STATE OF THE ART

In a seminal paperwork, entitled *Consuming Dark Tourism,* Phillip Stone and Richard Sharpley defines dark tourism as, any travel involving "the representation and consumption of death, in places that evoke "thanaptosis", which evinces the needs to meet with others' death. Policy makers embrace a great variety of dark tourism sites worldwide in which case it gave a lot of dispersed knowledge-production in literature (Stone & Sharpley, 2008). Although the studies in dark tourism have been proliferated over the recent years, three are the families of theories which need to be discussed: (e.g),

1. Profit-Oriented,
2. Interactional-Oriented,
3. Heritage-Oriented.

Profit-oriented theory confirms that tourism is jeopardized by the rise of new risks, disasters, and political instability. Oscillating from terrorism to virus outbreaks, the turn of new century brought many threats for the well-functioning of industry. Since communities have developed a potential of resiliency to better the lives of their members, tourism would be a conduit not only revitalizing the value of lands, but also accelerating the times proper of recovery-process. A fairer distribution of wealth, produced by tourism (and derived profits) corresponds with a sustainable mechanism to mitigate the negative effects of disasters. Tourism not only seems to be a resilient industry, it ascribes to be part in the process of resiliency of human groups. Based on pedagogic goals, dark tourism sites offer a valid message to avoid a next tragedy or at least the underlying factors, which ushered community into an state of disaster, to be tackled off (Stone & Sharpley, 2008; Cohen, 2011; Korstanje & Ivanov, 2012).

However, some voices eloquently have exerted a considerable criticism on the following axiom. Whether business and profits are monopolized by private actors, the real reasons of disasters will be forgotten, even biased (Bowman & Pezzulo, 2009; Reijinders, 2009). While visiting spaces of slums or dark tourism, as R. Tzanelli observed, first world citizens elude any responsibility for the historical duties of European Empires during Colonialism (Tzanelli, 2016). To overcome the conceptual limitation given by profit-oriented theory, basically, an emergent family arose. Based on the contribution of Richard Sharpley and Phillip Stone, from the University of Central Lancashire UK, these approaches envisaged the interactional dynamic of dark tourism. Since death causes a serious disruption between past and present, these scholar argue that consuming other's death situates as a valid attempt to imagine the own end. By the orchestration of dark sites, humans not only intend to grasp death, but also to understand its effects. Centered on the concept of "thanaptosis", people who had the experience of visiting dark tourism shrines or sites manifest a much deeper sensation, which opens their emotions to others who they do not know. Surfing through the channels of pain or mourning helps interpreting the proper life. After all, we have dubbed this academic wave as "interactional", simply because visitors are abstractly interacting with "the absent other" (following Giddens' conception of postmodernity), interrogating the self through the others' death. To date, this theory resonated within the circles of dark tourism researchers. The psychology of experience plays a vital role in this process (Stone, 2012, 2011, 2013; Sather Wagstaff, 2011; Raine, 2013; Yankovska & Hannam, 2014; Dalton, 2014; Jonhston, 2013; Marshall, 2014; Podoshen et al 2015; Collins-Kreiner, 2015; Gnoth & Matteucci, 2014; Sharpley & Sundaram, 2005).

Last but not least, the third group of theorists devoted their resources to conform what we termed, *Heritage-Oriented family.* Even if studies in this field emphasize on the importance of experience, they focus on heritage as the touchstone of dark tourism practices. Tourists not only need to be in contact with human suffering, what is more important, they are in quest of past. Following Dark Tourism as Heritage explanations, these specialists dissect the cultural background of death. Still, they found some evidence that people, no matter the age, have developed a strange attachment to death. Medieval Pilgrimages started following the interests of parishioners for visiting Saint's Tombs in the same way, battlefront or war celebrations crystalized in form of Heritage. One of its authorative voices was A V Seaton, who claimed that death situates as "one heritage" everyone has in common, then, death is the epicenter of heritage. Therefore, dark tourism would be conducive to mediate between constructed memory and present so that the community may reflection about events that belongs to its bloody past (Seaton, 1996; Lennon & Folley, 1999; Strange & Kempa, 2003; Winter, 2009; Dann & Seaton, 2001; Timothy & Boyd, 2006; Wight 2006; Tarlow, 2005; Biran, Poria & Oren, 2011; Hyde & Harman, 2011; Hartmann, 2014).

To here, two assumptions should be made. On one hand, these three ideal types are not exhaustive and in the same destination can be combined in major or lesser degree. For example, while some shrines are commoditized more prone to Heritage-oriented subtype, in other cases as Cromañón, the interactional dynamic prevails. Though each one of these theories shed light in some aspect of this topic, the question whether an excess of emphasis in the utterance of tourists remains unchecked. Doubtless, what tourists say or think leads to confusing outcomes when fieldworkers do not alternate with other methodologies. This happens because tourism-related researchers often embrace obtrusive methodologies such as open-ended questionnaires or interviews which only reflects the peak of iceberg. Reasons for this are twofold. Under some contexts, interviewees lie to protect their interests whereas in others simply are not cognizant of their emotional lives. This is the reason why, some qualitative ethnographies are further recommendable. At a first blush, interesting advances are found in the book *Heritage that hurts,* authored by Joy Sather-Wagstaff, who follows a self-ethnography in ground zero. As we will discuss in next section, she has a negative connotation around heritage, since it alludes to a biased impression of disasters, covering the reasons behind. On another, trauma opens the doors for empathy, which leads towards solidarity. This escapes from the monopoly of meaning imposed by Heritage.

Dark Tourism and Emotions

Joy Sather-Wagstaff (2011), lecturer at University of Illinois at Urbana-Campaign, presents in her book *Heritage that hurts,* where she defends a ground-breaking argument in basis formation and evolution of Ground-zero. In this interesting work, the author highlights that Ground Zero leaves a mark of tragedy, a disaster imposed to construct circuits of fear and loss, which needs to be deciphered by social scientists. The memoryscape of 9/11 not only woke up an emotional solidarity of the world to USA, but formed a collective sentiment of loss which merits to be discussed. Those who visit these places enter in connection with the others' suffering experiencing what others lived. Although some voices have claimed a sentiment of this nature is not authentic since dark tourism commoditizes emotions, culture and places, she adds, from Hiroshima to Pearl Harbor selling disasters to a global audience that has not faced them, consists in a valid attempt to diminish the negative effects of trauma. Starting from the premise that trauma and mourning are controlled by human spirituality, these sites administer empathy to conform what she dubbed as "*Heritage that hurts*".

There is no reason to suppose Ground Zero is unreal because it never reveals the roots of 9/11, rather, it confers "an allegory" in some nations which had no previous experience with terrorism; endorsing their support to US other nations paved the ways for an international solidarity. This is exactly the empathy, dark tourism sites generate. Its outstanding status, 9/11 subordinated the periphery to perform a shared experience to overcome the barriers of ethnocentrism. While tourists are influenced by their previous beliefs, prejudices and stereotypes, trauma and dark tourism open the doors for changing dogmatic one-sided gazes.

As the previous argument given, Sather Wagstaff argues convincingly that dark tourism operates by mediating between past and future. Conducting a self-ethnography, where she picked up stories, testimonies which intersected with individual biographies, it is important not to lose the sight that the contemporary ethnocentrism is forged by "the climate of false cosmopolitanism" which is promoted by "heritage" (not dark tourism). In this respect, since emotions go universally defying the hegemony of nation-state or even crossing the borderlands imposed by modernity, real ethnocentric discourse emerges whenever people are forced to remember events within one direction alone. While standardized discourses are posed by politicians, crystalizing what she calls heritage, the construction of dark sites facilitates a multi-sectorial gaze of the same event, which is helpful to democratic spirit. To put this in slightly terms, once disasters have taken place in community, the reconstruction is subject to severe controversy. The monopoly of meaning and significance of what occurred is at stake by many actors that oscillates from victims, or survivors, towards investors or tourists. At the time, heritage alludes to a much deeper dogmatic framing sometimes conducive to the interests of status quo, emerging peripheral voices are re-channeled to perform a new gaze that encourages various expressions of emotionality, when dark tourism sites surface. This happens because tourists should be understood as proactive actors who negotiate fresh and alternatives meaning(s) of tragedy, confronting with Governments. As stated, Sather Wagstaff innovatively takes distance from the studies of heritage, emphasizing on its alienatory nature. Heritage, far from helping visitors to understand past, commoditizes trauma to offer a great spectacle revitalizing our attachment for nation-hood. Emotions are the only conduits which break the hegemony of nation-state. At the time, political authorities urge to manipulate the message of disasters (in their benefit) or even with ends of enhancing further profits, dark sites set the pace to ethnocentrism and heritage. In this vein, she is strongly concerned not only by the effects of 9/11 but derived allegories forming tourist experience. Unlike other authors who envisage in dark tourism as a fashioned alienatory practice, or an obsessive quest to reach (staged) authenticity, she sees the problem from another lens. Based on the theory of "Kodak culture", as it was formulated by Chalfen in 1987, Sather Wagstaff holds that our memories are contained by the dispositiffs as albums, filed boxes, or even computers used to ritualize an event. These types of real archives correspond with yielding identity to reinforce the belonging to in-group. It is not surprisingly that the exchange (or dissemination) of images, feelings and experiences are determined by "the invention of souvenirs", which was replaced by photograph. Both work as instrument that helps circulating "memories" as well as narratives of certain "experiences". This logic not only is enrooted in the needs of visiting dark tourism sites, but also in keeping material connection with some places or feelings no matter the time. Doubtless, she adheres, tourism contributed to the visual culture of consumption playing a leading role by disseminating these types of experiences, engaging to far-way cultures and places which are reminded by the introduction of historiography.

She toys with the idea that:

the Material and visual culture of travel come not only to represent place but also to act as a memory aids, allowing us to re-perform place procesually as context change and time passes. The ongoing narratives performed through my conversations with participants revealed the ways in which tourists' on-site experiences are indeed remembered in dialogue with present contexts through engagement with photographs and souvenirs, constructing new contexts of meaningfulness not only for the WTC site but also for the ongoing aftermath of events of 9/11 (Sather Wagstaff, 2011: 189).

By means of performing 9/11 in this way, many people who had not visited or experienced this traumatic event, may share their emotions with victims. For her viewpoint, places certainly are phenomenologically drawn by much earlier travel experiences which are mutually exchanged as a conduit of communication. It is unfortunate 9/11 did not marked the end but the start of terrorism. This means that similar events can be organized in the same way, 9/11 and ground zero is memorized. This point paves the ways for a "new culture of commemorations" (p 193) produced by the rise of violence worldwide. At some extent, far from being limited to an alienatory force, tourism allows a much wider redefinition as places as "commemorative" not profitable, spaces of struggle to evoke traumatic events. Fieldworkers, in the years to come, should take seriously into consideration how tourists' stories and their consequent reactions are significant for victims, or people who had suffered a great loss. Dark tourism sites, as 9/11, offer radical transformations not only for tourists but for survivors in the way landscape is internalized. Following this explanation,

Sather Wagstaff explains that further investigation is needed in the interactions of global tourists and organizers of these sites. It is preferably to see WTC as a unified icon for victims, who remind their pain, and visitors interested in the event. Sather Wagstaff adamantly insists in the fact that tourists are symbolically and emotionally attached to Ground-Zero as many others Americans.

...whereas the rest of the visiting population may not be mourning specific victims, they will be engaging in the commemoration of victims both in the museum and the memorial spaces." (p 196).

At least, this above-noted hypothesis is evinced by the multiplications of museums which pay homage to victims after 9/11 country-wide. Through a global and material culture where visual plays a pivotal role mediating between people and "commemorative landscapes". During her fieldwork, needless to say, she met with different voices, persons and interviewees who provided a robust framework which lead her towards "engagement" with dark tourist sites.

Even though, Sather-Wagstaff sheds light on some interesting points unchecked by current specialized literature, in next section, we will place her argument under the critical lens of scrutiny, to understand how quite aside from any emotionality; visitors are in quest of something different in the ongoing quest for identity by confirming their societies are the best of feasible worlds. To put this in bluntly, Sather Wagstaff ignores the intersection of curiosity and pleasure. This means that no matter how authentic the experience unfolds, dark tourists feel pleasure from others' death while they affirm their supremacy "as chosen race", a sacred-aura inherited to those who are in competition in the race of life.

Dark Tourism in the Days of Thana Capitalism

One of the troublesome aspects omitted by Sather Wagstaff is the functionality of pleasure within the structuration of self. Tourists are not in quest of empathy, but only oriented to maximize their pleasure. As R. Duncan (1978) puts it, tourism needs from "the culture of shock" to sanitize strangers and any potential threat they represent into the romantic figure of "the good-tourist". Subject to a rite of passage, tourists are subject to the tutelage of locals. Since tourists pay for that sponsorship, they are condemned to see the world (not as a native) but as a guest. The same serves to explain the paradox of authenticity, which is discussed in the following lines,

If the tourists emerges from a visit to a foreign country with his own categories largely intact, the experience will have done little to demystify his reified worldview. The tourist furthermore may return from his travels with his previous reified, stereotyped

images of the peoples and places visited. This may be due in part to the tourist business, which profits from providing the tourists what that with he wished to see (Duncan 1978: 275)

Indeed, the commercialized hospitality places tourists into a tramp, simply because at the same time they launch far from home to appreciate the world as it stands in other geographies, he is marked as an strangers. Once he is accepted by native as "other who is different to us", typically native should offer hospitality in order for him to avoid any harm but at the same time, he renounces to feel an authentic experience. Guest will never experience the world as natives do, and here is where inauthenticity surfaces. The contact of tourists, far from being authentic, is with no-body unless by their expectances or dreams, in terms of MacCannell as empty-meeting grounds (MacCannell 1992). The virtuality of dark tourism is not determined by the instrument to consume death, but by the fact, its fictional nature as an emptied encounter with the otherness. This suggests the evolution of curiosity (an emotion, neglected by anthropology) but very important to explain tourist behaviour.

On one hand, Timothy Schroeder (2006) traces back to the roots of pleasure and curiosity. Per his outcomes, the concept of pleasure cannot be divorced from surprise, which turns out the stepping stone. What people expect -in a future that is not taking room in present- depends upon "a modular system" that receives the name of gut-level expectations, where probabilities are separated from beliefs. Schroeder's upshot is very illustrative to our discussion simply because he connotes a intersection of pleasure, the main emotion following tourism, with the necessary expectances which are conducive to regulate "the sense of pleasure". In other terms, we have to contemplate the possibility likely dark tourists move only by pleasure-maximization goals, instead of altruist interests as Sather Wagstaff said.

In a seminal book, *Imaginative Horizons* Vincent Crapanzano (2004) dissects the roots of imagination, which mediates between humans and their conception of future. Since the rites of passage marks the beginning of a new status for self, it represents a serious risk for its ontological sense of security. Imagination not only serves to reduce this sentiment of sensed risk, but to give continuance to human existence. For this anthropologist, each attempt to memorize past, covers the real reasons of the event, one want to remember. It is important to discuss, Crampanzano adds, our societies are prone to produce "negative monuments" which while remembers some events, paradoxically accelerate the oblivion of what is ritually remembered. To put this slightly in other terms,

We live in an age of negative monuments - those that focus on loss, death, war, and holocaust- rather than positive ones, commemorating victory, success and heroism, which fail to move us the way the monuments of loss do. We find the positive ones

anachronistic. We recognize their artifice and are suspicious of the values they proclaim. Unlike the negative ones, they are not sustained by an aesthetics of loss, whose effectiveness is derived from a mourning that so easily bleeds into our own terrors that it blinds us, momentarily at least, to artifice and suspicion... (Crapanzano 2004: 170)

Each time, we try to symbolize our discontent for the loss of values, we are unable to find a way to restore such values unless by a sad acknowledgement of the loss, which paradoxically perpetuates the loss.

On another, it is interesting to discuss Christopher Lasch's conceptualization of the *culture of narcissism* to expand our current understanding how Thana Tourism has arisen and finally evolved to the current stage of production. Lasch discussed capitalism from the lens of narcissism, a pathological state where the sense of the past is replaced by the sensual world of desires and pleasure. American society is facing substantial changes in which case citizens not only set the pace to consumers, but also people need to be validated by what others see. As Lasch observed,

Narcissism represents the psychological dimension of this dependence. Notwithstanding, his occasional illusions of omnipotence, the narcissist depends on others to validate his self-esteem. He cannot live without an admiring audience. His apparent freedom from family ties and industrial constraints does not free him to stand alone or to glory in his individuality (p 10).

Following this, since self is frustrated to understand the world as it is, the subject extrapolates its inner life to the external world paving the ways for the production of a fictional landscape. Starting from the premise that a narcissist personality is enmeshed with a narcissist culture, Lasch argues that narcissists not only look rapid gratifications, but also they are unable to cooperate with others, leading their behaviour to an extreme individualism (Lasch 1991). In his book, *The Rise of Thana Capitalism and tourism,* Korstanje (2016) explains that beyond a surface interest for the others, dark tourists cover a sentiment of solipsism which is fed by others' suffering. Basically, the life is seen as a long race, where only few participants win. Visitors feel pleasure to sense others' suffering because in this way, they reinforce the belief they are part of "chosen people". Of course, this will be not expressed overtly in an interview, but a closer look, it is evident that the consumption of death is not limited to tourism, it expands to other cultural entertainment as realities, TV programs, Movies and Journalism. In days of Thana Capitalism, consumers are prone to gaze others' death to affirm they live in the wonderland. The citizens of Thana-capitalism receives the term of Death Seekers and their main traits are being sketched below,

- Death seekers appeal to claim how bad the world is, only to highlight their wellness or their particular situation. News on crimes, disasters, and sad events are used as a pretext to tell others how happy they are.
- They did not understand reality unless by fact that events reinforce their cognitive background or previous beliefs.
- Serious problems to understand the otherness.
- Sites of mass-death, disaster or suffering (Thana-Tourism) are often selected as the primary destinations for visiting in holidays.
- Since they are special, death consumers feel they have the right to interact with others well-skilled like them.
- Death seekers support social Darwinism where the survival of strongest is the main cultural value.
- Consuming others suffering they feel special, superior or more important.
- They do not take part of charitable organizations or political militancy, unless by what they visually consumed through TV.
- Although they boast how altruist they are, they follow individual and instrumental ends in their life. It opens the doors to dissociation between what they say and what they really do.
- Excessive endorsement to democracy which became Western civilization as a superior ladder in the process of evolution.
- Psychologically they feel problems can be solved only speaking. They are not pragmatist persons. Narcissism is enrooted in the psychological trait of death seekers.
- Frightful personalities that think the world is a dangerous place.
- Death seekers entertain witnessing how others struggle. Very open to mythical conflagrations as goodness against evilness, they symbolically associate death to "condemnation". For them, the correct persons should not die.
- Pathological problems to understand death.

As discussed above, death seekers which are enrooted in a narcissist culture, believe they are part of a super race, supporting social Darwinism as one of the mainstream cultural values. One of the examples that explains further how these types of societies work, are the movies *Hunger Games, the Purge, or even the classic Reality Big Brother* inspired in Orwell's novel 1984. The plots of these films bespeaks of an exemplary centre that oppresses a down-trodden and pale periphery. This symbolizes the dependency of workforce with financial elite within capitalist societies. These centres organize a bloody game where participants, coming from this restricted periphery are confronted to struggle against others to take the glory. Since only one participant will win, this suggests that all the rest will die. Of course, participants over-valorise their own skills thinking they had probabilities to win. Far from being truth, the likelihood to defeat are slim in view of how background was drawn. This seems to be exactly how modern world works. Only few concentrated elite gathers almost all produced surplus while the rest of society is pressed to survive. The material asymmetries produced by the global capitalism are ideologically transformed in forms of entertainment. If you pay attention to tourism, we will realize that our grand-parents spent their vacations in paradisiacal destinations. Dark tourism suggests that not only the apollonian sense of beautiness has changed, but also the patterns of holiday-making. A new emergent growing segment of tourists opt for spaces of mass death or mourning to visit instead of the sun and beach products. Dark tourism is an indicator among many others respecting to the fact we are passing from the risk society to Thana Capitalism (Korstanje 2016). In consequence, death has transformed in a mediator between citizens and their social institutions. What does feel visitors of dark tourism?.

Indeed, visitors of dark tourism feel the same global audience of CNN, Fox or any global media when witnessing the last attack of ISIS or how an hotel has been bombarded. In a society where God has unfortunately died, feeling that they are fortunate because (as participant of Hunger Games) they are in competition, death-seekers maximize their pleasure consuming others' death. In doing so, a Hobbesian atmosphere of social Darwinism remains. In this case, citizens devote their resources to demonstrate privilege and status. This mechanism of discipline is conducive to elite which fragments the possibilities of workers to confront their legitimacy in an ever changing state of exploitation that enlarges the gap between have and have-nots day to day.

As this previous argument given, Thana Capitalism operates in a new facet of capitalism, where protection or security set the pace to other terms, as death or competence. Doubtless this change was assisted by the 9/11 insofar terrorists showed their accessibility to the modern means of mobility. From that moment on, nobody felt safe anytime and anywhere. Since, 9/11 was the founding event that marked the start of Thana Capitalism, death was commoditized as a exchangeable good that supported economic policies otherwise would be rejected. Following Baudrillard, the "spectacle of Disaster", which never takes place in reality, paved the pathway for the advance of a culture of witnessing (Howie, 2010).

The founding allegory of Thana Capitalism comes to "the myth of Noah's ark". Beyond the romanticism created by Hollywood around this biblical hero, it is important to discuss his role in the first genocide perpetrated against humankind. The legend tells us that God, annoyed by the corruption of human beings, mandated to Noah to construct an ark. Noah's divine mission consisted of gathering and adding a pair per species to his ark so as to achieve the preservation of natural life. The world was destroyed by the great flood, but life diversity survived. At first glance, the myth's moral message is based on the importance of nature and the problem of sin and corruption. But when examined more carefully, the myth poses the dilemma of competition: at any "tournament" or game, there can be only one winner.

In the *Universal Flood*, Noah and the selected species stand as the only witnesses of everything and everyone else's death. The problem of curiosity and fascination for death comes from "the principle of selection" Noah activates. Secondly, secrecy plays a vital role neglecting humankind its possibility to change God's decision. The principle of irreversibility, present in death, stems from the human impossibility to forecast its own end.

While Noah never reveals the unfortunate destiny of humankind, which is next to be purged, he introduces principle of selection as one of chief cultural values of rationality and Western thought. From that moment on, with the support of Noah, God divided the world in two, *the victims and witnesses*. The same logic will be applied for his Son's Crucifixion, where victimhood melts into curiosity.

Once again, Noah is the first survivor and the only chosen by God to continue with humankind on the earth. Doubtless, the force and influence of this myth in capitalist system is stronger than other cultures, simply because paves the ways for the configuration of a sentiment of exemption where the destruction of all is based in the salvation of few ones. Ideologically speaking, Noah's story leads to "a much process of social Darwinism", in which case capitalism was successfully reproduced worldwide. This dynamic reflects an asymmetrical system where a privileged group amasses almost 80% of produced wealth while the rest is pressed to live with limited resources. The richest people emulate the goals of rationality in the same way that, they set goals to fulfil, focusing to one thing at a time. In any case, slumming or poverty is not explained by the basic contradictions of capitalist system, but in their cosmology, they resulted as a reminder of their virtuousness, strengths, or skills.

As the previous backdrop, the culture of disaster within modern capitalism aims at disorganizing the social ties. In so doing, the derived narcissism is adopted as the main cultural value of society. The question whether capitalism expanded faster than analysts precluded correspond with two key factors: *the needs of being different and the needs of protection.* The society of risk sets the pace to a new capitalism, (thana-capitalism), where the presence of death allows changes otherwise would not be feasible. In days of Thana Capitalism, the life is seen as a long trace where only one will be the winner, whereas the otherness is seen as an rival to defeat. The death of others, which is represented through cultural entertainment and Media not only make us to feel special because we are in trace after all, but also remind how special we are. This is the reason why disasters captivate today to global audience. At the time, they exhibit the disgrace in Others news reinforce the supremacy of West over other cultures. Secondly, leisure practices as classic Sun and Sea tourism is changed to new forms where mass-disaster or mourning spaces are the main attraction. This new segment, known by some specialists as Thana-Tourism or Dark

Tourism, recycles spaces of disasters or mass-death to be visually commoditized to international consumers who need to be close to Other's death. If older leisure practices embraced an apollonian view of beautiness that invited workers to spend time and money in paradise-alike destinations, now we are witness of the rise of a new class, *death-seekers*.

CONCLUSION

This chapter debated not only the robust conceptual framework around dark tourism studies, but also placed the book *Heritage that hurts,* under the critical lens of our scrutiny. Because neither empathy nor solidarity are the key factors that determine "dark tourism", we hold the thesis that the curiosity for witnessing others' death represents an illustrative indicator how suffering is commoditized in capitalist societies. At the time, elite avoids any responsibility by the produced pain (as Tzanelli eloquently noted), death is commoditized as a sign of weakness, in a culture that proposed to live forever. It is important to clarify first that this position does not represent any attack to any voice or author, but an attempt to build an all-encompassing model that helps understand this much deep seated issue. Based in an in-depth review of the theory of emotions, we opted to go for another path, recovering the contributions of Christopher Lasch from the dust of oblivion. In days of Thana Capitalism, death seekers maximize their pleasure by gazing others' death, since in this way, they affirm as "a privilege class".

REFERENCES

Biran, A., Poria, Y., & Oren, G. (2011). Sought experiences at (dark) heritage sites. *Annals of Tourism Research*, *38*(3), 820–841. doi:10.1016/j.annals.2010.12.001

Bowman, M. S., & Pezzullo, P. C. (2009). Whats so darkabout dark tourism?: Death, tours, and performance. *Tourist Studies*, *9*(3), 187–202. doi:10.1177/1468797610382699

Cohen, E. H. (2011). Educational dark tourism at an in populo site: The Holocaust Museum in Jerusalem. *Annals of Tourism Research*, *38*(1), 193–209. doi:10.1016/j.annals.2010.08.003

Collins-Kreiner, N. (2015). Dark tourism as/is pilgrimage. *Current Issues in Tourism*, 1–5.

Cooper, J. M. (1984). Plato's theory of human motivation. *History of Philosophy Quarterly*, *1*(1), 3–21.

Crapanzano, V. (2004). *Imaginative Horizons: literary-philosophical anthropology*. Chicago: University of Chicago Press.

Dalton, D. (2014). *Dark tourism and crime* (Vol. 34). Abingdon, UK: Routledge.

Dann, G. M., & Seaton, A. V. (2001). Slavery, contested heritage and thanatourism. *International Journal of Hospitality & Tourism Administration*, *2*(3-4), 1–29. doi:10.1300/J149v02n03_01

Duncan, S. (1978). The Social construction of unreality: an interactionists approach to the Tourist's cognition of Environment. In D. Led & M. Samuels (Eds.), *Humanistic Geography* (pp. 262–282). Abingdon, UK: Routledge.

Faucher, L., & Tappolet, C. (2006). *Introduction: modularity and the nature of emotions* (L. Faucher & C. Tappolet, Eds.). Alberta, Canada: University of Calgary Press.

Foley, M., & Lennon, J. J. (1996). JFK and dark tourism: A fascination with assassination. *International Journal of Heritage Studies*, *2*(4), 198–211. doi:10.1080/13527259608722175

Giddens, A. (1990). *The Consequences of Modernity*. Cambridge, UK: Polity Press.

Gnoth, J., & Matteucci, X. (2014). A phenomenological view of the behavioural tourism research literature. *International Journal of Culture, Tourism and Hospitality Research, 8*(1), 3-21.

Hartmann, R. (2014). Dark tourism, Thana-Tourism, and dissonance in heritage tourism management: New directions in contemporary tourism research. *Journal of Heritage Tourism*, *9*(2), 166–182. doi:10.1080/1743873X.2013.807266

Heuermann, K., & Chhabra, D. (2014). The Darker Side of Dark Tourism: An Authenticity Perspective. *Tourism Analysis*, *19*(2), 213–225. doi:10.3727/108354214X13963557455766

Howie, L. (2010). *Terror on the Screen: Witnesses and the Re-animation of 9/11 as Image-event, Popular Culture*. Washington, DC: New Academia Publishing, LLC.

Hyde, K. F., & Harman, S. (2011). Motives for a secular pilgrimage to the Gallipoli battlefields. *Tourism Management*, *32*(6), 1343–1351. doi:10.1016/j.tourman.2011.01.008

Illouz, E. (2008). *Saving the modern soul: Therapy, emotions, and the culture of self-help*. Berkeley, CA: University of California Press.

Johnston, T. (2013). Mark Twain and The Innocents Abroad: Illuminating the tourist gaze on death. *International Journal of Culture, Tourism and Hospitality Research*, *7*(3), 199–213.

Jones, K. (2006). Chapter In L. Faucher & C. Tappolet (Eds.), Quick and Smart? Modularity and the Proemotion (pp. 3–28). Alberta, Canada: University of Calgary Press.

Korstanje, M. E. (2016). *The Rise of Thana-Capitalism and Tourism*. Abingdon, UK: Routledge.

Korstanje, M. E., & George, B. (2015). Dark Tourism: Revisiting Some Philosophical Issues. *E-review of Tourism Research*, *12*(1-2), 127–136.

Korstanje, M. E., & Ivanov, S. H. (2012). Tourism as a form of new psychological resilience: The inception of dark tourism. *Cultur-Revista de Cultura e Turismo*, *6*(4), 56-71.

Lasch, C. (1991). *The culture of narcissism: American life in an age of diminishing expectations*. New York: WW Norton & Company.

Lennon, J. J., & Foley, M. (1999). Interpretation of the unimaginable: The US Holocaust Memorial Museum, Washington, DC, and dark tourism. *Journal of Travel Research*, *38*(1), 46–50. doi:10.1177/004728759903800110

MacCannell, D. (1992). *Empty meeting grounds: The tourist papers*. London: Routledge. doi:10.4324/9780203412145

Marschall, S. (2014). Tourism and remembrance: The journey into the self and its past. *Journal of Tourism and Cultural Change*, *12*(4), 335–348. doi:10.1080/14766825.2014.890208

Miles, W. F. (2002). Auschwitz: Museum interpretation and darker tourism. *Annals of Tourism Research*, *29*(4), 1175–1178. doi:10.1016/S0160-7383(02)00054-3

Podoshen, J. S. (2013). Dark tourism motivations: Simulation, emotional contagion and topographic comparison. *Tourism Management*, *35*, 263–271. doi:10.1016/j.tourman.2012.08.002

Podoshen, J. S., Venkatesh, V., Wallin, J., Andrzejewski, S. A., & Jin, Z. (2015). Dystopian dark tourism: An exploratory examination. *Tourism Management*, *51*, 316–328. doi:10.1016/j.tourman.2015.05.002

Raine, R. (2013). A dark tourist spectrum. *International Journal of Culture, Tourism and Hospitality Research, 7*(3), 242-256.

Reijnders, S. (2009). Watching the detectives inside the guilty landscapes of Inspector Morse, Baantjer and Wallander. *European Journal of Communication, 24*(2), 165–181. doi:10.1177/0267323108101830

Roochnik, D. (2008). *Beautiful city: the dialectical character of Plato's" Republic.* Ithaca: Cornell University Press.

Ryan, C., & Kohli, R. (2006). The Buried village, New Zealand–An example of dark tourism? *Asia Pacific Journal of Tourism Research, 11*(3), 211–226. doi:10.1080/10941660600753240

Sather-Wagstaff, J. (2011). Heritage that hurts: Tourists in the memoryscapes of September 11 (Vol. 4). Left Coast Press.

Schroeder, T. (2006). Chapter. In L. Faucher & C. Tappolet (Eds.), An unexpected pleasure (pp. 255–272). Alberta, Canada: University of Calgary Press.

Seaton, A. V. (1996). Guided by the dark: From thanatopsis to thanatourism. *International Journal of Heritage Studies, 2*(4), 234–244. doi:10.1080/13527259608722178

Seaton, A. V. (1999). War and thana-tourism: Waterloo 1815–1914. *Annals of Tourism Research, 26*(1), 130–158. doi:10.1016/S0160-7383(98)00057-7

Sharpley, R., & Sundaram, P. (2005). Tourism: A sacred journey? The case of ashram tourism, India. *International Journal of Tourism Research, 7*(3), 161–171. doi:10.1002/jtr.522

Stocker, M., & Hageman, E. (1996). *Valuing Emotions.* Cambridge, UK: Cambridge University Press.

Stone, P. (2013). Dark tourism scholarship: A critical review. *International Journal of Culture. Tourism and Hospitality Research, 7*(3), 307–318.

Stone, P., & Sharpley, R. (2008). Consuming dark tourism: A thanatological perspective. *Annals of Tourism Research, 35*(2), 574–595. doi:10.1016/j.annals.2008.02.003

Stone, P. R. (2011). Dark tourism: Towards a new post-disciplinary research agenda. *International Journal of Tourism Anthropology, 1*(3-4), 318–332. doi:10.1504/IJTA.2011.043713

Stone, P. R. (2012). Dark tourism and significant other death: Towards a model of mortality mediation. *Annals of Tourism Research, 39*(3), 1565–1587. doi:10.1016/j.annals.2012.04.007

Strange, C., & Kempa, M. (2003). Shades of dark tourism: Alcatraz and Robben Island. *Annals of Tourism Research, 30*(2), 386–405. doi:10.1016/S0160-7383(02)00102-0

Tarlow, P. E. (2005). Dark tourism. Niche Tourism, 47. In Niche tourism: contemporary issues, trends and cases. London, Routledge.

Timothy, D. J., & Boyd, S. W. (2006). Heritage tourism in the 21st century: Valued traditions and new perspectives. *Journal of Heritage Tourism, 1*(1), 1-16.

Tzanelli, R. (2016). *Thana-Tourism and Cinematic Representations of Risk: Screening the End of Tourism*. Abingdon, UK: Routledge.

Verma, S., & Jain, R. (2013). Exploiting Tragedy for Tourism. *Research on Humanities and Social Sciences, 3*(8), 9–13.

White, L., & Frew, E. (2013). *Dark tourism and place identity: managing and interpreting dark places* (Vol. 37). London: Routledge.

Wight, A. C. (2006). Philosophical and methodological praxes in dark tourism: Controversy, contention and the evolving paradigm. *Journal of Vacation Marketing, 12*(2), 119–129. doi:10.1177/1356766706062151

Wilson, J. Z. (2008). *Prison: Cultural memory and dark tourism*. New York: Peter Lang.

Winter, C. (2009). Tourism, social memory and the Great War. *Annals of Tourism Research, 36*(4), 607–626. doi:10.1016/j.annals.2009.05.002

Yankovska, G., & Hannam, K. (2014). Dark and toxic tourism in the Chernobyl exclusion zone. *Current Issues in Tourism, 17*(10), 929–939. doi:10.1080/13683500.2013.820260

ADDITIONAL READING

Aries, P. (1975). Western attitudes toward death: From the Middle Ages to the present (Vol. 3). Maryland, VE: John Hopkins University Press.

Ariès, P. (2013). *The hour of our death*. New York, NY: Vintage.

Augé, M. (1995). *Non-Places: An introduction to an anthropology of supermodernity* (J. Howe, Trans.). New York: Verso.

Baudrillard, J. (1985). "Intellectual Commitment and Political power: an interview with Jean Baudrillard". *Thesis Eleven.*

Baudrillard, J. (1986). *America*. New York: Verso.

Baudrillard, J. (1995a). *The Systems of the Objects*. Mexico: Siglo XXI.

Baudrillard J (1995b). The Gulf War Did Not Take Place. Sydney: Power Publications

Baudrillard, J. (1996). *The perfect crime*. London: Verso.

Baudrillard, J. (1997). Aesthetic illusion and virtual reality. *Jean Baudrillard: Art and Artefact*, 19-27.

Baudrillard, J. (2001). *Imposible Exchange*. New York: Verso.

Baudrillard, J. (2002). *Screened Out*. New York: Verso.

Baudrillard, J. (2003). *The Spirit of Terrorism*. New York: Verso.

Baudrillard, J. (2006). Virtuality and Events: the hell of power. *Baudrillard Studies,3*(2).

Bauman, Z. (1998). *Globalization: The human consequences*. New York, NY: Columbia University Press.

Bauman, Z. (2007). *Consuming Life*. Cambridge: Polity Press.

Bigley, J. D., Lee, C. K., Chon, J., & Yoon, Y. (2010). Motivations for war-related tourism: A case of DMZ visitors in Korea. *Tourism Geographies*, *12*(3), 371–394. doi:10.1080/14616688.2010.494687

Brunsma, D., & Picou, J. S. (2008). Disasters in the twenty-first century: Modern destruction and future instruction. *Social Forces*, *87*(2), 983–991. doi:10.1353/sof.0.0149

Bryant, W. C. (1948). The Genesis of Thanatopsis. *The New England Quarterly*, *21*(2), 163–184. doi:10.2307/361747

Buda, D. M., & McIntosh, A. J. (2013). Dark tourism and voyeurism: Tourist arrested for "spying" in Iran. *International Journal of Culture. Tourism and Hospitality Research*, *7*(3), 214–226.

Cohen, E. (2016). The Permutations of Thailand's "Floating Markets". *Asian Journal of Tourism Research*, *1*(1), 59–98.

Collins-Kreiner, N. (2010). Researching pilgrimage: Continuity and transformations. *Annals of Tourism Research*, *37*(2), 440–456. doi:10.1016/j.annals.2009.10.016

Collins-Kreiner, N. (2016). The lifecycle of concepts: The case of Pilgrimage Tourism. *Tourism Geographies*, *18*(3), 322–334. doi:10.1080/14616688.2016.1155077

Freire-Medeiros, B. (2009). The favela and its touristic transits. *Geoforum*, *40*(4), 580–588. doi:10.1016/j.geoforum.2008.10.007

Frenzel, F., & Koens, K. (2012). Slum tourism: Developments in a young field of interdisciplinary tourism research. *Tourism Geographies*, *14*(2), 195–212. doi:10.1080/14616688.2012.633222

Frenzel, F., Koens, K., Steinbrink, M., & Rogerson, M. (2014). Slum tourism: State of the Art. *Tourism Review International.*, *18*(4), 237–252. doi:10.3727/154427215X14230549904017

Freud, S. (1920). *Beyond the Pleasure Principle*. London: International Psycho-Analytical Press.

Friedman, M. (1982). *Capitalism and Freedom*. Chicago, IL: University of Chicago Press.

Fuchs, G., & Reichel, A. (2004). Cultural differences in tourist destination risk perception: An exploratory study. *Tourism (Zagreb)*, *52*(1), 21–37.

Hay, B. (2015). Dark hospitality: Hotels as places for the end of life. *Hospitality & Society*, *5*(2-3), 233–248. doi:10.1386/hosp.5.2-3.233_7

Korstanje, M. E., & Ivanov, S. H. (2012). Tourism as a form of new psychological resilience: The inception of dark tourism.

Makarem, S. C., & Jae, H. (2016). Consumer boycott behavior: An exploratory analysis of twitter feeds. *The Journal of Consumer Affairs*, *50*(1), 193–223. doi:10.1111/joca.12080

Mamoulaki, E. (2016). In search of the exile past: Pilgrims and visitors to the island of Ikaria and their bearing on the historical past. *International Journal of Tourism Anthropology*, *5*(3-4), 204–220. doi:10.1504/IJTA.2016.081773

O'Rourke, P. (1988). Holidays in Hell. London: Picador Ed.

Podoshen, J. S. (2013). Dark tourism motivations: Simulation, emotional contagion and topographic comparison. *Tourism Management*, *35*, 263–271. doi:10.1016/j.tourman.2012.08.002

Raine, R. (2013). A dark tourist spectrum. *International Journal of Culture, tourism and hospitality Research, 7*(3), 242-256.

Rolfes, M. (2010). Poverty tourism: Theoretical reflections and empirical findings regarding an extraordinary form of tourism. *GeoJournal, 75*(5), 421–442. doi:10.1007/s10708-009-9311-8

Russell, F. H. (1977). *The just war in the Middle Ages*. Cambridge: Cambridge University Press.

Russell, J. B. (1986). *Lucifer: The Devil in the Middle Ages*. Ithaca, NJ: Cornell University Press.

Ryan, C. (2005). Dark Tourism – an introduction. In C. Ryan, S. Page, & M. Aitlen (Eds.), *Taking Tourism to the limits: issues, conceptys and managerial perspectives* (pp. 187–190). Oxford: Elsevier. doi:10.1016/B978-0-08-044644-8.50020-5

Ryan, W. (1971). *Blaming the Victims*. New Jersey, NJ: Vintage Books.

Tang, Y. (2014). Dark touristic perception: Motivation, experience and benefits interpreted from the visit to seismic memorial sites in Sichuan province. *Journal of Mountain Science, 11*(5), 1326–1341. doi:10.1007/s11629-013-2857-4

Thomas, S., Seitsonen, O., & Herva, V. P. (2016). Nazi memorabilia, dark heritage and treasure hunting as alternative tourism: Understanding the fascination with the material remains of World War II in Northern Finland. *Journal of Field Archaeology, 41*(3), 331–343. doi:10.1080/00934690.2016.1168769

Tinson, J. S., Saren, M. A., & Roth, B. E. (2015). Exploring the role of dark tourism in the creation of national identity of young Americans. *Journal of Marketing Management, 31*(7-8), 856–880. doi:10.1080/0267257X.2014.995207

Walter, P. G. (2016). Travelers experiences of authenticity in hill tribe tourism in Northern Thailand. *Tourist Studies, 16*(2), 213–230. doi:10.1177/1468797615594744

Winter, T., Teo, P., & Chang, T. C. (Eds.). (2008). *Asia on tour: Exploring the rise of Asian tourism*. Abingdon: Routledge.

Wright, D. (2014). *Residents' perceptions of dark tourism development: the case of L'aquila, Italy* (Doctoral dissertation, University of Central Lancashire).

Wu, M. Y., & Pearce, P. L. (2014). Chinese recreational vehicle users in Australia: A netnographic study of tourist motivation. *Tourism Management, 43*, 22–35. doi:10.1016/j.tourman.2014.01.010

Zheng, C., Zhang, J., Zhang, H., & Qian, L. (2017). Exploring sub-dimensions of intrapersonal constraints to visiting dark tourism sites: A comparison of participants and non-participants. *Asia Pacific Journal of Tourism Research*, *22*(1), 21–33. doi:10.1080/10941665.2016.1175489

KEY TERMS AND DEFINITIONS

Capitalism: Signals to an economic system centered not only in private ownership, but also in the circulation and capital exchange. The main assets of capitalism include capital accumulation, profits, voluntary exchange, and private property which lead to a price system.

Consumption: In sociology consumption was defined as the touchstone of capitalist system, which consisted in as a central every-day life form of identity or class structuration.

Dark Tourism: This entails a subtype of tourism which involves sites of mass death or disasters.

Globalization: It refers to a much deeper process that connects disperse cultures, nations and economies, into the same platform where the exchange of worldviews, products or ideas is integrated.

Mobilities: This represents an academic paradigm born from social sciences that explores the socio-economic background that facilitates the peoples' movements.

Thana Capitalism: Neologism coined by Maximiliano Korstanje to denote a new state of capitalism, which replace the risk society. In thana-capitalism the others' death is the main commodity to trade off.

Chapter 2
Museums of Dark Mythologies in the Tourist Place

Oleg E. Afanasiev
Russian State University of Tourism and Service, Russia

Alexandra V. Afanasieva
Oles Honchar Dnepropetrovsk National University, Ukraine

ABSTRACT

The present chapter focuses on the role of museums as producer of dark myths, which means the cultural background that leads visitors to consume "other´s death". Anthropologically speaking, museums are symbolic instrument that helps understanding traumatic events. For this reason, it is important to deepen the connection between tourism consumption and disasters. Over centuries, positivism trivialized mythology as a fictional story, or rumors proper of primitive cultures; rather, not only myths play a leading role in configuring culture, but also the borders between life and death. Here we propose an alternative fresh methodology to study dark tourism issues in the decades to come.

INTRODUCTION

In our days, allegories and myths are inherently associated and exploited to profit-oriented goals in tourism industry. Without these imagined landscapes, tours, attractiveness and other forms of commoditized territories, as museums, dark-shrines or hot-spot of consumption would have prospered and flourished (MacCannell, 1976). In this respect, in the culture of gazing, museums and tourism seem to be inextricably intertwined (Urry, 2002; Urry & Larsen, 2011). The same applies for

DOI: 10.4018/978-1-5225-2750-3.ch002

dark tourism and consumption of haunted castles, houses or spaces of mass-death (Holloway, 2010; Levitt, 2010; Korstanje, 2011). Many tourists pay fortune to visit bewitched museums to hear the stories of cursed spirit, ghost which materializes in a moment or any others macabre experiences that alluded to massacre of innocent people (Tzanelli, 2016). Visitors of these types of sites not only are in quest of something new, exciting, they look to consume events (enrooted in the pastime) which helps them to interpret their present life (Stone & Sharpley, 2008; Stone 2006; Korstanje & George, 2015). In dark tourism consumption, as Sather Wagstaff puts it, there is a type of new emergent solidarity between tourists and victims which remains unchecked (Sather-Wagstaff, 2011). Many important museums allow to infer interesting forms of communication, attracting a large audience of people who is interested in the problem of death, spirituality and even ghosts. The world famous castles with ghosts that have become the museums now – inhabited by ghosts of Henry VII and his wives Hampton Court in London, the Mikhailovsky Castle with a ghost of Paul I, the Hermitage, the Louvre Museum and many are the evident examples. Today, virtually every museum has its mysterious legends and special secrets, primarily due to the specifics of such institution. Thus, there is the situation, when, along with the rich museum collection the new collection of legends is being established and used in excursion activities.

As this backdrop, one might speculate there is a type of Dark mythology which merits to be studied, an organization of legends, myths, stories around others` death, unjust death, or on-slaughters that current generations should remember. At some extent, dark tourism alludes to a much deeper stage of remembrance in order for next generations to learn from post disasters scenarios (Cohen, 2011; Dalton, 2014). Following this reasoning, a new class of "non-traditional" museums – museums of legends is formed. Here the genre of folklore is beyond the scope of mysticism inherent to any museum and becomes a separate object of tourist interest. While Museums which are based on "dark mythology" - at first glance - are new and interesting phenomena recently surfaced in the modern tourism industry, no less true is that other legendary or epic museums are traditional dispositifs to hold memory in community. For example, "Glade of fairy tales" near Yalta is long well-known iconic attraction of Crimean tourism industry. Although this open-air museum is not positioning itself as a representative of legends, storylines of its exposition are constructed after Russian folk tales based on Slavic legends and myths. Here, among the others, the negative, dark and mystical folk characters of the ancient mythological space of the East European Plain appear affordable to tourists. Whatever the case may be, this chapter explores not only ghost tourism or dark tourism as a new emergent issue, but also the connection of museums into the social imaginary from where dark consumption buttressed.

PRELIMINARY DISCUSSION

It is interesting to discuss to what extent how classic museums started to emerge in the last decade as a result of an rising demand in high-culture, pieces of arts, or masterworks in painting which paved the ways for the rise and expansion of mass-tourism in Europe and US. Tourists who visited these types of places, were interested in modern arts adjoined to the needs of consuming culture as a form of emancipation from the alien climate of urban cities (MacCannell, 1976). The degree of authenticity they demanded, as MacCannell observed, reminded how important aesthetics was for tourism industry (Urry, 2002). In earlier studies Korstanje and Busby proposed an all-encompassing model to understand how mythologies and legends, far from being mere fictions, paved the pathways for the maturation of modern tourism and the industry of services (Korstanje & Busby, 2010). Following this outcome, we discuss in this chapter the possibility to forge a "dark mythology", which is understood as a orchestration of discourses, allegories, points of convergence previously centered in a dark legend which explains "trauma" or "traumatic events" for community. Further attention should be given to the study of dark mythology as recently appeared in the horizons of tourism fields. The question whether, dark myths and legends play a leading role in the allegorical formation of dark tourism sites is a point which remains unexplored in English speaking journals and books. In part, this is because, positive science undermines mythology as a serious option, though anthropology has historically pivoted and reached interesting results using mythology as an object of study; secondly, specialized literature prefer to administer open and closed ended questionnaires to visitors, instead of delving into profound cosmology of death. Some of the most relevant works, but not all because of time and space issues, will be reviewed in this section. This will help expand our understanding of this slippery matter, at the same time, it echoes the reasons why, a new fresh alternative is needed. The "dark mythology" offers, in this vein, a fertile ground for next scientific approaches.

Originally, A. Chronis (2012) and O. Jenkins (2003) have devoted considerable attention to tourist-travel stories as conduits in order for psychological experience to be expressed from inner to external world. Tourists not only remind what they experience, but social researchers can understand tourism by inquiring in such an experience. In this token, Razak accomplished an interesting content analysis of myths and legends using brochures published from 1962 to 2007 as a main methodology. He starts from the premise that each ethnicity updates their own myths in order to forge a dissipated and specific identity respecting to neighbours. Following this, while J. Mendes analyzed online brochures from the official tourism center in the Algarve with the purpose of evaluating the use of myths and legends in its communication, M. Banyai showed how different destination images are associated fictional landscape of fear as Dracula tourism in Transylvania. This research revealed as well that locals and tour guides respond to these images according to wider stereotypes disseminated by media and literature. Further pungent investigations shed light on how founding parents, or mythical heroes who are enrooted in the national folklore are exploited by tourism industry to enhance the destination attractiveness (Shackley, 2001; Inglis & Holmes, 2003; Strange & Kempa, 2003; Gentry, 2007; Light, 2007; Wilbert & Hansen, 2009; Holloway, 2010; Moscardo, 2010). What is most important, dark tourism serves as a mechanism of resilience not only for community to learn from adversities, but also to accelerate post disaster recovery processes (Korstanje & Ivanov, 2012; Mugnano & Carnelli, 2017). Last but not least, D.N. Zamyatin (2013), I.I. Mitin (2006), O.E. Afanasiev and A.V. Trotsenko (2013) noted the importance of conceptual framework produced and created by culture to understand the engagement of self with territory. Per this study, what would be more than interesting to discuss is to what extent, marketing would use mythology to understand human geography, travels and the gravitation of tourism in modern world.

As the previous argument given, Korstanje and George (2015b) called the attention to the power of myths not only by forming the psychological landscape in tourism demand, but in reproducing mythical allegories which stems from founding parents. As social construes, beaches, sun-bathing, and thermals corresponds with myths of origins which are expressed in the biblical trauma of Lost paradise. While humankind was debarred from Eden, the recovery of lost paradise was the obsession of Western World. This was recently confirmed by Cantallops and Cardona (2015) who present an interesting thesis. The archetype of lost paradise not only was profoundly associated to tourism, but to the figure of Island, which captivated readers in literature over centuries. It is possible to link mythology to brochures, as well as other promotional material to captivate consumers` attention. The dichotomy paradise-islands take a leading point of discussion in Cantallops and Cardona`s development. In a new seminal book Korstanje (2016) found the origin of dark tourism stems from the Noah`s ark myth. This myth was certainly the symbolic epicenter by God divided the world in two, victims who succumbed to universal flood, and survivors (who played the role of witnesses). From that moment on, Western civilization appealed to create a more death-oriented culture, where the other`s suffering posed as the main exchanged commodity. For that reason, it is not surprisingly, the same can be said of dark mythology, which means the expression of mythological stories, legends, aimed to produce a referential image of death. This is the direction, dark mythology should take in the years to come.

METHODOLOGICAL DISCUSSION

While we have reviewed in depth the specialized literature, it is interesting to discuss some of limitations in these studies. At some extent, there is a fashion in tourism research to apply questionnaires as the only valid method to understand social issues. The same happens in dark tourism issues. Researchers and fieldworkers administer questionnaires to visitors organizing and tabulating the information according to their previous stereotypes. This leads to serious misunderstanding and saturation of information, which obscure more than it clarify. Not only sometimes, interviewee are unfamiliar with their behavior or the deepness of their consciousness, but also in other occasions they lie to protect their interests. This is the reason behind the needs of thinking new alternative approaches to study these types of matters.

An anthropocentric vector preferably is needed to understand a Mehta-discourse of dark mythology as it was discussed in precedent sections. These vectors exhibit not only the priorities of museum, curators, even the interests of tourists as well as their demands and needs. This method evinces a complementary method to current fieldworkers and tourism researchers. While culture is underwent to significant transformation, an ever increasing demands of dark sites are bringing the model of dark mythology into the foreground. Leisure, entertainment and educational needs take center stage among the socio-cultural requests of museum visitors. In this regard, a museum is no longer acts only as a scientific institution, but uses all the means of modern service as a part of its communicative instrument. All this leads to the emergence of a new generation of museums – interactive, entertaining museums, including dark mythology.

The function of cultural entertainment is given by introducing a sense of escapement from humdrum routine. In so doing, interactive museum can be deemed as producer of myths and controlled-risk which is crystallized in urban folklore. These sites facilitate an atmosphere of perplexity, no less true is that visitor of dark sites are intellectually sophisticated consumers, who defy the classic products. More oriented to story and pastime, dark tourists valorize the importance of being in connection with others` suffering to understand their proper lives. In addition, dark myths plays a crucial role in the development of societies and their mainstream cultural values. Museums are instruments for these myths to be offered to citizens and of course this does not represents a new phenomenon. What is most interesting, myths are embedded with the national symbol exhibitions, as well as artifacts, object, or arts which conforms the national-being; a point of existence which paradoxically endorses identity and exclusivity for those who do not meet the requirements of in-group. For example, Russian National-being corresponds not only to those who speak Russian as main language, but excludes dramatically a lot of people who does not have fluency in such a language. Even learning Russian, it is almost impossible to dominate the language as a native does. This is the main paradox of language, which represents the sensible world, and culture, which serves as a shelter to "the dangerous other". Though museums were historically used by Science to show the supremacy of rationality over other values, myths represents a foundational part of museums which merits to be discussed.

In this respect, modern society with its urban folklore (the so-called postfolklore), including, inter alia, the myths, legends and fairy-tale characters – symbols of cities and countries, in theory continues that tradition. Our modern system of world perception is mythologized no less, and perhaps even more, than the system of ancient man. Based on the approval of Russian philosopher A.F. Losev (2001) that myth – it is a reality for its subjects, we can say that these modern myths as real for the present man as were real the gods of Olympus to the ancient Greeks. After all, a myth – is not only ancient, pre-existent to religious, perception form of the surrounding reality, and not just a form of non-positive knowledge. Myth is a way of knowing and understanding the world by man, largely explaining the inexplicable from a rational point of view of things and phenomena. In contrast to the archaic myth, dominant in all spheres of activity, a modern myth – the prerogative of mass culture, art and literature. According to the Russian scientist-folklorist S.Y. Neklyudov (n.d.), "Science in its purest form – the lot of few professionals, but science that came to mass man through school, through popular publications, through television, is very often used for the construction of very archaic mythological phantoms". In this sense, museums of legends, on the one hand, continue a long-standing museum tradition, and on the other, transformed according to needs of modern socio-cultural system of the human being, profess revolutionary new methods of museum communication. Thus, the dark mythology – is not just entertainment facilities aimed at getting money from inexperienced tourists. They are, above all, the guardians of modern myths and legends, their representants, carrying a hidden message to a modern museum visitor.

Often institutions or organizations, calling themselves "museum" is actually the usual shop that sells souvenir or ornamental products without any semantic loading, exhibition and developed sightseeing and entertainment programs. The "Museum of Bogies" in the Crimea, or even mentioned in the List-Verse site rating of museums, devoted solely to the mythical and legendary characters, "Fairies Museum" in California are the examples. All of this is de facto conventional shops of arts and crafts. Therefore, for studying dark mythology as an important component of modern tourism industry, there are need for conceptualization of the term of "a museum myths and legends," and its variant "a museum of legends and myths" associated to death, the establishment of its main functional features, the classification of such museums, the determination of their place in the tourism and the importance for dark tourism, and also compiling a database and rating top-20 museums of allegories or legends.

The Study Description

The definition of "dark mythology" should be based on an understanding of "traumatic legend" as a part of national folklore and post-folklore that is involved in tourism, and, especially, on the visions of "dark myth" and "dark legend" as most solicited in current tourism industry. This statement is based on the fact that all museums of myth and legends are a form of submission of latter to a modern tourist. Any museum of legends, using folklore, forms a part of the tourism space. It acts as an intermediary between a myth and a tourist at the same time being one of the most important components of marketing tourism areas. Mythology of tourism space is gaining particular recognition nowadays. It creates new meanings based on ancient and modern myths and legends. The concept of "tourist legend" lies at the core of mythology of tourism space. Let us consider this concept in detail. Tourism legend – it is a complete concise literary work that has potential and/or being actively used in tourist activities; it is based on the rational and emotional interpretation of information about the native lands by community of people (ethnic, economic, political, etc.), who inhabit a specific territory. Tourism legend, as a rule, claims to be truth, but cannot be checked accurately, its authorship is very difficult or even impossible to determine, and as a literary work, it has the logic and consistency of presentation, specific "tourism" goal, from which the style of presentation of information depends. Tourism legend – it is a same tourism resource, as a monument to history and culture, or as a natural object, having recreational properties. Tourist legends are intangible (or information) resources; they cover part of the "mythological" space, involved in the tourism sector, thematically embracing the diversity of folklore (myths, legends, epics, fables, fairy tales, beliefs, stories, historical jokes, etc.), as well as non-folklore components (retellings of stories and rumors, false or unreliable public opinion, "marketing" legend), which are integrated over time and acquire properties of the tourism legends.

The concept of myth in tourism is interpreted broadly. In most cases, myth is the form of worldview that has come down to us from ancient cultures by means of fables, legends, traditions and beliefs. In this case, myth is the object of cultural studies and ethnography and is used in tourism as an intangible historical and cultural resource. Then its functions are very similar to the functions of tourism legends, and often in the course of engaging in tourism the first is converted into the second. Also, current studies in the field of humanitarian geography understand myth as a kind of information about the territory, which has been transformed through the prism of the public perception of the world. This myth forms the basis of the image of space, and at competent use is able to positively affect the image of the tourism territory. Myth in tourism can also be understood as misconceptions about something that is unproductive from the perspective of this study. As stated, we propose to use the term of "tourist legend" as the main", as it covers myths, converted according to tourist needs. Detailed classification scheme of tourism legends has been developed by us earlier. However, we note especially among the tourism legends the dark legends and myths. According to adopted concept of "dark tourism" as a form of tourism activity connected with presentation and consumption of death and disaster places and attractions, enjoy the human suffering, the cruelty, the consequences of natural and technogenic catastrophes and social disasters, etc. (M. Foley and J. Lennon, 2000; E. Alexander, 2015; D. Dalton, 2015 and others), dark mythology seems to be distinguished by the following features: connection of plot with disaster, death or human pains that left a peculiar mark on the territory of modern destination and/or caused to emergence of mystical events or phenomena. The destination having own dark legends and myths make tourist feel the "power of place" in higher degree, get especial experience, to sense involvement in mystical phenomena and gloomy events, and in some cases, be directly involved in them.

Centered on the premise that dark mythology is a part of national folklore, involved in tourism activities, all legends, "exhibited" in a "museum of legends", are comparable to dark tourism. At the same time, the folklore forms adjacent to the legends – fables, myths, fairy tales, etc., and also literary works that have become legendary, in such museums turn into tourism legend. It separately has to be said about the literary works. They themselves do not belong to the genre of legends, as they are not part of the national folklore and have a specific author, the events described in them are often fictitious (only if it is not documentary). But there is a part of the works, which can be roughly attributed to the category of tourism legends. For example, the works of A. Conan Doyle glorified 221b Baker Street (where Sherlock Holmes Museum is now open), literature heritage of M.A. Bulgakov reflected in legendary places that are visited by many tourists now: "bad apartment" – Bulgakov Museum today, Patriarch's Ponds, the building of the museum of medicine in Kiev, etc.), literary character of Bram Stoker, Dracula, became the mythological tourism brand of Romania). These literary works are well-known, have a territorial binding and are widely involved in the tourism life. Today, all over the world established museums of individual works, literary characters, and so forth, which may be considered as museums of legends, and are also the subject of our research. Museums are constructed to remember a traumatic event, which oscillates from battle celebrations to natural disasters. Museums exhibits the human needs of disciplining time and death.

For what has been discussed, it is safe to formulate the common definition of a museum of dark (mythology) legends of as a museum-type institution, in which a legend is the main object of exposition, conservation and research. In this mythological space, part of which a tourist legend is, is represented mediated through the physical artifacts, as well as by means of interactive and theatrical forms of museum communication. Museum of dark legends – it is a form of preservation, presentation and involving tourism legends and other forms of folklore in the tourist activity. In the following based on a general definition we will consider in more detail museums of dark legends.

The main features of a museum of dark legends are:

- Thematic specificity (fairytale, myth, legend, and other forms of folklore, interesting in terms of dark tourism – superstitions, beliefs, etc. act as the main object of study and exhibition);
- Form of presentation the information (objects of arts and crafts, painting and drawing, theatrical and animation activities, which in itself is part of the cultural expression);
- Using advanced information technologies in museum communication and expositions;
- Clearly expressed entertainment function.

The presence of well thought-out exposition, and also excursion and entertainment work with visitors is a mandatory condition for the existence of museum of legends. Inconsistency with this condition automatically excludes the object from this category of museums.

Studying the dark legends museums' activity requires their typology. Museums of legends can be combining in types by the following criteria: form of organization of a museum, the presentation of information, organization of the exhibition, the dominant forms of museum communication, objects of museum research and preservation, etc. Let us consider some of them.

Typology of museums according to the method of presenting information. Tourism legend it is rather unusual museum exhibits, because unlike of them the former cannot be seen or touched by virtue of intangible nature. Therefore, the museums often resort to reification of a legend.

The types of exhibits that are shown in museums of legends:

- Sculptures of fantastic and mythical characters (Children's Museum of Mythology and Forests in Zaslawye, Russia; Museum of Myths and Legends in Prague, Czech Republic);
- Objects of everyday life of a certain epoch, the legendary hero's attributes (for example, Sherlock Holmes' pipe of the XIX century, which he could use, if he only existed);
- Image of fairy and mythical heroes on paper, canvas, in lacquer miniature (The case of First Museum of Slavic Mythology in Tomsk, Russia);

- Theatrical performances, staging and reconstruction, interactive shows (as illustrated by Torun House of the Legends, Poland);
- Texts in the form of manuscripts, brochures, text on the monitor screens (e.g., the Prague Museum the legends are presented in the "Book of Legends", and also it is given to visitors in different languages in print);
- Computer graphics (as illustrated by The Horrors of St. Petersburg Interactive Museum).

Typology of museums by the method of exposition construction and the form of museum organization:

- Open-air museum (e.g., the Glade of Fairy Tales in Yalta, Crimea);
- Indoors museum with the classic form of the exhibition organization (Museum of Kazan Legends and Fairy Tales, Loch Ness Center and Exhibition, Bran Castle, National Leprechaun Museum of Ireland, Dublin, etc.);
- Indoors museum with the use of interactive technologies (Mothman Museum in Point Pleasant, Museum of the Living Dead in Monroeville, Museum of Mythical Monsters in Waxahachie, etc.);
- Virtual museum (Northwest Museum of Legends and Local History in the United States).

Typology of museums by the objects of museum research and preservation:

- Museum of the legendary, mythological and fairy-tale characters;
- Museum of the legendary literary works, and individual characters;
- Museum of urban legends (including historical) and modern myths;
- Horror museums (subject to the involvement of existing legends in them).

Also the museum of dark legends can be classified by the form of property, but most of considered by us museums are private and corporate, with the exception of only the State Historical and Cultural Museum-Reserve "Zaslawye", part of which is the Children's Museum of Mythology and Forests, and the museum "Glade of Fairy Tales" in Yalta.

We compiled the top-20 museums legends when identifying and exploring them. They are ranked by the popularity (references on thematic tourism sites, blogs, and visitors' reviews on the site TripAdvisor.com) and by the attendance (Table 1).

This table describes the potentiality of Dark Mythology or Dark Legends as the conceptual background that engage tourists with others` death.

Table 1. Top 20 world museums of legends

Rating Position	Name	Web-site	Location
1	Glade of Fairy Tales	polyana-skazok.org.ua	Yalta, Crimea
2	Prague ghosts and legends museum	muzeumpovesti.cz	Prague, Czech Republic
3	Bran Castle, Dracula Museum	bran-castle.com	Romania
4	Torun House of Legends	domlegend.pl	Torun, Poland
5	Sherlock Holmes Museum	sherlock-holmes.co.uk	London, United Kingdom
6	National Leprechaun Museum	leprechaunmuseum.ie	Dublin, Ireland
7	Loch Ness Center and Exhibition	lochness.com	Drumnadrochit, Scotland
8	Mothman Museum	mothmanmuseum.com	Point Pleasant, USA
9	Museum of Witchcraft and Magic	cornishwitchcraft.co.uk/museum.html	Boscastle, United Kingdom
10	Museum of Kazan Legends and Fairy Tales	kazanlegend.info	Kazan, Russia
11	The Horrors of St. Petersburg Interactive Museum	museum.spbhorror.ru	Saint Petersburg, Russia
12	Vampire Museum	cryptozoologymuseum.com	Paris, France
13	Museum of Superstition and Witchcraft	sueverija.narod.ru	Uglich, Russia
14	Museum of Russian Superstitions	dom-domovogo.ru	Villa Lesnoye, Russia
15	First Museum of Slavic Mythology	slav-museum.ru	Tomsk, Russia
16	Children's Museum of Mythology and Forests	ru.zaslaue.by/muzeynye-ekspozicii/detskiy-muzey-mifologii-i-lesa	Zaslawye, Belarus
17	Museum of the Living Dead	monroevillezombies.com	Monroeville, USA
18	Museum of Mythical Monsters	huntmonsters.com	Waxahachie, USA
19	House of Legends (museum and restaurant)	-	Lviv, Ukraine
20	Northwest Museum of Legends and Local History (virtual museum)	nwlegendsmuseum.com	Washington state, USA

Glade of Fairy Tales is the oldest among the museums of legends. The legend is already connected with its own appearance. In 1923, the future sculptor, and then petroleum engineer Pavel Bezrukov arrived in Crimea for the tuberculosis treatment. After visiting different places, he stopped near Yalta, at Wuchang-Su waterfall. Crimean mountain air positively influenced the engineer's organism, and like a fairy tale, a miracle of healing happened. After the war, aged Bezrukov came here and turned this place into a fairy glade. Today, Glade of fairy tales – it is an open air museum, which brought together the works of different artists. A special place here is given to the negative and evil characters of Russian folk tales. They particularly attract the visitors of all ages. A variety of excursions and thematic programs is held in the museum. This is one of the most visited places in Crimea.

Prague ghosts and legends museum it is a classical museum of legends. It focused on presentation of Prague myths and legends in a "tangible" form. Here, the interactive exhibition presents the most authentic Prague legends, heroes of which, according to local residents, are real or actually existed. The museum is located in a historic residential building on two floors. The sculptures of characters and scenes of Prague fabulous stories, legends' texts in different languages, and so forth are presented here.

The most visited castle in the Romania is Bran, so-called Dracula Castle, although there are any historical evidences about staying here this mythical character. But there are many legends connecting life of Vladislav the Impaler (Tepes), the Dracula prototype, with this castle. According to tradition, the Romanian Count not only visited this place passing through, but even he was imprisoned in the dungeon, falling into disfavor to the Hungarian King Matthias Hunyadi. During its existence, Bran changed a lot of owners, was the imperial residence and a museum of the Middle Ages. The famous film director Francis Coppola gave money for the restoration of the castle and made here his version of "Dracula." After that, the castle has become the pilgrimage destination for fans of this legendary literary character. There is a legend that a few decades ago tourists, who are have come in Romania in search of famous vampire's traces, discovered a striking similarity of the castle with one described in Stoker's novel. After that, the castle became the "Dracula residence".

On another hand, *Sherlock Holmes Museum*, offers a literary character, which has become the hallmark of London. Fictional apartment 221b Baker Street (at the time of releasing the works about Sherlock Holmes this address didn't exist), has situated as one of the most famous places in London among fans of dark and criminal tourism and general travelers. Since the extension of streets, address was given to the building of construction society Abbey National, and because of the huge flow of letters, the organization introduced a special post of secretary, processing incoming mail addressed to Sherlock Holmes. Still, in 1990 this museum was opened to be visited by tourists. It is interesting that on the museum building was hanged the typical London memorial plaque, so-called "Blue plaque", which is installed on the buildings, which are associated with episodes of the life of real historical figures. In this point, fiction and reality blurs. The plaque points out that detective-consultant Sherlock Holmes lived here from 1881 to 1904. The interior of the museum fully meets the situation of fictional apartments, it also presents the well-known due to Arthur Conan Doyle's works Sherlock Holmes objects – his pipe, hat, violin, hunting whip, by means of which he drove from his living room unmasked villain, Watson's army revolver and many more.

American museums, mentioned in the above table, incorporated into their activities largely generated by the mass culture characters of horror films that have become iconic attractions of the certain territories. For example, Mothman Museum combines urban legend and the plot of the same movie, the Museum of the Living Dead reflects popular in the genre of horror motifs of zombies, etc.

Traditional folklore characters, witches, gnomes (leprechauns), fairies, vampires and others are more specific for museums in Northern Europe.

Souvenir production is a special form of interaction between museums of legends and tourists. It is also intended to reify intangible legends, consolidate the positive image created with their help, and motivate tourists to re-visit, not only a museum, but a city, a region and a country as a whole. For example, in the Museum of Superstition and Witchcraft in Uglich the various amulets are sold as souvenirs. The souvenir production that plays the vampire theme is sold in the castle Bran. Museums of national mythology and fairy-tale characters (leprechauns and gnomes, Loch Ness, etc.) by means of souvenirs popularize the territory's image, introducing in its brand fabulously and legendary component.

Besides the already existing museums of dark legends, there are those that are only forming or exist informally, outside the official tourism statistics. *The Chernobyl exclusion zone in Ukraine* is de facto open-air museum of dark legends, but not de jure. There are a well thought-out "exposition" with exhibits (cities, infrastructure facilities, buildings, abandoned things), many of which have been restored and prepared for presentation to visitors, the logic of tourist route, forms of museum communication and education. And undoubtedly it is of great interest for fans of dark tourism. Chernobyl exclusion zone in Ukraine is most enigmatic, mysterious territory that overgrown with myths and legends of the post anthropogenic nature. Because of the greatest secrecy, the history of the Chernobyl disaster has acquired suppositions and falsifications, transformed into a global information myth, which reflected in popular culture (mainly in the style of horror) and became iconic tourist attraction for dark tourism followers. Time stood still here, and we can observe interrelationship between nature and the remains of human-made systems. In the world today is very popular alarmist concept as "What would happen if Human suddenly disappeared?". Exactly, in the Chernobyl zone we can clearly see how natural ecosystem answers this question: how the once wide avenues and streets are overgrowing, buildings are being destroyed, forest, forest is gradually replacing man-made landscape. Since 2012 the territory of the Chernobyl zone is opened for visits by organized groups of tourists. Here on the tour route abandoned city of Pripyat is demonstrated, where Chernobyl nuclear power plant employees once lived, as well as destroyed reactor plant, the city of Chernobyl with a series of memorials in memory of the man-made disaster are the sightseeing objects. Abandoned houses are of particular interest. Each of them has own sad story or dark legend. Thus, in

Figure 1. The house, abandoned in 1986, with an inscription on the wall, "Forgive and goodbye, my house!", Chernobyl
(©2013, O. Afanasiev. Used with permission)

one of those houses visitors can see a very sad and heartbreaking inscription left by former residents during the eviction in 1986.: "Forgive and goodbye, my house!" (Figures 1-5). In addition to organized tourist groups visiting the Chernobyl zone quite legally, this area attracts particular attention of 'illegal tourists "- a variety of member of an unofficial organization, representatives of subcultures, stalkers, diggers, enthusiasts of extreme tourism, etc. Although a visit to Chernobyl zone cannot be determined truly as extreme tourism, but this is space of classic "dark tourism" in the open air, a peculiar post-apocalyptic tragic shaking event, which is memorized as a sign of human irrationality as the paradox of existence. One of the aspects that defines Chernobyl consist in the following dilemma. At the time, technology would play a role in making of this life a safer place to live, risk-perception was prone to zero-sum game. Chernobyl reminds how the introduction of technology may mitigate some risks, but opening the doors to others, only by the fragilities of human existence, which means "human error".

Figure 2. Tour group near the destroyed 4th power unit of Chernobyl nuclear power plant, Chernobyl
(©2013, O. Afanasiev. Used with permission)

Figure 3. The abandoned city of Pripyat. Former House of Culture "Energetic" and the attraction "Ferris wheel"
(©2013, O. Afanasiev. Used with permission)

Figure 4. Former Lenin prospect in Pripyat – once the widest street of the city (©2013, O. Afanasiev. Used with permission)

Figure 5. A former hotel "Polesie" in Pripyat
(©2013, O. Afanasiev. Used with permission)

CONCLUSION

Museum of dark (mythology) legends – it is a key factor of tourist performance in dark tourism shrines and sites. It provides not only with a mythological haven which confers meaning to human existence (an ontological sense of stability respecting to external world) but also explain our obsession by these type of products. At the time, we perceive the environment as more hostile to us, further needs of prefiguring death by the lens of others. Besides, Museums hold influence on the borders between death and life. They are memorizing events of the past, for appreciating life. Quite aside from this, Museums contain legends (death mythologies) which are orchestrated in forms of myths, fables, stories, and folklore, to be incorporated into the symbolism of human existence. In fact, fieldworkers have adamantly trivialized the role of tourism as producer of myths interacting between the needs of entertainment-escapement and curiosity-conquest.

In this context, museums usually represent the most important legendary, fantastic plots and characters, which are specific and recognizable for a city, region or the entire country. Museums and (dark) myths are vital for the development of attractiveness, which s necessary for destination branding process. This is the reason why dark tourism offers a fertile ground for next investigation in the years to come. Thus, a museum of legends – it is important mechanisms of tourism brand formation based on the legends of tourism areas. In addition, such museums as new institutions best meet tourism demand, satisfy the socio-cultural needs of modern visitor, save and externalize intangible legend in material form and manner. Museum of dark myths and legends – it is a form of legalization of informal cultural mythological space through local people`s eyes. Dark mythology objects, transforming into a museum space, become the factors of attraction and enhance profits and attractiveness of the destinations.

REFERENCES

Afanasiev, O., & Afanasieva, A. (2015). The functional significance and place of tourist legends in creating attractive destination properties. *Universities for Tourism and Service Association Bulletin*, *9*(1), 52–59. doi:10.12737/7943

Afanasiev, O. E., & Trotsenko, A. V. (2014). Category “legend” in the regional toponymic space (by the example of the Dnepropetrovsk region in Ukraine). *Pskovskij regionologicheskij zhurnal*, *17*, 67-77. (in Russian)

Alexander, E. (2016). *Dark tourism of the Bosnian screen*. Retrieved September 04, 2016, from http://www.worldcat.org/title/dark-tourism-of-the-bosnian-screen/oclc/948964947

Banyai, M. (2009). The image of tourism destinations: A case of Dracula tourism. University of Waterloo.

Cantallops, A. S., & Cardona, J. R. (2015). Holiday destinations: The myth of the lost paradise? *Annals of Tourism Research*, *55*, 171–173. doi:10.1016/j.annals.2015.10.002

Chronis, A. (2012). Between place and story: Gettysburg as tourism imaginary. *Annals of Tourism Research, 39*(4), 1797–1816. doi:10.1016/j.annals.2012.05.028

Cohen, E. H. (2011). Educational dark tourism at an in populo site: The Holocaust Museum in Jerusalem. *Annals of Tourism Research, 38*(1), 193–209. doi:10.1016/j.annals.2010.08.003

Dalton, D. (2014). *Dark Tourism and Crime*. Florence, Italy: Taylor and Francis.

Gentry, G. W. (2007). Walking with the Dead: The Place of Ghost Walk Tourism in Savannah, Georgia. *Southeastern Geographer, 47*(2), 222–238. doi:10.1353/sgo.2007.0023

Holloway, J. (2010). Legend-tripping in spooky spaces: Ghost tourism and infrastructures of enchantment. *Environment and Planning D: Society and Space Environ. Plann. D, 28*(4), 618–637. doi:10.1068/d9909

Inglis, D., & Holmes, M. (2003). Highland and other haunts. *Annals of Tourism Research, 30*(1), 50–63. doi:10.1016/S0160-7383(02)00031-2

Jenkins, O. (2003). Photography and travel brochures: The circle of representation. *Tourism Geographies, 5*(3), 305–328. doi:10.1080/14616680309715

Korstanje, M., & Busby, G. (2010). Understanding the Bible as the roots of physical displacement: The origin of tourism. *E-Review of Tourism Research, 8*(3), 95–111.

Korstanje, M. E. (2011). Detaching the elementary forms of dark-tourism. *Anatolia, 22*(3), 424–427. doi:10.1080/13032917.2011.620800

Korstanje, M. E. (2016). *The Rise of Thana Capitalism and Tourism*. Abingdon, UK: Routledge.

Korstanje, M. E., & George, B. (2015a). Dark Tourism: Revisiting Some Philosophical Issues. *E-review of Tourism Research, 12*, 127–136.

Korstanje, M. E., & George, B. P. (2015b). The media or the message? An examination of myths as resources to understand the tourism phenomenon. *International Journal of Tourism Anthropology, 4*(2), 122–141. doi:10.1504/IJTA.2015.070055

Korstanje, M. E., & Ivanov, S. H. (2012). Tourism as a form of new psychological resilience: The inception of dark tourism. *Cultur-Revista de Cultura e Turismo, 6*(4), 56–71.

Lennon, J. J., & Foley, M. (2009). *Dark tourism: The attraction of death and disaster*. London: South Western Cengage Learning.

Levitt, L. (2010). Death on display: reifying stardom through Hollywood's dark tourism. *The Velvet Light Trap*, (65), 62-70.

Light, D. (2007). Dracula tourism in Romania Cultural identity and the state. *Annals of Tourism Research*, *34*(3), 746–765. doi:10.1016/j.annals.2007.03.004

Losev, A. F. (2001). *Dialectics of Myth*. Moscow: Mysl'. (in Russian)

MacCannell, D. (1976). *The tourist: A new theory of the leisure class*. Berkeley, CA: University of California Press.

Mitin, I. I. (2006). Tourist myths and complex characteristics of the territory in human geography. *Turizm i kul'turnoe nasledie*, *3*, 103–110.

Moscardo, G. (2010). The Shaping of tourist experience: the importance of stories and themes. In M. Morgan, P. Lugosi, & J. R. Ritchie (Eds.), *The tourism and leisure experience: Consumer and managerial perspectives* (pp. 43–58). Bristol: Channel View Publications.

Mugnano, S., & Carnelli, F. (2017). A "New Normality" for Residents and Tourists: How Can a Disaster Become a Tourist Resource? In Tourism in the City (pp. 321-332). Berlin: Springer Int. Publ.

Nekljudov, S. (n.d.). *FAQ: Mythology in the culture: 7 facts about the role of myth in the history of culture and myth-making in the modern world*. Retrieved September 4, 2016, from http://postnauka.ru/faq/6599

Sather-Wagstaff, J. (2011). Heritage that hurts: Tourists in the memoryscapes of September 11 (Vol. 4). Left Coast Press.

Shackley, M. (2001). *The legend of Robin Hood: myth, inauthenticity, and tourism development in Nottingham, England. In Hosts and guests revisited: Tourism issues of the 21st century* (pp. 315–322). Cognizant Communication.

Slyusareva, N. A. *(2015).* The conflict of myth's interpretations in the modern museum practice. *Cennosti i smysly*, *6*(40), 138-146. (in Russian)

Stone, P. (2006). A dark tourism spectrum: Towards a typology of death and macabre related tourist sites, attractions and exhibitions. *Tourism: An Interdisciplinary International Journal (Toronto, Ont.)*, *54*(2).

Stone, P., & Sharpley, R. (2008). Consuming dark tourism: A thanatological perspective. *Annals of Tourism Research*, *35*(2), 574–595. doi:10.1016/j.annals.2008.02.003

Stone, P., & Sharpley, R. (2009). *Darker Side of Travel: The Theory and Practice of Dark Tourism (Aspects of tourism)*. Channel View Publications.

Strange, C., & Kempa, M. (2003). Shades of dark tourism. *Annals of Tourism Research, 30*(2), 386–405. doi:10.1016/S0160-7383(02)00102-0

Tzanelli, R. (2016). *Thana tourism and the representation of risk*. Abingdon, UK: Routledge.

Urry, J. (2002). *The tourist gaze*. London: Sage.

Urry, J., & Larsen, J. (2011). *The tourist gaze 3.0*. London: Sage. doi:10.4135/9781446251904

Wilbert, C., & Hansen, R. (2009). *Walks in spectral space: East London crime scene tourism. In Strange spaces: Explorations into mediated obscurity* (pp. 187–203). Farnham, UK: Ashgate Pub.

Zainal, A. (2012). *Current issues in hospitality and tourism research and innovations: Proceedings of the International Hospitality and Tourism Conference, IHTC 2012*. Boca Raton: CRC Press.

Zamyatin, D. (2013). Geo-cultural branding of territories: the conceptual grounds. *Labirint. Zhurnal social'no-gumanitarnyh issledovanij, 5*, 11-23. (in Russian)

ADDITIONAL READING

Bowman, M. S., & Pezzullo, P. C. (2009). Whats so dark about dark tourism?: Death, tours, and performance. *Tourist Studies, 9*(3), 187–202. doi:10.1177/1468797610382699

Bristow, R. S., & Newman, M. (2004). *Myth vs fact: An exploration of fright tourism. Proceedings of the Northeastern Recreation Research Symposium.*

Brown, J. (2013). Dark tourism shops: Selling "dark" and "difficult" products. *International Journal of Culture. Tourism and Hospitality Research, 7*(3), 272–280. doi:10.1108/ijcthr-05-2012-0039

Chelminski, R. (2003, April). The Curse of Count Dracula: The Prospect of a Tourist Bonanza from a Dracula Theme Park in Transylvania Excites Some Romanians, But Opponents See Only Red. *Smithsonian*. Retrieved December 20, 2016, from http://www.smithsonianmag.com/travel/the-curse-of-count-dracula-79837910/

Cohen, J. (2002). The Contemporary Tourist: is Everything Old New Again. In S. M. Broniarczyk & K. Nakamoto (Eds.), *Advances in Consumer Research* (Vol. 29, pp. 31–35). Valdosta, GA: Association for Consumer Research.

Coote, D. (2010, June 12). Exploitation or healthy interest? An analysis of dark tourism. *Jeju Weekly.* Retrieved December 21, 2016, from http://www.jejuweekly.com/news/articleView.html?idxno=776

Hartmann, R. (2014). Dark tourism, thanatourism, and dissonance in heritage tourism management: New directions in contemporary tourism research. *Journal of Heritage Tourism*, *9*(2), 166–182. doi:10.1080/1743873X.2013.807266

Hooper, G., & Lennon, J. J. (2017). *Dark tourism: practice and interpretation.* London: Routledge.

Korstanje, M. (2011). Detaching the elementary forms of dark-tourism. *Anatolia, an International Journal of Tourism and Hospitality Research, 22*(3), 424-427. doi: 10.1080/13032917.2011.620800.

Korstanje, M. (2014). Dark tourism and place identity: Managing and interpreting dark places (contemporary geographies of leisures, tourism and mobility). *Journal of Tourism and Cultural Change*, *12*(4), 369–371. doi:10.1080/14766825.2014.892560

Korstanje, M. (2015). *The anthropology of dark tourism. Exploring the contradictions of Capitalism.* Leeds, UK: CERS, School of Sociology and Social Policy, University of Leeds.

Korstanje, M. (2017). England and the Culture of Achievement: The Roots of Dark Tourism. In M. Korstanje (Ed.), *Gazing at Death: Dark Tourism as an Emergent Horizon of Research.* New York: Nova Science Publ.

Korstanje, M., & Ivanov, S. (2012). Tourism as a Form of New Psychological Resilience: The Inception of Dark Tourism. *Cultur: Revista de Cultura e Turismo*, *6*(4), 56–71.

Korstanje, M. E., & George, B. P. (2016). Craving for the consumption of suffering and Commoditization of Death: the evolving facet of Thana Capitalism. In M. Korstanje (Ed.), *Terrorism in a Global Village: How Terrorism Affects Our Lives.* New York: Nova Science Publ.

Lang, P., & Tanas, S. (2014). Tourism 'Death Space' and Thanatourism in Poland. *Current Issues of Tourism Research*, *3*(1), 22–27.

McKercher, B., & Prideaux, B. (2014). Academic myths of tourism. *Annals of Tourism Research*, *46*, 16–28. doi:10.1016/j.annals.2014.02.003

Poade, D. (2015). Dark Tourism and Crime. *Tourism Management, 50*, 255–256. doi:10.1016/j.tourman.2015.02.015

Seaton, A. V. (2014). Guided by the dark: From thanatopsis to thanatourism. *International Journal of Heritage Studies*, *2*(4), 234–244. doi:10.1080/13527259608722178

Skinner, J. (2012). *Writing the dark side of travel.* New York: Berghahn Books.

Skinner, J. (2016). Theatricality, dark tourism and ethical spectatorship: Absent others. *Journal of Tourism and Cultural Change, 1-2*. doi:10.1080/14766825.2016.1149902

Stone, P. R. (2005). Dark Tourism Consumption – A call for research. *e-Review of Tourism Research, 3*(5), 109–117.

Werdler, K. (2013). Dark tourism and place identity: Managing and interpreting dark places. *Journal of Heritage Tourism*, *9*(4), 360–362. doi:10.1080/1743873X.2013.861984

KEY TERMS AND DEFINITIONS

Dark Mythological Space: A type of mythological tourism space, which is based on localities, places and objects associated with the mysterious and massive deaths, tragedies, murders, natural and technological catastrophes, etc. As a result of these events the human community gives to these places a mysterious power, dark reputation, finds confirmation of suffering and casualties occurred here once in mysterious and unexplained phenomena. They are explained by dark legends and myths that constitute irrational part of the mythological dark space.

"Dark Mythology": Based on an understanding of "traumatic legend" as a part of national folklore and post-folklore that is involved in tourism, and, especially, on the visions of "dark myth" and "dark legend" as most solicited in current tourism industry.

Dark Tourism: (also black tourism or grief tourism): A kind of tourism, that allows visitors to see by their own eyes places and sites historically associated with peoples death, tragedy, suffers, disasters, etc.

Disaster: A great accident, that can be occurred in nature and humane-made landscapes, it lead to the serious disruption of the society functioning, causes human victims, material, economic or environmental loss and impacts, which exceeds the ability of the affected community or society to cope using its own resources. The territories that have affected by disasters are the dark tourism destinations.

Museum of Legend: It is a museum institution, where a legend is the main object of display, preservation and study. With that, the mythological space, part of which a tourism legend is, is mediately represented through tangible artifacts and interactive and theatrical forms of museum communication. Museum of legends – is a form of preservation, presentation and involving of tourism legends and other forms of national folklore in the tourism activity. Museum of dark legend is kind of museum institution that represents legend, based on dark mythology.

Mythological Tourism Space: A special type of space, based on the mythologization territory by community. Rational basis of mythological tourism space is a territory, region, and spiritual, irrational background – tourist legends.

Tourism Legend: It is a complete concise literary work that has potential and/or being actively used in tourist activities; it is based on the rational and emotional interpretation of information about the native lands by community of people (ethnic, economic, political, etc.), who inhabit a specific territory. Tourism legend, as a rule, claims to be truth, but cannot be checked accurately, its authorship is very difficult or even impossible to determine, and as a literary work, it has the logic and consistency of presentation, specific "tourism" goal, from which the style of presentation of information depends. Tourism legend – it is a same tourism resource, as a monument to history and culture, or as a natural object, having recreational properties. Tourist legends are intangible (or information) resources; they cover part of the "mythological" space, involved in the tourism sector, thematically embracing the diversity of folklore (myths, legends, epics, fables, fairy tales, beliefs, stories, historical jokes, etc.), as well as non-folklore components (retellings of stories and rumors, false or unreliable public opinion, "marketing" legend), which are integrated over time and acquire properties of the tourism legends.

Chapter 3
Going to the Dark Sites With Intention:
Construction of Niche Tourism

Bintang Handayani
President University, Indonesia

ABSTRACT

This chapter discusses construction of niche tourism in postmodernism. It aims to give a flavour on how the arguments are presented. Utilising death sites and Voluntourism, coupled with proliferation of Information and Communications Technology (ICT) as backdrop, this chapter sets to the layer of dark tourism as the revelation and contemplation, it bridges the nexus between visiting the death sites and extreme poverty areas, and hospitality features as core essence attributed to authentic experience. This chapter thus is an agreement of the previous studies which suggest authentic experience derived from cool authenticity and existential authenticity. It would emerge as not only the answer for searching authentic experiences but also most importantly it could extend the niche tourism formation and deepen Voluntourism conceptualisation. Findings of this study provide practitioners in the tourism and hospitality industries with clues to position death sites and Voluntourism as premium market offerings. Eventually, some directions for future study are discussed.

INTRODUCTION

While virtual traumascapes and the roots of dark tourism indicate 'describing facts' associated with death and destruction to critically examining the designs that give meaning to historical and quasi-historical events e.g. death sites, Voluntourism

DOI: 10.4018/978-1-5225-2750-3.ch003

revolves around the role of participation, social movements, and social networks. Voluntourism (also known as volunteer tourism) can be traced its roots in alternative and ecotourism (Wearing and McGehee, 2013b). In tourism experiences, both death sites and Voluntourism are attributed to darkness elements. They offer authentic experience through actively involved in global community activities and destruction past events. It is likely that individuals choose to participate because they wish to expand their activist identities into their leisure travel. Presumably, this would not only indicate construction of niche tourism in postmodernism but also would strengthen the need to be coexisted. Arguably, development and management of dark tourist sites focus on technology driven virtual traumascapes, and is also to knit together insights from various partial perspectives, derived from pure disciplines like psychology, sociology, and economics to applied fields like ecology, technology, and management studies. Considering postmodern world is looking for new existential identity and motivation, the branches of dark tourism i.e. visiting death sites and Voluntourism have emerged as the current state of tourism. In this sense, development and management of dark tourist sites and Voluntourism are likely about individuals choose to participate because they wish to expand their activist identities into their leisure travel.

Utilising death sites and Voluntourism, coupled with proliferation of Information and Communications Technology (ICT) as backdrop, this chapter sets to the layer of dark tourism as the revelation and contemplation, it bridges the nexus between visiting the death sites and extreme poverty areas, and hospitality features as core essence attributed to authentic experience. In other words, visitation to death sites and Voluntourism revolve around the spectrum of going to the dark sites with intention. Therefore, the statement that set as the research problem is how the proposed variables i.e. death sites and Voluntourism, and ICT could be attributed to Virtual Traumascapes and the Roots of Dark Tourism?

LITERATURE REVIEW

As postmodern world is looking for new existential identity and motivation (Zotic, Alexandru & Dezsi, 2014), the branches of dark tourism i.e. visiting death sites and Voluntourism have emerged as the current state of tourism (Handayani, Ivanov & Korstanje, 2017). In this sense, visiting death sites and Voluntourism which embedded with tourism experience revolves around the role of participation, social movements, and social networks (McGehee & Santos, 2005). Further, in tourism experiences, it is likely that individuals choose to participate because they wish to expand their activist identities into their leisure travel (McGehee & Norman 2002; McGehee & Santos, 2005). In this token, the movement of more environmental friendly and minority issues as commodification could not be the newest form of postmodernism spectrum anymore. As Fife (2004) suggests (re) enactment and active participation of tourists have promoted the framing of niche tourism in postmodernism. Further, Zotic et al., (2014) expound that tourism trend from modernism to postmodernism, which indicates the shift from mass tourism (defined as conventional tourism involving large number of tourists in staged settings) - niche tourism (the symbolic stage wherein demassification of mass tourism, focuses on searching for authenticity) – nootourism (defined as the next phase wherein tourism focuses on knowledge and virtual tourism) - nontourism (the phase wherein tourism is associated with commonness new philosophy of life, lifestyle revisited). On the other hand, Wearing and McGehee (2013b) point out volunteer tourism as one of forms of tourism which defined as alternative ways of tourism development. It is believed that alternative ways of tourism development that are being championed including mass tourism, sustainable tourism, ecotourism, alternative tourism and pro-poor tourism (PPT).

Another inevitable phenomenon which intertwined dark tourism in the postmodernism spectrum is that its relationships with technology advancement i.e. proliferation of ICT, which is inseparable with people lives nowadays. Korstanje (2014) points out that Virtual Dark Tourism (VDT) which leads to the discourse on virtual-touring, represents a common practice in post-industrial societies which seems to be a "simulation" generated by special software, where the user meets with fictitious landscapes or pictures taken by other visitors of real landscapes. Further, he suggests that the experience of this, though it is manipulated by the multimedia, is authentic by some people. In line with that, Clarke (2005–2006: 154) argues 'in the absence of personal experience with death people rely on the media, among other things, for information, attitudes, beliefs and feelings about death and its meanings'. However, is this (i.e. experience of visitation to the dark sites which is manipulated by the multimedia) theoretically in line with what Wang (1999) suggested as the existential authenticity, which is defined as "a special existential state of being in which individuals are true to themselves".

The proliferation of ICT in the dark tourism spectrum specifically in the context of death sites is revolved around the growth of demand on applying: (1) free Wi-Fi in the tourist destination; (2) in terms of Augmented Reality (AR) tourist's experience; (3) in terms of enriching the values of attraction through technological application e.g. application of Wayfinding (Baker, 2016), application of re-enactment of rituals of the death, etc., This kind of development and management of niche tourism is presumably not only adapt proliferation of ICT e.g. application of digital ecosystem (Gretzel, 2016), would add values for business and enhances tourists' experiences and other elements which makes everything in an interface. With digital ecosystem, business could forecast trend through the Big Data. This may be applicable for development and management of dark tourist sites and Voluntourism, which would be focused on the predictive Tourism.

In addition, past studies suggest ICT development for optimising the potential of dark tourism namely: (1) AR technology, it displays objects such as buildings even after the remnants are erased; (2) 3-D data, technology which is useful for many purposes such as the reconstruction of buildings; (3) local e-government, which provides adequate information for dark tourism information related to local area and its community; (4) Digital archives, technology that provides information inside digital archives possesses certain tags; (5) Digital Map, which provides geography Information System (Ide, 2014). On the other hand, Reed (2009) denotes that volunteers' working on ICT is concurrently in line with the trend that people travel spends their vacations or gap years volunteering for NGOs in developing countries. This is the term that Clemmons (2011) points out as Voluntourism, i.e. a nexus between volunteering and tourism. This activist identities and their leisure travel in Voluntourism is attributed to pro-poor tourism (PPT) which is an approach to the industry that aims to provide opportunities for the poor (Wearing & McGehee, 2013b), is considered as Voluntourism settings i.e. commodification of poverty areas.

Reed (2009) further explains that social positioning theory, which offers a window into understanding how social roles change i.e. in the context of Voluntourism. For instance, voluntouirst may take benefit from emphasizing their identity as tourists which position them opposite to the homogenous locals or deemphasizing their similarity to the package tourist to gain more detailed information from locals. These may explain the authentic experience that makes Voluntourism as another type of niche tourism and could be emerged as the newest premium touristic market offerings. With this viewpoint, construction of tourism perspectives in general and construction of niche tourism in particular is profoundly inevitable to be examined.

This essay aims to scrutinise construction of niche tourism in postmodernism i.e. death sites and Voluntourism. Literature review about the death sites and Voluntourism are used as objects of the study. With this viewpoint, i.e. niche tourism in postmodernism as a backdrop, I posit that the shape of dark tourism to come are the growing phenomenon of death sites and Voluntourism, coupled with ICT proliferation e.g. Augmented Reality (AR) for the case of death sites which would position death sites and Voluntourism as premium market offerings. Presumably, it would emerge as not only the answer for searching authentic experiences but also most importantly could be the zeitgeist to come (Uriely, 2005). The structure of this essay is as follows. Briefly it discusses death sites and Voluntourism, not as comprehensive review but serve to give a flavour on how the arguments are presented. Next, discussion and the shape construction of death sites and Voluntourism to come are presented. Eventually, the concluding thoughts and future research directions are outlined.

Construction of Tourism in Postmodernism

Construction of tourism as industry in postmodernism indicates the inseparable relationships with authenticity, commodification, and empowerment. Research suggests the nexus among variables of authenticity, commodification, and empowerment pretty much revolves around construction on dichotomy of premodern, modern (see Cole, 2007), and postmodern (Zotic et al., (2014). The fact that postmodern society searches for authentic experience which derived from the new layer of touristic market offerings, which revolves around cultural activities and heritage, forces the market to provide touristic market offerings that fulfils the needs to be attached with active involvement (Lyons & Wearing, 2008; Ong, Lockstone-Binney, King, & Smith, 2014; Godfrey, Wearing & Schulenkorf, 2015; Heron, 2011; Holmes, Smith, Lockstone-Binney & Baum, 2010; Ong, Pearlman, & Lockstone-Binney, 2011; Smith & Font, 2014; Clemmons, 2011; Heron, 2011) and the needs of re-enactment of tragedy (Korstanje & George, 2015). Specifically, McGehee & Santos (2005) suggest that volunteer tourism organization's claims that expeditions improve ''global citizenship'' and participants become more involved in changing the world. This new layer specifically denotes the higher stages of experience for not only involving issues such as "go green", environmental friendly and sustainability, humanity and minority issues (see Anholt, 2007), but also most importantly is the authentic experience which makes them feeling able to avoid tragedy, to be safer, to feel that they are not only privileged but able to have contemplation and revelation (Korstanje, 2014).

As the postmodernism focuses on being self-referential, Zotic et al., (2014) suggest in their thesis, debate on tourism in postmodernism would be pretty much bridging the nexus between a new tourism, nootourism, and non-tourism, thus the shift from nootourism to non-tourism would be revolved around seeking the feeling akin to the host community and its whole package of cultural and heritage activities; which presumably would provide the authentic experience, signifies the feeling that tourist able to avoid tragedy, to be safer, to feel that they are not only privileged but also able to have contemplation and revelation. This kind of touristic market offerings can be derived from death site and the Voluntourism. For that reasons, overview about the death site and Voluntourism is as follows.

Death Tourism and Voluntourism

Visiting death sites and the extreme poverty areas is not a new phenomenon but it is profoundly a growing trend in the spectrum of postmodernism. Studies indicate the huge interest of tourists for seeking the authentic experiences to witness how people died (Foley & Lennon, 1996; Seaton, 1996; Miles, 2002; Strange & Kempa, 2003; Wight, 2006; Jamal & Lelo, 2011; Robb, 2009; Stone & Sharpley, 2008; Sharpley, 2005; Wilkinson, 2010; Stone, 2012; Kang, Scott, Lee, & Ballantyne, 2012; Holdenrid, 2013; Crozier, 2013; Korstanje, 2014) e.g. visiting the death sites and to gain authentic experience to see the world and to be actively participating to the issue of sustainability, preservation & conservation, humanity e.g. the Voluntourism (see Lyons and Wearing, 2008; Clemmons, 2011; Heron, 2011).

Research into niche tourism in relation with authentic experience in general and in the context of less-developed country e.g. Indonesia has been examined through the lens of authenticity (see Meschkank, 2011) and commodification in general (see Cohen, 1988; Cole, 2007) and in Asia-Pasific in particular (see Lovelock, 2003; Ong, Lockstone-Binney, King & Smith, 2014; Mowforth & Munt, 2015). On the other hand, niche tourism as the new layer for tourism research has been discussed by Yeoman & Beeton (2014) and Lyons and Wearing (2008) which allude the growing of Voluntourism. Further, Voluntourism is an example of niche tourism which is considered as a form of the distinguish desire for development (Heron, 2011, 2007, 1999). Specifically, it indicates Voluntourism, which combines defining features of the work of volunteers and tourism, is revolved around working on the domains such as health, education and community development (Clemmons, 2011; Heron, 2011). McLennan (2014) points out that volunteers focuses on providing services, in particular services related to health, education and community development. Health care projects include organizations that operate permanent clinics, do health promotion activities, and that organize and facilitate medical brigades (short term medical teams). Education includes charitable schools, adult education and support for existing public and private schools. Community development is a fuzzy term which encompasses construction projects (of houses, schools and other community buildings), water and sanitation projects, and micro-credit and small business support programs. The link between "volunteers" and "tourism" seems to be in the spectrum wherein volunteers are combined with the tourism. In this sense, Stephen Wearing (2005) suggests that term 'volunteer tourism' refers to tourists who, for various reasons, volunteer in an organized way to undertake vacations that might involve: (1) aiding or alleviating the material poverty of some groups in society; (2) restoration of certain environments; (3) research into aspects of society or environment. Further, Wearing explains:

Volunteer tourism can take place in varied locations such as rainforests, biological reserves, or bustling cities. Activities can vary across many areas, such as scientific research (wildlife, land and water), conservation projects, medical assistance, economic and social development (including agriculture, construction and education), and cultural restoration. Hence the volunteer tourist contribution is bilateral, in that the most important development that may occur in the volunteer tourist experience is that of a personal nature, that of a greater awareness of self. That is, they are seeking a tourist experience that is mutually beneficial, that will contribute not only to their personal development, but also positively and directly to the social, natural and/or economic environments in which they participate. In principle, volunteer tourism as a leisure experience offers the potential for increased understanding between guest and host nations of the local community and economy in a decidedly decommodified manner.

In this sense, Voluntourism can be defined as a way to promote sustainable tourism which at the same time offers leisure experience from its volunteering activities. Research into Voluntourism as the alternative of niche tourism is explored from the perspectives of developing countries as object of the areas to be assisted (see Lyons & Wearing, 2008; Ong, Lockstone-Binney, King, & Smith, 2014). In this vein, Voluntourism is a particular research which combines social work and tourism which seems to be examined from the lens of (a) medical Voluntourism (e.g. see Godfrey, Wearing & Schulenkorf, 2015; Heron, 2011; Holmes, Smith, Lockstone-Binney & Baum, 2010; Lockstone-Binney, Holmes, Smith & Baum, 2010; Lockstone, Smith & Baum, 2010; Ong, Pearlman, & Lockstone-Binney, 2011; Smith & Font, 2014); (b) Voluntourism in general, which focuses on literacy e.g. teaching English in non-English speaking country and/or that focuses on conservation and preservation e.g. in South Africa region (Clemmons, 2011; Heron, 2011; McLennan, 2014).

A death site is most probably seen from the lens of religion and spirituality. The essence of spirituality, according to Krentzman (2013) and Willson, McIntosh, & Zahra (2013) revolves around such questions as (1) where do we find meaning? (2) how do we feel connected? and (3) how should we live?. On the other hand, in religion, the questions are: what is true and right? The interconnection between religion and spirituality lies on belief, comfort, reflection, ethics, and awe. These variables that construct religion and spirituality may explain why the need for visitation on the death sites and the extreme poverty areas. Dark tourism lovers find the belief, comfort, reflection, ethics, and awe on God and their relationships with other people and enables them to understand the meaning of life, love, and living, that it's the coexist perspectives.

WHERE DO WE GO FROM HERE?

Although, past studies denote the critics on the dichotomy between a premodern (authentic) and modern (inauthentic) (see Meethan 2001; Olsen 2002), and further analyses have attempted to deconstruct the notion of authenticity (see MacCannell, 1976), the shape of niche tourism to come would be pretty much relying on the form of cool authenticity (i.e. refers to the real, original, or genuine), not the hot authenticity (i.e. accepted but enjoyed fake versions) (Cole, 2007; Selwyn, 1996). This in line with Wang (1999) studies which points out the existential authenticity, which is defined as "a special existential state of being in which individuals are true to themselves". As a result, niche tourism, which in this study refers to dark tourism, has to be embedded with cool authenticity and existential authenticity. In this vein, death sites and Voluntourism emergence as niche tourism imprints features on the current and future society that are looking for new existential identity and motivation, which presumably is provided by the "darkness" elements of death sites as revelation and contemplation as mentioned by Seaton (1996); and the "lightness" elements of purity of coexist perspectives (Hayano, 2011), is led to the hospitality attributed to kindness, rightness, and interdependency with other people. This "rightness attitude" derived from hospitality which is projected towards the visitors would denotes the interrelationships among people as society, which emerges as the coexist perspectives (Korstanje, 2011; Hayano, 2011; Takahashi, 1988). Importantly, the role of significant other(s) in terms of the rituals that conducted in the death sites setting suggests interdependency with other people e.g. ritual of Trunyan cemetery in Bali and/or ritual of Aokigahara-Jukai is to extinguish one's existence, not only substantially but also symbolically. Trunyan cemetery and Aokigahara-Jukai suicide forest are the dark attractions which deeply revolves around philosophical role of significant other(s) and the coexist perspectives. More so, on the other side of niche tourism spectrum in postmodernism i.e. Voluntourism denotes hospitality elements, they are that attributed to the spectrum of Voluntourism perhaps also be in line with the perspectives of human interdependency with other people and the coexist perspectives (Clemmons, 2011; Heron, 2011; Hayano, 2011; Takahashi, 1988). As Krentzman (2013) puts it, some people find the belief, comfort, reflection, ethics, and awe in spirituality or some people may find it in religion. This positions death sites and extreme poverty areas as the most thought-provoking dark tourism layers in general, that shifts the religious society into secular society, and they are the most distinguished niche attractions.

The Shape Construction of Death Sites and Voluntourism to Come

As discussed, death sites and Voluntourism could be the next layers of attraction for dark tourism lover. Coupled with the ICT, several studies indicate that re-enactment in the context of death sites would potentially positions the popularity of it as a remarkable attraction. However, considering the deconstruction of niche tourism petty much relies on the cool authenticity and existential authenticity, this proliferation of ICT that intended to be applied for death site seems to be daunting albeit in tourism studies, hot authenticity (i.e. accepted attributes but enjoyed fake versions) is existed. Likewise, ICT application on the voulntourism seems to be make sense if it is used for Social Networking for Development (see McLennan, 2014) For that reason, proliferation of ICT that intended to be applied for death sites should be not diminishing the "true" darkness elements attributed to the brand image of the dark sites. In this vein, some of proliferations of ICT could be applicable when presumably is related with the accessibility. For instance, Wayfinding application could assist tourist in finding the comfy way to reach the destination, without being too stand in the way of the authenticity of the attraction as main essence of unique proposition. Wayfinding not only plays role in connecting the physical environment with the needs and emotions of visitors and/or residents but also it assists the visitors, residents, and/or local people in recalling the branded communications that has been exposed by the aspiration of the producer and/or by the online community reviews (Baker, 2016). This is in line with current research that intertwines Smart Tourism and Innovation that Gretzel (2016) indicates as the uses of digital ecosystem in Smart Destination. In this sense, digital ecosystem in Smart Destination i.e. in the context of death sites and Voluntourism could adapt the intertwined relationships between Smart Mobile phone and sensor, enables networked (business, consumers, technologies, things, experiences) which may enhance not only the destination values but also adds values to business (Gretzel, 2016).

CONCLUDING THOUGHTS AND FUTURE RESEARCH DIRECTIONS

The objective of this essay is to scrutinise construction of niche tourism in postmodernism i.e. death sites and Voluntourism. Without claiming to capture all of the developments in study of the construction of niche tourism in postmodernism, this essay identifies the layer of dark tourism as the revelation and contemplation, bridges the nexus between visiting the death sites and extreme poverty areas, and hospitality features as core essence attributed to authentic experience. Thus, this essay is an agreement of the previous studies which points out the significance nexus between visitation for revelation and desire for development. The findings of the current research provide insight into a key construction of niche tourism in postmodernism, in adopting approach of unique and emotional selling propositions of touristic market offerings to dealing with development and planning on death sites and Voluntourism. In this sense, visitation to the dark sites are done with intention for not only searching for revelation and contemplation but also aimed to fulfil the desire for development, which involves not only philosophical experience of avoiding troubled thoughts by maintaining quality relationships with significant other(s) in particular and to actively interact & involve with global community. In terms of Business perspective, the development and management of dark tourist sites and Voluntourism should be focused on the predictive Tourism. In sum, visitation to death sites and Voluntourism revolve around the spectrum of going to the dark sites with intention. Future research direction should focus on replication of this conceptualisation and test it empirically. With this in mind, it would enable further testing of this link and the inclusion of associated constructs.

REFERENCES

Anholt, S. (2007). *Competitive Identity: The New Brand Management for Nations, Cities and Regions*. New York: Palgrave Macmillan. doi:10.1057/9780230627727

Baker, B. (2016, April 27). What Does Wayfinding Add to City Branding? *Small City Branding Around the World*. Retrieved 27 April 2016, from http://citybranding.typepad.com/city-branding/2016/04/what-does-wayfinding-add-to-city-branding.html

Berridge, K. (2001). *Vigor mortis: the end of the death taboo*. London: Profile Books.

Clarke, J. N. (2005). Death under control: The portrayal of death in mass print English language magazines in Canada. *Omega*, *52*(2), 153–167.

Clarke, L. (2006). *Worst cases: terror and catastrophe in the popular imagination*. Chicago: University of Chicago Press.

Clemmons, D. (2011). *Voluntourism*. Retrieved 1 September 2016, from http://www.Voluntourism.org/contact.html

Cohen, E. (1988). Authenticity and commodization in tourism. *Annals of Tourism Research*, *15*(3), 371–386. doi:10.1016/0160-7383(88)90028-X

Cole, S. (2007). Beyond authenticity and commodification. *Annals of Tourism Research*, *34*(4), 943–960. doi:10.1016/j.annals.2007.05.004

Crozier, J. (2013). *The Dark Tourism Lecture JC v2*. Retrieved 1 September 2016, from https://www.youtube.com/watch?v=E52W8GA4DKA

Fife, W. (2004). Penetrating Types: Conflating Modernist and Postmodernist Tourism on the Great Northern Peninsula of Newfoundland. *Journal of American Folklore, 117*(464), 147–167. doi:10.1353/jaf.2004.0036

Foley, M., & Lennon, J. J. (1996). JFK and dark tourism: A fascination with assassination. *International Journal of Heritage Studies, 2*(4), 198–211. doi:10.1080/13527259608722175

Godfrey, J., Wearing, S., & Schulenkorf, N. (2015). Medical volunteer tourism as an alternative to backpacking in Peru. *Tourism Planning & Development, 12*(1), 111–122. doi:10.1080/21568316.2014.960602

Gretzel, U. (2016). *Smart Tourism*. Retrieved 28 Dec 2016, from https://www.youtube.com/watch?v=tlGvJgTqtmo

Handayani, B., Ivanov, S., & Korstanje, M. E. (2017). Smart Tourism for Dark Sites: The Sacred Site of the Dead, Trunyan Cemetery. In M. E. Korstanje & B. Handayani (Eds.), *Gazing at Death: Dark Tourism as an Emergent Horizon of Research* (pp. 15–42). New York: Nova Publishers.

Hayano, A. (2011). Suicide Forest in Japan. *VICE News*. Retrieved 15 August 2016, from https://www.youtube.com/watch?v=4FDSdg09df8

Heron, B. (2007). *Desire for development: Whiteness, gender, and the helping imperative*. Wilfrid Laurier Univ. Press.

Heron, B. (2011). *Voluntourism: Helping or Hurting? The Agenda with Steve Paikin*. Retrieved 1 September 2016, from https://www.youtube.com/watch?v=uzeM3DqEzXw

Heron, B. A. (1999). *Desire for development, the education of white women as development workers* (Doctoral dissertation). National Library of Canada, Bibliothèque nationale du Canada.

Holdenrid, C. (2013). *Dark Tourism*. Retrieved 1 September 2016, from https://www.youtube.com/watch?v=ZWO5U1dtfqE

Holmes, K., Smith, K. A., Lockstone-Binney, L., & Baum, T. (2010). Developing the dimensions of tourism volunteering. *Leisure Sciences, 32*(3), 255–269. doi:10.1080/01490401003712689

Ide, A. (2014). Dark tourism and information technology. Information Processing Society of Japan research report. *Computers and the Humanities Research Group report, 2014*(4), 1-6. Retrieved 13 June 2016, from https://ipsj.ixsq.nii.ac.jp/ej/?action=pages_view_main&active_action=repository_view_main_item_detail&item_id=101443&item_no=1&page_id=13&block_id=8

Jamal, T., & Lelo, L. (2011). Exploring the conceptual and analytical framing of dark tourism: From darkness to intentionality. *Tourist Experience: Contemporary Perspectives*, 29-42.

Kang, E. J., Scott, N., Lee, T. J., & Ballantyne, R. (2012). Benefits of visiting a 'dark tourismsite: The case of the Jeju April 3rd peace park, Korea. *Tourism Management, 33*(2), 257–265. doi:10.1016/j.tourman.2011.03.004

Korstanje, M. (2014). *Conceptual discussion of dark tourism: suffering, egoism and the depersonalization of death*. Conference, GOA University India. 02-03 May 2014. "Globalization of tourism, opportunities and challenges".

Korstanje, M. E. (2011). Influence of history in the encounter of guests and hosts. *Anatolia, 22*(2), 282–285. doi:10.1080/13032917.2011.597991

Korstanje, M. E., & George, B. (2015). Dark Tourism: Revisiting Some Philosophical Issues. *E-review of Tourism Research, 12*, 127–136.

Krentzman, A. R. (2013). *What Is Spirituality?* Retrieved 15 July 2015, from University of Minnesota, Center for Spirituality and Healing and Charlson Meadows website: http://www.takingcharge.csh.umn.edu/enhance-your-wellbeing/purpose/spirituality/what-spirituality

Lockstone, L., Smith, K., & Baum, T. (2010). Volunteering flexibility across the tourism sector. *Managing Leisure, 15*(1-2), 111–127. doi:10.1080/13606710903448202

Lockstone-Binney, L., Holmes, K., Smith, K., & Baum, T. (2010). Volunteers and volunteering in leisure: Social science perspectives. *Leisure Studies, 29*(4), 435–455. doi:10.1080/02614367.2010.527357

Lovelock, B. (2003). A comparative study of environmental NGOSperspectives of the tourism industry and modes of action in the South and South-East Asia and Oceania regions. *Asia Pacific Journal of Tourism Research, 8*(1), 1–14. doi:10.1080/10941660308725451

Lyons, K. D., & Wearing, S. (2008). Volunteer tourism as alternative tourism: Journeys beyond otherness. *Journeys of discovery in volunteer tourism: International case study perspectives*, 3-11.

MacCannell, D. (1976). The Tourist: A New Theory of the Leisure Class. New York: Schocken. 1984 Reconstructed Ethnicity: Tourism and Cultural Identity in Third World Communities. *Annals of Tourism Research, 11*(3), 375–391. doi:10.1016/0160-7383(84)90028-8

McGehee, N., & Norman, W. (2002). Alternative Tourism as Impetus for Consciousness-Raising. *Tourism Analysis, 6*, 239–251.

McGehee, N. G., & Santos, C. A. (2005). Social change, discourse and volunteer tourism. *Annals of Tourism Research, 32*(3), 760–779. doi:10.1016/j.annals.2004.12.002

McLennan, S. (2014). Networks for Development: Volunteer Tourism, Information and Communications Technology, and the Paradoxes of Alternative Development. *PoLAR: Political and Legal Anthropology Review, 37*(1), 48–68. doi:10.1111/plar.12050

Meethan, K. (2001). *Place, Culture, Consumption.* Basingstoke, UK: Palgrave. doi:10.1007/978-1-349-87747-8_8

Meschkank, J. (2011). Investigations into slum tourism in Mumbai: Poverty tourism and the tensions between different constructions of reality. *GeoJournal, 76*(1), 47–62. doi:10.1007/s10708-010-9401-7

Miles, W. (2002). Auschwitz: Museum interpretation and Darker Tourism. *Annals of Tourism Research, 29*(4), 1175–1178. doi:10.1016/S0160-7383(02)00054-3

Mowforth, M., & Munt, I. (2015). *Tourism and sustainability: Development, globalisation and new tourism in the third world.* Routledge.

Olsen, K. (2002). Authenticity as a Concept in Tourism Research. *Tourist Studies, 2*(2), 159–182. doi:10.1177/146879702761936644

Ong, F., Lockstone-Binney, L., King, B., & Smith, K. A. (2014). The Future of Volunteer Tourism in the Asia-Pacific Region Alternative Prospects. *Journal of Travel Research, 53*(6), 680–692. doi:10.1177/0047287514532365

Ong, F., Pearlman, M., & Lockstone-Binney, L. (2011). An examination of not-for-profit volunteer tourism sending organisations guiding considerations that influence volunteer tourism programmes. *World Leisure Journal, 53*(4), 296–311. doi:10.1080/04419057.2011.630787

Reed, K. (2009). The social construction of volunteer non-governmental organization worker identities: Preliminary analysis of effects and implications for information behaviors. *Proceedings of the American Society for Information Science and Technology, 46*(1), 1–4. doi:10.1002/meet.2009.1450460336

Robb, E. M. (2009). Violence and recreation: Vacationing in the realm of dark tourism. *Anthropology and Humanism*, *34*(1), 51–60. doi:10.1111/j.1548-1409.2009.01023.x

Seaton, A. V. (1996). Guided by the dark: From thanatopsis to thana-tourism. *International Journal of Heritage Studies*, *2*(4), 234–244. doi:10.1080/13527259608722178

Selwyn, T. (1996). Introduction. In T. Selwyn (Ed.), In the Tourist Image. Myths and Myth Making in Tourism (pp. 1–32). Chichester, UK: Wiley.

Sharpley, R. (2005). Travels to the edge of darkness: towards a typology of dark tourism. *Taking tourism to the limits: Issues, concepts and managerial perspectives*, 217-228.

Smith, V. L., & Font, X. (2014). Volunteer tourism, greenwashing and understanding responsible marketing using market signalling theory. *Journal of Sustainable Tourism*, *22*(6), 942–963. doi:10.1080/09669582.2013.871021

Stone, P. (2012). Dark tourism as mortality capital. *Annals of Tourism Research*, *39*(3), 1565–1587. doi:10.1016/j.annals.2012.04.007

Stone, P., & Sharpley, R. (2008). Consuming Dark-Tourism a Thanatological Perspective. *Annals of Tourism Research*, *35*(2), 574–595. doi:10.1016/j.annals.2008.02.003

Strange, C., & Kempa, M. (2003). Shades of dark tourism: Alcatraz and Robben Island. *Annals of Tourism Research*, *30*(2), 386–405. doi:10.1016/S0160-7383(02)00102-0

Takahashi, Y. (1988). Aokigahara-jukai: Suicide and Amnesia in Mt. Fujis Black Forest. *Suicide & Life-Threatening Behavior*, *18*(2), 164–175. doi:10.1111/j.1943 278X.1988.tb00150.x PMID:3420643

Uriely, N. (2005). The tourist experience: Conceptual developments. *Annals of Tourism Research*, *32*(1), 199–216. doi:10.1016/j.annals.2004.07.008

Wang, N. (1999). Rethinking Authenticity in Tourism Experience. *Annals of Tourism Research*, *26*(2), 349–370. doi:10.1016/S0160-7383(98)00103-0

Wearing, S., & McGehee, N. G. (2013a). Volunteer tourism: A review. *Tourism Management*, *38*, 120–130. doi:10.1016/j.tourman.2013.03.002

Wearing, S., & McGehee, N. G. (Eds.). (2013b). *International volunteer tourism: Integrating travellers and communities*. CABI. doi:10.1079/9781845936969.0000

Wearing, S. (2005). *Voluntourism - Can It Influence Mass Tourism?* Retrieved 1 September 2016, from http://www.Voluntourism.org/news-studyandresearch1105.htm

Is Voluntourism, W. (2013). *Storm Warriors International.* Retrieved 29 August 2016, from https://www.youtube.com/watch?v=MyR1nZbAWH0

Wight, A. C. (2006). Philosophical and methodological praxes in dark tourism: Controversy, contention and the evolving paradigm. *Journal of Vacation Marketing, 12*(2), 119–129. doi:10.1177/1356766706062151

Wilkinson, P. F. (2010). *Review of* "The darker side of travel: The theory and practice of dark tourism", by Sharpley and Stone. *e-Review of Tourism Research, 8*(1).

Willson, G. B., McIntosh, A. J., & Zahra, A. L. (2013). Tourism and spirituality: A phenomenological analysis. *Annals of Tourism Research, 42*, 150–168. doi:10.1016/j.annals.2013.01.016

Yeoman, I. S., & Beeton, S. (2014). The State of Tourism Futures Research: An Asian Pacific Ontological Perspective. *Journal of Travel Research, 53*(6), 675–679. doi:10.1177/0047287514551054

Zotic, V., Alexandru, D. E., & Dezsi, Ş. (2014). Debate on tourism in postmodernism and beyond. *Turističko poslovanje*, (13), 79-93.

ADDITIONAL READING

AP. (2007). Township Tourism booming as visitors want to see ''real'' South Africa. USA

Bellini, N., Grillo, F., Lazzeri, G., & Pasquinelli, C. (2017). Tourism and regional economic resilience from a policy perspective: Lessons from smart specialization strategies in Europe. *European Planning Studies*, 1–14.

Biran, A., Poria, Y., & Oren, G. (2011). Sought experiences at (dark) heritage sites. *Annals of Tourism Research, 38*(3), 820–841. doi:10.1016/j.annals.2010.12.001

Davis, M. (2006). *Planet of slums*. London: Verso.

Dunkley, R., Morgan, N., & Westwood, S. (2011). Visiting the trenches: Exploring meanings and motivations in battlefield tourism. *Tourism Management, 32*(4), 860–868. doi:10.1016/j.tourman.2010.07.011

Freire-Medeiros, B. (2007). A Favela que se ve^ e que se vende. Reflexo˜es e pole^micas em torno de um destino turıstico. *Revista Brasileira de Ciencias Sociais, 22*(65), 62–72. doi:10.1590/S0102-69092007000300006

Freire-Medeiros, B. (2009). The favela and its touristic transits. *Geoforum*, *40*(4), 580–588. doi:10.1016/j.geoforum.2008.10.007

Hatane, L. M. (2016). *" Understanding the costs and benefits of short term international volunteerism": exploring the benefits and potential harms with regard to short-term international volunteer service in Cape Town* (Doctoral dissertation, University of Cape Town).

Laing, J., & Frost, W. (2017). *2 Nature and Wellbeing*. Nature Tourism.

Leslie, D. (Ed.). (2012). *Responsible tourism: Concepts, theory and practice*. CABI. doi:10.1079/9781845939878.0000

Onda, T. (2011). *"Helping Them Help Themselves": Where Development Meets Tourism in Bali* (Doctoral dissertation, Wesleyan University).

Pleumarom, A. (2012). *The politics of tourism, poverty reduction and sustainable development*. Penang, Malaysia: Third World network (TWN).

Pleumarom, A. (2012). The politics of tourism and poverty reduction. *Responible tourism: Concepts. Theory into Practice*, 90–106.

Podoshen, J. S. (2013). Dark tourism motivations: Simulation, emotional contagion and topographic comparison. *Tourism Management*, *35*, 263–271. doi:10.1016/j.tourman.2012.08.002

Rolfes, M. (2010). Poverty tourism: Theoretical reflections and empirical findings on an extraordinary form of tourism. *GeoJournal*, *75*(5), 421–442. doi:10.1007/s10708-009-9311-8

Scheyvens, R. (2012). *Tourism and poverty*. Routledge.

Stone, P., & Sharpley, R. (2008). Consuming dark tourism: A thanatological perspective. *Annals of Tourism Research*, *35*(2), 574–595. doi:10.1016/j.annals.2008.02.003

Stone, P. R. (2010). *Death, dying and dark tourism in contemporary society: A theoretical and empirical analysis* (Doctoral dissertation, University of Central Lancashire).

Today. January 9, 2007. http://www.usatoday.com/travel/destinations/2007-01-04-south-africa-township-tourismx.htm. Accessed 10 June, 2016.

Wakeford, S. (2013). *The motivations, expectations and experiences of secondary school students involved in volunteer tourism: a case study of the Rangitoto College Cambodia house building trip* (Doctoral dissertation, Auckland University of Technology).

Walter, T., Pickering, M., & Littlewood, J. (1995). Death in the news: The public invigilation of private emotion. *Sociology*, *29*(1), 579–596. doi:10.1177/0038038595029004002

Wearing, S. (2001). *Volunteer tourism: Experiences that make a difference*. Cabi. doi:10.1079/9780851995335.0000

Wright, D. W. M. (2016). Hunting humans: A future for tourism in 2200. *Futures*, *78*, 34–46. doi:10.1016/j.futures.2016.03.021

Yeoman, I. (2012). *2050–tomorrow's tourism*. Bristol: Channel View Publications.

Zheng, C., Zhang, J., Zhang, H., & Qian, L. (2017). Exploring sub-dimensions of intrapersonal constraints to visiting dark tourism sites: A comparison of participants and non-participants. *Asia Pacific Journal of Tourism Research*, *22*(1), 21–33. doi:10.1080/10941665.2016.1175489

KEY TERMS AND DEFINITIONS

Death Tourism: A journey to places that are identified with death and suffering which aims for seeking the authentic experiences to witness how people died.

ICT: Technological and communication application (and/or term that includes any communication device or application, encompassing: radio, television, cellular phones, computer and network hardware and software, satellite systems and so on) that is used as tool to process data and information.

Niche Tourism: A sub-domain of Tourism Management is usually developed around visitors' particular interests or needs.

Postmodernism: A broad movement which marked a departure from modernism and is influenced by the proliferation of ICT.

Voluntourism: A combination of volunteering and tourism (sightseeing), allows international travel to contribute to sustainable development while exploring a new country and culture.

Chapter 4
On the Use of Qualitative Comparative Analysis to Identify the Bright Spots in Dark Tourism

Hugues Seraphin
The University of Winchester, UK

Vanessa Gowreesunkar
Mauritius Institute of Education, Mauritius

ABSTRACT

As Haiti lacks visitor attractions, the development of an authentic event programme is going to be an essential part of the on-going tourism strategy. Culturally rich events are part of the appeal of a destination and can be cost efficient to organise. Furthermore it is well documented that planned events have the ability to improve national pride in small developing countries. From our findings we have highlighted the fact that Voodoo has helped the Haitian people to maintain its true nature and culture and now offer economic development options to the destination. The development of voodoo events will enhance Haiti's tourism and provide opportunities for locals to embrace their cultural heritage and come to terms with their past. That said, unless the 'blind spots' of the destination are removed, there is no empirical evidence to confirm that tourism will bring prosperity to Haiti nor that voodoo can play a significant role in the country's tourism sector.

DOI: 10.4018/978-1-5225-2750-3.ch004

INTRODUCTION

The term 'dark tourism' was first coined by Lennon and Foley (2000) to define the relationship between dark tourism attractions and a specific interest in death, the macabre and the paranormal. Other academics such as Seaton (1996) have referred to this activity as 'thanatourism', 'morbid tourism' and 'black spots'. These terms have been used to describe a fascination for travelling to places where death or tragedy has occurred. As for Dalton (2015), he outlines how dark tourism sites are typically places of genocide and mass murders, locations where terrorist's acts have been executed or places where basic human rights have been violated. Based on the above interpretations of dark tourism, it becomes difficult to imagine that something positive can be worked out from this activity, and hence our research question: What are the bright spots of dark tourism? With this as background, the objective of this book chapter is to provide evidence that when an activity, product or service, as a key component of the daily life of locals, is used for tourism purpose, the activity, product or service is likely to be sustainable. The findings of this paper can be helpful for DMOs as they can influence destination marketing strategies in terms of products to be developed. Also, the findings of this book chapter helps to develop an understanding on the tourism industry which has often been blamed for the commodification of heritage sold to tourists as products and services (Park, 2014). To some extent, we are going to challenge Park (2014) statement. This book chapter covers both end of research spectrum: 'There are two types of research that can be considered. At one end of the spectrum is pure research, which is undertaken only to gain a better understanding of an issue with no other purpose than intellectual curiosity. At the other end of the spectrum is applied research. This research is undertaken specifically to offer a solution to a practical issue' (Fox, Gouthro, Morakabati & Brackstone, 2014: 9). In order to achieve our objectives, a qualitative comparative analysis (QCA) will be adopted. This approach is mainly used to study four issues: Internal organisational process; organisational external environment; overlap within and between organisational environments and finally promoting a methodological alternative (Kan, Adegbite, El Omari & Abdellatif, 2016). This book chapter falls into all four categories. Still regarding the methodology, Haiti, a post-colonial, post-conflict and post-disaster destination (Séraphin, Butcher & Korstanje, 2016) which also a well is known destination for Voodoo (Séraphin & Nolan, 2014), will be utilised as a case study. From a structural point of view, the chapter is going to be largely but not exclusively inspired by Kan, Adegbite, El Omari & Abdellatif (2016), a methodological paper that focuses on Qualitative Comparative Analysis (QCA).

Table 1. Anatomy of dark tourism

Lennon and Foley	1996	Death / Macabre / Paranormal
Seaton	1996	Tragedy
Daams	2007	Educational experience
Stone	2007	Education / entertainment
Bowman & Pezzulo	2010	Reflection on mortality
Garcia	2012	Ethics
Dalton	2015	Genocide / mass murders / terrorist acts / violation of human rights
Korstanje	2017	Tourism / Culture

Source: The author (adapted from various sources)

ANATOMY OF INVESTIGATED TOURISM PHENOMENON: VOODOO AND DARK TOURISM

Dark Tourism

Dark tourism is not a new phenomenon. According to Stone and Sharpley (2008), it refers to travel and experience of places, sites, attractions or events linked in one way or another with death, suffering, violence or disaster. Despite increasing academic attention paid to dark tourism, understanding of the concept remains limited, particularly with respect to its perception in tourism. Table 1 below, provides some information on how dark tourism is perceived:

Despite the fact dark tourism is an aggregate of different area, Table 1, shows an evolution in the way dark tourism is perceived. Daams (2007, cited in Niemelä, 2010, [Online]) describes how educational experiences are one of the key motives for attending these types of events. He outlines how visiting death and disaster sites can raise awareness of historical events and prompt the visitor to understand the world in more clarity – ultimately creating an educational experience (cited in Niemelä, 2010, [Online], p. 16). Likewise, Stone (2010) describes how dark tourism genocide sites such as Auschwitz allow visitors to learn about the history on the conditions under which individuals were tortured to death. Whilst the educational aspect of dark tourism is apparent, Bowman and Pezzullo (2010) describe another major motivation related to the contemplation of death. They posit that sites like Auschwitz enable people to come to terms with the fragility of life. A further reason attributed to this form of tourism is related to the entertainment factors. In this respect, Stone (2010) proposes the London Dungeons as an attraction utilised in the form of entertainment to exploit death and the deceased. Bowman and Pezzullo (2010) also describe how visits to dark tourism attractions can encourage a person to reflect on their own mortality. However, there is an ethical issue related to dark tourism. Stone (2007) describes how travelling to destinations where people are known to have suffered or passed can raise issues relating to exploitation for business, education or entertainment purposes. As a result, Garcia (2012) describes how the sensitive nature of dark tourism attractions poses many challenges to practitioners. To this, Rachel Noble, a representative of the charity Tourism Concern, suggests that sites associated with dark attributes should be avoided for numerous, ethical reasons. She describes how tourists visiting counties which have suffered in any way, whether this be through natural disaster or genocide, should contemplate the appropriateness of this (cited in Stokes, 2015 [Online]). However, other dark tourism attractions such as museums are considered to provide the experience and education in a more sophisticated manner (cited in Stokes, 2015 [Online]).

Voodoo (in Haiti)

This sub-section identifies articles and book chapters on dark tourism using *Academia*, *ResearchGate* and *Google Scholar* as database. The sample comprises 26 entries from aggregate databases. To obtain these 26 entries, the study used 'Voodoo' 'Haiti' as the two keywords and only considered research with the two keywords in their title. The results are as follow (Table 2):

Voodoo is mainly viewed as a religion and to a lesser extent, as a cultural elements; as a political and tourism tool and finally as a cure in medicine. Based on Park's (2014) definition, voodoo can be considered as a form of cultural heritage. As explained by Séraphin and Nolan (2014) in: '*Voodoo in Haiti: A Religious Ceremony at the Service of the 'Houngan' Called 'Tourism,'* voodoo is derived from the West African religion Vodun and was developed (almost solely) in Haiti by the imported African slaves. The religion was used a means to cope with the degradations of slavery including being forced to convert to Christianity and to speak Créole. Voodoo became a way for the slaves to keep a connection with their African roots and also to retain some of their humanity (Damoison & Dalembert, 2003). It also helped slaves to resist their master's cultural oppression (Saint-Louis, 2000) and to adapt to their new environment. Modern voodoo is said to have derived from a mixture of the master's religion and African Vodun (Metraux, 1958). As a religion, voodoo is based on the belief in a *Grand Maître*, a Great Master or Creator, as well as several *loa* or spirits. The practise of voodoo involves ritual celebrations led by a *Houngan* or priest. Metraux (1958) explains that a good Houngan should be able to perform many roles: priest, healer, fortune teller, exerciser and entertainer. And as such it can be argued that as a religion, voodoo is perfectible. This flexibility, combined with the origins of voodoo (a means to survive difficult conditions) – demonstrates that voodoo is perfectly able to adapt to its environment and the needs of the market

Table 2. Anatomy of voodoo

Grenier	2002	Culture
Potter	2010	Culture
Hebblethwaite	2015	Culture
Largey	2006	Culture
Williams	1969	Culture
Rippmann	**2000**	Medicine
Gustafson	1990	Medicine
Laguerre	**2016**	Politics
Garrisson	2000	Politics
Trouillot	1991	Politics
Rotberg	1990	Politics
Feguson & Laguerre	1990	Politics
Armitage	**2014**	Religion
Gobin	2012	Religion
Clark	2009	Religion
McGee	2008	Religion
Louis	2007	Religion
Taylor	2004	Religion
Glazier, Leland & Richards	1993	Religion
Matsua	1992	Religion
Homiak	1991	Religion
Hicks	1982	Religion
Bourguignon	1970	Religion
Carrasco	2015	Religion
Séraphin & Nolan	2014	Tourism
Goldberg	1983	Tourism

Source: The authors (adapted from various sources)

without losing its authenticity. Thomson (2004) explains that when he visited Haiti in 1990, he witnessed many voodoo ceremonies being staged for tourists at hotels 'Friday night in the Oloffson [hotel]) was traditionally the night for a voodoo extravaganza carefully choreographed by (...) the showgirls' (Thomson, 2004:46). During this decade Haiti received few tourists because of the political and economic situation of the country (Séraphin, 2013ab) but voodoo ceremonies were successfully staged for those who were desirable of it. Although the hotel environment may have staged the authenticity of the ritual, the Houngan were content to perform and the visitors pleased to watch. This commercialisation of voodoo described by Thomson (2004) in *Bonjour Blanc, a journey through Haiti,* has highlighted the importance of involving the locals in the tourism sector as they have contributed to the visitor experience (Séraphin, 2013c). As voodoo is an integral part of the Haitian culture, sharing with visitors can also contribute to a better self-awareness, understanding and acceptance of this heritage. From the above, it is clear that the role of Voodoo has changed throughout the years.

Can we come to the conclusion that dark tourism and Voodoo (as a form of dark tourism) are both moving away from the dark pain and suffering to something brighter, enjoyable and profitable?

METHODOLOGY

Multi Criteria Decision Analysis

Botti and Peypoch (2013: 109) explain that 'MCDA is a general term for methods providing a quantitative approach to support decision making in problems involving several criteria and choices'. Botti and Peypoch (2013:108) also propose that what tourists are doing when selecting a destination for their holidays: 'Tourists who wish to enjoy a satisfying experience try to select one destination from a set of *n* possible alternatives and on the basis of *m* criteria'. A MCDA could therefore be considered as a method falling under Qualitative Comparative Analysis (QCA).

Taking the example of countries economic performance, Vis, Woldendorp and Keman (2007) pointed out a few research gaps in the field of QCA: First of all, they are very limited. Second, most comparative analyses research rely or a single case study. This approach is not rigorous as 'studying single cases hardly help to discern best practices' (Vis et al, 2007: 532). As a result, Vis et al (2007) are promoting the fuzzy-set theory combined with ideal type analysis as a potential solution to address the lack of good practice in terms of comparative analysis. 'This approach provides more precise information on the case under investigation (...) and is easily interpretable (Vis et al, 2007: 537). As for Stokke (2007), he completes the list of advantages of using qualitative comparative analysis (QCA) by adding the fact that this technique can help the investigator to consider more cases than he would usual do. For instance, Chang, Tseng and Woodside (2013) used this technique to analyse 645 self-administered questionnaires. For Ordanini, Parasuraman and Rubera (2013), QCA makes better sense of the data in research contexts. To the list of benefits of this method can be added achieving accuracy and generalisation (Woodside and Baxter, 2013), it is more informative and structured (Loane, Bell & McNaughton, 2006). Last but not least, this method can be applied to a variety of areas like education (Schneider, Bentrop & Paunescu, 2010); health (Chang, Tseng & Woodside, 2013); ICT (Loane & Bell, 2006); hospitality (Ordanini, Parasuraman and Rubera, 2013), in B2B context (Woodside & Baxter, 2013), countries economic performance (Vis, 2007), politics (Stokke, 2007) to name a few. If Ordanini & Parasuraman (2013) introduced QCA into a luxury hotel context to investigate how customers' perceptions of new service attribute influence adoption intentions in order to evidence that QCA can help make better sense of the data in research contexts, it is however very important to highlight the fact, QCA is not the only research technique advocating the use of more than one source of information or data. The ELECTRE method developed by Ritchie and Crouch, 2003 (cited in Botti & Peypoch, 2013) integrates all the relevant factors that might typify the competitiveness of a destination, namely: Core resources and attractors; supporting factors and resources; destination management; destination policy, planning and development; qualifying and amplifying determinants. (Ritchie & Crouch, 2003 cited in Botti & Peypoch, 2013). This method is one of the most cited in academic research related to tourism (Botti & Peypoch, 2013). The ELECTRE method is part of a more general term for method providing support for decision making in problem involving several criteria and choices, namely Multi-Criteria Decision Analysis (Botti & Peypoch, 2013). Still in a tourism marketing context, Séraphin, Gowreesunkar and Ambaye (2016) used the Blakeley Model (2007), a multi criteria model to determine the blind spots of Haiti as a tourist destination. Séraphin, Ambaye, Gowreesunkar and Bonnardel (2016) also developed a multi-criteria model for Destination Marketing Organisation to determine the right color for their logo. Woodside and Baxter (2013) in their quest to achieving accuracy and therefore the possibility to generalise results, pointed out that Case Study Research (CSR), degrees-of-freedom analysis (DFA), fs/QCA and decision system analysis (DSA) are tool helping to achieving excellence in the quality of results. It is legitimate to wonder whether MCDA can reach this level of accuracy. Woodside and Baxter (2013) used DSA in a context where manufacturers, distributors and customers were involved in the decision. In other words, many stakeholders involved in decision making. To some extent, this tool presents many similarities with MCDA. We can also come to the conclusion that QCA, a method theorized by John Stuart Mill in 1843 and popularised by Ragin in 1987 (Kan, Adegbite, El Omari & Abdellatif, 2016) and used in many sectors opened the door to many other approaches, stream of thoughts and more importantly, accurate and precise research tool. Among these are the Blakeley Model (2007) mentioned earlier in this sub-section.

ABOUT THE BLAKELEY MODEL AND ITS APPLICATIONS

There are many barriers to learning, some of which are systemic (e.g. lack of opportunity, a culture that does not support learning, lack of exposure to environmental change) and some rooted in individual psychology such as cognitive dissonance (Festinger, 1957) or Freudian defense mechanisms (Illeris, 2009). When an individual (or system) fails to learn, representations and understandings of reality no longer function effectively as changes that have taken place in the environment fail to be incorporated into the learner's mental representations of the world (Barr, Stimpert & Huff, 1992).

There is a general consensus that people defend themselves against learning when the content of that learning is in some way uncomfortable or threatening to the self. Failure to learn then results in blind spots which can be defined as 'a regular tendency to repress, distort, dismiss or fail to notice information, views or ideas in a particular area that results in…[failure] to learn, change or grow in responses to changes in that area' (Blakeley, 2007: 6).

There are many models of learning in adulthood (Mezirow, 1990; Argyris, 1976; Schön, 1983) but the one elaborated on here is Blakeley's, which places the issues of 'blind spots' and defense mechanisms as central to the understanding of learning process (Blakeley, 2007). Learning, according to this model, comprises four key processes: paying attention to a cue, experiencing emotions, sense-making and generating behavior in a way that results in new or changed beliefs, behavior or emotional orientations (such as increased self-confidence or openness to change). Learning only results when the individual notices new and different cues, or makes sense of cues in a way that generates new constructs, beliefs, emotions or behavior. When individuals pay attention to familiar cues, experience emotions, make sense and take action in ways that involve no change, then they are in the comfort zone, drawing on existing knowledge and skills in order to survive and achieve goals within the environment. When they pay attention to new cues, learn new emotions in relation to cues (e.g. increasing self-confidence in relation to a skill), make sense in ways that expand understanding and change behavior, they step outside of the comfort zone and into the learning zone; here they start to experience a range of emotions, depending on how novel the learning is, or how threatening it is to the self. If people do not step outside the comfort zone and engage with these emotions however, they do not learn. The greater the ability to do this, the greater the learning that takes place. This then contributes towards the expansion of cognitive, emotional and behavioral resources that enable learners to adapt and be ready for the complex, changing world in which they live.

Because the Haitians have no dreams or hopes and they live with past memories (Wagner, 2015), 'emotions' and 'change of emotions' are problematic. The same can be said for 'action' and 'change of behavior' as the leaders don't care about the well-being of their people. Subsequently nothing has been done to improve their standard of living, resulting in a population for whom basic needs are not fulfilled (Wagner, 2015). As a result, this situation has led to a 'brain-drain' (Wagner 2015) and it has been very difficult for Haiti to keep up with all the changes in the tourism industry and in other sectors. For instance, informality of businesses is still a norm in Haiti (Wagner, 2015). Based on this analysis, it is obvious that Haiti as a destination has remained in its comfort zone (Maguire 2014; Thomson, 2004). The population is a key ingredient to the success of the tourism industry as a sector. But, because the Haitian population is faced with unfavorable living conditions, quite understandably they have other concerns than welcoming tourists. Haiti is not ready for the tourism industry yet (Darwling-Carter, 2010).

The Blakeley model applied to Haiti revealed that the problem of the tourism industry goes beyond tourism management skills. It is first of all a human issue that needs to be addressed (the primary needs of the locals need to be met); the human aspect needs to be fixed (a sense of community needs to be developed and the locals need to be able to dream); and finally, Haiti needs visionary leaders (the right context needs to be put in place and the 'yes, we can spirit' encouraged). It is the improvement of the well-being of Haitians that is going to lead to the improvement of the performance of Haiti as a destination (Séraphin, Gowreesunkar & Ambaye, 2016)

The Blakeley Model Applied to Dark Tourism (Voodoo) in Haiti to Identify the Bright Spot of Dark Tourism

The deductive method seeks to draw valid conclusions from initial premises. It follows the logic of syllogy (Hammond & Wellington, 2013:40). Therefore, if the blind spot is all about a context that stop people to be able to release their full potential and also a context where there is a discrepancy between how a destination perceive itself and how potential visitors perceive this destination, the bright spot can therefore be a context that facilitate people self-actualisation and where the view of visitors and locals are similar about a destination. This latest approach is to be related to interpretivism 'which takes the world as capable of multiple interpretations and seeks to uncover the meaning that human beings invest in social activity' (Hammond & Wellington, 2013:120). In post-colonial, post-conflict and post-disaster destinations like Haiti, Séraphin, Butcher and Korstanje (2016) highlighted the importance of education of tourists at pre-visit stage as a way to remove blind spots and potentially improve the negative perception of visitors about a particular destination. Based on a deductive approach, we can also come to the conclusion that education contribute to identify and shed light on the bright spots. Can Voodoo be considered as an education tool? If the answer is 'yes', Voodoo could be considered as a bright spot in the economic, social development of Haiti and above all could give potential visitors a better understanding of the destination and its history and change their negative perception. Thus, using the information about Voodoo provided in section 2, we understand that Voodoo is actually quite 'bright' always supported by an interesting story of life. Voodoo helped Haitian people to maintain a sense of unity; maintain their African roots; to free themselves and making history by becoming the first black republic in the world. Because of the negative image of Haiti (Séraphin et al, 2016a,b) tourists do not really know and therefore understand the importance of this religion in Haiti. This leads to the conclusion that Voodoo can be an even brighter spot when it is made visible.

FINDINGS AND DISCUSSIONS

Voodoo as a form of dark tourism presents many bright spots that are hidden by blind spots. This situation explains why Voodoo is still not a driver for tourism development in Haiti. Also, concerns about the impacts of tourism on local culture could explain why Voodoo has not really been pushed forward as a tourism product. Tourism offers destinations an opportunity for economic diversification (Holden, 2013), and experiences and products to tourists (Page, 2013). However, because of touristic practice, ethics and moral concerns have become prominent topics. The environmental impacts of the industry and implications for developing societies are some of the key focus. Subsequently, many ethical codes and code of conducts have been developed like the Global Code of Ethics for Tourism adopted in 1999 with the objective of minimising the negative impact of tourism on the environment and on cultural heritage while maximising the benefits of tourism in promoting sustainable development and poverty alleviation as well as understanding among nations (Edgell & Swanson, 2013), and a number of alternative forms of tourism (responsible tourism; pro-poor tourism; fair trade in tourism; volunteer tourism; reality tours; transnational solidarity activism) have been developed in an attempt to reduce the negative impacts of the industry and more importantly to ensure that good is being done (Lovelock & Lovelock, 2013). Alongside these initiatives, many definitions of sustainable tourism have been developed. In this book chapter we adopt the one developed by East Carolina University's Centre for Sustainable Tourism: 'Sustainable tourism contributes to a balanced and healthy economy by generating tourism-related jobs, revenues and taxes while protecting and enhancing the destination's social, cultural, historical, natural, and built resources for the enjoyment and well-being of both residents and visitors' (Edgell Sr & Swanson, 2013: 149). As a results of all the information provided in this sub-section, we come to the interim conclusion that non-purpose tourism products and activities (like Voodoo) which we define as: 'any activity which main purpose is deeply rooted into the local livelihood therefore not purposely designed and created for tourism but that can be used and experienced also by visitors, with an in fine objective to enhance the tourist experience while positively impacting on the locals at various levels', are the most sustainable form of tourism as they benefit the tourists and the locals. Taking the example of street-food, Bellia, Pilato and Séraphin (2016) provide evidence that non-purpose tourism products and activities are sustainable. Street-food is a common way of eating in emerging countries (or destinations) like Africa, Asia and Latin America (Kowalczyk, 2014; Marras, 2014 cited in Global Forum on Food Security and Nutrition). Beyond being a way of eating, street-food is also an entrepreneurial and social activity that provides employment (street food vendors) to a huge percentage of the population in emerging countries (Fellow & Hilmi, 2011). Street-food can also be a tourism tool. Studies show that food represents an attraction in its own right, as tourists are more interested to experience authenticity (Tinker, 1997; Kowalczyk, 2014). Indeed, food (taste, ingredient, accompaniment, preparation, form of serving the dish and the way of consuming the dish), is an important motivator that push people to travel the world. Food and tourism are therefore inextricably linked, given that eating is a physical necessity for every tourist and food and beverage in tourism do generate substantial revenues (Hjalger and Richards, 2002).

Following this compelling information explaining why street could be considered as a non-purpose tourism product and activity but also a sustainable activity, we come to the same conclusion about Voodoo in Haiti (Séraphin, 2017). However, it is also important to highlight the fact that 'authenticity is regarded as the most important criterion for the development of heritage tourism' (Xie & Wall, 2003 in Park, 2014: 62). Dark tourism can therefore play an important role in heritage tourism in Haiti while maintaining the authenticity of the product.

CONCLUSION

As Haiti lacks visitor attractions, the development of an authentic event programme is going to be an essential part of the on-going tourism strategy (Séraphin & Nolan, 2014). Culturally rich events are part of the appeal of a destination and can be cost efficient to organise. Furthermore it is well documented that planned events have the ability to improve national pride in small developing countries (O'Toole, 2011). From our findings, we come to the conclusion that Voodoo has helped Haitian people to maintain their cultural authenticity and now offer economic development options to the destination. The development of voodoo events may enhance Haiti's tourism and provide opportunities for locals to embrace their cultural heritage and come to terms with their past (Séraphin & Nolan, 2014). That said, unless the 'blind spots' of the destination are removed, there is no empirical evidence to confirm that tourism will bring prosperity to Haiti (Séraphin et al., 2016) nor that voodoo can play a significant role in the country's tourism sector (Séraphin & Nolan, 2014).

FUTURE RESEARCH

After applying the cointegration theory to the Haitian context, Dupont (2009) came to the conclusion that this destination should focus first on developing the condition of leaving of its people before thinking about tourism development as it is the reduction of poverty that is going to trigger the development of tourism and not the other way round. Future research (empirical and conceptual) could therefore be directed towards the investigation of real potential economic impacts of Voodoo with focus on the prerequisites that would make it an effective agent of development for Haiti and destinations with a similar profile.

REFERENCES

Argyris, C. (1976). Single loop and double loop models in research on decision making. *Administrative Science Quarterly, 21*(3), 363–375. doi:10.2307/2391848

Barr, P. S., Stimpert, J. L., & Huff, A. S. (1992). Cognitive change, strategic action, and organizational renewal. *Strategic Management Journal, 13*(1), 15–36. doi:10.1002/smj.4250131004

Blakeley, K. (2007). *Leadership blind spots and what to do about them*. Chichester, UK: Wiley.

Botti, L., & Peypoch, N. (2013). Multi-criteria ELECTRE method and destination competitiveness. *Tourism Management Perspectives, 6*, 108–113. doi:10.1016/j.tmp.2013.01.001

Bowman, M. S., & Pezzullo, P. C. (2010). Whats so Dark about Dark Tourism? - death, tours, and performance. *Tourist Studies, 9*(3), 187–202. doi:10.1177/1468797610382699

Chang, C. W., Tseng, T. H., & Woodside, A. G. (2013). Configural algorithms of patient satisfaction, participation in diagnostics, and treatment decisions influences on hospital loyalty. *Journal of Services Marketing*, *27*(2), 91–103. doi:10.1108/08876041311309225

Dalton, D. (2015). *Dark tourism and crime*. Abingdon, UK: Routledge.

Damoison, D., & Dalembert, L. P. (2003). *Vodou. Un tambour pour les anges*. Paris: Editions Autrement.

Darwling-Carter, G. (2010). Quand on parle de tourisme. *Antilla*, *1415*, 38–40.

Dupont, L. (2009). Cointegration et causalité entre développement touristique, croissance économique et réduction de la pauvreté: Cas de Haïti. *Etudes Caribéennes*. Available from: http://etudescaribeennes.revues.org/3780

Edgell, D. L. Sr, & Swanson, J. R. (2013). *Tourism policy and planning. Yesterday, today, and tomorrow*. Abingdon, UK: Routledge.

Fellow, P. & Hilmi, M. (2011). *Selling street and snack foods*. FAO diversification booklet 18.

Festinger, L. (1957). *A theory of cognitive dissonance*. Palo Alto, CA: Stanford University.

Fox, D., Gouthro, M. B., Morakabati, Y., & Brackstone, J. (2014). *Doing events research from theory to practice*. Abingdon, UK: Routledge.

Garcia, B. R. (2012). Management Issues in dark tourism attractions: The case of ghost tours in Edinburgh and Toledo. *Journal of Unconventional Parks Tourism and Recreation Research*, *4*(1), 14–19.

Global Forum on Food Security and Nutrition. (2014). *Street food and urban and periurban agriculture and horticulture: perspectives for a strategic coalition towards food security*. Discussion No. 110 from 17 November to 12 December. Author.

Hammond, M., & Wellington, J. (2013). *Research Methods. The Key Concepts*. London: Routledge.

Hjalger, A. M., & Richards, G. (2002). *Tourism and gastronomy*. London: Routledge.

Holden, A. (2013). *Tourism, poverty and development*. Abingdon, UK: Routledge.

Illeris, K. (2009). A comprehensive understanding of human learning. In K. Illeris (Ed.), *Contemporary Theories of Learning – Learning theorists... in their own words*. Abingdon, UK: Routledge.

Kan, A. K. S., Adegbite, E., El Omari, S., & Abdellatif, M. (2016). On the use of qualitative comparative analysis in management. *Journal of Business Research, 69*(4), 1458–1463. doi:10.1016/j.jbusres.2015.10.125

Korstanje, M. E., & Handayani, B. (2017). *Gazing at death, New-York.* Nova Science Publishers, Inc.

Kowalczyk, A. (2014). *From street food to food districts – Gastronomy services and culinary tourism in an urban space*. Retrieved from www.turystykakulturowa.org

Lennon, J., & Foley, M. (2000). *Dark Tourism – The Attraction of Death and Disaster*. London: Thomson.

Loane, S., Bell, J., & McNaughton, R. (2006). Employing information communication technologies to enhance qualitative international marketing enquiry. *International Marketing Review, 23*(4), 438–455. doi:10.1108/02651330610678994

Loane, S., Bell, J., & McNaughton, R. (2006). Employing information communication technologies to enhance qualitative international marketing enquiry. *International Marketing Review, 23*(4), 438–455. doi:10.1108/02651330610678994

Lovelock, B., & Lovelock, K. (2013). *The ethics of tourism: Critical and applied perspectives*. Routledge.

Maguire, R. (2014). The limits of Haitian so sovereignty: Haiti through clear eyes. *The Journal Haitian Studies, 20*(2), 165–177. doi:10.1353/jhs.2014.0027

Metraux, A. (1958). *Le vodou haitien*. Paris: Gallimard.

Mezirow, J. et al. (1990). *Fostering critical reflection in adulthood: A guide to transformative and emancipatory learning*. San Francisco, CA: Jossey Bass.

Niemelä, T. (2010). *Motivation Factors in Dark Tourism - Case: House of Terror*. Available from: http://www.theseus.fi/bitstream/handle/10024/14984/Niemela_Titta.pdf

O'Toole, W. (2011). *Events Feasibility and Development*. Oxford, UK: Elsevier.

Ordanini, A., Parasuraman, A., & Rubera, G. (2013). Service innovation viewed through a service-dominant logic lens: A conceptual framework and empirical analysis. *Journal of Service Research, 14*(1), 3–23. doi:10.1177/1094670510385332

Page, S. J. (2013). *Tourism management. An introduction* (4th ed.). Abingdon, UK: Routledge.

Park, Y. P. (2014). *Heritage Tourism*. Abingdon, UK: Routledge.

Pilato, M., Bellia, C., & Séraphin, H. (2016). *Street food and food safety: A driver for tourism?* PEEC2016 International Conference, Bucharest University of Economic Studies, Bucharest, Romania.

Pilato, M., Bellia, C., & Séraphin, H. (2016). *Street food and food safety: A driver for tourism?* PEEC2016 International Conference, Bucharest University of Economic Studies, Bucharest, Romania.

Schneider, M. R., Schulze-Bentrop, C., & Paunescu, M. (2010). Mapping the Institutional Capital of High-Tech Firms: A Fuzzy-Set Analysis of Capitalist Variety and Export Performance. *Journal of International Business Studies*, *41*(2), 246–266. doi:10.1057/jibs.2009.36

Schön, D. A. (1983). *The reflective practitioner: how professionals think in action*. London: Temple-Smith.

Seaton, A. (1996). Guided by the dark: From thanatopsis to thanatourism. *International Journal of Heritage Studies*, *2*(4), 234–244. doi:10.1080/13527259608722178

Séraphin, H. (2017). Assessing dark tourism as a sustainable economic activity for emerging destinations using a multi criteria approach. In M. E. Korstanje & B. Handayani (Eds.), *Gazing at death*. Nova Science Publishers, Inc.

Séraphin, H., Butcher, J. & Konstanje, M. (2016). Challenging the negative images of Haiti at a pre-visit stage using Visual Online Learning Materials. *Journal of Policy Research in Tourism, Leisure and Events*. doi: 10.1080/19407963.2016.1261146

Séraphin, H., Gowreesunkar, V. & Ambaye, M. (2016). The Blakeley Model applied to improving a tourist destination: The case of Haiti. *Journal of Destination Marketing Management*. doi: 10.1016/j.jdmm.2016.07.004

Séraphin, H., & Nolan, E. (2014). Voodoo in Haiti: A Religious Ceremony at the Service of the 'Houngan' Called 'Tourism'. In Rituals and traditional events in the modern world. New-York: Routledge.

Stokes, R. (2015). *Can dark tourism ever be a good thing?*. Available from: http://newint.org/features/web-exclusive/2013/01/21/dark-tourism/

Stokke, O. S. (2007). Qualitative comparative analysis, shaming, and international regime effectiveness. *Journal of Business Research*, *60*(5), 501–511. doi:10.1016/j.jbusres.2007.01.003

Stone, P. (2007). *Dark tourism: the ethics of exploiting tragedy*. Available from: http://works.bepress.com/cgi/viewcontent.cgi?article=1020&context=philip_stone

Stone, P. (2010). *Death, Dying and Dark Tourism in Contemporary Society: A Theoretical and Empirical Analysis*. Available from: http://clok.uclan.ac.uk/1870/1/StonePPhD_thesis_final.pdf

Stone, P., & Sharpley, R. (2008). *Consuming Dark Tourism: A Thanatological Perspective*. Academic Press.

Thomson, I. (2004). *Bonjour blanc, a journey through Haiti*. London: Vintage.

Tinker, I. (1997). *Street Foods: Urban Food and Employment in Developing Countries*. New York: Oxford University Press.

Vis, B., Woldendorp, J., & Keman, H. (2007). Do miracles exist? Analyzing economic performance comparatively. *Journal of Business Research*, *60*(5), 531–538. doi:10.1016/j.jbusres.2007.01.006

Wagner, L. R. (2015). *Hold tight, don't let go*. New York: Amulet Books.

Woodside, A. G., & Baxter, R. (2013). Achieving accuracy, generalization-to-contexts, and complexity in theories of business-to-business decision processes. *Industrial Marketing Management*, *42*(3), 382–393. doi:10.1016/j.indmarman.2013.02.004

ADDITIONAL READING

Korstanje, M. E., & Handayani, B. (2016). *Gazing at death, New-York*. Nova Science Publishers, Inc.

Korstanje, M. E., & Séraphin, H. (2016). Revisiting the Sociology of Consumption in Tourism. In S. K. Dixit (Ed.), *Handbook of Consumer Behaviour in Hospitality and Tourism*. Abingdon: Routledge.

Korstanje, M. E., & Tarlow, P. (2012). Being lost: Tourism, risk and vulnerability in the post-9/11entertainment industry. *Journal of Tourism and Cultural Change*, *10*(1), 22–33. doi:10.1080/14766825.2011.639455

Powell, C., Dosquet, F., & Séraphin, H. (2015) Guide pratique de l'organisateur d'évènements, Mesnil: EMS Management Saurabh Kumar Dixit (Ed.), Handbook of Consumer Behaviour in Hospitality and Tourism. Abingdon: Routledge

Séraphin, H. (2014). *Le tourisme: L'ouverture pour le peuple de Toussaint*. Paris: Publibook.

Séraphin, H. (2017). Assessing dark tourism as a sustainable economic activity for emerging destinations using a multi criteria approach. In M. E. Korstanje & B. Handayani (Eds.), *Gazing at death, New-York*. Nova Science Publishers, Inc.

Stone, P. (2010) Death, Dying and Dark Tourism in Contemporary Society: A

Theoretical and Empirical Analysis. Available from: http://clok.uclan.ac.uk/1870/1/StonePPhD_thesis_final.pdf [Accessed: 17.12.16].

Volcic, Z., Erjavec, K., & Peak, M. (2014). Branding post-war Sarajevo. Journalism. *Journalism Studies*, *15*(6), 726–742. doi:10.1080/1461670X.2013.837255

KEY TERMS AND DEFINITIONS

Blind Spot: Failure to learn then results in blind spots which can be defined as 'a regular tendency to repress, distort, dismiss or fail to notice information, views or ideas in a particular area that results in…[failure] to learn, change or grow in responses to changes in that area' (Blakeley, 2007: 6).

Dark Tourism: Seaton (1996) have referred to this activity as 'thanatourism', 'morbid tourism' and 'black spots' used to describe a fascination for travelling to places where death or tragedy has occurred.

Qualitative Comparative Analysis (QCA): This approach is mainly used to study four issues: Internal organisational process; organisational external environment; overlap within and between organisational environments and finally promoting a methodological alternative.

Chapter 5
Research Methods in Dark Tourism Fields

Maximiliano Emanuel Korstanje
University of Palermo, Argentina

ABSTRACT

The current chapter delves into the methodologies as well as limitations of used method in dark tourism fields. As fieldworkers are familiar, sometimes interviewees not only are incognizant of their inner-world, but in other occasion, they simply do not say the truth to protect their own interests. Though in tourism and dark tourism fields, researchers are prone to administer questionnaires or interviews as the main methodological option, no less true is that results are far from being clear or have very problems to be organized in an all-encompassing model.

INTRODUCTION

Dark Tourism situated as one of most intriguing issues in tourism research over the recent years. In fact, it represents not only a new fertile ground to understand how authenticity works but the fascination for others' death (Lennon & Foley, 2000). For some voices, dark tourism is both, a result of the rise of twentieth century as well as the consolidation of postmodernism that ushered society into a solipsist individualism (Korstanje, 2016). What is even more important seems to be the connection of death and secularization. While for some scholars, dark tourism can be defined as a form of new heritage (Poria, Reichel & Biran, 2006; Cohen, 2011), for others, it can be framed under the logic of consumption (Stone & Sharpley, 2008; Stone, 2013).

As this backdrop, no less true is that this emergent subfield shows some methodological limitations in how the fieldwork is conducted as well as samples

DOI: 10.4018/978-1-5225-2750-3.ch005

are drawn. In a seminal manuscript, Philip Stone (2011) questioned despite the advance of applied research in last years, there is a clear fragmentation in the produced knowledge which leads very well to misunderstanding and confusion. In this respect, it is necessary to posit a clear agenda to forge multidisciplinary and unified methods of study. In this chapter, we explore not only the main limitations of current research in dark tourism fields, but also focuse on the multiplication of different meanings about the phenomenon. Under the same connotation, there is no consensus what dark tourism means. While some specialists allude to "dark tourism" (Stone, 2011; 2013), others prefer other nomenclatures as "Thana Tourism" (Knudsen, 2011), Morbid tourism (Blom, 2000), Tragedy Tourism (Verma & Jain, 2013), among many others. This essay-review is not ended to ignite a debate in what what has been written but only to focus in the methodological approaches followed by professional fieldworkers up to date.

Our main thesis is that applied-research in dark tourism issues show three main problems, which obscure part of obtained results. At a first glance, beside the lack of coherence to use methodologies, there is a tendency to abuse from open-ended or close-ended questionnaires, which often are applied to tourists on the visited sites. Since dark tourism is defined exclusively as "an experience", in a whole portion of literature, professional researchers allude to what tourists think, feel or surmise to elaborate further indicators that help understanding the issue from an all-encompassing way. But quite aside from this, these approaches ignore sometimes people are unfamiliar with their inner-world while in others they simply lie to protect their interests. This means that there is a great dissonance between what people do and really think. The second problem consists in replicating the logic of destination-management in the resulted diagnosis. Since dark tourism revitalizes the resources of affected community to boost their economies, dark tourism sometimes is viewed as a vehicle towards improvement. This particularly seems to be true, but the profit-oriented approach leaves behind other important factors that determine dark tourism. More interested in protecting the interests of destinations and investors, than in explaining facts, these approaches sometimes become in marketing plans. As a result of this, the interests for studying dark tourism are not associated to its socio-cultural nature, but only to added-value these destinations promise. The previous assumption suggests that only a partial view of the issue is obtained. Last but not least, further discussion is necessary to forge an all-comprising epistemology of dark tourism that escapes from the re-visited caveats. In the section "towards an epistemology of dark tourism" We review the role of ideology as a cultural matrix that not only co-determines what people feel, but also the ways the world is reached. It reproduces a paradoxical situation simply because epistemologically speaking; interviewees are unable to respond beyond the cultural borders of ideology, which mold the cosmologies of *interviewee and interviewer.*

STATE OF THE ART

What is Dark Tourism?. This question not only has posed as a difficult point to grasp, but also misled many observers to present a coherent discussion which can be articulated in a comprehensible model. The fact is that the ways our grand-parents made tourism differed notably from current ones. The rise and consolidation of new emergent segments as doom-tourism, disaster-tourism or dark tourism not only defied the apollonian concept of beautiness, but contemplates morbid forms of consumption (Koch, 2005). As this argument given, it is not surprising policy makers see in dark tourism an efficient instrument to accelerate recovery-process in post-disaster contexts (Lennon & Foley, 2000; Miles, 2000; Stone & Sharpley, 2008; Korstanje & Ivanov, 2012). From this wave, tourism is more than a resilient activity or industry it paves the ways for society to enhance its resiliency to face disasters and obstacles. Dark tourism gives a lesson to affected community, so that the same tragedy does not repeat in a near future. Some sociologists, as Naomi Klein (2007), have criticized the current fashion to commoditize disasters because it triggers policies oriented to marginalize the local "Others". While disasters affect the lives of more pour classes of society, elite not only slides its responsibilities but also takes the opportunity to implement economic policies otherwise would be never accepted. In this respect, one of the risks of selling disaster as tourist attractions consists in ignoring the real causes of the event. The culture of simulacrum (spectacle) is surely opposed to a much deeper understanding of the disaster (Baudrillard, 1996).

Rather, tourism scholars kept distance from the critical voices of dark tourism, whereas the question of heritage plays a major role as an efficient instrument for affected people to revitalize their deteriorated identity. Since these traumatic events occurred in past, dark tourism would be defined as "an anthropological attempt to seek "heritage", by international visitors who are interested in historical events. Starting from the premise that "fascination for death" is universal supporters of dark-heritage suggest that pilgrims in Medieval Times as well as any expression of religiosity is based on the needs of being in contact with others' death. Far from an alienatory activity, dark tourism brings some benefits and positive consequences for local community (Poria, 2007; Chauhan & Khanna, 2009). In that way, death consumption means an escapement to visit other realties where dark tourists may interpret their own lives (Stone, 2012). Whatever the case may be the role of experience in the process if vital in order for understanding the engagement of visitors with the site. Biran, Poria and Oren (2011) acknowledge that visitors escape from their routines to experience authentic sensations, many of them derived as unfamiliar to their daily lives. Like Heritage-Seekers, visitors who chose dark destinations as their main option, are in quest of answers, which remain enrooted in pastime.

As this backdrop, Dorina Buda and Alison McIntosh (2013) toyed with the idea that dark tourism should be framed into the logic of voyeurism. Taking their cues from psychanalytic theory, which delved into desire as a catalyst for movement, they explain that experiences as dark only may be molded through consumption of the danger. Embedded within a wider logic of emulation where visitors want to feel like or what victims felt, dark tourism still opens the doors for interesting investigation in the fields of psychology, sociology and education. In addition, E. H. Cohen (2011) has observed that dark tourism serves as an educational instrument which gives a message to society. The meaning conferred to territory plays a vital role at this stage. Visitors tend to think as authentic those sites where the memorized event took room. Instead, whether museums or shrines are built on allegorical reasons in sites that nothing has to do with the founding trauma, they are pondered as inauthentic. Cohen's outcomes not only reveal the political root of dark tourism, but also the importance of location whenever the self encounters with tragedy. Dark tourism sites are politically designed to express a message to community. Victims and their families not only have diverse ways of negotiating that message but also by appropriating an interpretation of social trauma. Dark tourism alludes to a psychological need of figuring one death by imagining the other's death. Nonetheless, the myopia of scholars to understand dark tourism rests on two primary aspects. There are no clear boundaries or indicators to mark a unified site of memory which cannot be subject to political struggle. Furthermore, starting from the premise heritage depends on the political interests, sometimes the national discourse around dark sites are not accepted one side of community (White & Frew, 2013; Korstanje, 2011).

At some extent, dark tourism divides scholarship in two main sides, detractors and supporters. Quite aside from this, there are some methodological caveats which will be discussed in the next section. Let's clarify that this does not represent any attack or criticism to any position, rather, it situates as complementary discussion that will hopefully help epistemologists in tourism in the years to come.

METHODOLOGICAL PROBLEMS OF DARK TOURISM

The history of science reveals two important assumptions. On one hand, what is scientific knowledge in some periods can be pseudo-science in others. It is safe to say that the modern project of science, which is based on the intersection of causes and explanation, derives from Aristotelian philosophy (Wallace, 1972). As differentiated from other forms of knowledge, science (Scientia est cognitio) was thought in view of previous causes that mold the object. As a result of this, Aristotle was a pioneer in envisaging that causalities cannot be divorced from explanations. For this period, since mathematics and quantitative methods played a vital role in constructing a bridge between perception and physical world, later developments focused on "reasoned facts" and a much deeper process of demonstration as the main criterion of credibility for science (Wallace, 1972). This paved the ways for the adoption of "ocular-centrism" to classify "scientific facts". The power of gazing, for medieval scientists, consisted in the revelation of the causes behind facts. The medieval conception of methodology was characterized by an over-valorization of mathematics as the valid instrument towards true. The medieval legacy not only accompanied epistemologists even in the rise of modernity, but also exerted a notable influence to date. Experimenters became in discoverers of a reality, just put outer the individual mode of perception (Longino, 1990). By the mid of twentieth century, the Austrian-British philosopher Karl Popper introduces the concept of "empirical falsification" to validate the outcome of science. Such an epistemological method consisted in a radical division between empirical-basis and theories. Upon its formulation, each theory should be placed on falsifiability (refutability) in order for observer to know if the belief is or not validated. Without this condition, "the scientific object" dilutes into speculation and abstract thinking (Popper, 1968, 1993, 2013). Due to space and time, it is almost impossible to reduce the history of science in this section, as I would wish, but what is important to discuss seems to be the role of "ocular-centrism" as the main cultural value of modern reason. D. Levin (1999) calls the attention to "western philosophy" as an intellectual movement associated to "light", "enlightenment" and "truth" while "the darkness" was relegated as residual position in the struggle for grasping the sensible world. Doubtless, the rise of "phenomenology", as well as the arrival of feminism in the fields of epistemology, posited a radical criticism to science as a social construal, derived from the needs of patriarchal order to segregate women and children from the means of production. As Sandra Harding (1986) puts it, science and its preexisting values not only were originally formulated by white men, but also expressed only a portion of reality, which is conducive to female's exploitation. Phenomenology as a project interrogated the sense of reality from a point of view which adjusts to individual perception. Each person holds a different configuration of the external world according to a previous cognitive structure which is cemented by its biography (Merleau-Ponty, 2002).

Recently, some ethnographers highlighted the subject nature of hermeneutics, not as a limitation, but as stronghold. What fieldworkers should take care, is avoiding a cult of experience as the only valid source of information. Since ethnographers understand that there is a clear dissociation between what people utter and their real behaviour, fieldworkers should enter in the field, living as natives, feeling what they feel. In this respect, asking to key-informants is only a limited method to understand the complexity of social world. Good ethnography combines techniques of interviews, with direct observations that helps validating ethnographers' hypotheses (Geertz, 1982, 1994).

The question whether hermeneutics flourished as an acceptable theory in epistemology was brilliantly assessed by British geographer David Harvey (1989) in his book *The Condition of Postmodernity.* For Harvey, the economy (means of production) and epistemology are inextricably intertwined. While "the full scale production" persisted in the core of Western nations in twentieth century, Science kept an "all-encompassing" view of the world, which was centered on medieval conceptions, as discussed. The oil embargo that took place in 1972 not only pressed to industrialized economies to segment their economies, but also paved the pathways for the advance of a new more decentralized epistemology of the world. Adapted to each person, epistemologists do not refer to a unique world, but to many parallel worlds (Harvey 1989). In consequences, science faced a rapid fragmentation and the ideals of Enlightenments as they were coined in Paris or Padua sets the pace to the hegemony of experience (Thirkettle & Korstanje, 2013).

In tourism fields, John Tribe (2010) thematized on the ever-increasing level of knowledge-fragmentation in the discipline, as a result of the indifference between Academy and academicians. Though this may be partially true, the fact is that Tribe puts the cart before the horse because he ignores that as academic discipline tourism lacks of a clear and shared epistemology. For the sake of clarity, neither an object of study nor a method, tourism-related scholars failed to coordinate a basic definition of what tourism means. As a result of this, tourism adopted a profit-oriented conceptualization of scientific research, which conducive to managerial disciplines. The tourist was mistakenly contemplated as the only source of information in order for the hypothesis of researchers to be validated. Secondly and most important, questionnaires and other obtrusive techniques were employed to reveal the feelings of interviewees. Since the psychological experience was the tug-of-war of these emergent schools, many of them surfaced in US and England, experts in tourism adopted "the voice of tourist" as an unquestionable-truth. Originally-designed as opinion polls, instead of scientific research, tourism-led researchers singled out the complex dynamic and nature of experience (Korstanje, Mustellier & Herrera, 2016). If a clear epistemological original sin happened some decades back, dark tourism tended to replicate the same original vicious. The use and abuse of questionnaires for fieldworkers to corroborate their beliefs not only obscured part of their outcomes, but led towards to contradictories landscapes. Based on "what ought to be", dark tourism research started to produce investigation to be fruitful to the logic of destination-management or it was self-oriented to create further segments to boost local economies. With the benefits of hindsight, whether the meaning of experience was a hard concept to grasp harder was the sense of death.

THE USE OF QUESTIONNAIRES AND OBTRUSIVE METHODS

Recently, Jonathan Skinner edited by book entitled *Writing the Dark Side of Travel* where invited authors discuss to what extent we can homogenize a great variety of subthemes. At time of studying dark tourism, many marginal topics as battlefront commemorations, genocides and disaster converge. Based on a post-Marxist position, Skinner dangles the possibility postmodernism cements the rise of a new hedonist experience, where the others' suffering revitalizes the deteriorated ego. Genocide museums not only remember a moral tragedy but disseminate a code enrooted in politics. The role of ethnologist consists in deciphering that code by writing and describing the context. The written word (text) is of paramount importance to understand the allegory of dark tourism sites. The discrepancies among authors who conform this book respecting to the archetype of death represents a serious problems to arrive to a all-embracing theory which allows expanding the current understanding of the issue. Editor J. Skinner warns that chapters included in this project do not examine the death but how it is interpreted by local cultures or story tellers. These tales are embedded in the text, not in history (Skinner 2012).

Although this book exhibits a strong sensibility in the role played by the ethnography to unearth covered voices, some limitations and doubts arise. Skinner and his collaborators start from the premise of Seaton or Sharpley who posit an exaggerated trust in the perception, emotions and opinion of visitors or tourists. This point begs two interesting questions, how may we know interviewees are not lying or simply they are not familiar with the psychological laws of their behavior?

It is unfortunate that the epistemology of tourism has some limitations to dissociate interpretation (emotionally-oriented) from perception (cognitive-oriented). To put this in other terms, risks perception stems from the cognitive structure while fear comes from the deepness of emotionality. I can perceive a destination as unsecure, but this does not impede I travel there in my holidays (Korstanje, 2016). Besides, these investigations are designed to take tourists as the main source of veracity in the field. Although social anthropologists have already recognized that this represents one of the problems of positivism, which assumes asking is only pathway towards truth, somehow approaches in dark tourism alludes to what tourists feel to reconstruct the epistemological object of dark tourism. Such a stance ignores that likely people lie to protect their interests, or in other they are not cognizant of their real emotions, in which case all information we gathered can be biased by our prejudices (Korstanje, 2016).

My anecdotes as fieldworkers in Cromañón Sanctuary, a site (night-club) where a fire suffocated almost 194 youth attendants in 2004, would be pertinent as an entry in this discussion. One day, a teenager came to me to explain me further on the slippery matter I was involved. I kindly accepted his invitation and switched on my tape recorder. While I supposed he was much to say, the interview lasted almost 6 hours. The information I obtained from this young was very important for me at a preliminary stage. Nonetheless, with the passing of months I have advanced my ethnography comparing the collated information by what I can hear and see. Not only I realized that the original interview was completely false, because the involved key-informant wanted to attract attention and exaggerated his stories, but he felt the needs to tell something to me. The importance of this story was not determined by its credibility. He had not lost anyone in the disaster of Cromañon, though developed a strange attachment for the event, for the other's suffering. This empathy led him to alter his sense of reality. Paradoxically, although this interview was a fake, it underpinned the main hypotheses in my research opening the doors to new cosmologies and opportunities to be empirically validated. This story though false shed light on my investigation, reminding exactly what we have discussed. Not always, what people swear is real. What is a psychological experience rests on shaky foundations, and it should not be deciphered using "open, closed-ended questionnaires or interviews" alone.

DARK TOURISM AS AN INSTRUMENT FOR PROFIT-ORIENTED POLICIES

Some studies have widely showed how tourism not only serves as a mechanism that revitalizes economies in post disaster conjunctures, but contributes with further profits to groups which have been historically segregated (Korstanje & Ivanov, 2012; Boyd, 2000). This poses a more than intriguing question, what are the dangers of commoditizing Dark Tourism sites?

In a seminal book, entitled *The Future of the Holocaust,* Berel Lang calls the attention to the current uses and abuses of human rights after Auschwitz. He acknowledges that thinking Nazis as "demons" or "hatred-filled maniacs" not only is an ethical error because they slide their responsibilities for committed crimes, but paved the pathways for oblivion. Demons are outside the jurisdiction of law, and their acts are catalogued as pure evils. Rather, humans are subject to the law and their behaviour codified. One of the most troubling aspects that accompany genocides, ethnic cleansing and other murders seems to be associated to a spectacularization of disaster, which obscures more than it clarifies (Lang 1999). Not only there are many risks in commoditizing disasters, simply because the real causes of disasters are forgotten, but also the responsibilities avoided. Nicole Guidotti Hernandez (2011) formulated the term "unspeakable violence" to refer to the ideological dispositions of nation-state to narrate history. Based on a study-case of borderlands between Mexico and US, she alludes to how nationhood is constructed under silenced genocides and acts of extreme violence, which not only are covered, but sometimes biased to be offered to visitors and tourists. Last but not least, in earlier studies Korstanje (2014) analyzes the show Chile Ayuda a Chile after the strong quake hit Chile a couple of years ago. At some extent, when the disaster is commoditized, there are serious problems to understand the reasons behind the traumatic event, if the cultural background that facilitated disasters is not corrected, the probabilities of a repetition turns out higher (Korstanje, 2014).

TOWARDS AN EPISTEMOLOGY OF DARK TOURISM

To what extent, the current literature is useful to prospect a future epistemology of dark tourism remains unanswered. One of the limitations of current methods consists in the application of questionaries' and intrusive techniques to gather information. Though this was discussed in earlier section, some concerns arise. At a first glance, if we start the premise (as specialized literature suggests) that people look in dark tourism a type of escapement to alleviate the burden or their routines, or simply the urban alienation, we have to take into consideration that alienation does not work without ideology. While people are subject to ideology, they not only fleshed out a biased understanding of external world, but also they culturally replicate the mandate of elite. Following this, what interviewees feel, or think is far from being true, but only a product of wonderland. In fact, it is a very important contradiction of many studies in dark tourism fields considering that dark tourism alleviates alienation, while the only valid source to gather reliable information is interviewing the same alienated agents.

If psychoanalysis has left a legacy, it relates to the fact that the self never reconstructs things as they really happen, but only interpret combining deep unconscious forces with "the narcissist object", as Haydèe Faimberg (2005) observed in her book *The Telescoping Generations.* Since Freud formulated the "Oedipus complex", which was based on Oedipus myth, we started to understand not only the profundity of mind, but the role played by secrecy in individual behaviour. While Oedipus was defenseless trapped in a grim future, which resulted from a bloody past, his problem was not associated to the horrendous crime he perpetrated but to deceit (which means the secret he carried during his life). What this myth reminds, Faimberg explains, is that a most part of our acts are determined by the figure of our parents, likely even not remembering events as they happened in history, but only in the way they were deciphered by us. Our cognition as well as everything we say about us stems from a fake-story which is fabricated by our emotional inner-world.

We usually acknowledge after Freud, from a psychoanalytical perspective, that the Oedipus myth concerns Oedipus parricidal and incestuous desires and we view them as a paradigm of the unconscious desires felt by all men for their parents. The paradigm is usually called the direct Oedipus complex. Let us repeat it once again, Oedipus` destiny is not governed solely by the prophecy- by what, according to what just has been said, can legitimately be called the Oedipus complex- but also by an unspoken message (Faimberg, 2005: 67)

As this backdrop, many disciplines emerged during XXs decade, are prone to hear from interviewees as valid source of information to reconstruct an all-encompassing explanation that obscures rather than clarifies. In some circumstances, obtained information is misunderstood, duplicated, or exaggerated according to the cognitive frames of fieldworkers. Many other projects pursue diffuse goals. While improving the condition of life of communities castigated by disasters is a valuable goal, this places us far away from a real understanding of dark tourism. It is true that policy makers should read what social scientists produce, but in our discipline the borders between tourism-management and scientific-research are blurred.

CONCLUSION

Many of the problems of dark tourism studies come from a much deeper background, originated in the proliferation fragmented knowledge. Even, the concept of death is a concept very hard to decipher. In this line, we take the opportunity to exert a radical criticism not only to the current literature but also to the future of discipline in the years to come. We have developed three clear guidelines in this chapter. The main limitation of researchers contends in applying standardized questionaries' to visitors, believing that asking is the only way to reach truth. This method, far from allowing coherent outcomes, leads to misunderstanding and contrasting findings. Secondly, there exist many ethical risks in commoditizing disasters because survivors may forget the preexisting causes. In that way, the likelihoods for the disaster to take room again are higher. Last but not least, many of dark tourism works emphasizes on the alienatory nature of the topic, ignoring that if people are alienated, questionnaires and interviews are not good option to understand the problem. While lay-people, who is consulted by fieldworkers, use dark tourism to escape from alienation implies invalidating their answers respecting to what dark tourism means.

REFERENCES

Baudrillard, J. (1996). *The perfect crime.* London: Verso.

Biran, A., Poria, Y., & Oren, G. (2011). Sought Experience at Dark Heritage sites. *Annals of Tourism Research, 38*(3), 820–841. doi:10.1016/j.annals.2010.12.001

Blom, T. (2000). Morbid tourism-a postmodern market niche with an example from Althorp. *Norsk Geografisk Tidsskrift, 54*(1), 29–36. doi:10.1080/002919500423564

Boyd, S. W. (2000). 'HeritageTourism in Northern Ireland: Opportunity Under Peace. *Current Issues in Tourism, 3*(2), 150–174. doi:10.1080/13683500008667871

Buda, D. M., & McIntosh, A. J. (2013). Dark tourism and voyeurism: Tourist arrested for "spying" in Iran. *International Journal of Culture. Tourism and Hospitality Research, 7*(3), 214–226.

Chauhan, V. & Khanna, S. (2009). Tourism: a tool for crafting peace process in Kashmir, J&K, India. *Tourismos: An International Multidisciplinary Journal of Tourism, 4*(2), 69-89.

Cohen, E. H. (2011). Educational dark tourism at an in populo site: The Holocaust Museum in Jerusalem. *Annals of Tourism Research, 38*(1), 193–209. doi:10.1016/j.annals.2010.08.003

Faimberg, H. (2005). *The Telescoping Generations: listening to the narcissistic links between generations.* East Sussex, UK: Routledge.

Geertz, C. (1982). The way we think now: Toward an ethnography of modern thought. *Bulletin - American Academy of Arts and Sciences. American Academy of Arts and Sciences, 35*(5), 14–34. doi:10.2307/3823993

Geertz, C. (1994). Thick description: Toward an interpretive theory of culture. In M. Martin & C. McIntyre (Eds.), Readings in the philosophy of social science. Cambridge, MA: MIT Press.

Guidotti-Hernández, N. M. (2011). *Unspeakable violence: Remapping US and Mexican national imaginaries.* Durham, NC: Duke University Press. doi:10.1215/9780822394495

Harding, S. G. (1986). *The science question in feminism.* Ithaca, NY: Cornell University Press.

Harvey, D. (1989). *The condition of postmodernity* (Vol. 14). Oxford, UK: Blackwell.

Klein, N. (2007). *The shock doctrine: The rise of disaster capitalism.* New York: Macmillan.

Knudsen, B. T. (2011). Thana-tourism: Witnessing difficult pasts. *Tourist Studies, 11*(1), 55–72. doi:10.1177/1468797611412064

Koch, A. (2005). Cyber citizen or cyborg citizen: Baudrillard, political agency, and the commons in virtual politics. *Journal of Mass Media Ethics, 20*(2-3), 159–175. doi:10.1080/08900523.2005.9679706

Korstanje, M. E. (2011). Detaching the elementary forms of dark-tourism. *Anatolia, 22*(3), 424–427. doi:10.1080/13032917.2011.620800

Korstanje, M. E. (2014). Chile helps Chile: Exploring the effects of earthquake Chile 2010. *International Journal of Disaster Resilience in the Built Environment, 5*(4), 380–390. doi:10.1108/IJDRBE-01-2012-0002

Korstanje, M. E. (2016). *The Rise of Thana Capitalism and Tourism.* Abingdon, UK: Routledge.

Korstanje, M. E., & Ivanov, S. (2012). Tourism as a Form of New Psychological Resilience: The Inception of Dark Tourism. *Cultur: Revista de Cultura e Turismo, 6*(4), 56–71.

Korstanje, M. E., Mustelier, L. C., & Herrera, S. (2016). Understanding the Indiscipline of Tourism: A Radical Critique to the Current. In *Global Dynamics in Travel, Tourism, and Hospitality* (pp. 208–221). Hershey, PA: IGI-Global. doi:10.4018/978-1-5225-0201-2.ch012

Lang, B. (1999). *The future of the Holocaust: Between history and memory.* Ithaca, NY: Cornell University Press.

Lennon, J. J., & Foley, M. (2000). *Dark tourism.* Cornwall, UK: Cengage Learning EMEA.

Levin, D. M. (1999). *The philosopher's gaze: Modernity in the shadows of enlightenment.* Berkeley, CA: University of California Press.

Longino, H. E. (1990). *Science as social knowledge: Values and objectivity in scientific inquiry.* Princeton, NJ: Princeton University Press.

Merleau-Ponty, M. (1996). *Phenomenology of perception.* New Dehli: Motilal Banarsidass Publisher.

Miles, W. (2002). Auschwitz: Museum interpretation and Darker Tourism. *Annals of Tourism Research, 29*(4), 1175–1178. doi:10.1016/S0160-7383(02)00054-3

Popper, K. (1993). *Unended Quest: An Intellectual Autobiography, Karl Popper*. London: Routledge.

Popper, K. (2013). *Realism and the aim of science: From the postscript to the logic of scientific discovery*. Abingdon, UK: Routledge.

Popper, K. R. (1968). Epistemology without a knowing subject. *Studies in Logic and the Foundations of Mathematics*, *52*, 333–373. doi:10.1016/S0049-237X(08)71204-7

Poria, Y. (2007). Establishing cooperation between Israel and Poland to save Auschwitz Concentration Camp: Globalising the responsibility for the Massacre. *International Journal of Tourism Policy*, *1*(1), 45–57. doi:10.1504/IJTP.2007.013897

Poria, Y., Reichel, A., & Biran, A. (2006). Heritage site management: Motivations and expectations. *Annals of Tourism Research*, *33*(1), 162–178. doi:10.1016/j.annals.2005.08.001

Skinner, J. (2012). *Writing the dark side of Travel*. New York: Berghan Books.

Stone, P. (2012). Dark tourism as mortality capital. *Annals of Tourism Research*, *39*(3), 1565–1587. doi:10.1016/j.annals.2012.04.007

Stone, P. (2013). Dark tourism scholarship: A critical review. *International Journal of Culture, Tourism and Hospitality Research*, *7*(3), 307–318. doi:10.1108/IJCTHR-06-2013-0039

Stone, P., & Sharpley, R. (2008). Consuming dark tourism: A thanatological perspective. *Annals of Tourism Research*, *35*(2), 574–595. doi:10.1016/j.annals.2008.02.003

Stone, P. R. (2011). Dark tourism: Towards a new post-disciplinary research agenda. *International Journal of Tourism Anthropology*, *1*(3-4), 318–332. doi:10.1504/IJTA.2011.043713

Thirkettle, A., & Korstanje, M. E. (2013). Creating a new epistemiology for tourism and hospitality disciplines. *International Journal of Qualitative Research in Services*, *1*(1), 13–34. doi:10.1504/IJQRS.2013.054342

Tribe, J. (2010). Tribes, territories and networks in the tourism academy. *Annals of Tourism Research*, *37*(1), 7–33. doi:10.1016/j.annals.2009.05.001

Verma, S., & Jain, R. (2013). Exploiting Tragedy for Tourism. *Research on Humanities and Social Sciences*, *3*(8), 9–13.

Wallace, W (1972). *Causality and Scientific explanation*. Ann Arbor, MI: The University of Michigan Press.

White, L., & Frew, E. (2013). *Dark Tourism: place and identity: managing and interpreting dark places*. London: Routledge.

ADDITIONAL READING

Biran, A., Poria, Y., & Oren, G. (2011). Sought experiences at (dark) heritage sites. *Annals of Tourism Research*, *38*(3), 820–841. doi:10.1016/j.annals.2010.12.001

Carrigan, A. (2014). Dark tourism and postcolonial studies: Critical intersections. *Postcolonial Studies*, *17*(3), 236–250. doi:10.1080/13688790.2014.993425

Heidelberg, B. A. W. (2015). Managing ghosts: Exploring local government involvement in dark tourism. *Journal of Heritage Tourism*, *10*(1), 74–90. doi:10.1080/1743873X.2014.953538

Isaac, R. K., & Çakmak, E. (2014). Understanding visitors motivation at sites of death and disaster: The case of former transit camp Westerbork, the Netherlands. *Current Issues in Tourism*, *17*(2), 164–179. doi:10.1080/13683500.2013.776021

Korstanje, M. (2015). Heritage that hurts: Tourists in the memoryscapes of September 11. *Journal of Heritage Tourism*, *10*(1), 91–92. doi:10.1080/1743873X.2014.888816

Korstanje, M. E., & Clayton, A. (2012). Tourism and terrorism: Conflicts and commonalities. *Worldwide Hospitality and Tourism Themes*, *4*(1), 8–25. doi:10.1108/17554211211198552

Korstanje, M. E., & Olsen, D. H. (2011). The discourse of risk in horror movies post 9/11: Hospitality and hostility in perspective. *International Journal of Tourism Anthropology*, *1*(3-4), 304–317. doi:10.1504/IJTA.2011.043712

Light, D. (2014). Tourism and toponymy: Commodifying and consuming place names. *Tourism Geographies*, *16*(1), 141–156. doi:10.1080/14616688.2013.868031

Muzaini, H., Teo, P., & Yeoh, B. S. (2007). Intimations of postmodernity in dark tourism: The fate of history at Fort Siloso, Singapore. *Journal of Tourism and Cultural Change*, *5*(1), 28–45. doi:10.2167/jtcc082.0

Raine, R. (2013). A dark tourist spectrum. *International Journal of Culture, tourism and hospitality Research, 7*(3), 242-256.

Reijnders, S. (2009). Watching the detectives inside the guilty landscapes of Inspector Morse, Baantjer and Wallander. *European Journal of Communication*, *24*(2), 165–181. doi:10.1177/0267323108101830

Ryan, C., & Kohli, R. (2006). The Buried village, New Zealand–An example of dark tourism? *Asia Pacific Journal of Tourism Research*, *11*(3), 211–226. doi:10.1080/10941660600753240

Sharpley, R. (2005). Travels to the edge of darkness: Towards a typology of dark tourism. *Taking tourism to the limits: Issues, concepts and managerial perspectives*, 215-226.

Tzanelli, R. (2003). Casting the Neohellenic Other: Tourism, the Culture Industry, and Contemporary Orientalism inCaptain Corellis Mandolin(2001). *Journal of Consumer Culture*, *3*(2), 217–244. doi:10.1177/14695405030032004

Tzanelli, R. (2004). Constructing the cinematic touristThe sign industryof The Lord of the Rings. *Tourist Studies*, *4*(1), 21–42. doi:10.1177/1468797604053077

Tzanelli, R. (2013). *Heritage in the Digital Era: Cinematic Tourism and the Activist Cause*. Abingdon: Routledge.

Young, C., & Light, D. (2016). Interrogating spaces of and for the dead as alternative space: Cemeteries, corpses and sites of Dark Tourism. *International Review of Social Research*, *6*(2), 61–72. doi:10.1515/irsr-2016-0009

Yuill, S. M. (2004). *Dark tourism: understanding visitor motivation at sites of death and disaster* (Doctoral dissertation, Texas A&M University).

KEY TERMS AND DEFINITIONS

Dark Tourism: This is a subtype of tourism characterized by the consumption of death or the interests for visiting spaces of mass death and disasters.

Death: This is the termination or end of all biological functions. Within philosophy, the concern for death was the epicenter for the rise and expansion of Existentialism.

Globalization: This can be defined as an economic project of social integration among nations.

Ideology: It exhibits the collection of allegories, ideas and beliefs that conform the social ethos. Though ideology took different meanings depending on the sociological wave, Marxists argue that ideology works as a mechanism of social control.

Methodologies: This represents the set of methods, beliefs, hypothesis and ideas that help forging analytical instrument to be scientifically validated.

Science: It signals to a specific way of organizing knowledge as well as the set of methods to test or nullifying hypotheses.

Truth: For common parlance, truth is a term often used to denote reality or facts.

Chapter 6
Political Reflections on Dark Tourism:
The Case of Turkey

Funda Çoban
Aksaray University, Turkey

ABSTRACT

This paper argues the popular black spots of Turkey, which are really few, initially serve as a political instrument to construct and deepen the national identity. Gallipoli, Anıtkabir, National Park for Commander-in-chief, the deathbed of Ataturk, Ulucanlar Prison, and Sakarya Earthquake Museum are well-known black spots in Turkey which could be addressed to improve this argument. The discourse of sterile interior designs, introductory brochures, official web pages, digital presentation and the quantitative gap between domestic and foreign visitors are some proofs, supporting the claim. On the other side of the coin, however, the construction of realms of memory, belonging to the "others" is continuously is suspended and included in official ideology through normalization processes. Diyarbakır Prison, Madımak Hotel Aşkale are the discursive given "darker sites," exemplifying the counter-discursive black spots in this sense. So, it can be concluded that the initial function of few samples of dark tourism sites in Turkey is mainly political rather than being economic or cultural.

DOI: 10.4018/978-1-5225-2750-3.ch006

INTRODUCTION

Battles, diseases, disasters, genocide, accidents and the rest of all tragic events which are the imprint of humane mortality... No matter what the cause, people have always had a special interest in such events, affirming their being isn't eternal. Funeral ceremonies, memorials, visits to cemeteries are direct reflections of this interest which has been part of the anthropological concern. However, appeal, connecting this interest to a touristic context is quite fresh (Stone, 2013). This "new" touristic field is called as black spot tourism (Rojek, 1993), milking the macabre (Dann, 1994); dark tourism (Foley & Lennon, 1996, 2000), thanatourism (Seaton, 1996, 2009a) or morbid tourism (Blom, 2000). It is also variously defined as "the commercial [touristic] developments of grave sites and sites in which celebrities or large numbers of people have met with sudden and violent death" (Rojek, 1993, p.136); "the presentation and consumption of real and commoditized death and disaster sites" (Foley & Lennon, 1996, p.198); ''to travel to a location wholly, or partially, motivated by the desire for actual or symbolic encounters with death'' (Seaton, 1996, p. 240); ''traveling to touristic sites focusing on sudden death and which quickly attracts large numbers of people and, on the other an attraction-focused artificial morbidity-related tourism" (Blom, 2000, p.32), "visitation to sites associated with death, disaster, and depravity" (Lennon & Foley, 2000, p.46), ''the act of travel to sites associated with death, suffering and the seemingly macabre'' (Stone, 2006, p.146), "traveling to the sites concerned with encountering spaces of death or calamity that have political or historical significance, and that continue to impact upon the living" (Stone, n.d.); or "one of a number of institutions which mediate between the living and the dead' (Walter, 2009a, p. 39). Regarding the variety of the definitions, many issues arise, not excluding the question if dark tourism is truly new. In this context, Seaton (1996) and Stone (2006) develop the claim that human concern on tragic sites dates back to Roman gladiatorial games, public executions of the medieval period, the guided morgue tours of the Victorian period and thus, ask in which way dark tourism is new as a respond to the pioneering researchers, Foley and Lennon (2000) asserting dark tourism is intrinsically a post-modern phenomenon. On the other hand Ashworth and Isaac (2015) question the assumption, "rising demand of dark consumer" (Lennon & Foley, 2000; Stone, 2008) by adding "the apparent growth of interest may have more to do with the growth in the investigators than with the phenomenon investigated" (p. 317). Also, "dark tourism" which logically sets a dichotomy between dark and light, triggers some other debates, stressing "dark" itself assumes that the black spots are "ill-conditioned, abnormal, disturbing, troubling, suspicious," (Browman & Pezzullo, 2010, pp. 190–191; Seaton, 2009b; Ashworth & Isaac, 2015) and consequently pathological and exceptional (Clarke et al., 2014, p. 228). Indeed, there seems to be no compelling reason to articulate death with dark-light dualism, especially by thinking of Asiatic "yin-yang" philosophy and, also Islamic belief regarding death as a kind of redemption to unite with *Allah*. From a similar perspective, Sharpley and Stone (2009b) state "dark tourism simplifies and hides a multitude of meanings and purposes with respect to both their production and consumption" (p.250). Alternatively, Seaton (1996) proposes "thanatopsis" and explains the fascination with death appears as a kind of mediator between deceased and living. Along similar lines, Stone and Sharpley (2008) claim "thanatourism" is a way of keeping "ontological security." For them, visits to sites of death and tragedy make possible one to confirm his/her own existence through "catharsis." "Thus, dark tourism contributes to neutralize the fear of (unexpected) death through the significant other death via entertainment, education, or memorialization" (Stone, 2012). In parallel to them, Korstanje and Ivanov (2012) consider dark tourism, which is based upon masculinity, outrage, heroism, and strength, as a kind of management of fear (Korstanje, 2015). In this context, motivations to visit those sites come into focus. As a rebuttal to this point, supply-sided explanations in the framework of culture industry (see Seaton & Lennon, 2004; Stone & Sharpley, 2008) in one hand, demand-sided explanations (see Dann, 1998; Seaton, 1996) on the other appear as the leading approaches. Nevertheless, demand or supply-oriented explanations tend to be negated in the vast range of black spots. Miles' (2002) relatively dark places, Stone's (2006) spectrum of supply from the lightest to the darkest, and Sharpley's (2009a) shades of dark tourism have partly been negated in different case studies (see Cohen, 2011; Tucker, 2016). Indeed it is a hard task to theorize inclusively why people choose a spot for which reasons. Also, it is another fact digitalization in tourism blurs the limits of shades of dark tourism (Miles, 2014). As a result, the categorizations remain mainly descriptive (Sharpley, 2009b, p.11). So, the abundance of the spots causes the differentiation of the reasons while there always remains a matrix of possible motivations. In other words, "not surprisingly, the range of motives identified is as broad as the range of sites explored" (Biran, Yaniv&Oren, 2011, p.825). Moreover, the proposed motivations are always being mediated by ethnicity, religion, and gender. For instance, Sharpley and Baldwin's (2009) research also shows female visitors to battlefields are keen on searching for family ties which exclusively proves gender is a correlative dynamic.

In conclusion, the issue to define dark tourism continually re-appears. Despite the growing number of studies in twenty years, there is no commonly accepted definition of it (Young&Light, 2016, p. 68; Ashworth&Isaac, 2015). Even, for Young, "if the motives for visiting sites associated with death are little different from those for visiting heritage places, then it is questionable whether it is appropriate to identify 'dark tourism' as a distinct form of tourism demand" (Young, 2016, p. 69).

Yet, current research appears to validate the view that "dark tourism" has a unique place in modern societies. Because evidence for dark tourism shows that new black spots are being opened/created every year, as well as the number of visitors is growing (Stone, 2006, 2013; Powell&Iankova, 2016), media attention and the number of web pages on dark tourism rise. The growing chances to communicate and travel in a cheaper and fast way undoubtedly support this vacuum. People in a post-modern era travel intercontinentally and get info about the "unknown places" via the internet. As Stone (2005) states "fascination with scenes of death and disaster are old and quite possibly universal, but what is new is the way in which there is a commercialized and functional tourism industry able to make very much more available to very many more people than was the case in the past."

At that point, it is important to clarify the role of politics overdetermined by economics. In other words, the course of being an attractive touristic spot is deeply related to political economy. That is why dark tourism is also regarded as a branch of heritage tourism (Biran et al., 2011). As Ashworth (1996) puts forward atrocity heritage tends to transfer of political and social messages while it is also both a highly marketable combination of education and enjoyment. That is, "tragedies, atrocities and disasters have the potential, through their representation and commemoration, to be exploited not only for commercial gain through tourism but also to convey political messages; as a consequence, questions arise with respect to what or whose story should be told." (Sharpley, 2009b, p. 147). As a matter of fact, heritage tourism also deals with which part of history is to be accepted as "heritage," and in which context the heritage will be presented (Ashworth & Hartmann, 2000) as dark tourism does. So, dark tourism's limits expand to the realm of the regarding state's the capacity to face with nasty history. For instance, in KwaZulu Natal, South Africa, British colonial authorities commemorate members of the British Army, fallen in the Zulu Wars of the late 1870s on memorial stones across the battlefields, although until the 1990s no memorials have been allowed for the Zulu dead (as cited in Seaton 2009b, p.96, Moeller, 2005). As a similar dissonance, Jewish genocide has been Americanized through the values, liberty, equality and pluralism in Holocaust Museum in the USA (Yuill, 2005).

Consequently, it is quite open that political mechanism is a substantial fact behind the question why a spot becomes an attractive touristic site whereas another similar spot, carrying heaviness of history on its shoulders, doesn't attract tourists as the former does. Nevertheless, there has been relatively little research on the political dimension of dark tourism. Apart from a few studies (e.g. Ashwort & Hartmann, 2005; Ryan & Kohli, 2006; Seaton & Lennon, 2004), dark tourism's political aspect hasn't been inclusively discussed whilst the pioneering theorists deal with naming, conceptualization and categorization issues. In rare instances, the main argument about political side revolves around the problem how national identity is constructed. Regarding this, this study particularly attempts to contribute them by asking how dark spots are nationally used as a political tool. Moving from this point, it argues there are black spots, dedicated to constructing and supporting the state ideology while there are also "unrecognized" and "unnamed" black spots whose non-existence reinforces the mainstream ideology. In this sense, the discussion centers on discursive conflict among different spaces. As a result, it brackets the discussions which stress the rarity and immaturity of Turkish black spots arise from the decision-makers' unawareness and negligence and, focuses on the discourses on the existent black spots and the "other" ones. In this sense, the foregoing discussion implies that Turkish black spots mainly fulfill some political targets rather than economic and cultural ones whilst the unrecognized/ignored black spots in Turkey are closely tied to politics of identity. To support these claims, the research regards the number of black tourists; the black spots' representations in media, touristic brochures, on web pages and lastly the current spots' narratives. On the basis of this data, it also addresses to Madımak Hotel and Diyarbakır Prison as two characteristic case studies which give possibility to discuss the counter-discursive structure of "alternative" black spots. Hence, the study consists of three sections. The first section discusses the equivalent dimensions of dark spots in Turkish politics by considering the relevant Turkish literature. In the following section, it scrutinizes the discourses of the existent Turkish black spots on the grounds of the currently available qualitative and quantitative data. The last section supports the previous section's arguments by discussing Madımak Hotel and Diyarbakır Prison cases which have the capacity of producing counter-identity-discourses. Finally, this study purports dark tourism could offer an opportunity to face with tragic historical events and thus, contribute to the improvement of civic society if its educational role is seriously taken into consideration.

BACKGROUND

In a broader scope, the issue of dark tourism is directly related to history of capitalism and its political dimensions. In this context, it is essential to consider the connection among profit-making circulation in the markets, its relationship with nation-state building and finally, dark tourism as a form of cultural industry.

POLITICAL DIMENSION OF DARK TOURISM AND THE SCENE IN TURKEY

History is written by victors. Yet, survivors always have the potentiality to rewrite history from the perspective of quasi-defeated. In this sense, historical heritage has a political dimension related to the questions about "what is heritage? who decides what is heritage?, why and for whom, is heritage created?" (Ashworth & Tunbridge,

1996, p. 5). In other words, "what is commemorated is not synonymous with all that has gone on in the past; what is defined as memorable or historically significant is open to social control, contest, and negotiation" (Alderman, 2010, p.90). In line with this, black spots with their over-shadowed authenticity are the products how history is politically interpreted. On these grounds, the evidence of the interpretation can also be observed in the representations of those spots as well as in their non-existence. For instance, the spots representing slave trade in the USA has just recently been "created." Not to use of the word, "slavery" in the plantation museums of the South and instead, focusing on the social life, achievements, and possessions of the white planter class (Eichstedt &Small, 2002) are examples of such selective representation of history. Moreover, how the fact is presented is pre-determined. "Experience and what we 'gaze' upon is not only socially and culturally constructed by our own history and circumstance, but also framed by what the tourist industry wants us to see" (Ellis, 2009, p.3). Today, simulators are commonly used to offer an authentic experience in many spots. Thus, the selected history's reconstruction reproduces the imagined character (see also Anderson, 1983) of a black spot as a "simulacrum" (Baudrillard, 1994). Accordingly, the consuming tourist considering his/her experience as authentic and, believing to overcome the gap between the tragedy and his/her self, makes an unquestioned distinction between the past and present (see also Ellis, 2009). This imaginary confrontation with death and tragedy is also supported by kitschification (Sharpley & Stone, 2009a) and Disneyfication (Solomon, 2015) processes. Kitsch souvenirs with a message "I was there," snow globes telling "everything gonna be all right" (Stone & Sharpley, 2009), Chernobyl as a playground (Yankovskaa & Hannamb, 2014, p.934), the shopping mall opposite the entrance to Auschwitz are the instances, revealing a similar essence despite their geographical diversity. Thus, as Foucault (2003) argues, power relations feed life instead of death through various dispositions although they also commercialize death via normalization and, normalize it via commercialization.

However, it is worth to note dark spots don't only serve for thanatouristic (Seaton, 1996) desires or dark tourists aren't necessarily "fascinated with death." From the lightest to the darkest (Seaton, 1996) dark touristic motivations are various. According to Dann (1998) "the desire to overcome phantom, search for novelty, nostalgia, celebration of crime and deviance, basic bloodlust and interest in challenging one's sense or mortality," to Seaton and Lennon (2004) "shadenfreude and thanatopsis," to Rojek (1997) "collective sense of identity or survival," to Biran et al. (2011) "desire to learn and understand the history presented, a sense of 'see it to believe it," to Mowatt (2011) "interest in having an emotional heritage experience personal identity and history," to Walter (2009a, 2009b) memento mori, to Baldwin and Sharpley (2009) and secular pilgrimage (see also Dunkley, 2011, Collins-Kreiner, 2016) identify why people visit those spots. On the other hand, it is another fact the motivational categorizations' explanatory power is limited because touristic visits to dark spots are generally organized as a part of a longer journey. Besides, many of tourists make a visit just because that is a must-see-spot (Stone, 2010; Seaton, 2011). In this sense, it is even suspicious if there is a consciously motivated tourist (Miles, 2014). So, it can be more appropriate to address to those findings as an output instead of motivation (reason). At that point, it can be claimed the key to turn a dark spot into an international "must-see-spot" is hidden in the success of the relevant state and decision-makers in presenting or popularizing the "tragedy of the locals" as the universal tragedy of mankind. As a matter of fact "nation-states frequently adopt international tourism as a vehicle for their enhancing national cultural identity and international profile or, in some cases, in an attempt to legitimize themselves within the global community" (Sharpley, 2009b, p.149). Thus, the spots such as the place where Princess Diana died, the grave of Marilyn Monroe, Alcatraz Prison, Pompeii, Sixth Floor in Mexico, Auschwitz-Birkenau and Robben Island attract many foreigners, while slave castles in Ghana, Palestine camps or Ulucanlar Prison (Turkey) aren't promoted in a global community. Also, it is another fact the supposedly dark tourists have pre-determined thoughts about what to see at a black spot in a globalized local context (Seaton, 2009b). The visitor primarily verifies his/her own ideas during the visit despite each space's discursive plurality. As a result, there is always a gap between what is displayed and what is seen. The way how to fill the gap is invented or imagined (Ellis, 2009). "The interpretation may be ideologically influenced, conveying broader political messages beyond the immediate significance of the site, again distorting the narrative or diminishing its authenticity for the visitor" (Sharpley & Stone, 2009a, p.118). Thus, the issue still lies in the political interpretation how and in which way the "space" between the presented and the comprehended is rationalized. The emotions of pro-Nazi tourists during a visitation to a concentration camp, the unpleasant feelings triggered by a women wearing a t-shirt in German flag colors at Holocaust Museum (Tinson et al, 2015, p.872), the different meanings referred to Gallipoli by Turkish and Anzac visitors indicate how a spot can overlap power relations and create discursive conflicts (see also, White, 2015). Moreover, the initial aims of dark tourism are stuck to construct and reproduce national identity when the degree of globalization process of local tragedy gradually decreases. Specifically, dark spots which primarily speak to "their own nations," generate a totality, namely "us," while they can't reach foreigners' life worlds easily. No doubt a visitor isn't a simple consumer who takes whatever is presented. He/she is also an active part of the visit. Stone, for example, shows (2009b) the visitors of dark dungeons in London don't only enjoy the place, but also make connections among the dungeons, Holocaust and Guantanamo. Yet, the visitor's potential to pluralize the meanings embedded in the distance between signifier and signified diminishes when the spot has a more nationalistic tone.

Turkey is a good example of the latest case. Dark spots of Turkey are mainly related to Atatürk, Independence War, the war-related monuments and museum in a national context. With a correlation, Turkish black spots primarily call domestic tourists. Following these facts, Turkish researchers predominantly address to dark tourism in a managerial logic. Hence, a bunch of studies about dark tourism in Turkish context mainly introduce Turkey's dark spots and attempt to answer "how to attract more tourist" (see Boz, 2016; Birdir, Dalgıç, Güler & Kayaalp, 2015) while some other make descriptive lists regarding "Turkey's dark tourism potentials" (see Aliağaoğlu, 2004; Taş, 2016, Yıldız, Aytemiz & Yıldız, 2015, Ilgar, 2015; Çetinsöz & Temiz, 2016). In total, the related case studies stress dark tourism is undeveloped in Turkey and conclude "negligence and unconsciousness" are the possible reasons for this situation. These facts undoubtedly explain one side of the picture. Indeed, dark tourism in Turkey is a new-born sector and there isn't economic, political or cultural consciousness enough. However, the fact that dark tourism is just considered as a mediator to feed national identity indicates the other side of the picture. "Other" dark spaces which have capacity to democratically deconstruct the hegemonic discourse are ignored or normalized in some cases. Moreover, the related Turkish literature perpetuates not to problematize the tension between them. Instead, improvement of Turkish dark tourism is correlated with (victorious) Ottoman or close-Turkish history. Thus, dark tourism in Turkey initially serves for national identity instead of economical or cultural purposes indifference with many other international counters.

However, it is also a duty to avoid from short-cuts till reaching this point. Because each specific spot constructs its own fuzzy-discourse through various messages and means. So, every spot's presentation and the narrative is different from another although they serve similar purposes. In this sense, the following section attempts to give concrete details about the complete picture of Turkish black spot panorama and thus, deepen the discussion from a political view.

POPULAR BLACK SPOTS IN TURKEY AND THEIR POLITICAL EVALUATION

Turkey's black spot tourism is undeveloped although there are many battle museums and monuments which can be classified as darker (Stone, 1996). The number of attractive ones is also limited. Atatürk's Mausoleum, Atatürk's death-bed in Dolmabahçe, Gallipoli battlefields and monuments, Commander-in-chief National Park in Afyon, Earthquake Museum in Sakarya and Ulucanlar Prison in Ankara are the primary inviting spots.

Anıtkabir, located in Ankara and established on a 3000 square meter columned area, is a huge complex which consists of Ataturk's mausoleum, Museum of Independence War and Ataturk's comrade, Inonu's tomb. This complex is understandably well-kept and sterile to honor Ataturk's commemorative and thus, also represents modern Turkey's shine discursively. When it is reviewed the official website, a systematic presentation, which keeps the same sense of perfection, can be followed from one page to another. Keeping the same sense on the introduction page of the site, it is promised "the history of War of Independence and establishment of the Republic will conspicuously be told through different exhibition techniques during the visit; and "the difficulties experienced on the way to independence and the foundation of the new Turkish Republic are animated for the visitors" with panoramas (http://www.anitkabir.tsk.tr). While vaults, busts, and models "provide a different atmosphere" in 18 different galleries, the effect of Atatürk's tomb's photos are supported by two wall panels with photos related to his death, funeral and tomb (http://www.anitkabir.tsk.tr). Besides, "the live image of the tomb is made public through TV right in front of the tomb" (http://www.anitkabir.tsk.tr). Additionally, there is wax statue of Ataturk at his desk; Ataturk's dog, Fox's stuffed body, his books and fourteen "touch-screen computers" at the work office section of Anıtkabir.

The data appears to suggest that the presentation of Anıtkabir as a black spot aims visitors to have an authentic experience about Independence War. Digital techniques used in the complex support the relevant feelings. However, this authenticity is cut up because of the oscillation which carries the tension between historical facts regarding Ataturk's life and struggle, and Anıtkabir's official atmosphere which keeps the state's distance from visitor/citizen. The photos and videos on the official website, which represent Anıtkabir as a building and show soldiers on duty rather than crowded ceremonies at the place, support the argument. Just only about 169,000 foreign visitors to 5 million domestic visitors in 2015; increasing visits on national holidays are some other evidence for enriching it. Thus, it is fair to state that visit to Anıtkabir turns into a national ritual affirming citizenship mediated by soldier-state symbolism beyond being a visitation to Ataturk's tomb. Furthermore, "visit certificate service" organized by the museum administration gives the possibility to interpret the visit to Anıtkabir as a secular pilgrimage. Because, for an "average" Turkish citizen visiting Anıtkabir is a kind of citizenship duty and sign of respect rather than a touristic tour (compare with Kang, Scott, Lee&Ballantyne, 2012, p. 257). Regarding the visit, expression in Turkish, "coming into Ataturk's presence" also emphasizes the same spiritual experience. Additionally, the fact that Anıtkabir isn't placed on the list of the most visited national museums infers that Anıtkabir isn't acknowledged as a "usual" tourist spot. So, Anıtkabir as a black spot is the first step to construct national identity.

Another popular black spot frequently visited to commemorate the death of Atatürk is his room and death-bed in Dolmabahçe. This "private room" has been kept as it is, with the Turkish flag over the bed where Atatürk passed away. Every day, thousands of people, especially students, visit the room in twenty-minute tours. According to the tour guides, domestic visitors want to see the place much more than foreign tourists. In particular, the room every year is flooded with visitors on 10th November, the date of Ataturk's death, and the domestic visitors break into tears. During these days, emotions of respect, longing, and loyalty to Ataturk are intensively expressed. In this sense, the visit to the death-bed in Dolmabahçe can be considered as a micro-extension of "secular pilgrimage experience" in Anıtkabir. As a matter of fact, Dolmabahçe allows visitors of "private room" to experience spiritual closeness to Atatürk in comparison with Anıtkabir in a more indirect way, and also enables a captivating experiment which reveals the fact that Ataturk is mortal in body. Thus the cool cosmopolitan Istanbul portraits Ataturk in a more humanistic scene mediated by the state-based, cold capital Ankara. Dolmabahçe in this frame corresponds to the nostalgic dark spot of Rojek (1993), while Anıtkabir meets his "sensitive dark spot."

Another black spot destination of Turkey is Gallipoli, which is undoubtedly well known all over the world. Gallipoli, which is visited by more than two million local and foreign tourists every year, is the name of the region where hundreds of thousands of Anzac soldiers and Turkish soldiers lie together under the ground. Gallipoli Peninsula Historical National Park with an area of 33,490 hectares has been declared as a National Park in 1973, resembles an open-air museum with its cemetery and monuments, war constructions, archaeological and historical sites. 56 local monuments and martyrs, 35 foreign burials and monuments have been dedicated to the more than 250.000 Turkish and more than 250,000 British, French, Australian and New Zealand casualties. In this respect, the area has a distinctive meaning for Turkey, New Zealand, and Australia. Following this, Gallipoli War is regarded as an epilog on the way to the War of Independence, which would provide the foundation of modern Turkey. On the other hand, the New Zealanders see this war as a turning point in terms of awakening of national consciousness and thus, "Gallipoli probably represents something more than thanatourism for them" (Slade, 2003, p. 780). From this point of view, the region from both perspectives is important in terms of being a secular pilgrimage as well as being a "must-to-go-spot." However, it should be noted that this experience is a constructed and an imagined in large scale. Because the stones of the martyrdoms and other monuments representing the brutality and violence of war were erected later (Ilgar, 2015, p.7). Although there are 22.000 burials in 31 war cemeteries on the peninsula, only about 9.000 of them could be identified. The remaining 13.000 people lie in unidentified cemeteries, and 14.000 people, not even remnants, are mentioned at the monumental tombs of the British, Australian and Indian monuments of the peninsula (Aliağaoğlu, 2004). These monuments, in particular, are important in the context of determining the topography of the collisions and mass deaths and, establishing a representative relationship. On the other hand, the arrangements of Anzac Cove Memorial Ceremonies and Dardanelles Victory Ceremonies on different dates imply the existence of two separate discourses still struggle on the Gallipoli battlefield. The concentration of Anzac martyrdom and monuments in the north whereas the concentration of Turkish martyrdom in the south geographically confirms this discursive struggle. Indeed, neither the Turks visit northern nor the Anzacs visit southern with sufficient interest (Yeşildağ, 2010). Thus, "the dialogical forms of memorialization and tourism at Gallipoli have resulted in the reenchantment of national history (West, 2010, p. 222).

On the other hand, it may be appropriate to relate the development of the region as a dark spot, especially after the 1990s (especially for Anzacs), with the technological and communicative developments of 90s. Turkey has only been able to open the local tragedy to the international tourism sector after those years. The March 18th, Commemoration of Dardanelles and the April 25th, Anzac Ceremonies have become increasingly host the "heroic performance" recently. The cultural commemoration events including rock and pop song clips, guitars, scrolls, pieces from the Bible, independence anthems, aboriginal taps, laser light shows, fog and smoke in Anzac Cove at 5.30 a.m. on the night that connects April 24 to April 25 each year contribute to local tourism (Ilgar, 2015, p.9) even if this cacophony can be thought in terms of "society of spectacle." Additionally, tourists are invited to visit Gallipoli with the summons of "after the dawn service, get a breakfast package while watching the coast" (Kızılırmak, Alrawadieh, Küçükali & Atsız, 2016). As a respond to the "invitations," by the end of 2013, approximately 1.5-2 million local and foreign tourists; 450.000 Anzacs, 600.000 foreign visitors in total (Birdir, et al., 2015) came to Gallipoli. In this respect, it can be asserted that Turkey's most attractive black spot, which doesn't serve only national tourists but also invites foreign tourists, is Gallipoli. However, the reason Gallipoli's attractiveness for tourists isn't only about its spiritual and nationalistic value. Tourists coming to Gallipoli, especially Anzacs, plan their visit included in a longer Turkey tour with sun-beach arrangements. They averagely stay one day in Çanakkale. Therefore, even if there is a dark touristic motivation for Gallipoli, it is possible to claim that an intentional visit is not "planned" to some extent by foreigners. However, the story is quite different for Turkish tourists. Turks visit Gallipoli with a sense of duty and special planning every year. Here, motivations such as spiritual experience, respect to martyrs, learning history are at the forefront (Yeşildağ, 2010). Visit to the Çanakkale martyrdom is especially recommended by the Ministry of Education. In memorial ceremonies, sense of awe and superiority of Turkish history together with gratitude to the martyrs come to the forefront. Therefore, for Turkish tourists, Çanakkale is a national identity mediator which affirms the emergence of national consciousness by the allegory of "victory."

Another black spot that can be evaluated in the black spot category, when the same narrative is followed, is the Commander-in-chief National Park. There are parks, martyrs, and monuments in which place the major battlegrounds of the War of Independence exist. The region is visited by local tourists rather than foreigners (45.000-50.000 domestic visitors to 500-600 foreigners) (Alaeddinoğlu & Aliağaoğlu, 2007). At the area, it is aimed that visitors get information about the history of Independence War together with the Museum of Independence War and, see what kind of difficulties have been gone through on the way to the victory. There are 10 monuments and various martyrs, 1 publicity park and 2 museums within the national park boundaries. Kocatepe Monument, which is the most gorgeous, is made of bronze in a weight of 4 tons and it is 7.50 meters high. The cemetery of Dumlupınar Battle and Mustafa Kemal Atatürk Monument are surrounded by symbolic tombs, and there are 500 martyr gravestones erected in memory of 2425 martyrs. In this context, on the Park's website (http://bolge5.ormansu.gov.tr/5bolge/AnaSayfa/BTMParki.aspx?sflang=tr) Park is introduced as the place "in which 137,000 our martyrs lay and through which we again become FLAG." Subsequently, it is expressed "these lands are the place we once again show the power of TURKEY to the whole world." In accordance with this narrative, an elegant introduction stressing awe and victory, a gigantic Atatürk sculpture and military memorials are presented on the site. In this sense, Park's discourse is based upon a narrative emphasizing a righteous victory rather than displaying the atrocity of wars. Just as it is in other important battlefields around the world, the fact inland farming is stopped and sanitized and peaceful presentation of the area (Winter, 2009, p.614) also keeps the brutality of the war out of sight. Museum of Independence Museum, while exhibiting historical materials that support the narrative of the battlefield, uses a direct exhibition scheme arranged for didactic purposes, attempting to ensure that the visitor "imagines" the war. Thus, insecurity, gratitude, humility, and superiority are interactively tried to be evoked (Tarlow, 2005).

The popular black spots mentioned so far generally consist of battlefields and national museums, created by the themes of Atatürk and the War of Independence. However, two different black spots, which have been established in recent years, also make sense to make a comparison with different concepts.

The first one is Sakarya Earthquake Culture Museum. In the massive earthquake that hit Turkey in 1999, tens of thousands of people were killed, injured and lost their homes. This museum which was opened to commemorate this earthquake was built with curved and ruined columns to the memory of thousands of buildings destroyed. The museum's narrative, thus, intends to make visitors feel the shape of the building in a demolished place. This effect is also reflected in the tiny plates on which the names of the deceased names are written; in a three-dimensional plan showing destroyed Adapazarı; and inside "an art gallery" with photos, tables, and pictures. However, the most striking element in the museum is the virtual earthquake platform where the similar magnitude of the tremor of 7.4 is sustained. So, it is aimed visitor to have an authentic experience and to "take a lesson" from the tragedy. On the other hand, the fact that the museum has no foreign language statement in the exhibition halls; emphasizes "we" in its general narrative and mainly attracts domestic tourists (Yamaç, 2015) indicate the place gives priority to national identity, solidarity and unity even if the theme is different from those mentioned before. Notes written in the visitors book such as "Allah'ım (My God), you protect us our country," "they are our martyrs," "As Turkish youth, we have never forgotten our martyrs, our past," "this pain is always our past," (Depremin acısı anı defterinde ölümsüzleşiyor, 2016) reveal earthquake is recognized as a threat to national history and national unity. Yet, it is also worth to note those who come to see the Adapazarı earthquake's sufferings far from visiting it just for the sake of memorial, because Adapazarı is not an important tourist destination in its own right. Adapazarı is a place just dropped by. Therefore, even the exhibition techniques appealing sensuality such as earthquake simulator or curved columns cannot prevent the oscillation between real and virtual regarding the earthquake. Moreover, the sterility, discipline, and order of the museum strengthen simulacrum while the earthquake itself symbolizes downfall. There is no obstacle to go to McDonalds' and eat after visiting this representative area mediated by national consciousness, national solidarity and the reality of death.

Lastly, Ulucanlar Prison Museum opened to serve as a highly promising project in terms of Turkey's black spot resources, presents itself as a historic confrontation space. Ulucanlar Prison, Turkey's first prison, where detainees, convicts, and prisoners were held, tortured and even executed in inhumane conditions, represent one of the dark faces of history. However, from the website of Ulucanlar Prison Museum, it can be inferred even this torture place has been portrayed as a ring of the national "progress" of Turkey. As the prison's promotional site emphasizes that the "famous people were hosted in Ulucanlar," (http://www.ulucanlarcezaevimuzesi.com/eng/) visitors are being invited to the place with descriptive and attractive calls. For example, "the misty corridors that ended with the "Hilton," the waxy sculpted cells designed according to their original form, the isolation rooms, private belongings of the prisoners, their letters, court letters, and the scaffold on which 18 prisoners were executed…" (http://www.ulucanlarcezaevimuzesi.com/eng). This introduction, however, ends with the following sentence connotatively: "A cafeteria and the cultural center wait for you at the prison yard." Hence the museum promises authenticity, frightening, awakening the senses, empathy, but ultimately to be rested and cultured. In this sense, the warning that many parts of the museum are to be visited within a certain route also completes how the visitor's body and mind are open to be correlated/ disciplined within the narrative of the prison.

Reading all the introduction pages together, it is even natural a person to visit the museum with great enthusiasm. Yet, from a critical point of view, it is fair to claim the mode of presentation of the museum makes the torture and ill-treatment deprived of their subject. In the museum, "confrontation with history" is mentioned; but who the confronted subject is not certain. Moreover, the romanticized and nostalgic promotion pushes the visitor into a state of consciousness that "no such things are happening anymore." As a matter of fact, lightening the cells and corridors with shiny fluorescent lamps and keeping the place sanitized, which were supposedly renovated in their original forms, support the sense of "everything is all right" (compare Mowatt, 2011). Besides, the wax sculptures which have been situated to strengthen the experience make the environment kitsch. Although "kitsch, of course, can manifest itself in many disparate forms and techniques, although the overriding factor appears to be objects of interpretation which transmit feelings of comfort, safety and hope, when tragedy and the macabre are pre-packaged and interpreted for mass consumption, melancholic sentiments are not only engaged at the individual level but, perhaps more importantly, are politicized and rendered" (Sharpley & Stone, 2009a, p.127). Additionally, the fact the pieces sold in prison gift shop are produced by real prisoners gives the message "torture and ill-treatment is over." Thus, the experience of the visitor oscillates between real and virtual again. On the other hand, the empty space between unimaginable tortures and the place's power to awaken empathy tends to ignore unimaginable (Norridge, 2009).

If all these popular black spots of Turkey are evaluated together, it is possible to say, whatever their categorization is, the existing areas stand at a position which will actually reinforce one political discourse, "we." So they don't pursue economic goals as in many cases in Europe and in the world - either free or under $ 2-. But still, the process operated here is not straightforward. Each spot includes internalization, alienation and normalization processes in its own characteristics. Because such a consideration of death supports one-sided narrative about the deceased and the tortured, while blessing to be alive (Strange, 2003; Dunkley, 2015).

Undoubtedly, the variety of the visitors and the remembered pieces after the visit can't be read undivided. The outputs vary according to the closeness to the deceased, the person's historical knowledge or the meaning that the person attributes to the space. Besides, whatever the ethical concerns about the commercial side of dark tourism, the position of the spots are not necessarily unethical (Stone, 2009a) especially in consideration with the various motivations such as education or/and remembrance. That is, dark spots tend to help for constructing social consciousness, too (Stone, 2009a). As a matter of fact, the fact that national pride is illuminated in various spots from martyrdoms to the prisons in Turkish context reinforces unity in their multi-dimensionality. From this perspective, the following section will go along with this claim despite focusing on the "other" spots.

WHAT ABOUT "OTHERS": CONTROVERSIAL BLACK SPOTS IN TURKEY

Until now, the discourses of the popular black spots in Turkey have been examined. However, there are also areas of massacres and atrocities in which the "other stories" arise although either their existence has been ignored or their capacity to become a "real" black spot has been softened. Of these, two cases are particularly noteworthy, which have caused great public debate.

The first one is Diyarbakır Prison. The place has been one of those atrocity spots in which Kurdish people were enclosed largely and tortured unimaginably between 1980-1984 after military the coup in Turkey (Diyarbakır Cezaevi Gerçekleri Araştırma ve Adalet Komisyonu Raporu, 2012). Briefly, Diyarbakır Prison is known as Alcatraz of Turkey. Therefore, the relatives of the victims and the different non-governmental organizations struggle the place to be turned into a museum. Yet, the decision-makers in Turkey don't lean towards the idea. Instead, several plans, including turning the place into a school or destroying it wholly, has been kept on the agenda. However, it is a fact this prison has a symbolic meaning for Kurdish population of Turkey and, also for those who fight against the violation of human rights. From this standpoint, the idea of a museum is deliberated in terms of being a chance to face with nasty parts of history. In this respect, it is worth to remind "historic penal sites may be gloomy, but their interpretation provokes debate when frames of remembrance, forged by external political pressure and internal policies, illuminate disturbing practices and institutions" (Strange, 2003:402). Yet, the building is still used as a prison.

Another place which can be regarded as a black spot is Madımak Hotel. During the Pir Sultan Abdal Memorial Festival in 1992, 35 people, including intellectuals, poets, and scholars, were burned alive at the hotel, which was set on fire by radical Islamists. The fact that the tragic event happened at a time of an Alevi ritual and that the vast majority of the deceased are Alevis, however, give a political character to the tragedy. As a consequence, Madımak Hotel is a symbol of the hostility to "otherness," especially in the memory of Alevis. So, the leading Alevi associations are insistent on turning this place into a memory museum. However, political decision-makers were transformed it into a Science and Culture Center. In this Science and Culture Center, the ground floor was designed as children's library and the first floor was arranged as the scientific center where the scientific experiment equipment was located. At the ex-hotel-lobby in the right part of the floor, 37 fountains were made to name each of the casualties. From the fountains, water is circulated in the form of water, which means "life." On the corner where Atatürk bust was also erected, for the names of the dead on a marble pedestal "37 people lost their lives in the painful event that took place on 2 July 1993. Hoping that such painful events will not happen again" was written. Under the bust of Atatürk in the corner of the memorial, Ataturk's words "there are no obstacles for a nation knowing how to act in national unity and solidarity, no matter what different beliefs in society exist" were added. "We have tried to create a place where all Sivas and our people can express themselves, and we tried to focus on the main themes of human-centered peace and brotherhood," said Governor of Sivas (Yalçınkaya, 2011) and emphasized that the place hasn't been organized for a "particular group." Besides, in terms of "mechanical production" of the massacre, in a documentary on the state television TRT, the perpetrators of the massacre have been represented as deviant and pathologic people (Yalçınkaya, 2011).

The data yielded by these facts provides convincing evidence that Madımak is a complete example of dissonant heritage in terms of Ashworth, because the idea of turning this place into a science and culture center makes the history of a great tragedy obscure. On the other hand, the fact that two perpetrators' names are written in the corner of the memorial and, that they are at the top of the list of victims make the victim equal to the perpetrator discursively. Besides, the Alevi identity of the deceased has particularly been muted and excluded from the narrative of the memorial, thus the event has been normalized. This is as absurd as Judaism isn't mentioned in a concentration camp. So, the phenomenon is presented only as a crime against humanity. The articulation of Atatürk's words also strengthens the context of mystification by inferring differences are in conflict with national solidarity. The governor's words emphasizing "peace and brotherhood," also normalize identity politics embedded in the massacre towards the Alevis. In this context, as Alderman (2010) states officials are aware of that marginalized social actors -such as Alevis- "can use memorials and monuments to challenge dominant narrations of the past (Alderman, 2010). However, it is Alevis' duty to understand museumification can also operate as a mechanism which draws a veil between past and present and thus, museum itself freezes the facts at a present time organized by the governmentality techniques while it also reaffirms the domination of political power (Yalçınkaya, 2011, p.377). In this sense, it is worth to note dominant power relations reproduce normalization practices through exclusion while they normalize the excluded facts through inclusion.

Not surprisingly, in this context, another black spot of Turkey is Aşkale although it is non-existent as a visitation place. Aşkale was a working camp and had founded for the people who couldn't pay their property taxes in the framework of tax laws in 1941. However, it is also a historical fact the affected people from high property taxes in those years was mainly the non-Muslim population of Turkey. As a matter of fact, hundreds of non-Muslim Turkish citizens suffered from cold weather and life conditions in Aşkale while eighteen of them passed away. Despite this tragic history, it seems there is nobody willing to face with this tragic event as well as there is no debate about the arrangement of this place as a black spot. As a result,

Aşkale's non-existence as a black spot reinforces the dominant political discourse, hiding nasty facts.

By evaluating the whole picture together, finally, the political direction of creation and arrangement of black spots is clearer. That is, official ideology doesn't equally take care of the pains and memories of the citizens who have specifically been exposed to brutality due to their identity differences. In other words, good active history, such as past actions undertaken by "my" social group which inspire positive feelings, such as pride is illuminated while bad active history, such as past actions undertaken by "my" social group which inspire negative feelings, such as shame (Sharpley, 2009b, p.162) are not adequately addressed. In this sense, ignorance of the demands -as in the case of Diyarbakır Prison-, mystification the symbolic meaning of the space through normalization practices –as in the case of Madımak Hotel, and lastly behaving as if never happened –as in the case of Aşkale- are the same story's different faces. Thus, dark tourism as a political tool melts or ignores the others' tragic experiences in official ideology.

Of course, it is not possible to arrange every place, where death and massacre happened, as a black spot in hot geographies like Turkey. However, if the most meaningful aspect of black tourism is to learn from the pains and thus, to prevent tragic events from happening again, then it is beneficial to illuminate some spots with a common sense of history with respect to those who suffered or lost their lives. As Stone and Sharpley (2008) state "dark tourism may offer a new social institution whereby the functional value of death and mortality is acknowledged, its precariousness is appreciated, and efforts to assure ontological well-being and security become a source of not only playfulness, humor and entertainment but also education and memorial" (p. 588). Hence it is important to recognize that "different one" is also the citizen of the same country if it is aimed to build a more democratic society. As long as the difference is considered as a feature reinforcing the integrity, making effort to arrange some dark spots in terms of sites of memory instead of commercial aims will contribute to strengthening such a democratic culture.

FUTURE RESEARCH DIRECTIONS

Although this research finally considers black spots as a potential resource to improve civic society and proposes the "other black spots" should be narrated in a democratic way, it is also another question if educational and cultural contribution of the black spots is limited to the democratic culture of the relevant society. Morever, it is also another awaiting research question what remains in the visitor's mind after a visit. In this respect, it seems understanding dark scene in Turkey requires more quantitative data apart from this theoretical attempt.

CONCLUSION

As the number of dark spots in the world increases, so does the quest for dark tourism rises and deepens. However, much of the current debate revolves around on dark tourism's descriptive dimensions. Thus, it seems the efforts of theorizing are inadequate and incomplete. Undoubtedly, one of the reasons for the situation is that dark tourism is acknowledged from the perspective of tourism management, especially as an economic tool. On the other hand, the critical approaches, which stress dark tourism just reproduces simulacrum and commercializes death and atrocity, also underestimate its educational, psychological and cultural importance.

However, there is not a single dark tourism, nor is there any single purpose of dark tourism. Yet, heritage tourism's assumptions as an overarching approach may contribute to understanding the political nature of the dark spots. From that perspective, dark tourism should be regarded in terms of nation- state formation, especially by thinking of non-written/hidden histories.

In that framework, this study attempted to meet such a need by presenting a general panorama of Turkey. The popular and excluded "other" dark spots of Turkey were discussed in connection with the political discourse which is constructive and normalizing. It was found out there has been a line regarding the national identity in the logic of the arrangement and promotion of Turkish dark spots. It has also been determined that Turkish decision-makers give priority to the themes, War of Independence and Ataturk. However, it has also been shown the "national identity" line can be followed at recent instances of dark spots although these have been arranged to fulfill different purposes. On the other hand, it has been displayed the dark spots of "others" are ignored or normalized through various discursive practices. So, it is fair to conclude the potentiality of dark tourism to contribute to a pluralistic civic society in Turkey case is faint.

On the other hand, the rapidly growing literature on dark tourism indicates that the objective interpretation and presentation of historical heritage is an important means for realizing democratic whether it is from Turkey's or from other countries' perspectives. Therefore, it is necessary to confront history without kitschification, Disneyfication or commercialization. Preventing the rise on xenophobia, nuclear weapons, nuclear power plants, internal and regional wars, namely preventing new Auschwitzs, World Wars and Chernobiles, are the debt of living to the deceased.

REFERENCES

Alaeddinoğlu, F., & Aliağaoğlu, A. (2007). Savaş alanları turizmine tipik bir örnek: Büyük Taarruz ve Başkomutan Tarihî Milli Parkı. *Anatolia: Turizm Araştırmaları Dergisi*, *18*(2), 215–225.

Alderman, D. H. (2010). Surrogation and the politics of remembering slavery in Savannah, Georgia (USA). *Journal of Historical Geography*, *36*(1), 90–101. doi:10.1016/j.jhg.2009.08.001

Aliağaoğlu, A. (2004). Sosyo-kültürel miras turizmi ve Türkiye açısından örnekler. *Coğrafi Bilimler Dergisi*, *2*, 50–64.

Anderson, B. (1983). *Imagined communities: Reflections on the origin and spread of nationalism*. London, UK: Verso.

Ashworth, G., & Hartmann, R. (2005). *Horror and human tragedy revisited: The management of sites of atrocities for tourism*. Elmsford, NY: Cognizant Communication Corporation.

Ashworth, G., & Tunbridge, J. E. (1996). *Dissonant heritage*. New York, NY: Wiley.

Ashworth, G. J., & Isaac, R. K. (2015). Have we illuminated the dark? Shifting perspectives on dark tourism. *Tourism Recreation Research*, *40*(3), 316–325. doi: 10.1080/02508281.2015.1075726

Baldwin, F., & Sharpley, R. (2009). Battlefield tourism: Bringing organized violence back to life. In R. Sharpley & P. R. Stone (Eds.), *The darker side of travel: The theory and practice of dark tourism* (pp. 186–206). Bristol, UK: Channel View Publications.

Baudrillard, J. (1994). *Simulacra and simulation*. Michigan, MI: University of Michigan Press.

Biran, A., Yaniv, P., & Oren, G. (2011). South experiences at (dark) heritage sites. *Annals of Tourism Research*, *38*(3), 820–841. doi:10.1016/j.annals.2010.12.001

Birdir, K., Dalgıç, A., Güler, A., & Kayaalp, Y. (2015). Hüzün turizmi: Gelibolu yarımadası tarihi milli parkını ziyaret eden yabancı turistlerin deneyimleri. *Journal of Tourism and Gastronomy Studies*, *3*, 12–23.

Blom, T. (2000). Morbid tourism: A postmodern market niche with an example from Althorp. *Norwegian Journal of Geography*, *54*, 29–36.

Boz, M. (2016). Turizm destinasyonu olarak Gelibolu. *Karadeniz*, *31*, 63–74.

Browman, M. S., & Pezzullo, P. C. (2009). Whats so dark about dark tourism? Death, tours, and performance. *Tourist Studies*, *9*(3), 187–202. doi:10.1177/1468797610382699

Çetinsöz, B. C., & Temiz, G. (2016). *Alternatif bir turizm türü olarak Türkiye'nin karanlık (dark) turizm potansiyeli.* Paper presented at International Multidisciplinary Congress of Eurasia. Retrieved From: https://www.researchgate.net/publication/309591517_Alternatif_Bir_Turizm_Turu_Olarak_Turkiye'nin_Karanlik_Dark_Turizm_Potansiyeli

Clarke, R., Dutton, J., & Johnston, A. (2014). Shadow zones: Dark travel and postcolonial cultures. *Postcolonial Studies*, *17*(3), 221–235. doi:10.1080/13688790.2014.993426

Cohen, E. (2011). Educational dark tourism at an in populo site: The Holocaust Museum in Jerusalem. *Annals of Tourism Research*, *38*(1), 193–209. doi:10.1016/j.annals.2010.08.003

Collins-Kreiner, N. (2016). Dark tourism as/is pilgrimage. *Current Issues in Tourism*, *19*(12), 1185–1189. doi:10.1080/13683500.2015.1078299

Dann, G. (1994). Tourism: The nostalgia industry of the future. In W. Theobald (Ed.), *Global tourism: The next decade* (pp. 55–67). Oxford, UK: Butterworth-Heinemann.

Dann, G. (1998). *The dark side of tourism. Etudes et rapports, se'rie L.* Aix-en-Provence: Centre International de Recherches et d'Etudes Touristiques.

Depremin acısı anı defterinde ölümsüzleşiyor. (2016). Retrieved from: http://aa.com.tr/tr/turkiye/depremin-acisi-ani-defterinde-olumsuzlesiyor/629373

Diyarbakır Askeri Cezaevi Gerçekleri Araştırma ve Adalet Komisyonu Raporu. (2012). Retrieved From: http://bianet.org/files/doc_files/000/000/370/original/111203-DC-Sempozyum_Sunum_%C3%96zetleri.pdf

Dunkley, R. (2015). Beyond temporal reflections in thanatourism. *Annals of Tourism Research*, *52*, 172–179. doi:10.1016/j.annals.2015.03.007

Dunkley, R., Morgan, N., & Westwood, S. (2011). Visiting the trenches: Exploring meanings and motivations in battlefield tourism. *Tourism Management*, *32*(4), 860–868. doi:10.1016/j.tourman.2010.07.011

Eichstedt, J., & Small, S. (2002). *Representations of slavery: Race and ideology in southern plantation museums.* Washington, DC: Smithsonian Books.

Ellis, R. (2009). *Experiencing "dark tourism": The real Auschwitz?* (Unpublished undergraduate thesis). University of Bristol, UK. Retrieved from: http://www.bristol.ac.uk/history/media/docs/ug-dissertations/2009ellis.pdf

Foley, J., & Lennon, M. (1996). JFK and dark tourism: A fascination with assassination. *International Journal of Heritage Studies*, *2*(4), 198–211. doi:10.1080/13527259608722175

Foucault, M. (2003). *Society Must Be Defended* (D. Macey, Trans.). New York, NY: Picador.

Hally, M. B. (2009). *A guide for international nursing students in Australia and New Zealand*. Sydney, Australia: Elsevier.

Hewison, R. (1987). *The heritage industry*. London, UK: Methuen.

Ilgar, R. (2015). Mabetleşen bir mekân: Gelibolu yarımadası tarihi savaş alanları turizmi. *Çanakkale Araştırmaları Türk Yıllığı, 13*(19), 1-20.

Kang, E., Scott, N., Lee, T., & Ballantyne, R. (2012). Benefits of visiting a dark tourism site: The case of the Jeju April 3rd Peace Park, Korea. *Tourism Management*, *33*(2), 257–265. doi:10.1016/j.tourman.2011.03.004

Kızılırmak, İ., Alrawadieh, Z., Küçükali, S., & Atsız, O. (2015). *Çanakkale'de düzenlenen Anzak tur programlarına yönelik bir içerik analizi.* Research Paper. Retrieved from: https://www.researchgate.net/publication/299599754_Canakkale%27de_Duzenlenen_Anzak_Tur_Programlarina_Yonelik_Bir_Icerik_Analizi

Korstanje, M. (2015). *The anthropology of dark tourism, exploring the contradictions of capitalism.* Centre for Ethnicity & Racism Studies. Retrieved from: http://cers.leeds.ac.uk/files/2015/02/Korstanje_CERS_15.pdf

Korstanje, M., & Ivanov, S. (2012). Tourism as a form of new psychological resilience: The inception of dark tourism. *Cultur*, *6*(4), 56–71.

Lennon, M., & Foley, J. (2000). *Dark tourism: The attraction of death and disaster*. London, UK: Continuum.

Massey, D. (2005). *For space*. London, UK: Sage.

Miles, S. (2014). Battlefield sites as dark tourism attractions: An analysis of experience. *Journal of Heritage Tourism*, *9*(2), 134–147. doi:10.1080/1743873X.2013.871017

Miles, W. (2002). Auschwitz: Museum interpretation and darker tourism. *Annals of Tourism Research*, *29*(4), 1175–1178. doi:10.1016/S0160-7383(02)00054-3

Moeller, M. (2005). *Battlefield tourism in South Africa with special reference to Isandwlana and Rorke's drift KwaZulu-Natal* (Unpublished MPhil Thesis). Faculty of Economic and Management Sciences, University of Pretoria.

Mowatt, R. A. (2011). Visiting death and life: Dark tourism and slave castles. *Annals of Tourism Research*, *38*(4), 1410–1434.

Norridge, Z. (2009). Finding a home in Hackney? Re-imagining narratives of slavery through a multicultural community museum space. *African and Black Diaspora: International Journal (Toronto, Ont.)*, *2*(2), 167–179.

Pollock, G. (2003). Holocaust tourism: being there, looking back and the ethics of spatial memory. In D. Crouch & N. Lübbren (Eds.), *Visual culture and tourism* (pp. 175–190). Oxford.

Powell, R., & Iankova, K. (2016). Dark London: Dimensions and characteristics of dark tourism supply in the UK capital. *Anatolia*, *27*(3), 339–351. doi:10.1080/13032917.2016.1191764

Rojek, C. (1993). *Ways of escape*. Basingstoke, UK: Macmillan. doi:10.1057/9780230373402

Rojek, C. (1997). Indexing, dragging and the social construction of tourist sights. In C. Rojek & J. Urry (Eds.), Touring cultures: Transformations of travel and theory (pp. 52–74). London, UK: Routledge.

Ryan, C., & Kohli, R. (2006). The buried village, New Zealand: An example of dark tourism? *Asia Pacific Journal of Tourism Research*, *11*(3), 211–226. doi:10.1080/10941660600753240

Seaton, A. (1996). Guided by the dark: From thanatopsis to thanatourism. *International Journal of Heritage Studies*, *2*(4), 234–244. doi:10.1080/13527259608722178

Seaton, A. (2011). *Social affiliations and emergent motivations in thanatourism behaviour at Lansdown Tower and Cemetery*. Paper presented at Tourism Imaginaries, Berkeley University of California, Berkeley, CA. Retrieved From: http://www.tourismstudies.org/tourismimaginariesAuthors.htm

Seaton, A., & Lennon, J. (2004). Thanatourism in the early 21st century: Moral panics, ulterior motives and alterior desires. In T. V. Singh (Ed.), *New horizons in tourism: Strange experiences and stranger practices* (pp. 63–82). Wallingford, UK: Cabi. doi:10.1079/9780851998633.0063

Seaton, T. (2009a). Thanatourism and its discontents. An appraisal of a decade's work with some future issues and directions. In J. Tazim & M. Robinson (Eds.), *The sage book of tourism studies* (pp. 521–542). London, UK: Sage. doi:10.4135/9780857021076.n29

Seaton, T. (2009b). Purposeful otherness: Management implications. In R. Sharpley & P. R. Stone (Eds.), *The darker side of travel: The theory and practice of dark tourism* (pp. 75–109). Bristol, UK: Channel View Publications.

Sharpley, R. (2009a). Shedding light on dark tourism: An introduction. In R. Sharpley & P. R. Stone (Eds.), *The darker side of travel: The theory and practice of dark tourism* (pp. 3–22). Bristol, UK: Channel View Publications.

Sharpley, R. (2009b). Dark tourism and political ideology: Towards a governance model. In R. Sharpley & P. R. Stone (Eds.), *The darker side of travel: The theory and practice of dark tourism* (pp. 145–166). Bristol, UK: Channel View Publications.

Sharpley, R., & Stone, P. (2009a). Representing the macabre: Interpretation, kitschification and authenticity. In R. Sharpley & P. R. Stone (Eds.), *The darker side of travel: The theory and practice of dark tourism* (pp. 109–128). Bristol, UK: Channel View Publications.

Sharpley, R., & Stone, P. (2009b). Life, death and dark tourism: Future research directions and concluding comments. In R. Sharpley & P. R. Stone (Eds.), *The darker side of travel: The theory and practice of dark tourism* (pp. 247–251). Bristol, UK: Channel View Publications.

Slade, P. (2003). Gallipoli thanatourism: The meaning of ANZAC. *Annals of Tourism Research, 30*(4), 779–794. doi:10.1016/S0160-7383(03)00025-2

Solomon, A. (2015). Authenticity and simulation in post tourism. *Synergy, 11*(1), 41–53.

Stone, P. (2005). *Review: Dark tourism –cashing in on tragedy?* Paper presented at the Tourism Society Seminar Event, London, UK. Retrieved from: www.dark-tourism.org.uk

Stone, P. (2006). A dark tourism spectrum: Towards a typology of death and macabre related tourist sites, attractions and exhibitions. *Tourism: An Interdisciplinary International Journal, 54*(2), 145–160.

Stone, P. (2009a). Dark tourism: Morality and new moral spaces. In R. Sharpley & P. R. Stone (Eds.), *The darker side of travel: The theory and practice of dark tourism* (pp. 56–72). Bristol, UK: Channel View Publications.

Stone, P. (2009b). "It's a bloody guide": Fun, fear and a lighter side of dark tourism at the dungeon visitor attractions, UK. In R. Sharpley & P. R. Stone (Eds.), *The darker side of travel: The theory and practice of dark tourism* (pp. 167–185). Bristol, UK: Channel View Publications.

Stone, P. (2010). *Death, dying and dark tourism in contemporary society: A theoretical and empirical analysis* (Unpublished doctoral dissertation). University of Central Lancashire, UK. Retrieved from: http://clok.uclan.ac.uk/1870/

Stone, P. (2012). Dark tourism and significant other death: Towards a model of mortality mediation. *Annals of Tourism Research, 39*(3), 1565–1587. doi:10.1016/j.annals.2012.04.007

Stone, P. (2013). Dark tourism scholarship: A critical review. *International Journal of Culture. Tourism and Hospitality Research, 7*(3), 307–318.

Stone, P. (n.d.). Enlightening the "dark" in dark tourism. *AHI,* 22-24.

Stone, P., & Sharpley, R. (2008). Consuming dark tourism: A thanatological perspective. *Annals of Tourism Research, 35*(2), 574–595. doi:10.1016/j.annals.2008.02.003

Strange, C., & Kempa, M. (2003). Shades of dark tourism: Alcatraz and Roben Island. *Annals of Tourism Research, 30*(2), 386–405. doi:10.1016/S0160-7383(02)00102-0

Tarlow, P. (2005). Dark tourism: The appealing "dark" side of tourism and more. In M. Novelli (Ed.), *Niche tourism: Contemporary issues, trends and cases* (pp. 47–57). Oxford, UK: Elsevier. doi:10.1016/B978-0-7506-6133-1.50012-3

Taş, İ. (2016). Türkiye'nin hüzün turizmi profili. *The Journal of Academic Social Science Studies International Journal of Social Science, 48,* 183–198.

Tinson, J., Saren, M. A. J., & Roth, B. E. (2015). Exploring the role of dark tourism in the creation of national identity of young Americans. *Journal of Marketing Management, 31*(7-8), 856–880. doi:10.1080/0267257X.2014.995207

Tucker, H. (2016). Empathy and tourism: Limits and possibilities. *Annals of Tourism Research, 57,* 31–43. doi:10.1016/j.annals.2015.12.001

Türkiye Diyarbakır Askeri Cezaevi İle yüzleşiyor. Diyarbakır Askeri Cezaevi Gerçekleri Araştırma ve Adalet Komisyonu Raporu. (n.d.). Retrieved From: http://bianet.org/files/doc_files/000/000/370/original/111203-DC-Sempozyum_Sunum_%C3%96zetleri.pdf

Walter, T. (2009a). Dark tourism: Mediating between the dead and the living. In R. Sharpley & P. R. Stone (Eds.), *The darker side of travel: The theory and practice of dark tourism* (pp. 39–55). Bristol, UK: Channel View Publications.

Walter, T. (2009b). Disaster, modernity, and the media. In K. Garces-Foley (Ed.), *Death and religion in a changing world* (pp. 265–282). Armonk, NY: Sharpe.

West, B. (2010). Dialogical memorialization, international travel and the public sphere: A cultural sociology of commemoration and tourism at the First World War Gallipoli battlefields. *Tourist Studies, 10*(3), 209–225. doi:10.1177/1468797611407756

White, G. M. (2015). Is Paris burning? Touring Americas good war in France. *History & Memory, 27*(2), 74–103. doi:10.2979/histmemo.27.2.74

Winter, C. (2009). Tourism, social memory and the great war. *Annals of Tourism Research, 4*(36), 607–626. doi:10.1016/j.annals.2009.05.002

Yalçınkaya, A. (2011). Hafıza savaşlarından sahiplenilmiş şehitliğe: Madımak katliamı örnek olayı. *Mülkiye, 66*(3), 333–394.

Yamaç, Z. (2015). Sakarya destinasyonunun imaj algısına yönelik bir araştırma. *İşletme Bilimi Dergisi, 3*(2), 85-61.

Yankovskaa, G., & Hannamb, K. (2014). Dark and toxic tourism, dark and toxic tourism in the Chernobyl exclusion zone. *Current Issues in Tourism, 17*(10), 929–939. doi:10.1080/13683500.2013.820260

Yeşildağ, B. (2010). *Savaş alanları turizmi ve Gelibolu Yarımadası Tarihi Milli Parkı örneği* (Unpublished MA Thesis). Çanakkale 18 Mart University, Social Sciences Institute. Retrieved from: http://acikerisim.lib.comu.edu.tr:8080/xmlui/bitstream/handle/COMU/668/Baris_Yesildag_Tez.pdf?sequence=1

Yıldız, Z., Yıldız, S., & Aytemiz, L. (2015). Kara turizm, terör turizmi ve Türkiye potansiyeli. *İnsan ve Toplum bilimleri Araştırmaları Dergisi, 4*(2), 390-407.

Young, C., & Light, D. (2016). Interrogating spaces of and for the dead as alternative space: Cemeteries, corpses and sites of dark tourism. *International Review of Social Research, 6*(2), 61–72. doi:10.1515/irsr-2016-0009

Yuill, S. M. (2003). *Understanding visitor motivation at sites of death and disaster* (Unpublished MA Thesis). Office of Graduate Studies of Texas A&M University. Retrieved from: http://oaktrust.library.tamu.edu/bitstream/handle/1969.1/89/etd-tamu-2003C-RPTS-Yuill-1.pdf?sequence=1&isAllowed=y

ADDITIONAL READING

Beech, J. (2001). The marketing of slavery heritage in the UK. *International Journal of Hospitality & Tourism Administration*, *2*(3/4), 85–105. doi:10.1300/J149v02n03_04

Butler, D. L. (2001). Whitewashing Plantations: The commodification of a slave-free Antebellum South. *International Journal of Hospitality & Tourism Administration*, *2*(3/4), 163–175. doi:10.1300/J149v02n03_07

Church, A., & Coles, T. (2007). *Tourism, power and space*. New York, NY: Routledge.

Cole, T. (1999). *Selling the Holocaust: From Auschwitz to Schindler: How history is bought, packaged, and sold*. New York, NY: Routledge.

Corsane, G. (2005). *Heritage, museums and galleries: An introductory reader*. London, UK: Routledge. doi:10.4324/9780203326350

Dann, M. S., & Seaton, A. V. (2001). Slavery, contested heritage and thanatourism (Eds). New York, NY: The Hawthorn Hospitality Press.

Dicks, B. (2004). *Culture on display: The production of contemporary visitability*. Maidenhead, Berkshire, England: McGraw-Hill Education.

Farmaki, A. (2013). Dark tourism revisited: A supply/demand conceptualisation. *International Journal of Culture. Tourism and Hospitality Research*, *7*(3), 281–292. doi:10.1108/IJCTHR-05-2012-0030

Foley, M., & Lennon, J. (1997). Dark tourism – An ethical dilemma. In M. Foley, J. J. Lennon, & G. Maxwell (Eds.), *Strategic Issues for the hospitality, tourism and leisure industries* (pp. 153–164). London, UK: Cassell.

Hall, C. H. (1994). *Tourism and politics: policy, power and place*. New York, NY: John-Wiley.

Kirshenblatt-Gimblett, B. (1998). *Destination culture: Tourism, museums, and heritage*. Berkeley, UK: University of California Press.

Knapp, S. (1989). Collective memory and the actual past. *Representations (Berkeley, Calif.)*, *26*(1), 123–149. doi:10.1525/rep.1989.26.1.99p0284y

Light, D. (2000). An unwanted past: Contemporary tourism and the heritage of communism in Romania. *International Journal of Heritage Studies*, *6*(2), 145–160. doi:10.1080/135272500404197

Mayo, J. (1988). War memorials as political memory. *Geographical Review*, *78*(1), 62–75. doi:10.2307/214306

O'Rourke, P. J. (1989). *Holidays in hell.* London, UK: Picador.

Staiff, R. (2013). *Re-imagining heritage interpretation: Enchanting the past-future.* Farnham, Surrey, England: Routledge.

Tzanelli, R. (2016). *Thanatourism and the cinematic representation of risk.* London, UK: Routledge.

Urry, J. (2002). *Tourist gaze.* London, UK: Routledge.

Webster, C., & Stanislav, I. (2016). Political ideologies as shapers of future tourism development. *Journal of Tourism Futures*, *2*(2), 109–124. doi:10.1108/JTF-05-2015-0029

Wilson, J. (2008). *Prison: Cultural memory and dark tourism.* New York, NY: Peter Lang.

Winter, C. (2011). Battlefield visitor motivations: Explorations in the Great War town of Ieper, Belgium. *International Journal of Tourism Research*, *13*(2), 164–176. doi:10.1002/jtr.806

KEY TERMS AND DEFINITIONS

Counter-Discursive Black Spots: A term referring there are "other" black spots clashing with the mainstream discourse narratively.

Dissonant Heritage: The heritage which narratively distorts the past events and thus, creates an incoordination with visitors' expectations and past knowledge.

National Identity Construction: A term proposing national identity is a product of an economic and political process related with the history of capitalism.

Normalization Practices: A Foucauldian term, emphasizing that the power relations perform in a productive way which disciplines, controls and reproduces everyday life by turning the "anomaly" into an idealized norm of behavior.

Others' Dark Spots: An expression referring there are some other potential dark spots belonging to the ethnical, religious or cultural groups excluded from the hegemonic political discourse.

Secular Pilgrim: Pilgrim, stressing the spiritual purification after visiting a place although the place hasn't got any religious root.

Turkish Black Spots: The umbrella name to indicate the black spots in Turkey, disregarding the ethnical background.

Chapter 7
Dark Tourism as a Form of Governmentality of Fear

Funda Çoban
Aksaray University, Turkey

ABSTRACT

Although dark tourism attracts many scholars from different backgrounds, there is no consensus about its definition. Yet still, it is possible to classify the discussions revolving around the definition issue: The first group focuses on the descriptive side of dark tourism in terms of "sudden death and disaster," while a second group gives priority to the existential dimension of the dark touristic interest in terms of "never-ending death and disaster." However, fear appears as a surrounding component of both approaches. At that point, this study questions the relationship between the rise of dark touristic interest since the 1990s and the notion of governmentality of fear. In this respect, the study attempts to make bridge between the existential context of dark tourism and its political dimension with the Foucauldian terms, especially by shedding light on dark tourism in terms of "biopower technology."

INTRODUCTION

Fear as an evolutionary emotion (Solomon, 2008) is one of the basic emotions to survive. Also, people are even delighted to feel fear to a certain extent. The horror movies or the amusement park facilities such as high-speed roller coaster are the concrete forms of this satisfaction embodied in popular culture. In this context, it is fair to assume that fear is a significant component of the contemporary social life shaped and diffused by it. On the other hand, dark tourism with its cultural and psychological, but also commercial aspects is distinctively related to the sociological dimension of fear because fear is one of the constitutive elements of dark tourism.

DOI: 10.4018/978-1-5225-2750-3.ch007

From this vein, the relationship between the ontology of dark tourism and the socio-political context of the fear has the capacity to explain why dark tourism has recently become an attractive sector. In other words, it is possible to make a connection between the fact that the dark tourism sector has started to develop since the 1990s -if its other historical forms are bracketed- and the idea that the fear is a substantial phenomenon which particularly has been constructing and reproducing Western societal order especially since the 1990s. However, in order to establish this relationship firmly, the scope of dark tourism must first be discussed, and then the nature of this scope in the West's fear culture should be investigated.

From this perspective, the study at hand opens up with a literature discussion on how to interpret dark tourism. Thus, different perspectives on dark tourism are traced to put the case clearly. Then, it is claimed that the constituent element of these debates, classified as epistemological and ontological ones, is fear. From this point of view, the following section of the study assesses fear as a governmental technique in the Foucaldian sense after tackling it with its ontological extensions. So, the section addresses the issue as a functional departure with its extreme politico-economic returns instead of assuming there is no connection between the development of dark tourism and the current political scene in the world. In this context, the leading questions of the section are what the breaking point causing the current age is called "age of fear" is and how this point has affected dark tourism to emerge as a separate sector. In parallel with these queries, the section deepens the main question how dark tourism plays a functional role for mobilizing, disciplining, and controlling the people. By using Stone's (2006) dark tourism classification, finally, the last section discursively analyses how the dark touristic spots run as a tool for governmentality of fear. Hence, the ultimate goal of the study is to review the definition problems of dark tourism by using a constituent element in addition to explaining the functions of fear through the political construction and production of contemporary society within a touristic realm. Thus, it is aimed to provide an interdisciplinary approach to the study of dark tourism as a political economic area.

BACKGROUND

In psychology, fear is considered as one of the basic emotions that enable the living beings to survive. However, it has a socially constructed dimension like other emotions. On the other hand, proposing fears can be socially constructed means that they are also manageable and routable. In this sense, fear can be assessed as a foundational component which connects dark tourism to (post) modern world at the intersection of psychology, sociology, and politics.

UNDERSTANDING DARK TOURISM WITHIN THE LITERATURE

One of the most important problems that humankind is desperate for, is fear of death and the death itself. War, famine, outbreaks, natural disaster etc. are some cases that make this desperation collectively real. In other words, any kind of disaster – natural or human-made – causing people to suffer brings about a social/collective respond originating from the individual fears. The collective rituals to eradicate plague in the Middle Ages, the taboo objects and the sacred places are some examples of these kinds of societal reflections. However, the response of the 20th century Western people to such fears has gained a very commercial dimension, along with the traces of the previous periods. The name of this dimension is dark tourism.

Considering the frequently referred definitions of dark tourism (Foley & Lennon, 1996) or black spot tourism (Rojek, 1993), it is "the commercial [touristic] developments of grave sites and sites in which celebrities or large numbers of people have met with sudden and violent death" (Rojek, 1993, p.136); "the presentation and consumption of real and commoditized death and disaster sites" (Foley & Lennon, 1996, p.198); ''to travel to a location wholly, or partially, motivated by the desire for actual or symbolic encounters with death'' (Seaton, 1996, p. 240); ''traveling to touristic sites focusing on sudden death and which quickly attracts large numbers of people and, on the other an attraction-focused artificial morbidity-related tourism" (Blom, 2000, p.32), "visitation to sites associated with death, disaster, and depravity" (Lennon&Foley, 2000, p.46), "the act of travel to sites associated with death, suffering and the seemingly macabre'' (Stone, 2006, p.146), "traveling to the sites concerned with encountering spaces of death or calamity that have political or historical significance, and that continue to impact upon the living" (Stone, n.d.); or "one of a number of institutions which mediate between the living and the dead" (Walter, 2009a, p. 39). Also, Seaton (2009) preferring the term thanatourism defines it as "tourism motivated by the desire to visit places . . . associated with death, whether or not death is seen to be a principle motivation" (p. 522). Regarding the various definitions, there is a long and complex list of dark spots, such us graves of Marilyn Monroe or James Dean, martyrdoms, battlefields; disaster sites such Katrina or Chernobyl, London's dark dungeons, Auschwitz, Alcatraz Prison, Robben Island, which is far away to be comprehensive. However, the variety and the expansion of the dark sites prove the contemporary society is tremendously attracted by atrocity and suffering (Lennon & Folley, 2000) so that "the commodification of death for popular tourist consumption has become a focus for mainstream tourism providers" (Stone, 2013, p. 307). As a result, another new dark site is being added to the current dark spots list every each day in addition to the millions of dark touristic page which can be found on the internet (Sharpley, 2009a). In sum, it is hard to properly define the sector's scope and classify the extent of the dark touristic charm (Ashworth &

Isaac, 2015). No doubt there are individual and societal reasons to visit a site in addition to the politico-economic alternates. In other words, given the fact that dark tourism grows as a separate sector[1] at the cross point of supply and demand sides, determining which side causes the sector to develop varies according to the historical and the spatial context. Yet despite all difficulties, it is still possible to categorize the dark touristic studies under two topics in order to determine the constitutive component of dark tourism.

Epistemological Debates

At this side of the debates, the issues are mainly addressed to the representation and the authenticity of the dark spots (Lennon & Foley, 2000; Miles, 2002), interpretation of the authenticity with its ties to heritage tourism (Ashworth & Hartmann, 2005), and the economic, political and ideological consequences originating from that interpretation (see Ashworth& Turnbridge, 1996; Seaton & Lennon, 2004; Alderman, 2010). In this sense, the epistemological debates assume there is a post-modernistic propensity rooting in the gap between *the signifier* and *the signified* and ask how we know/interpret the reality. As Lennon and Folley (2000) has argued, most of the dark spots run as a tool which questions the progressiveness and the rationality of modernity while they eradicate the exact limits between the real and hyper-real, thus blur the sharpness of the tragedy. Hence "once tourists have physically arrived the sites and satisfied their curiosity through the narration of the tragedy, they demand something brighter, such as colorful cultural aspects, beautiful scenery and cheerful entertainment" (Yoshida, Bui & Lee, 2016). Indeed, "contemporary society increasingly consumes, willingly or unwillingly, both real and commodified death and suffering through audio-visual representations, popular culture and the media" (Stone & Sharpley, 2008, p. 580). In this sense, from the most entertaining to the most touchy sites, they embrace the tension between real and hyper-real, that is at the end connected to the presentation of the place (Rojek, 1997; Stone & Sharpley, 2008; Walter, 2009b). On the other hand, the main factor mediating this discussion is the visitor motivations because it is important why the tourists choose a spot to visit and what expectations they have before the visit despite the spot's semantic diffusion blurring the tragedy's cognitive, historical and interpretational aspects. In other words, the reason why a tourist is attracted by the dark touristic site beyond the charming presentation of the place as a form of cultural product within the capitalistic logic remains as a substantial topic. "The desire to overcome phantom, search for novelty, nostalgia, celebration of crime and deviance, basic bloodlust and interest in challenging one's sense or mortality" (Dann, 1998); "see it to believe it" (Biran, Yaniv & Oren, 2011), *schadenfreude* (Seaton & Lennon, 2004); sense of survival (Rojek, 1997), secular pilgrimage (Dunkley & Westwood, 2011), empathy

(Andermann & Simine, 2012; Rapson, 2012), confirmation of the personal identity and the history (Mowatt, 2011), "insecurity, gratitude, humility and superiority" (Tarlow, 2005), finding out *de facto* psychological and cultural origins (Slade, 2003), commemoration and education (Panakera, 2007), *memento mori* (Walter, 2009a) are some of those motivations determined in the relevant studies. In this sense, perhaps the most important reason why the dark touristic spots encompass an extensive spectrum is the diversity of those motivations. Representing this spectrum, Rojek's (1993) nostalgic and sensitive sites, Stone's (2006) spectrum of dark spots (from lightest to darkest), Miles's (2002) dark and darker spots, Sharpley's (2009a) shades of dark tourism, Cohen's (2011) *in populo* and *in situ* sites attend to offer comprehensive explanations within the matrix of the presentation, the history and the personal motivation. However, they woefully remain descriptive (Dann, 1998). Therefore, the motivational explanations are repeatedly intermingled and get more and more complex (Stone, 2012; Isaac & Ashworth, 2012).

Ontological Debates

The starting point of the ontological discussions, which analytically serves a basis for the descriptive epistemological debates, focuses on the question whether dark tourism is really a new sector. In this sense, Seaton (1996) dates back the history of dark tourism to the Middle Ages (compare Korstanje, 2015a) as a thanatoptic tradition, thus searches the roots of dark tourism in the human interest to death although he also recognizes the its new contemporary forms. From the same vein, the common argument of the ontological debates analyzes the existential concerns and anxiety from suffering (see Slade, 2003). As Stone stresses (2012), when people gaze upon the "others" death and tragedy they affirm their own existence and thus, satisfy psychologically as a survivor. However, the question how this ontological/psychological motive has turned into a special interest including entertainment can sociologically be traced through the process that dying has constantly been sequestrated by professionalization, medicalization, and privatization (Stone & Sharpley, 2008). Again Stone (2012) adds thanatourism is a "mediating" process which leaves space to understand mortality as a social construction. In this sense, "the public executions to see the condemned, the guided morgue tours of the Victorian period, the Chamber of Horrors exhibition of Madame Tussauds or the 'correction houses' of the nineteenth century where galleries were built to accommodate fee-paying visitors who witnessed flogging as a recreational activity are accepted as the first examples of black tourism" (Stone, 2006, p. 147). From a similar vein, Sharpley and Stone (2008) state "increasingly socially acceptable gaze upon death and its re-conceptualization for entertainment, education or memorial purposes offers both the individual and collective self a pragmatic confrontational mechanism to begin the process of neutralizing the impact of mortality, and consequently, this can help minimize the intrinsic threat that the inevitability of death brings" (p. 587). "Thus, contemplating death through a dark tourism lens allows tourists to view their own death as distant, unrelated to the dark tourism product that they consume, and with a hope that their own death will be a good Romantic death and their lives will be meaningful and ontologically secure" (Stone, 2012, 1574). So, the tourists want to avoid their own death (Korstanje, 2015a). In this sense, dark tourism at its top is related to the "work of mourning" which runs as a kind of libidinal economy in terms of Freud.

If two axes of dark touristic approaches are evaluated together, it is clear that each analysis has its own power for "shedding light on dark tourism." Because, the existence of man on the earth is shaky and perpetually under threat as the ontological approach explains whereas thinking of tragedy and disaster as an interest has emerged only in recent years will narrow the scope as the epistemological approach emphasizes. In other words, the increase in the number of the dark touristic spots, the improving techniques used in the presentation and the promotion of the areas, the rise in the number of the visitors are recognizable in comparison with the previous centuries although the existential concern has always been there at different levels. It is, then, meaningful to ask, "What has happened, causing dark anxiety to turn into a dark touristic attraction?" Putting it differently, it is necessary to investigate the socio-political context that transforms the individual / psycho-ontological interest of the 19th Century into a true tourist attraction in the late 20th Century

DARK TOURISM AS ECONOMY OF FEAR

It is commonly accepted that the world has become less secure after the 1990s. Despite the threats posed by the bipolar order, the world system, which had gained some stability in the face of the regional, economic and political conflicts, has left its place to the "new world order" after the collapse of the USSR (Bush & Scowcroft,1998). In this new world, the primarily respected factors threatening the security of the nation-states are "terrorism, ecological catastrophe and crime" and they have replaced the "threat of communism" although they have less political tone and direction in addition to their ambiguous nature. In this process, the developments in the communication and transportation sectors, the process transforming the world into a "glocal" village (Robertson, 1995), the adverse effects of the globalization such as rise of conservatism or harsh identity politics (Robertson, 1995) are the catalyzers aggravating and de-territorializing those risks. As a result, the postmodern individual of the 21st Century in a sort of hyper-reality (Baudrillard, 1994) within time-space compression (Harvey, 1990) is far from concrete threats such as famine, hot war, epidemics seen in the previous centuries, and lives in full of risks which are diffused, distributed and equalized (Beck, 1992).[2] In this sense, 21st century is uncanny for the laymen. Contemporary people's sense of security has changed and been reshaped since from Jefferson's "in pursuit of happiness" to Roosevelt's "freedom from fear."

On the other hand, fear as a primary emotion in terms of behavioral, cognitive and evolutionary psychology is a natural impulse that protects the human-beings from threats (Izard, 1991; Ekman & Davidson, 1994; Solomon, 2008). However, what sociologically striking is that fear is a social construction like other emotions. As Harré and Parrot (1996) states, "human psychology is a complex pattern of cultural practices, discursive conventions, and physiological processes (p. 20; see also Armon-Jones 1986; Bar-tal, 2001; Solomon, 2008). In other words, of what the people are afraid, when people feel uncanny and how people act varies according to the context of the given historical and cultural realm (Scruton, 1986; Svendsen, 2008). For example, according to Castel, the contemporary people feel much more insecure than the Middle Aged man, although they are exposed to a lesser extent of threat to a Middle Aged man (as cited in Korstanje, 2010). In this sense, the term, culture of fear (Furedi, 1997; Glassner, 1999), which has started to be used to characterize the world's condition after the 1990s (Brissett, n.d.), stresses such a socio-political context. Within this realm, the culture of fear reveals itself in many faces: fear from hormone in foods, car accident, rape, robbery, refugees, unemployment, divorce, long-lasting relationship, pedophilia, Islam, asylum seekers, aging, impoverishment, strangers, getting weight etc… The list is long. Modern people live in the age of phobias/fears. The web page, phobialist (http://phobialist.com/) lists hundreds of different phobia types. Resting upon these anxieties, different psychiatric branches and counseling services emerge; the coverage of insurance policies rises and the number of insured persons increase. Life-coaching, which is one of the most commercial reflections of a man's desire to control and cope with future, becomes more and more popular. As Giddens (1991) argues "people purchase ontological security through various institutions and experiences that protect themselves from direct contact with madness, criminality, sexuality, nature and death which at the end mean angst of disorder or chaos" (p. 156). In consequence, fear constantly produces its own economy (Flaxman & Rogerson, 2010). Besides, "mass-media reinforces the power of the invented external threats and thus, supports the policies and strategies providing control over the population" (Korstanje, 2010). As a remaining result, new power relations with their commercial and political aspects are created. However, what is more interesting is that the contemporary fears mostly don't have a subject, which in return causes to stress on the culture of anxiety instead of the culture of fear.

On the other hand, the theoretical roots of the culture of fear/anxiety can be found out in the Foucaldian term, governmentality which dates back late 17th Century.

For Foucault (2003) beginning from the end of the 17th Century, the concept of pastoral sovereignty of the 16th century has begun to leave its place to a different understanding of power, which disciplines, controls and reproduces the individual bodily and mentally through various internalization practices. In the framework of this new governmental logic, life and happiness (regarding the health of the body and mind) have been the rising values. What the disciplinary power has blessed is bodily and mental health, namely life in contrast to the death and the sickness. So, the main point of the governmentality is the man's survival, but survival as a capital which would serve for the dominant power relations. Moving cemeteries out of the cities (Foucault, 1984); medicalization of the death (Elias, 1985; Mellor & Shilling, 1993; Ira Byock, 2002), promoting youth, health and reproduction are the concrete forms of the governmental practices (Foucault, 1976, 1990, 1992). Besides, it is worth to note the power relations work in a productive way to overcome the governmental goals (Foucault, 1980). Here, the discourse of the power calls each individual distinctively and subjectifies them (Foucault, 1982) in a multiplying way.

In a similar vein, the risks which are subjectless, individualized and de-territorialized are in fact can be considered as governmental techniques within productive power relations if Foucault's governmentality and the notion of the culture of fear are articulated. Forasmuch as it is easier to control, discipline and normalize the individuals within a political atmosphere dominated by fears. In the contexts filled with fears, people are more attached to their beliefs, not being able to evaluate the past in a concrete way, and have a tendency to be more coercive (Bellah, 2005). In this sense, instead of considering fear as a sign of authoritarian or totalitarian regimes (Neumann, 1966), understanding the culture of fear as a functional dispositive which stabilizes and preserves the neoliberal power relations is more appropriate in order to comprehending the plurality of the contemporary fears/anxieties (Debrix & Barder, 2009, 2012).

At that point, a socio-economic connection can be found out between the rise of dark tourism and the culture of fear. More clearly, the fact that dark interest has been transformed into dark tourism after the 1990s can be considered as the product of economic-politic variation of the culture of fear which has intensified in the 1990s. In this sense, dark tourism is the correspondence of the neoliberal dispositive within the tourism sector. So, the chronological intersection between them is not a mere coincidence.

No doubt it is proper to presume that Seaton's analysis of thanatopsis is the constitutive component of such an economy of fear. As Ferraro (1995) also asserts fear is the constitutive element of life and the civilization is the result of the challenge to the death. Without paying attention to the existential concern about the temporality of the life, it is difficult to interpret the main axis of the various fears. However, the political and economic reflection of the culture of fear as a governmental technique is also meaningful under the assumption there is a historical intersection between dark tourism and the existential concern. As Korstanje (2015b) states "dark tourism is a result of the commoditization of two significant aspects, fear of death and need of intellectualizing the contingency" (p. 244). While "the postmodern fear is related to the interaction between tragedy and voyeurism, the former refers to the psychological effects of terrorism in audience while the latter works reifying the suffering of others in a good product of mass-consumption" (Korstanje, 2010, p. 168; see also Korstanje, 2015c). So, no matter how diverse the tourist motivations are, the increasing interest and institutionalization in dark tourism can be regarded in the context of the ontological desperation of finding an object for the diversified, atomized, de-socialized and secularized fears since the 18th century. While the West tries to overcome death through the strategies consisting of medicine and reversible death (Bauman, 1992), the instances of dark spots such as Chernobyl, Alcatraz, Auschwitz, battlefields, slave prisons are fed and multiplied with the same source, namely, fight with death. As Stone (2012) subtly depicts "dark tourism is part of wider death revivalism within popular culture, whereby dark tourism experiences help to de-sequester mortality and to mediate a range of contemporary relationships with the death which is recreated, where Other death is consumed at a distance and mediated through popular culture and the media" (p. 1582). Tourists look for emotional stimuli, and they "want to buy the feelings rather than products" (Minic, 2012, p. 81).

On the other hand, the fact that the dark tourism sector is more developed in the Anglo-Saxon world, especially in the United States and the UK, particularly about the quantity, technical- digital presentation, and promotion of the places is also non-accidental if it is also taken into consideration that these countries give respectable effort to govern the fears. In other words, the USA and its coalition partner the UK, which promise to struggle against the nuclear weapons, ecological threats and the rest of ambiguous evils are the most developed in dark tourism even if these two topics seems irrelevant. For example, the majority of prison museums (%60) are located in the United States (Ross, 2012, p. 116). The fact that Americans and British people don't feel safe while they travel foreign countries although they think they are superior and chosen as the ambassadors of life and happiness (Korstanje, 2015c) is the concrete reflection of the connection between dark tourism and the culture of fear. So, as a giant sector, the touristic aspect of the economy of fear with its insurance certificates, alarm systems, surveillance vehicles explains too much about how the most liberal/capitalist countries feed themselves with the fears. In this framework, it is again helpful to remind that the (re)producing and governing the fears aren't only relevant to the authoritarian/totalitarian regimes, but also to the neoliberal regimes in more subtle and undirected ways. Since capitalism inherently works in a productive and multiplying logic. The following section examines this productiveness in the framework of the spectrum of dark touristic spots.

DARK SPOT SPECTRUM IN ACCORDANCE WITH THE GOVERNMENTALITY

As mentioned earlier, dark spots cover a very wide range of spectrum whether from epistemological or ontological sides. However, Stone's (2006) classification from the lightest to the darkest provides a comprehensive view for the analysis of governmentality of fear through different instances. Based on Stone's classification, the concrete implementation of the theoretical evaluation above is as follows.

Dark Fun Factories

As Stone states (2006) "a dark fun factory alludes to those visitor sites, attractions and tours which predominately have an entertainment focus and commercial ethic, and which present real or fictional death and macabre events" (p.152). These types of dark spots give priority to the amusement by mediating the fear. Here, "family friendly exhibits portraying less savoury aspects of (past) life, such as the Black Death or Jack the Ripper, the London Dungeon offers a socially acceptable environment in which to gaze upon simulated death and associated suffering" (Stone, 2006, p.152).

In this respect, the dark fun factories mix entertainment and trade while they are mainly lack of educational mission. This situation offers a great deal of source to analyze their position in terms of governmentality of fear. Because, a visitor to a dark fun factory can cognitively constitute a distance between the horror of the fictional presentation of the past sufferings and his own existential situation, thus develop a cognitive economy that refers there is no similarity between the past and the present. The following lines on London's dark dungeon website are an excellent example of the discursive infrastructure of this economy:

"After being fitted by the Tailor it's time to leave the modern, working world behind and embark on a thrill filled journey through 1000 years of London's dark past – guided by a cast of London's infamous rogues and villains" (The London Dungeon, https://www.thedungeons.com/london/en/book-tickets/dungeon-lates.aspx).

Here, the objectless fears of the "modern and working world" are converted into another unknown anonymity which happened 1000 years ago within the commercial function of an entertainment economy. Thus, it is created a kind of catharsis and relaxation effect. However, Stone shows (2009) the visitors of dark fun factories in London don't only enjoy the place, but also make connections among the place, Holocaust and Guantanamo. Yet still, this effect is under control. On the other hand, the *stressed* family friendly environment builds the image there is no place for pain and tragedy in a middle-class family with a reversed discourse when the dungeon's atmosphere eliminates the decors, which might be horrific but would be contrary to the family life, such as incest. Taken together, the dark fun factories as a simulation beside their high profits make possible to *experience* the fears that can't find a way in ordinary life to pop-up. Thus, they guarantee the visitor to have a clear conscience within the discursive dichotomy referring to past and present, inside and outside, unreal and real.

Dark Exhibitions

"Dark Exhibitions offer products which revolve around death, suffering or the macabre with an often commemorative, educational and reflective message and they are manifested within an eclectic product range and are often located away from the actual site of death or macabre event" (Stone, 2006, p. 153). Some of the well-known samples of dark exhibitions are Holocaust Museum in the USA, Ground Zero and the Body Worlds Exhibition, but apart from the best-known instances, they are highly common in all over the world, because of their political functions in addition to the commercial benefits. The allegorical victory of a nation, the propaganda of the universal values, the respect for the ancestors and the glorification of history appear as some of those functions with their connection to the nation-state building policies. Undoubtedly it is an important detail in the fulfillment of these functions how the exhibition narrates the events as well as how death and suffering are museumized. The function of the dark exhibitions as an extension of the governmentality of fear arises at the point where the concrete history operates as a discursive mechanism. Here, the visitor confronts with a political-economic management which fragments the social reality in one hand, but on the other, he/she existentially confirms himself/herself through the knowledge that there is a distance between the exhibition area and the place where the tragedy has originally happened. Hence the visitor feeds his/her *self* with a free-floating cultural experience between the discursive "truth regime" produced by the exhibition and a consciousness which externalizes his/her own existence to this truth.

Dark Dungeons

"…with a mixture of dark and light elements, they refer to those sites and attractions which present by gone-penal and justice codes to the present day consumer, and revolve around (former) prisons and courthouses" (Stone, 2006, p.154). In this respect, the attractive side of the dark dungeons is that they promise experiences such as trial, quarantine, punishment and even going to jail in quasi-real places and thus, represent the reality as if it is the part of a game. Moreover, the real dungeons have even become an entertaining place. For instance, Robben Island, where Nelson Mandela was prisoned, as Shackley (as cited in Stone, 2006) notes " is part of the theme park, part shrine and part museum ... Deal in money." In this sense, from the more authentic forms to the more entertaining ones -such as Bodmin Jail Centre- the dark dungeons operate as a sort of panoptic[3] organization. The situation can be read as a hyper-internalization of the disciplinary society when the person accepts to be jailed and prisoned by his/her own choice, moreover, by paying money "for that service." Dark dungeons in this context are the allegory of the victory of the surveillance society. At this level, the imprisonment turns into *an object of desire* which confirms the logic of disciplining the body and the mind. Thus, the desire reflects the non-catchable essence of the embodiment of the objectless fears which are never be eliminated.

Dark Resting Places

These places consist of cemeteries and grave markers. In particular, the cemeteries presenting the excellent samples of Gothic and Romantic architectural styles attract many dark tourists -for instance, Père-Lachaise cemetery in Paris with over two million visitors a year-. Besides, this categorization also includes the famous people's graves and their death places.

At that point, the seductiveness of death is the clue for understanding the visits to the dark touristic graves with a touristic curiosity and concern, apart from the mourning for the beloved one. Forasmuch as death in disciplinary society has been so excluded from everyday life; life and health are so blessed; that is, the idea of death is coded as an anomaly. It is no coincidence in this respect that the impressive sculptures and architectural constructions end up in cemeteries. The disciplinary society is highly skilled in putting death out of the everyday life. From this perspective, the roots of a grave visit with a dark touristic interest underlie the gap between life and death. In other words, the fear of death combines itself with the happiness of being alive and thus, the objectless fears of the everyday life of the tourist, who is fascinated with the graves, overlap the consciousness of being alive. At that point, the visits to the tombs of celebrities, especially Hollywood stars, can be regarded as a popular form of a flow of fears as such, because the visitor compensates his/her sense of being alive at the expense of the "defeated" who is "popular and young but death" at the phenomenological gap revolving around the person's everydayness and the famous person's uniqueness.

Dark Shrines

They "are often constructed, formally or informally, very close to the site of death and within a very short time period of the death occurring and attracts attaching a higher level of political awareness and influence during the media period"

(Stone, 2006, p.155). In this sense, the dark shrines are the dark spots which carry entertaining and socializing aspects although they are short-lived. As Stone explains (2006) "whilst under the pretext of respect and reverence, they are serving as a focal point whereby rubbernecking is quickly becoming a recreational activity within contemporary society" (p.156). In parallel, the concreteness of the dark shrines as a governmental technique grounds on their temporality in addition to their capacity for "pornographisation" of dying as a sign of "spectacle of society" (Debord, 1994). The scandalous effect created by those kinds of "special-death-processes" which reveal almost all hidden private life secrets during the media period roots from the ordinariness of the tragedy. Thus, the proximity of the danger or the fear makes the person feel that the tragedy is just over there on one hand, but on the other, it swiftly turns into a free-floating emotion such as dread which could easily be canalized positively within a running political-commercial economy -think of the commemoration products- through the temporality of the public interest.

Dark Conflict Sites

"They revolve around war and battlefields, and are increasingly becoming more commercialized and as a result have an increasing tourism infrastructure" (Stone, 2006, p.156). In this framework, dark conflict sites narrate the tragedy, death and war in a political discourse just as dark exhibitions do. The governmental extension of dark conflict sites, however, relies on which such places present kind of peace and quietness. Indeed, battlefields are almost peaceful sites. There is no sign of skyscrapers, traffic-jam and city noise in those areas. The sanitized land contributes to the peaceful atmosphere. Moreover, most of the touristic packages offering visits to the battlefields include the promise of sea, sand, and sun. So, an antagonism appears: On one hand, there is the fact the destructiveness of the war, but on the other the beauty of the sterilized and sanitized land. In this context, the areas where hundreds of thousands of people have lost their lives and their opportunities for resting / recreation in and around provide the psychological facility to convert the objectless fears into the allegory of victory at the edge of the dichotomies between the countryside and the city, death and life. Thus, the narrative of the dark conflict sites romanticizes the past while it produces political discourses which bind the citizen to the "justified war." These places surrounded with the monuments, the martyrdoms, and the trenches, in return, narrate the greatness of the war rather than emphasizing the atrocity of it. Furthermore, this effect is strengthened by theatric shows and costumed actors. Thus, the horror of death is replaced by the glory of the victory. Hence the visitor confirms his/her thanatopsistic concern with the sense of being here-and-now and is subjectivized as a citizen who is ready to die, but also full of life.

Dark Camps of Genocide

They "represent those sites and places which have genocide, atrocity and catastrophe as the main thanatological theme although they also have touristic aspects with their intense political messages" (Stone, 2006, p.157). The most known genocide sites are the Jewish concentration camps in addition to the atrocity places in Rwanda, Cambodia, and Kosovo. The genocide camps which are the epitomes of dark tourism (Stone, 2006) are the places in which the economy of fear occurs in an intensified nature. In other words, the economy of fear finds its historical-cultural correspondence mostly in the genocide camps, because of their freshness and recentness. With these features, the genocidal places are like alarms reminding that the human-made death and the torture can knock the door momently. On the other hand, the fact that the visitor makes his/her visit as a must-do-thing in most cases blurs the consciousness about the urgency of the alarm. In other words, the reality of genocide sites which tell people can monstrously treat to each other gets over-shadowed by the fact the visit is a part of a longer journey. In parallel, the sites remain like an anomaly, abnormality or extremity which disrupts the routine and flow of the everyday life. So, the educational-cultural benefits stay limited. On the other hand, it is also worth to note that the genocide places have been renovated and been refigured according to the "historical needs" (Ellis, 2009). Thus, they have become more "attractive." Ellis (2009) analyzing case of Auschwitz warns "the notion that Auschwitz is actually aesthetically pleasing, and often at odds with what the tourist wants to see means that the photographs they capture do not reflect the true nature of the site as it stands now (Ellis, 2009). Additionally, the genocide has become de-territorialized and has remained subjectless in the history of the museumification of Auschwitz and Birkenau, which grounds on the political question whether the genocide sites belong to the Jews, the Polish people or humanity (Ellis, 2009).

On the other hand, the process of re-narration and anomalization of genocide cognitively finds its current partner within the idea that the terrorists are monsters. Following the same logic, the terrorism and terrorist are cursed instead of searching the reasons and sources of the violent behavior or the terroristic attack. Thus, terrorism is represented as something outside of the time arrow in terms of linear history. Just as putting the responsibility of genocide on the particular people and the institutions instead of settling an account with the Nazi era and, in particular, the rationality of the modernity… From this vein, the exposure of the genocide sites appears as a beneficial tool to produce the typology of a proper citizen who just curses the past instead of making the connections between the past and the present threats to the contemporary society.

FUTURE RESEARCH DIRECTIONS

Just as dark tourism is a quite fresh research area, sociology of emotions is also new. Additionally, the studies articulating both research areas are rare. Although the study at hand is an attempt as such, it still needs to be supported by more empirical data. On the other hand, the matrix of gender, ethnicity, and class would mediate the conclusions. For instance, it waits to be analyzed how gender plays a role while expressing the feels in a dark spot. So, it is also worth to undertake the identity differences at the intersection of dark tourism and economy of fear.

CONCLUSION

Dark tourism is a developing sector. So the relevant literature does. However, determining the distinctive features of dark tourism for recognizing it as an autonomous discipline is still an alive topic of discussion. In this sense, it is worth to note there is no consensus about the definition of the dark tourism. The relevant studies mostly focus on the tourist motivations and the touristification process of the spot while the rest points out the history of dark tourism by addressing the issue how human interest in horror, suffering, and atrocity is an old ontological problem.

At that point, dark tourism appears as a form of governmentality of fear at the intersection of the discussions which have been classified as ontological and epistemological. Since dark tourism is a branch of tourism which feeds itself with various fears, especially fear of death. Its emergence as a distinct sector dates back the 90s. On the other hand, the 90s under the name of "new world order," which has aroused after the collapse of the USSR, is also known as the "age of fears" which produces and increases objectless and subjectless fears, in particular, fear of terrorism. No doubt, the age of fears has brought about its own political and economic climate at the same time. One of the results of this climate, in this sense, is dark tourism. In other words, the intersection between the crystallization of the culture of fear and the rise of dark tourism isn't a mere coincidence. The increasing demand for dark tourism in the Anglo-Saxon world which has a high level of security concerns is the supportive fact of the claim.

On the other hand, the concrete form of this intersection, namely governmentality of fear produces an astonishing economy. Because, governmentally calls the individual desires, runs without excluding anybody from the system and thus, subjectifies people. As a result, most of the dark spots multiply and reproduce themselves by transforming death and torture into life. Hence the surplus within the variety of dark spots and tourist motivations is not an anomaly but a symptom. It is the symptom of the productive and inclusive neo-liberal logic. In this context, the analysis revolving around the spectrum of dark spots from the dark dungeons to the genocide sites indicates that dark tourism is a means which mirrors the fears of the contemporary world. The abstracted fear in the framework of the discourses and by the forms of subjectification at the sites embodies itself through an event, a place or a fragment. That concreteness, in return, functions to discipline, control and channel the emotion as an economy-politic investment. Forasmuch as the dark spots fragment time and space, produce "an effect of truth" through the discourses, and thus blur, normalize and eliminate the sharpness of death and tragedy. At the end, life becomes a flow in which fear of economy is channeled and aroused.

REFERENCES

Alderman, D. H. (2010). Surrogation and the politics of remembering slavery in Savannah, Georgia (USA). *Journal of Historical Geography*, *36*(1), 90–101. doi:10.1016/j.jhg.2009.08.001

Anderman, J., & Simine, A. (2012). Memory, community and the new museum. *Theory, Culture & Society*, *29*(1), 3–13. doi:10.1177/0263276411423041

Armon-Jones, C. (1986). The social functions of emotion. In R. Harré (Ed.), *The social construction of emotions* (pp. 57–82). Oxford, UK: Basil Blackwell.

Ashworth, G., & Hartmann, R. (2005). *Horror and human tragedy revisited: The management of sites of atrocities for tourism*. Elmsford, NY: Cognizant Communication Corporation.

Ashworth, G., & Isaac, R. K. (2015). Have we illuminated the dark? Shifting perspectives on dark tourism. *Tourism Recreation Research*, *40*(3), 316–325. doi: 10.1080/02508281.2015.1075726

Ashworth, G., & Tunbridge, J. E. (1996). *Dissonant heritage*. New York, NY: Wiley.

Bar-Tal, D. (2001). Why does fear override hope in societies engulfed by intractable conflict, as it does in the Israeli society? *Political Psychology*, *22*(3), 601–627. doi:10.1111/0162-895X.00255

Baudrillard, J. (1994). *Simulacra and simulation*. University of Michigan Press.

Bauman, Z. (1992). *Mortality, immortality, and other life strategies*. Stanford, CA: Stanford University Press.

Beck, U. (1992). *Risk society: Towards a new modernity*. New Delhi: Sage.

Bellah, R. (2005). Civil religion in America. *Daedalus, 134*(4), 40–55. doi:10.1162/001152605774431464

Biran, A., Yaniv, P., & Oren, G. (2011). South experiences at (dark) heritage sites. *Annals of Tourism Research, 38*(3), 820–841. doi:10.1016/j.annals.2010.12.001

Blom, T. (2000). Morbid tourism: A postmodern market niche with an example from Althorp. *Norwegian Journal of Geography, 54*, 29–36.

Brisset, W. (n.d.). Bibliographical essay on fear. *Hedgehog Review, 3*, 115-123. Retrieved from: http://www.iasc-culture.org/THR/archives/Fear/5.3JBrissett.pdf

Bush, G. H. W., & Scowcroft, B. (1998). *A world transformed.* New York, NY: Vintage Books.

Cohen, E. (2011). Educational dark tourism at an in populo site: The Holocaust Museum in Jerusalem. *Annals of Tourism Research, 38*(1), 193–209. doi:10.1016/j.annals.2010.08.003

Dann, G. (1998). *The dark side of tourism. Etudes et rapports, se'rie L.* Aix-en-Provence: Centre International de Recherches et d'Etudes Touristiques.

Debord, G. (1994). *Society of the spectacle.* New York, NY: Zone Books.

Debrix, F., & Barder, A. (2009). Nothing to fear but fear: Governmentality and the biopolitical production of terror. *International Political Sociology, 3*(4), 398–413. doi:10.1111/j.1749-5687.2009.00083.x

Debrix, F., & Barder, A. (2012). *Beyond biopolitics: Theory, violence and horror in world politics.* New York, NY: Routledge.

Document: New world order: George Bush's speech, 6 Mar 1999. (n.d.). Retrieved from: http://al-bab.com/albab-orig/albab/arab/docs/pal/pal10.htm

Dunkley, R. (2015). Beyond temporal reflections in thanatourism. *Annals of Tourism Research, 52*, 172–179. doi:10.1016/j.annals.2015.03.007

Dunkley, R., Morgan, N., & Westwood, S. (2011). Visiting the trenches: Exploring meanings and motivations in battlefield tourism. *Tourism Management, 32*(4), 860–868. doi:10.1016/j.tourman.2010.07.011

Ekman, P., & Davidson, R. J. (1994). Afterword. In P. Ekman & R. Davidson (Eds.), *The nature of emotion* (pp. 176–178). New York, NY: Oxford University Press.

Elias, N. (1985). *The loneliness of the dying.* Oxford, UK: Blackwell.

Ellis, R. (2009). *Experiencing "dark tourism": The real Auschwitz?* (Unpublished undergraduate thesis). University of Bristol, UK. Retrieved from: http://www.bristol.ac.uk/history/media/docs/ug-dissertations/2009ellis.pdf

Ferraro, K. (1995). *Fear of crime. Interpreting victimization risk.* New York, NY: Sunny Press.

Flaxman, G., & Rogerson, B. (2010). The economy of fear. *Symploke, 18*(1-2), 333–336.

Foley, J., & Lennon, M. (1996). JFK and dark tourism: A fascination with assassination. *International Journal of Heritage Studies, 2*(4), 198–211. doi:10.1080/13527259608722175

Foucault, M. (1975). *Discipline and punish. The birth of the prison.* New York, NY: Vintage Books.

Foucault, M. (1976). The history of the sexuality: Vol. 1. *An introduction.* London: Allen Lane.

Foucault, M. (1980). *Power and knowledge: Selected interviews and other writings 1972-1977* (C. Gordon, Ed.). New York, NY: Pantheon.

Foucault, M. (1982). The subject and power. *Critical Inquiry, 8*(4), 777–795. doi:10.1086/448181

Foucault, M. (1984). *Of other spaces. Architecture/Mouvement/Continuité.* Retrieved From: http://web.mit.edu/allanmc/www/foucault1.pdf

Foucault, M. (1990). The history of sexuality: Vol. 3. *The care of the self.* London: Penguin Books.

Foucault, M. (1992). The history of sexuality: Vol. 2. *The use of pleasure.* London: Penguin Books.

Foucault, M. (2003). *Society must be defended: lectures at the Collège de France, 1975-76.* New York, NY: Picador.

Furedi, F. (1997). *Culture of fear: Risk-taking and the morality of low expectation.* New York, NY: Continuum.

Giddens, A. (1991). *Modernity and self-identity. Self and society in the late modern age.* Cambridge, UK: Polity.

Glassner, B. (1999). *The culture of fear: Why Americans are afraid of the wrong things.* New York, NY: Basic Books.

Harré, R., & Parrot, W. G. (1996). *The emotions: Social, cultural and biological dimensions*. London, UK: Sage.

Harvey, D. (1990). *The condition of postmodernity: An enquiry into the origins of cultural change*. Cambridge, MA: Blackwell.

Ira Byock, M. D. (2002). The meaning and value of death. *Journal of Palliative Medicine*, *5*(2), 279–288. doi:10.1089/109662102753641278 PMID:12006230

Isaac, R., & Ashworth, G. (2012). Moving from the pilgrimage to dark tourism: Leveraging tourism in Palestine. *Tourism. Culture & Communication*, *11*, 149–164.

Izard, C. E. (1991). *Psychology of emotions*. New York, NY: Plenum. doi:10.1007/978-1-4899-0615-1

Korstanje, M. (2010). Profiling modern risks. An appraisal of the works of Bauman, Beck, Castel, Giddens, and Baudrillard. *Journal of Anthropology*, *6*(2), 161–172.

Korstanje, M. (2015a). *The anthropology of dark tourism, exploring the contradictions of capitalism*. Centre for Ethnicity & Racism Studies. Retrieved from: http://cers.leeds.ac.uk/files/2015/02/Korstanje_CERS_15.pdf

Korstanje, M. (2015b). The spirit of terrorism: Tourism, unionization and terrorism. *PASOS. Revista de Turismo y Patrimonio Cultural*, *13*(1), 239–250.

Korstanje, M. (2015c). *A difficult world: Examining the roots of capitalism*. New York, NY: Nova Science Publication.

Lennon, M., & Foley, J. (2000). *Dark tourism: The attraction of death and disaster*. London, UK: Continuum.

List of Phobias. (n.d.). Retrieved From: http://phobialist.com/

Mellor, A. P., & Shilling, C. (1993). Modernity, self-identity and the sequestration of death. *Sociology*, *27*(3), 411–431. doi:10.1177/0038038593027003005

Miles, W. (2002). Auschwitz: Museum interpretation and darker tourism. *Annals of Tourism Research*, *29*(4), 1175–1178. doi:10.1016/S0160-7383(02)00054-3

Minic, N. (2012). Development of dark tourism in contemporary society. *J. Geogr. Institute Cvijic*, *62*(3), 81–103. doi:10.2298/IJGI1203081M

Mowatt, R. A., & Chancellor, C. H. (2011). Visiting death and life: Dark tourism and slave castles. *Annals of Tourism Research*, *38*(4), 1410–1434. doi:10.1016/j.annals.2011.03.012

Neumann, F. (1966). *The democratic and the authoritarian state: Essays in political and legal theory*. New York, NY: Free Press.

Panakera, C. S. (2007). World War II and tourism development in Solomon Islands. In C. Ryan (Ed.), *Battlefield tourism: History, place and interpretation* (pp. 125–141). The Netherlands: Elsevier. doi:10.1016/B978-0-08-045362-0.50017-8

Rapson, J. (2012). Emotional memory formation at former Nazi concentration camp sites. In M. Robinson & D. Picard (Eds.), *Emotion in motion: Tourism, affect and transformation* (pp. 161–178). London, UK: Routledge.

Robertson, R. (1995). Glocalization: Time-space and homogeneity-heterogeneity. In M. Featherstone, L. Scott, & R. Robertson (Eds.), *Global modernities*. London, UK: Sage. doi:10.4135/9781446250563.n2

Rojek, C. (1993). *Ways of escape*. Basingstoke, UK: Macmillan. doi:10.1057/9780230373402

Rojek, C. (1997). Indexing, dragging and the social construction of tourist sights. In C. Rojek & J. Urry (Eds.), *Touring cultures: Transformations of travel and theory* (pp. 52–74). London, UK: Routledge. doi:10.4324/9780203427736

Ross, J. I. (2012). Touring imprisonment: A descriptive statistical analysis of prison museums. *Tourism Management Perspectives*, *4*, 113–118. doi:10.1016/j.tmp.2012.07.001

Scruton, D. (1986). *Sociophobics: The anthropology of fear*. Boulder, Colo.: Westview Press.

Seaton, A. (1996). Guided by the dark: From thanatopsis to thanatourism. *International Journal of Heritage Studies*, 2(4), 234–244. doi:10.1080/13527259608722178

Seaton, A., & Lennon, J. (2004). Thanatourism in the early 21st century: Moral panics, ulterior motives and alterior desires. In T. V. Singh (Ed.), *New horizons in tourism: Strange experiences and stranger practices* (pp. 63–82). Wallingford, UK: Cabi. doi:10.1079/9780851998633.0063

Seaton, T. (2009). Thanatourism and its discontents. An appraisal of a decade's work with some future issues and directions. In J. Tazim & M. Robinson (Eds.), *The sage book of tourism studies* (pp. 521–542). London, UK: Sage. doi:10.4135/9780857021076.n29

Sharpley, R. (2009a). Shedding light on dark tourism: An introduction. In R. Sharpley & P. Stone (Eds.), *The darker side of travel: The theory and practice of dark tourism* (pp. 3–22). Bristol, UK: Channel View Publications.

Slade, P. (2003). Gallipoli thanatourism: The meaning of ANZAC. *Annals of Tourism Research, 30*(4), 779–794. doi:10.1016/S0160-7383(03)00025-2

Solomon, R. (2008). *True to our feelings: What our emotions are really telling us.* New York, NY: Oxford University Press. doi:10.1093/acprof:oso/9780195368536.001.0001

Stone, P. (2006). A dark tourism spectrum: Towards a typology of death and macabre related tourist sites, attractions and exhibitions. *Tourism: An Interdisciplinary International Journal, 54*(2), 145–160.

Stone, P. (2009). "It's bloody guide" - Fun, fear and a lighter side of dark tourism at the dungeon visitor attractions, UK. In R. Sharpley & P. Stone (Eds.), *The darker side of travel: The theory and practice of dark tourism* (pp. 167–185). Bristol, UK: Channel View Publications.

Stone, P. (2012). Dark tourism and significant other death: Towards a model of mortality mediation. *Annals of Tourism Research, 39*(3), 1565–1587. doi:10.1016/j.annals.2012.04.007

Stone, P. (2013). Dark tourism scholarship: A critical review. *International Journal of Culture. Tourism and Hospitality Research, 7*(3), 307–318.

Stone, P. (n.d.). Enlightening the "dark" in dark tourism. *AHI,* 22-24.

Stone, P., & Sharpley, R. (2008). Consuming dark tourism: A thanatological perspective. *Annals of Tourism Research, 35*(2), 574–595. doi:10.1016/j.annals.2008.02.003

Svendsen, L. (2008). *A philosophy of fear.* Chicago: Reaktion Books.

Tarlow, P. (2005). Dark tourism: The appealing "dark" side of tourism and more. In M. Novelli (Ed.), *Niche tourism: Contemporary issues, trends and cases* (pp. 47–57). Oxford, UK: Elsevier. doi:10.1016/B978-0-7506-6133-1.50012-3

Walter, T. (2009a). Dark tourism: Mediating between the dead and the living. In R. Sharpley & P. Stone (Eds.), *The darker side of travel: The theory and practice of dark tourism* (pp. 39–55). Bristol, UK: Channel View Publications.

Walter, T. (2009b). Disaster, modernity, and the media. In K. Garces-Foley (Ed.), *Death and religion in a changing world* (pp. 265–282). Armonk, NY: Sharpe.

Yoshida, K., Bui, H. T., & Lee, T. J. (2016). Does tourism illuminate the darkness of Hiroshima and Nagasaki? *Journal of Destination Marketing & Management, 5*(4), 333–340. doi:10.1016/j.jdmm.2016.06.003

ADDITIONAL READING

Altheide, D. L. (2002). *Fear: News and the construction of a crisis*. New York, NY: Aldine De Gruyter.

Baker, D. (2014). The effects of terrorism on the travel and tourism industry. *International Journal of Religious Tourism and Pilgrimage*, *2*(1), 58–67.

Coffey, M. (2003). From nation to community: Museums and the reconfiguration of Mexican society under neoliberalism. In J. Z. Bratich, J. Packer, & C. McCarthy (Eds.), *Foucault, governmentality and cultural studies* (pp. 207–242). New York, NY: State University of New York Press.

Cooper, R. (2000). *The post-modern state and the world order*. London, UK: Demos Press.

Dillion, M. (1995). Sovereignty and governmentality: From the problematics of the "New World Order" to the ethical problematic of the world order. *Alternatives: Global, Local. Political*, *20*(3), 323–368.

Furedi, F. (2005). *Politics of fear: Beyond left and right*. New York, NY: Continuum Press.

Giddens, A. (1999). *Runaway world: How globalization is reshaping our lives*. London, UK: Profile.

Goleman, D. (1995). *Emotional intelligence*. New York: Bantam.

Hochschild, A. (1983). *The managed heart*. Berkeley, CA: University of California Press.

Hollinshead, K. (1999). Surveillance of the worlds of tourism: Foucault and the eye-of-power. *Tourism Management*, *20*(1), 7–23. doi:10.1016/S0261-5177(98)00090-9

Hurbert, D. (2001). Literary places, tourism and the heritage experience. Annals of Tourism Research, 28 (2), 312-333. Lee, M. (2007). Inventing fear of crime: Criminology and the politics of anxiety. New York, NY: Routledge.

Korstanje, M., & Babu, G. (2015). Dark tourism: Revisiting some philosophical issues. *Tourism Research,* 1(2), Retrievable from: https://www.researchgate.net/publication/283813368_Dark_tourism_Revisiting_some_philosophical_issues

Luhmann, N. (1993). *Risk: A sociological theory*. New York, NY: De Gruyter.

Nuryanti, W. (1996). Heritage and post-modern tourism. *Annals of Tourism Research*, *23*(2), 249–260. doi:10.1016/0160-7383(95)00062-3

Prinz, J. (2004). *Gut reactions*. New York, NY: Oxford University Press.

Scherer, K., Schorr, A., & Johnston, T. (2001). *Appraisal processes in emotion*. New York, NY: Oxford University Press.

Shackley, M. (2001). *Managing sacred sites: Service provision and visitor experience*. Nottingham: Cengage Learning Emea.

Skoll, G. (2010). *Social theory of fear: Terror, torture and death in a post capitalist world*. New York, NY: Palgrave MacMillan. doi:10.1057/9780230112636

Smith, N., & Croy, W. G. (2005). Presentation of dark tourism: Te Wairoa, the buried village. In C. Ryan, S. Page, & M. Aicken (Eds.), *Taking tourism to the limits: Issues, concepts and managerial perspectives* (pp. 199–213). Amsterdam: Elsevier. doi:10.1016/B978-0-08-044644-8.50022-9

Sturken, M. (2007). *Tourists of history: Memory, kitsch, and consumerism from Oklahoma City to Ground Zero*. Durham, NY: Duke University Press. doi:10.1215/9780822390510

Throsby, D. (2003). *Economics and culture*. Cambridge, UK: Cambridge University Press.

Uriely, N. (2005). The tourist experience. Conceptual developments. *Annals of Tourism Research*, *32*(1), 199–216. doi:10.1016/j.annals.2004.07.008

KEY TERMS AND DEFINITIONS

Disciplinary Power: A Foucaldian term, referring the 18th Century form of power which controls and disciplines its subordinates without repressing, but with the mechanisms for bodily and mental self-control.

Dispositive: A Foucaldian term, referring to the concrete heterogeneous arrangements consisting of the discourses, the institutions, the architectural forms, the laws, the administrative decisions, the philosophical and scientific proposals. Thus, a dispositive helps disciplinary power to operate.

Flows: A Deleuzian term, referring that capitalism runs as a machine which produces, channels, territorializes, de-territorializes, and re-territorializes the desires, and thus functions in a productive manner instead of repression and coercion.

Governmental Techniques: A Foucaldian term, referring to the disciplinary and productive socio-political apparatuses, such as surveillance and self-discipline, maintaining subjectification through the historical process.

Pastoral Sovereignty: A Foucaldian term, indicating the era of transcendent sovereignty of God, which is politically embodied in the body of the King. King, in this sense, is the concrete form of the monopolized power which punishes and represses in contrast to the disciplinary power.

Simulation: Baudrillard's term referring that the contemporary society *experience*s the events and the facts as a copy of the copy of the copy. Simulation is the losing the sense of truth because of the intense pressure of the media and the digitalization.

Subjectification: A Foucaldian term, referring to the socially constructed existence (of a person) in the matrix of power-knowledge relations which is historically shaped by non-centered different governmental techniques.

Time-Space Compression: David Harvey's term to indicate how time and space measurements have become irrelevant regarding to the developments in communication and transportation on one hand, and how the places under the effect of this challenge are exposed to an uncontrolled and unbalanced financial diffusion on the other.

ENDNOTES

1 However, it is also worth to note there are some approaches which don't consider dark tourism as an autonomous sector. They recognize dark tourism as the sub-branch of heritage tourism.

2 In the relevant literature, the concepts, risk, and threat are used differently. Risk indicates the possibilities determined by the person's own capacity consisting of reflexivity, decision-making and directing the events while threat means the instant dangers that person doesn't have a personal power to prevent. (Compare Beck, 1992 and Luhmann, 1993). For instance, a forest with full of bears is dangerous. If I go to that forest at the night, I take the risk by my own choice. If a bear "pays a visit" to my house in the village, it is a close threat to my life. However, risk and threat are used in the study without regarding the literature discussion, not to ramble.

3 The *Panopticon* is a kind of prison in which all prisoners are informed they are watched, but don't know when. So, all prisoners discipline and control their behavior as if they are watched, not to be punished. As a metaphor in *Discipline and Punish* by Foucault (1975) the panopticon indicates the condition of modern "disciplinary societies" which constantly surveil and discipline. In a panoptic logic, the chains or the locks aren't needed to control the individuals because they discipline themselves with the idea that they are being watched.

Chapter 8
Death and Culture:
Is Thana-Tourism Symptomatic of the End of Capitalism?

Maximiliano Emanuel Korstanje
University of Palermo, Argentina

Babu George
Fort Hays State University, USA

ABSTRACT

Taking cues from the surging popularity of thana-tourism, this paper argues that its prevalence echoes the end days of capitalism. The predominant forms of tourism in a society reflect the ethos of that society. What we once called 'mass tourism' reflected the spirit of classical capitalism; later, ecotourism and various other alternative forms of tourism reflected a critical turn in capitalism, often called the 'sympathetic capitalism'. These were incremental alternations, however. Thana-tourism is a qualitatively discontinuous form of tourism and its surge should thus correspond with a similarly discontinuous, radical, shift in capitalism. The authors present scholarly perspectives to bring home the view that thana-tourism might indeed be symptomatic of the end of capitalism

INTRODUCTION

Throughout the world, there is a growing tide to visit or organize tours on cemeteries where tourists learn further about the history of individual tragedies, or the life of celebrities who had died under strange circumstances. The same has been observed in England and US where hundreds of tourists visit haunted houses and castles. To

DOI: 10.4018/978-1-5225-2750-3.ch008

the fear factor these types of new emergent segments evinced, there is a morbid element which suggests that the conceptualization of tourism is changing. Here, some key questions arise: are capitalism and tourism entwined? Specifically, to what extent does the rise of dark tourism assume more fundamental changes in the societal scaffolding? Our position is that, if modern tourism is a reflection of the capitalistic forces, fundamental changes in the nature of tourism phenomenon that we notice more recently should be reflective of changes in capitalism itself. In this paper, we discuss this and a range of associated topics.

The classic Marxists emphasized on the advance of capitalism as an exploitative force that commoditizes relations, culture, customs and everything in their wake. Leisure and tourism, in this context, plays an alienatory role by mystifying the exploitative conditions where citizens are involved. As Dean McCannell (1976; 1992; 2001) observed, tourism and the productive system function in parallel preventing social fragmentation. Not only tourists emulate the cultural values of their respective societies, which are confronted in meeting others, but also tourism acts as a mediator between citizens and their institutions. In short, tourism revitalizes those frustrations experienced in day-to-day life in a way that lay-citizens foster their loyalties to the nation-state. The commoditization of culture, inevitably, not only molds the experiences of sightseers but also imposes a self-identity, which painstakingly interpolates locals. Paradoxically, while tourism produces further cultural commodities, less genuine the host-guest encounters turn. Recently, some specialists called the attention on the rise of a new form of tourism, more macabre, namely morbid emerged in zones of disasters, death or complete obliterations where the primary attraction is death and mourning; *Dark Tourism*. Though under different names, the onset of Thana or Dark Tourism interrogated social scientists on the possibilities the sense of beauty as it was aesthetically established were in jeopardy.

As the previous argument given, the present chapter centers on the ethical dilemma of dark tourism, which starts with a radical transformation in the means of production across capitalist nations. Our thesis here is that Thana tourism reflects the arrival of a new stage of production where the risk society sets the pace to a new capitalism, *Thana Capitalism*. One of the aspects that defines Thana Capitalism alludes to the consumption of other´s death as the main commodity to be exchanged.

In the first section of the chapter we discuss critically the intersection of capitalism with culture; though it remains as a well-discussed theme, not surprisingly, further interrogations are necessary. In so doing, we use the term Dark or Thana tourism indistinctively. Based on the advances and limitations of first Marxist studies, which oscillates from Marx to Bauman, we provide with an all-encompassing model to understand dark tourism as a unit of production, which is interconnected to a much deeper cultural matrix. Secondly, a short review of already existent literature in dark tourism is accomplished. The resistant sections aim to set forwards our theory on Thana-Capitalism as well as the ethical limitations of dark tourism. In sharp contrast with a whole portion of the scholarship, we finesse the epistemological borders of dark tourism as an individualistic-narcissist practice oriented to maximize the pleasure of visitors. Far from connecting with the other`s pain, these new "death-seekers" are insensitive to the alterity unless by the exacerbation of their supremacy. To sum, even if some voices have claimed that dark tourism triggers the sensibility for the others (Seaton, 2000; Wilson 2004; Stone 2012; Sather-Wagstaff 2016), we conclude the opposite, to say that, death-seekers use and abuse of the other to reaffirm their own privileged status. Also, this behavior is not limited to tourism but also is very well present in other forms of entertainment, as Television news, realities, movies or newspapers. We consume death every-time to reinforce our narcissism, but at the same time, no less true is that social ties are weakened. Paradoxically, though consternated and horrified by the disturbing news and death-related media contexts, we do not stop of consuming them.

PRELIMINARY DISCUSSION

While capitalist societies are highly mobile, creative and embracing competence as a positive cultural value, other non-western cultures are stagnant in the time (Maccannell, 1984). This prejudice which was originally coined during the nineteenth century not only endured up to date, but also cemented the possibility to colonize the non-western others through the articulation of European Paternalism. The first ethnographers were preoccupied with their determination that non-western cultures would disappear by the advance of industrialism. The collated information extracted from ethnographers´ notebooks was involuntarily conducive to the colonial governor who were familiar with native´s customs (Korstanje 2012; Korstanje 2017). From its inception, capitalism and heritage were inextricably intertwined.

The expansion of capitalism was based on the introduction of different allegories as race, blood, and nationhood, which were enrooted in the belief that natural selection divides maturate nations from tribal-based organizations. Most certainly, capitalism posed the discourse of natural selection as the strength that led nations towards progress. However, not all voices validate such a hypothesis. The discursive manipulation of natural selection acted as an instrument of control over the workforce.

By this way, Robert Frank & Phillip Cook (2010) refer to *the winner take all society* as trend where few concentrates increasing portion of wealth, while blue-collar workers come across with serious financial problems to confront with their living costs. The rising inequality, which is proper of capitalism, not only has unfortunately enlarged, but also seems to be difficult to be reversed. In the academy, some scholars focus on the natural inequalities of capitalism as a system, while others preferably explore globalization as an omnipresent force that offers better conditions for investment for capital owners. Both positions for authors rest on shaky conceptual foundations. Not only the workforce, but bourgeoisie elite are experiencing serious disruptions and pressures in their respective realms:

The growing inequality at the top is even more dramatic than at the bottom, as the most highly compensated corporate managers, lawyers, and physicals have pulled away from the pack. In short, growth in inequality does not appear to have resulted from growing market imperfections or just from increased outsourcing to lower-paid workers in developing countries. What, then, has been driving it? (p. x)

As this backdrop, Frank & Cook argue convincingly that information revolution buttressed a substantial shift in the ways economies evolved as well as the costs of travel and corporative control. As a result of this, capital markets have become more flexible, instable and competitive than other past decades since the executive mobility was pressed by a most extreme competence where nobody should have a safe place in the corporation. This tendency escapes from business and organizational Management it can be found in all spheres of society, where only a few win taking everything at stake. The aim of this society is exclusively oriented to protect the profits in the short run terms, though it creates further socio-economic problems in others classes. This suggests that the ethical question of inequality remains enrooted in the ideological core of capitalism, but for some reasons, it is inexpugnable from lay-citizen`s scrutiny. To what extent Marxism has something to say in this respect seems to be an interesting discussion which will take place in next section.

CULTURE AND CAPITALISM

Though capitalism was widely studied by different economic schools, we shall delve into Marxism because of two main reasons. At first glance, Marx was a pioneering in discovering the connection between labor force and commodities, but secondly, his utopian conception respecting to the end of class struggle paved the ways for the imposition of a capitalist culture, which he originally criticized. Such a capitalist subculture coincides with the adoption of instrumentality and competence as two pillars of production. This occurred in view of the fact that Marx saw capitalism as an irreversible force. After all he was not a political militant, but he was a scientist. The triumph of industrialism over agrarian cultural forms showed not only his efficiency in describing the process but his proficiency over the economic theory

(Fillipi, 1988). Whatever the case may be, as stated Marx conceived history as an articulation of four stages, *communism* which refers to an organization where the property was widely-shared by all members of the tribe, *Slave-society,* which was characterized by the systematic exploitation of slaves. For Marx, slave society situates as the precondition towards a class-society. In this respect, once slave society sets the pace for *feudalism society is organized under a theocratic conception of the world,* where power is protected by monarchs who inherit their position. Ultimately, Marx pays much heed to the rising *capitalism* not only as originally-determined by the arrival of bourgeois but also by the hegemony of private-properties (Marx 1973; Marx & Engels, 1902; 1959). Sooner or later, one his darkest prophecies were that the public life would be subdued not only to the logic of profit but also to private interests. Followers and detractors of Marx have widely discussed his main thesis, but accepting the principle of commoditization as a taken-for-granted diagnosis that explains the reasons behind the ever-increasing material asymmetries among classes within society (Giddens, 1971; Hyman 1975; Burawoy, 1984; Lowith, 2002; Berlin, 2013; Skoll, 2014). Given how Marx laid the foundations to a new understanding of human relations, which is inherited to production, further studies validated the idea that culture has been globally commoditized not only to stimulate consumption but to reinforce the centre-periphery dependency, discussed in earlier sections (Comaroff & Comaroff, 2009; Korstanje, 2012). Since bourgeois had very tough to prosper unless the classic instruments of production would be revolutionized, Marx says, social relations should be mystified to cover the real conditions of exploitation. Though originally people may think the state would work as a safeguard of working force, this seems to be an over-simplification for Marx. Nation-state, which emerged in the industrial age, devotes their resources to impose the law-making which is conducive to legalize the exploitation of rank-and-file workers. This begs a more than pungent point, how is this exploitation orchestrated?

Marx responds clearly that the fetishism of commodities and capital are two key factors that facilitated the expansion of capitalism. While workers are legally encouraged to work, there is a manifesting gap between money and commodities which are fulfilled by the economic value. In that way, the concept of *surplus-value* seems to be vital to understanding how work-force is despoiled from their rights to yield wealth. Capital-owners pay for workers a wage, which represents a minor portion of their real labor force invested to produce the commodities. Profits resulted from the possibility of capital owners to sell value-added commodities. This *swindle* remains inexpugnable by lay-citizens, because the conditions of exploitation are normalized by law. At the time, the produced wealth is increased, the prosperity of workers decline (Marx, 1967). Though Marx developed a negative but irreversible diagnosis of capitalism, his legacy showed amply that there is a founding mythical conflict between capital owners and labor class, which is the touchstone of the nation-state.

One of the most authoritative voices in Marxist studies, Richard Hyman, published in 1975 a seminal book entitled *Industrial Relations.* In this fascinating text, he unveils the sacred figure of industrial relations as a taken-for-granted as a reality. The work-force is subject to an invisible force the *ideology*, which is legitimated by the industrial system, well-integrated to the legal jurisprudence. In this respect, Hyman goes on to write:

Industrial relations is the study of processes of control over work relations, and among these processes, those involving collective worker organization and action are of particular concern. (Hyman, 1975: p. 12)

Bourgeoisie successfully pivoted in monopolizing the means of production because, in the legal contract, its obligations are constrained only to wages, paid holidays and some others minor issues whereas workers are subject to perform broader tasks which range from manual labor to administrative duties. In fact, workers' obligations vary anytime depending upon their master-will. In consonance with Hyman, Richard Hofstadter has widely coined a theory which combines the advances of Marxist theory with cultural analysis. In a seminal book *Social Darwinism in American Thoughts,* he complements previous Marxist approaches inasmuch as he ignites hotly a debate on the role of social Darwinism to stimulate an extreme competence among workers. In this respect, the axiom of survival of the fittest was not new, it was originally coined by Darwin, but this theory was limited only to biology. His nephew *Sir Francis Galton* adopted main Darwinian outcomes to the study of society, considering that while the animals are successfully adapted to environs, the same applies to human beings. However, not only Galton misjudged Darwinian theses but also fostered the creation of a racial interpretation to explain why and how ethnicities evolved. In this vein, Hofstadter discusses that Galton confused the "survival of the fittest" with the survival of strongest" in a way that his theory was politically manipulated. Put in the terms of Galton, Darwinism led very well towards one of the darkest ethnocentrisms, which paved the ways for the surge of Adolf Hitler in Germany but it was not constrained to Germany, it still remains alive in the ideological core of the United States, Hofstadter adheres. In opposition to pure Darwin, Dalton, Graham Sumner and other prominent Social Darwinists proposed *that natural selection* posed Anglo-Saxons to the top of a social pyramid which distinguished as most civilized race in comparison with other ethnicities. For Darwinists, the introduction of selection was crucial to explain why some cultures adapt successfully to the technological changes while others simply perish. Though originally pitted against Protestantism, Social Darwinism gradually was being accepted by elite not only in Northern Europe and in the United States but internalized by many other non-European cultures as well. Latin-

America was particularly receptive to Darwinist ideals. Hofstadter was not wrong when he confirms, authoritative voices in theology embraced Darwinism because it represented the triumph of ethical virtue over laziness, corruption, and sin. The idea of privilege entrepreneurs who distinguished from others was particularly attractive for Americans as a symbolic platform to develop a sentiment of exception over other cultures, and of course, this new ideology worked fine promoting the class struggle at the time capital owners monopolized the means of production. The sense of a creative destruction impedes bottom-up social cooperation. Equally important, Hofstadter reminds that the *competition,* which was historically fostered by the ideology of capitalism, offered the salvation for few ones, at the expense of the rest (Hofstadter, 1992).

As Korstanje (2016) puts it, by realizing the dream of joining the "selected people," we accept the rules. Whenever one of our direct competitors fails, we feel an insane happiness. We toy with the idea that a similar mechanism is activated during our visit to dark tourism sites: we do not strive to understand, we are just happy because we escaped death and have more chances to win the game of life. In some extent, social Darwinism never diluted, it replicated alongside capitalist nation-state in the threshold of time to date.

The thinker who better has captivated this point was the recently deceased philosopher, Zygmunt Bauman. To understand his sophisticated argument we have to discuss firstly the conception of *Liquid Modernity*. Bauman acknowledges that materialism is spot on when proclaimed that means of production, adjoined to productive system, shapes the moral consciousness as well as collective and individual behavior. Bauman contends that industrialism, as it emerged in former centuries, was based on a solid form, where merchandises were long-lasting, but this was radically altered by late-modernity. We are witnessing a society of hyper-consumption where the solid melts in the liquid form. In the society of liquid lives, as Bauman adheres, social ties are weakened by the introduction of more malleable forms of consumption (Bauman, 2003, 2005). Following this, not surprisingly these reflections bring with a new book into the foreground, which is published in 2007, entitled *Consuming Life*. His thesis starts from the premise that new tendencies in consumptions are overriding the current lifestyles. The full exposition of private life, which can be found in realities as Big Brother, corresponds with the outset in radical changes the process of control is articulated. The old panoptical gaze, where few were watching the inmates' lives in prisons, was replaced by a new term *Ban-option* where only a few are extensively exposed to be watched by a global spectatorship. In the liberal labor market, workers are transformed into commodities, which are consumed by capital. In consonance with Hofstadter, though uncited in his texts, Bauman clarifies that modern companies do not help those lagging workers who stand behind, nor those who does not satisfy the requirement of managerial performance. Since people are commoditized as a simple resource, they are discarded or spoiled from the productive system as a whole. Paradoxically, this reflects in the different types of mobilities a clear dissociation, where some global tourists are legally encouraged to travel worldwide, while those migrants, who knock the doors of First World, are persecuted and deported. He claims that modern consumers have become in a self-commoditization of the goods they elect. Even if the market has historically highlighted the encounter between supply and demand, hitherto the boundaries of both are being diluted. The pillars of capitalism are based on the attractiveness of elaborated products that can be sold to a wider net of consumers. Today´s market seems to impose to the sphere of the state, codifying a new set of rules, where the status of citizens depends upon what they can consume. As previously discussed, the consuming society has unclear the borders between the consumer and its commodity. The question whether in the society of consumers goods are elaborated not to endure the entire life, but only to be replaced annually, no less true is that the quest of novelty was introduced in form as a creative-destruction to erode the social trust. Ultimately, Bauman reminds readers that the society of consumers encourages values oriented to short-terms where self-identity, emotions, self-experimentation play a pivotal role. This type of narcissism produces an increase of fear and panic that drives them to a total consumerism. After all, fear is the only sentiment that has no bottom. Bauman's main thesis is that excess of consumption works as a ritual mechanism to the end of softening the uncertainness of a more hostile world. The lack of planning and long-term expectancy connote with anguish and reclusion (Bauman, 2007). Bauman contributions to our debate are manifold, but because of time and space, some of them can be detailed in next.

Firstly, capitalism has doubtless mutated to different forms that combine the strictest controls supported by the leaps and bounds of surveillance-related technology with a false liberality posed for citizens to maximize their pleasure. Secondly and most important, the quest of pleasure maximization allows the expansion of a new logic of exploitation where consumers are transformed in consumed-objects (commodities). Here, innovatively the old dialectics of youth Marx is upended into a new all-encompassing model. Though Bauman has advanced a lot in the understanding of capitalism, he (as Beck or other classic sociologists) paid too much attention to the role of risk in society. Though we agree with Bauman and others that capitalism is shaping into new versions, we are not enthusiastic with his diagnosis. To fulfill this gap, new further approaches in this direction are needy.

SITUATING DARK TOURISM

Over the recent years, dark tourism situated as an interesting object of study for many disciplines, which spans from sociology to philosophy (Lennon & Foley, 2000; Korstanje & Handayani, 2016). One of the most captivating utilizations of this type of tourism was associated with the process of resilience in post-disaster contexts (Korstanje & Ivanov, 2012; Shondell-Miller & Gonzalez, 2013). These emergent destinations help obliterated communities to concentrate the necessary funds to make further profits and businesses (Rojeck, 1993; Biran & Hyde, 2013). At some extent, such an economic-centric position integrates dark tourism with risk-management tradition (Tarlow, 2007). As M. Novelli (2007) puts it, not only the psychological experiences of tourists play a leading role in the configuration of attractiveness, but also in meeting the new demands, further exotic destinations are surfacing. Doubtless, tourism-research should interrogate on some of these new trends which include the morbid element as the main criterion of consumption (Stone 2011). Given that, professional well-experimented researchers came across with serious methodological problems at the time of entering in the fieldwork (Korstanje & Handayani 2016).

As this backdrop, the dispersion of produced knowledge, as well as the lack of coherent unified definitions, has led to a specialist to a misconception of dark tourism (Ryan, 2005; Stone & Sharpley, 2008; Miles 2014). P. Stone (2012) argued convincingly that dark tourism mediates between the self and its finitude, taking the others´ death as a form of psychological bridge between life and mortality. Visitors of these types of spaces are looking an authentic experience that helps understand their own lives. Although Stone recognizes that dark tourism research remains in its infancy, there is a further dispersion on how the concepts are handled and ultimately defined. Basically, it is important not to lose the sight that the same phenomenon receives many names as Dark Tourism (Seaton, 1996; Wight, 2006; Cohen 2011; Kang et al, 2012), Thana Tourism (Dunkley 2007; Holden & Novelli, 2011; Tzanelli 2016), Morbid-Tourism (Blom, 2000; 2007), Prison-Tourism (Wilson 2008; 2011), Black-Tourism (Goudie, Khan & Kilian, 1999) even War or Battlefield-tourism (Wise 2011) or alike. This creates not only a serious misunderstanding on the explored object, but also multiplicates a fragmentation of produced knowledge that obscures more than it clarifies. On his doctoral thesis, Stone (2010) defines dark tourism as a contemporary leisure activity which includes travel to sites of mass-death, destruction or mourning.

Though the proliferation of doctorate theses, books, and articles in dark tourism is evident, three main waves can be identified, *dark tourism as heritage, dark tourism as mediation with death, and the critical turn.*

Dark tourism as heritage emphasizes on the fact that the current fascination with death seems not to be news. There are historical evidence and testimonies in Medieval Times how pilgrimages traveled long distances to visit sacred-cities as Jerusalem or the Saints´ Thombs. Those studies which form this academic wave understand dark tourism as a subtype of heritage allows not only the commoditization of space but an instrument for communities to alleviate their living conditions. It is important not to lose the sight that dark tourism sites offer a pedagogic lesson to society, which in the form of heritage, should be passed to next generations (Strange & Kempa 2003; Collins-Kreiner, 2010; Cohen, 2011; Biran, Poria & Oren, 2011; Hartmann, 2014). The psychological experience of visitors, adjoined to the concept of authenticity appears to be crucial to finesse the methodological border of research which means that the experience of tourist situates as the only valid source to discover the nature of dark tourism. Applied-research is confined to open or close-ended questionnaires conducted in dark sites alone.

Dark tourism as mediation of death signals to the set of approaches that philosophically speaking takes dark tourism as a new emergent for of imagining own death through others. In a secularized society where death is at least neglected, consuming others´ death exhibits an anthropological attempt to domesticate death. Needless to say, thanatosis is the touchstone beyond the interests of visitors for death (Stone 2010, 2011, 2012; Dalton 2014; Tanas, 2014). Though this academic wave was initiated by P. Stone, it was continued by countless scholars. Today, this theory is gaining traction worldwide. It is tempting to say that researchers that embrace this position often allude to a combination of methods which ranges from interviews with visual observation.

The Critical Turn is a recently-arrived theory which discusses critically not only both earlier mentioned schools but outlines in dark tourism as an alienation mechanism of control, which helps elite to legitimate its own practices. For these scholars, the morbid fascination that dark tourism wakes up is associated with an internal sentiment of oppression that is liberated for consumers to maximize their pleasure. To be honest, scholars who adhere to this wave insist in that the others´ death allows the construction of an ideological discourse, which is tended to enforce the centre-periphery dependency. The Apollonian sense of beauty that characterized the classic sun and sea destinations set the pace to a more macabre form of entertainments which are proper of late-capitalism (Bowman & Pezzullo, 2009; Potts, 2012; Friedrich & Jonhston, 2013; Carrigan 2014; Korstanje & George, 2015; Sather-Wagstaff, 2016; Tzanelli 2016; Korstanje, 2016).

Quite aside from the above-noted description, dark tourism shows no fewer problems in the used methodologies, which needs further revision. First and foremost, dark tourism as heritage or as a mediation of death falls in similar caveats at delineating the methodology. At first blush, the specialized literature dedicated to the study of ancient history reveals that the travels towards Saints' Thombs have little to do with modern dark tourism consumptions. Moved by personal sickness or the irreversible downward health, medieval pilgrims reached these sites as a form of divine devotion to God, or as a proof of sacrifice. Instead, the motivations of modern tourists center on the needs of discovering new places, customs, and cultures, maximizing their experiences into a commoditized product (heritage). It is safe to say that visitors look for the pleasure maximization inasmuch as they are in quest of authenticity. Secondly, applying questionnaires and interviews to visitors does not methodologically reveal the inner-world of interviewees. Sometimes interviewees lie or simply are not familiar with their psychological emotions. As a result of this, though many of the produced knowledge aim to outline visitors are in quest of heritage consumption, likely this was only the peak of the iceberg. Authenticity, as we stated, has paradoxically dissociated from mass tourism. Besides, many supporters of heritage theory define dark tourism as a fertile emergent source for profits. In consequence, their outcomes are determined by specific interests, instead of reasoning the issue as it really is. In consonance with this, not surprisingly, applied research in dark tourism emphasizes the role of experience. This raises the question to what extent the field of experience molds epistemologically the object of study of dark tourism remains unanswered. By this way, paradoxically researchers have serious problems in tabulating obtained responses because each person nourished a particular impression of death, while they fail to create a unified epistemology that helps to study the issue (Korstanje, 2016). The question whether the common discourse of dark tourism sites are individually constructed but collectively negotiated has come with no fewer problems at the time of explaining how politicians take part of the process tergiversating the real reasons of disaster (Tzanelli, 2016; Korstanje, 2016). At some extent, the formation of dark shrines are legally determined by the intervention of the state, which fills its own impression of history (Guidotti-Hernandez, 2011). The imposition of heritage, as it was studied by Sather Wagstaff (2016) in the ground-zero, alludes to instill a simplified story-telling of real events. As an incipient field, dark tourism emerged as a new segment which is adjusted to the needs of the market. Though there would be multiple reasons why a person visits dark tourism sites, this does not respond why such a person is emotionally motivated to do so. Further combined methodologies should be necessary to expand the current understanding of thanatosis (Korstanje & George, 2015). This suggests that the romantic archetype of tourists as seekers of heritage or interrogating on moral disasters should -at least- re-considered. As we will see in next section, tourists seek to maximize their pleasure, and in so doing, they feed on others' suffering.

THE PROFILE OF DEATH SEEKERS

As a culture, we subconsciously crave to hear news about disasters. The magnitude of destruction gives us a curious sense of contentment. In this paper, we hypothesized that this has to do with cultural Darwinism. Based on prior experiences of dealing with doomsdays, a culture would have developed some agility which gets encoded in the genetic traits of that culture. Continued non-use means that it faces the risk of extinction. This will make that culture extremely vulnerable when a great calamity hits it unexpectedly. So, keeping the cultural genes associated with disasters is critically important for the survival of culture.

Fundamentally, it is this fascination with disasters that has given birth to the phenomenon of 'thana-capitalism.' Cultural expressions that keep the *thana genes* alive also include imagined disasters depicted in our various contemporary cultural forms. Also, there is no dearth of consumer products that exploit our anxieties about disasters. While none of us want disasters to hit us individually, keeping alive a sense of death and destruction by liminally going through them is the way our cultures have found to deal with disasters.

Capitalism signals to the constructions of allegories containing death prompting a radical rupture of self with others. At the time citizens believe they are special the trust in neighbors is undermined. This happens because narcissism not only is self-effacing and derogatory but subordinates the otherness to the empire of selfish desires. In a context of turbulences, the imposition of this discourse is conducive to the weakening of social fabric. Thematising disasters by dark-tourism consumption patterns entail higher costs if the disaster repeats in the near future. The political intervention in these sites covers the real reasons behind the event, which are radically altered to protect the interests of status quo. The political and economic powers erect monuments to symbolize sudden mass death or trauma-spaces so that society reminds a lesson, which allegory contains a biased or galvanized explanation of what happened. Though to some extent, community needs to produce these allegories to be kept in warning, the likelihoods the same disaster takes a hit again seems to be a question of time (Korstanje, 2016).

Thana capitalism offers death (of others) as a Spectacle not only to revitalize the daily frustrations but also to enhance a harmed ego. Visiting spaces of disasters during holidays, or watching the news on terrorist attacks at home, all represents part of the same issue: *the advent of a new class of death seekers.* In this respect, death seekers can be decomposed by shared patterns of behavior, which are shown below:

- Death seekers trumpet heritage only to reinforce the cultural values of their society;

- They believe democracy and liberal consumption are the best of feasible worlds;
- They show a pathological form to understand death which is considered as a sign of inferiority;
- They use people in an instrumental way, as a hostage to achieve their goals;
- Serious problems to understand the alterity;
- Beyond their discourse of altruism and concerns for tragedy, they never commit with the other´s suffering;
- Death seekers often support social Darwinism as a form of progress or self-achievement;
- Consuming others' pain affirms death seekers into a status of privilege class, at the time they feel special or outstanding;
- Regardless of their political affiliation, they embrace the theory of conspiracy to explain their failures.

The symbolic epicenter of this new stage of capitalism, doubtless, comes from two founding myths, Noah´s ark and the Cruxification of Christ. Both stories will help to expand the current understanding of Thana Capitalism. The legend tells us that Noah, who is one of the founding parents of Abrahamic tradition, is asked by God to construct an ark. His divine mission consisted in selecting two pars for species for life as it was created by God persists. Although the world will be destroyed by the human degeneration, Noah opts to keep the secret, dooming the rest of humankind to the extermination. Here two assumptions should be done. On the one hand, Noah keeps the secret validating the God-will. The universal flood is culturally represented as the first genocide, always reminding the importance of selection to redeem a clear division between victims and witnesses. On another hand, the sense of exclusiveness and division coined by Noah´s myth accompanied humankind towards the formation of puritanism. Unlike other Protestant groups, Puritans claimed not only the sense of predestination but also the idea that only few would be saved by God. This connotes to a sentiment of exclusivity, where suffering is the precondition for salvation. As S. Zizek (2003) puts it, Christianity is based on a macabre discourse, where betrayal situates as the mainstream cultural value. Our Slovenian philosopher attempts to decipher the mystery of Christ as a form of redemption, where Christ dissuades humans that the only ways of salvation are impotence and suffering. His main thesis is that Christianity conserves as perverse core, where God tolerates imperfection or sin to pose a message to humans, happiness can be only reached through suffering. Instead of eradicating the sin from human´s mind, Zizek adds, God needs from a desire to impose a disciplinary discourse, where the impotence to defy the stronger is replaced with love.

However, Zizek´s development is limited to a biased understanding of this slippery matter. This happens because of two main reasons. Firstly, he glosses over the myth of Noah as the precondition of Christianity, but in second terms, Christ´s crucifixion reinforces a long-dormant tendency deposited by Judaism. The cruelty of the God in Old Testament sets the pace to a new benevolent deity, who not only becomes human but also lives in conditions of poverty and humility. At time Christ is crucified, the world understood two things. One on hand, riches are not worthy to enter heaven, unless they discard all their wealth, which means they consume all their objects in earth (mass-consumerism). Secondly, the shocking figure of Christ as a tortured person not only expresses an extreme suffering, reminding that all who so-called messiahs and prophets should be placed to an unspeakable tribulation, cementing the possibilities to orchestrate a spectacle of pain, which was revitalized by Than-capitalism. Christianity is the only religion whose sacred figure is a dying subject barbarically hanging on a crux. Not surprisingly Christianity is the only religion that boasts his God martyrized in a Crux, as a spectacle or at least a reminder how suffering may be sublimated by love. Whatever the case may be, anthropologically speaking Christ ignites a discussion around the problem of suffering as never before, focusing on a division between victims and witnesses. Of course, while victims are tragically touched by fate, witnesses are invested by the sign of exception.

Finally, like Noah´s tribulation, Christ´s anathema divides the world in two, what falls victims of arbitrariness, and those who moved by curiosity only need to gaze the suffering of others. One world rests on the needs of sacrifice, which means the restriction of pleasure to achieve collective world. Rather, the second signals to the maximization of hedonism escaping through others´ pain to the one condition which is irreversible, death. Such a tendency that has been accelerated in late capitalism paved the ways for the advance of Thana-Capitalism, a tendency where the suffering of others is the main commodity or primary reason to consume disaster-related news in the media. Though insensitive to this, we live in a society which theatricalizes death to find meaning in life. If the medieval man lived to have a good death, which was the start of a new life in heaven, modern consumers resist adamantly to die simply because they do not believe in the hereafter. As a result of this, the life is conceived as a great race where –like Hunger Games- all enter in competition at the same time. Knowing beforehand that only one can win and of course the winner takes all, participants would make decisions taking their courses of actions in a post-Hobbesian World where the social cooperation is undermined. Additionally, the others´ death not only exhibits the superiority of those who are still in the race but also a reason of pleasure, because they are part of chosen peoples. This discursive logic which was discussed in detail replicates the material asymmetries produced by Thana Capitalism where few hands concentrate the wealth and the working class is pushed to live with basic needs met. The culture of narcissism not only legitimates a new stage of capitalism where the rights of the workforce have been taken away in a complex and more uncertain World, but the introduction of more flexible forms of productions only can be possible if citizens overestimate their possibilities of success. Though polemically, we have explained and detailed why the logic of *dark tourism* is not new, even though it is the first symptom of a new stage of capitalism: a stage where death plays a crucial role between salvation and doom. Of course, since tourism changed, many of other institutions will be changed too. Death consumption is not limited to tourism; it can be found in journalism, magazines, Realities, cinema and any other type of cultural forms.

THANA CAPITALISM AS A TENET OF POST-CAPITALISTIC SOCIETIES

The Old society of risk, technically, starts with the nuclear accident in Chernobyl, Ukraine. This event reorganized the already-existent hierarchal order to a new reflective logic. In decline, the classic institutions created by welfare state were unable to protect citizens no longer. Ulrich Beck, who was one of the pioneers in envisaging a radical change in political making up, argued that the sense of community is now based on the risk perception (Beck, 1992). In the society of risks, the process of knowledge production leads to a state of complexity that creates a paradoxical situation. The same technology originally designed to make safer the life of people, if unregulated it can result in a real disaster. The old Word of classes where the first Marxists exerted their radical critique has set the pace for a new one. The classic division between riches and pours, or have and have-nots has gone forever. Now, all citizens seem to be equal before to risk. The stage of globalization that accelerated the transport orchestrated a closed-system which is very well market-oriented to mass-consumption. For exegetes of Thana Capitalism, who echo social Darwinist, economic inequalities among class can be compared to the conception of life. If millions of spermatozoids compete for the fecundation of an ovule, this suggests that only one will be the winner. Unlike risk society, in this new age, few concentrates much while the rest live with lower resources.

The *society of risk* operated under the logic of protection. No matter neither the causes nor the ideological position, nation-state endorsed the market to function as protector of the citizenry. The means of production corresponded with a decentralized way, where the process of reflexibility played a crucial role. This ushered into the atomization of agents, which were segmented by marketing experts to be bombarded by different products. Of course, Chernobyl was the founding event that inaugurated risk society passing from an economy of producers to an economy of consumers.

As discussed, the paradigm of protection supported adamantly the over-valorisation of Science as the only instrument capable to provide and disseminate valuable information to make the life safer. Undoubtedly, Chernobyl posed a serious dilemma to the use of technology. The same took-kit used to protect society can be fertile towards a real disaster. Paul Virilio has envisaged this apocalyptic scenario in his book *The University of Disaster.* Starting from the premise that the produced knowledge that determined the interests of scientists at universities has changed, Virilio argues that there is an epistemological dispersion by means researchers fail to get an all-encompassing model to understand reality. At a closer look, science passed to lead a position to produce a precautionary platform to inseminate fear in the population. The days of science as an instrument towards a better world have passed. The greatest business corporations appeal to science not only to predict the weather, by the use of many climate catastrophe simulation mathematical algorithms but by introducing "an economic disaster modelling-geek." The nets of experts seem to be more interested in locating and eliminating all risks that may threaten the current means of production, than in helping others (Virilio, 2010). In the apocalyptic world of Virilio, which has gone, risk-neglect, risk perception and the industry of insurances have pivoted the interactions in the societal order.

The epicenter of Thana Capitalism comes from the attacks to World Trade Centre, an event that occurred on 11 September of 2001, purportedly propagated by Al Qaeda. This shocking blow represented a turning point where Islam radicalism showed not only the weaknesses of West but also how the means of transport which were the badge of US, were employed as mortal weapons directed towards civil targets. Educated and trained in the best western universities, jihadist showed the dark side of the society of mass consumption. Many of the steps followed by Al-Qaeda were emulated from a Management guidebook. This made-man disaster showed the proud US that regardless of strength, power or levels of development of the country, terrorism will be present in all central nations. From this moment on, nobody will feel safe anytime and in any place. As Catholic Church in Lisbon's Quake through 1755, the rational basis of risk experts or risk-related analysis was placed under the critical lens of scrutiny. Beyond what radical conservatives in the Bush`s administration precluded, this event initiated a new age where the concept of security and prevention started to dilute.

All these discussed indicators set the pace to a more complex scenario, where economy turns chaotic (unpredictable after financial stock and the market crisis in 2008) where the atomized demands become in a competence of all against all (in the Hobbesian terms). The Darwinist allegory of the survival of strongest can be found as the main culture value of thana capitalism in a way that is captivated by cultural entertainment industries and cinema. Films as Hunger Games portray an apocalyptic future where the elite govern with iron rule different colonies. A wealthy capital which is geographically situated in Rocky Mountain serves as an exemplary center, a hot-spot of consumption and hedonism where the spectacle prevails. The oppressed colonies are rushed to send their warriors who will struggle with others to death, in a bloody game that keeps people exciting. Although all participants work hard to enhance their skills, only one will reach the glory. The same can be observed in realities as Big Brother, where participants neglect the probabilities to fail simply because they over-valorise their strongholds. This exactly seems to be what engages citizens to compete with others to survive, to show "they are worth of surviving." In sum, the *sentiment of exceptionality* triggered by these types of ideological spectacles disorganizes the social trust.

THANATOURISM AS THE INFATUATION FOR MORBID CONSUMPTION IN THE WESTERN CAPITALISTIC SOCIETIES

In his recent book *The Rise of Thana Capitalism and Tourism,* Korstanje (2016) dissects on the theory of heritage which remains unfit to explain why dark tourism situated as an increasingly-accepted style of consumption. While our grand-parents enjoyed their holidays in paradisiacal destinations along with beaches, now it sets the pace to a new morbid trend where the others´ suffering is the main criterion of attraction. This confirms, Korstanje adheres, that our patterns of holiday-making not only are changing but our society too. The upsurge of Thana-Capitalism results from the decline of risk society, in post 9/11 days.

The others´ death not only is consumed through tourism but through other forms of cinema, cultural entertainment, journalism and video games. The roots of thana-capitalism rest on the resistance of secular society to accept death as an inevitable reality, adjoined to the introduction of social Darwinism which stimulates the war of all against all. It is important to discuss to what extent Thana Capitalism is ethical because as in the novel *Hunger Games,* it allows the exploitation of peripheral communities while an exemplary center offers a macabre spectacle. Korstanje indicates that the plot of *Hunger Games* reflects the logic of Thana Capitalism, which means a futurist World where a capitol oppresses the periphery using the divide and rule. Most certainly, the fearless participants overestimate their skills neglecting their genuine probabilities to win. Because they are unable to cooperate with others, President Snow establishes an empire which is based the convergence of spectacle of death and submission. In the liberal market, where few concentrates a major portion of produced wealth whereas the majority lives with nothing, by gazing through how others die, spectatorship maximizes its pleasure. In a secular society where God is dead, the life is imagined as a great race where only a few selected people will reach the end. The others´ death reminds not only how special we are, but also we are encouraged to struggle with others in a game where nobody real wins. To keep the workers under control, elite emulates a radical discourse, where the winner takes all. Dark tourism represents the signs of a society where others´ death became as its main commodity (Korstanje 2016; Korstanje & George, 2015). But how are social ties weakened?

Most likely, those who have made fieldwork in post-disaster communities know on the "syndrome of survivor." This explains how the sentiment of narcissism disorganizes the social cohesion in the days of Thana-Capitalism. Still furthermore, in post-disaster contexts, victims face a great mourning or extreme loss which disorganizes their feelings. However, they feel that after all, Gods have protected them. Despite the great obliteration, survivors develop a biased image of themselves, understanding they have survived by some supernatural strength-holds as a virtue, force, or any type of superior spirit. Just there where "Others" have been doomed, they were chosen by God(s), fate or destiny. Given this, these token follows a goal, which often is associated with violence resistance or the quest for justice. Reactions like this are typical of victims in post trauma conjecture, but if it is not regulated, pathological forms of behaviors as Nationalism, Chauvinism or disproportionate ethnocentrism can emerge. The idea of exceptionalism using survivors sublimate their pain leads towards *a state of narcissism,* where they feel special, superior, more civilized and outstanding respecting to Others. Precisely, this is the moot point that characterizes the ideological core of thana-capitalism, where the needs of gazing disasters with victimization coexist.

CONCLUSION

Symbolically the death of others equals to the exclusion of workers from the labor market. Those who are relegated from the competition for a job are seen as responsible for their own destiny in the same way how victims are co-responsible for their death. The allegory of social Darwinism ideologically legitimates the others´ misfortune naturalizing unemployment as a condition of inefficacy and lack of rational control by the side of the worker. The figure of death silences the natural ethics each person feel for the others, while all are pressed to compete with unknown others to prove themselves they are part of a *Special Race.*

Though the conception that society of risk has gone or mutated to a known form seems not to be widely accepted, we have found in this chapter considerable evidence respecting to the arrival of death as a mediator between consumption and political institutions. In Thana-Capitalism, which in consonance with a hyper-secularized society, death is conceived as a sign of weakness. Hence people not only are afraid of death but devote their skills and resources to expand their lives. In zones of total destructions or death, tourists come across with the others´ suffering, which is commoditized to maximize their pleasure. In the mid of twentieth century, one of the fathers of symbolic interactionism, George H Mead held the thesis that while paradoxically modern audience were disgusting with the bad news, they were particularly addicted to consuming them. For Mead, since the self is culturally configured to interact with others, the communicative process encompasses anticipation and interpretation. This means that the self feels happiness through the others´ pain because in this way, the misfortune is externally exorcised (Mead, 2009). Though Mead dangles the possibilities of self-feeding from bad news, less attention was given to the rise of a new culture of disaster, where death situated as the main exchanged commodity. The society of capitalism emulates the plot of Hunger Games, where the capitol subsumes peripheral districts. President Snow opts for organizing some bloody games, known as *the Hunger Games.* In this futurist competition, participants are far from cooperating with others because their narcissism. Each one exacerbates their skills to be the winner. This well-famous novel, which was put on the excellent film trilogies, shows how the consumption of other death, in Thana Capitalism, invests a sentiment of exemption which poses as our real iron curtain. Death not only is everywhere, in TV, cinema and magazines but also become in the centerpiece of a society which keeps pathological forms to understand life.

REFERENCES

Bauman, Z. (2003). *Liquid love: On the frailty of human bonds*. Cambridge, UK: Polity Press.

Bauman, Z. (2005). *Liquid life*. Cambridge, UK: Polity Press.

Bauman, Z. (2007). *Consuming Life*. Cambridge, UK: Polity Press.

Beck, U. (1992). Risk society: Towards a new modernity (Vol. 17). Thousand Oaks, CA: Sage.

Berlin, I. (2013). *Karl Marx*. Princeton, NJ: Princeton University Press.

Biran, A., & Hyde, K. F. (2013). New perspectives on dark tourism. *International Journal of Culture. Tourism and Hospitality Research*, *7*(3), 191–198.

Biran, A., Poria, Y., & Oren, G. (2011). Sought experiences at (dark) heritage sites. *Annals of Tourism Research*, *38*(3), 820–841. doi:10.1016/j.annals.2010.12.001

Blom, T. (2000). Morbid tourism-a postmodern market niche with an example from Althorp. *Norsk Geografisk Tidsskrift, 54*(1), 29–36. doi:10.1080/002919500423564

Blom, T. (2007). Morbid Tourism: The Case of Diana, Princess of Wales and Althorp House. *Royal tourism: Excursions around monarchy*, 142-158.

Burawoy, M. (1984). Karl Marx and the satanic mills: Factory politics under early capitalism in England, the United States, and Russia. *American Journal of Sociology, 90*(2), 247–282. doi:10.1086/228079

Carrigan, A. (2014). Dark tourism and postcolonial studies: Critical intersections. *Postcolonial Studies, 17*(3), 236–250. doi:10.1080/13688790.2014.993425

Cohen, E. H. (2011). Educational dark tourism at an in populo site: The Holocaust Museum in Jerusalem. *Annals of Tourism Research, 38*(1), 193–209. doi:10.1016/j.annals.2010.08.003

Collins-Kreiner, N. (2010). Researching pilgrimage: Continuity and transformations. *Annals of Tourism Research, 37*(2), 440–456. doi:10.1016/j.annals.2009.10.016

Comaroff, J. L., & Comaroff, J. (2009). *Ethnicity, Inc*. Chicago: University of Chicago Press. doi:10.7208/chicago/9780226114736.001.0001

Dalton, D. (2014). *Dark tourism and crime* (Vol. 34). Abingdon, UK: Routledge.

Dunkley, R. A. (2007). Re-peopling tourism: A 'hot approach' to studying thanatourist experiences. *The critical turn in tourism studies: Innovative research methodologies*, 371-385.

Fillipi, A. (1988). *Instituciones e Ideologías en la Independencia Hispano-americana*. Buenos Aires: Alianza Editorial.

Frank, R., & Cook, P. (2010). *The Winner-take-All Society: why the few at the top get so much more than the rest of us*. New York: Virgin Books.

Friedrich, M., & Johnston, T. (2013). Beauty versus tragedy: Thanatourism and the memorialisation of the 1994 Rwandan Genocide. *Journal of Tourism and Cultural Change, 11*(4), 302–320. doi:10.1080/14766825.2013.852565

Giddens, A. (1971). *Capitalism and modern social theory: An analysis of the writings of Marx, Durkheim and Max Weber*. Cambridge University Press. doi:10.1017/CBO9780511803109

Goudie, S. C., Khan, F., & Kilian, D. (1999). Transforming tourism: Black empowerment, heritage and identity beyond apartheid. *The South African Geographical Journal, 81*(1), 22–31. doi:10.1080/03736245.1999.9713658

Guidotti-Hernández, N. M. (2011). *Unspeakable violence: Remapping US and Mexican national imaginaries*. Durham, NC: Duke University Press. doi:10.1215/9780822394495

Hartmann, R. (2014). Dark tourism, thanatourism, and dissonance in heritage tourism management: New directions in contemporary tourism research. *Journal of Heritage Tourism*, *9*(2), 166–182. doi:10.1080/1743873X.2013.807266

Hofstadter, R. (1992). *Social Darwinism in American Thoughts*. Boston: Beacon Press.

Holden, A., & Novelli, M. (2011). *The Changing Paradigms of Tourism in International Development: Placing the Poor First—Trojan Horse or Real Hope?*. Academic Press.

Hyman, R. (1975). *Industrial Relations: a Marxist introduction*. London: The Macmillan Press. doi:10.1007/978-1-349-15623-8

Kang, E. J., Scott, N., Lee, T. J., & Ballantyne, R. (2012). Benefits of visiting a 'dark tourismsite: The case of the Jeju April 3rd Peace Park, Korea. *Tourism Management*, *33*(2), 257–265. doi:10.1016/j.tourman.2011.03.004

Korstanje, M. (2012). Reconsidering cultural tourism: An anthropologists perspective. *Journal of Heritage Tourism*, *7*(2), 179–184. doi:10.1080/1743873X.2011.639883

Korstanje, M., & Handayani, B. (2016). *Gazing at Death: dark tourism as an emergent horizon of research*. New York: Nova Science Pubs.

Korstanje, M. E., & George, B. (2015). Dark Tourism: Revisiting Some Philosophical Issues. *E-review of Tourism Research*, *12*(1-2), 127–136.

Korstanje, M. E., & Ivanov, S. H. (2012). Tourism as a form of new psychological resilience: The inception of dark tourism. *Cultur – revista de cultura e turismo*, *6*(4), 56-71.

Lennon, J. J., & Foley, M. (2000). *Dark tourism*. Cornwall, UK: Cengage Learning EMEA.

Lowith, K. (2002). *Max Weber and Karl Marx*. London: Routledge.

MacCannell, D. (1976). *The tourist: A new theory of the leisure class*. Berkeley, CA: University of California Press.

MacCannell, D. (1984). Reconstructed ethnicity tourism and cultural identity in third world communities. *Annals of Tourism Research*, *11*(3), 375–391. doi:10.1016/0160-7383(84)90028-8

MacCannell, D. (1992). *Empty meeting grounds: The tourist papers*. London: Routledge. doi:10.4324/9780203412145

MacCannell, D. (2001). Tourist agency. *Tourist Studies*, *1*(1), 23–37. doi:10.1177/146879760100100102

Marx, K. (1967). Capital Volume 1: the process of capitalist production. New York: International Publishers.

Marx, K. (1973). *Grundriss. Foundations of the Critique of Political Economy*. Harmondsworth, UK: Penguin Books.

Marx, K., & Engels, F. (1902). *Wage-labor and capital*. New York: Labor News Company.

Marx, K., & Engels, F. (1959). *The communist manifesto* (Vol. 6008). New York Labor News Company.

Mead, G. H. (2009). *Mind, self, and society: From the standpoint of a social behaviourist* (Vol. 1). Chicago, IL: University of Chicago press.

Miles, S. (2014). Battlefield sites as dark tourism attractions: An analysis of experience. *Journal of Heritage Tourism*, *9*(2), 134–147. doi:10.1080/1743873X.2013.871017

Novelli, M. (2007). *Niche Tourism: contemporary issues, trends and cases*. London: Routledge.

Potts, T. J. (2012). Dark tourism and the kitschification of 9/11. *Tourist Studies*, *12*(3), 232–249. doi:10.1177/1468797612461083

Rojeck, C. (1993). *Ways of Escape*. London: Routledge. doi:10.1057/9780230373402

Ryan, C. (2005). Dark tourism–an introduction. *Taking Tourism to the limits: issues, conceptys and managerial perspectives*, 187-190.

Sather-Wagstaff, J. (2016). *Heritage that hurts: Tourists in the memoryscapes of September 11*. Abingdon, UK: Routledge.

Seaton, A. V. (1996). Guided by the dark: From thanatopsis to thanatourism. *International Journal of Heritage Studies*, 2(4), 234–244. doi:10.1080/13527259608722178

Seaton, A. V. (2000). Another Weekend Away Looking for Dead Bodies…: Battlefield Tourism on the Somme and in Flanders. *Tourism Recreation Research*, *25*(3), 63–77. doi:10.1080/02508281.2000.11014926

Shondell Miller, D., & Gonzalez, C. (2013). When death is the destination: The business of death tourism–despite legal and social implications. *International Journal of Culture, Tourism and Hospitality Research*, *7*(3), 293–306.

Skoll, G. (2014). *Dialectics in Social Thought: The Present Crisis*. New York: Palgrave Macmillan. doi:10.1057/9781137387066

Stone, P., & Sharpley, R. (2008). Consuming dark tourism: A thanatological perspective. *Annals of Tourism Research*, *35*(2), 574–595. doi:10.1016/j.annals.2008.02.003

Stone, P. R. (2010). *Death, Dying and Dark Tourism in contemporary society: the theoretical and empirical analysis* (Doctoral Thesis). University of Central Lancashire. Available at https://core.ac.uk/download/pdf/6677.pdf

Stone, P. R. (2011). Dark tourism: Towards a new post-disciplinary research agenda. *International Journal of Tourism Anthropology*, *1*(3-4), 318–332. doi:10.1504/IJTA.2011.043713

Stone, P. R. (2012). Dark tourism and significant other death: Towards a model of mortality mediation. *Annals of Tourism Research*, *39*(3), 1565–1587. doi:10.1016/j.annals.2012.04.007

Tanaś, S. (2014). Tourism 'Death Space' and Thanatourism in Poland. *Current Issues of Tourism Research*, *3*(1), 22–27.

Tarlow, P. E. (2007). Dark tourism: the appealing dark side of tourism and more. In M. Novelli (Ed.), *Niche tourism* (pp. 47–58). London: Routledge.

Tzanelli, R. (2016). *Thana Tourism and the cinematic representation of risk*. Abingdon, UK: Routledge.

Virilio, P. (2010). *University of disaster*. Cambridge, UK: Polity Press.

Wight, A. C. (2006). Philosophical and methodological praxes in dark tourism: Controversy, contention and the evolving paradigm. *Journal of Vacation Marketing*, *12*(2), 119–129. doi:10.1177/1356766706062151

Wilson, J. (2011). Australian prison tourism: A question of narrative integrity. *History Compass*, *9*(8), 562–571. doi:10.1111/j.1478-0542.2011.00789.x

Wilson, J. Z. (2004). Dark tourism and the celebrity prisoner: Front and back regions in representations of an Australian historical prison. *Journal of Australian Studies*, *28*(82), 1–13. doi:10.1080/14443050409387951

Wilson, J. Z. (2008). *Prison: Cultural memory and dark tourism*. New York: Peter Lang.

Wise, N. A. (2011). Post-war tourism and the imaginative geographies of Bosnia and Herzegovina and Croatia. *European Journal of Tourism Research*, *4*(1), 5.

Žižek, S. (2003). *The puppet and the dwarf: The perverse core of Christianity*. Cambridge, MA: MIT Press.

ADDITIONAL READING

Beech, J. (2000). The enigma of holocaust sites as tourist attractions-the case of Buchenwald. *Managing Leisure*, *5*(1), 29–41. doi:10.1080/136067100375722

Freire-Medeiros, B. (2009). The favela and its touristic transits. *Geoforum*, *40*(4), 580–588. doi:10.1016/j.geoforum.2008.10.007

Frenzel, F., & Koens, K. (2012). Slum tourism: Developments in a young field of interdisciplinary tourism research. *Tourism Geographies*, *14*(2), 195–212. doi:10.1080/14616688.2012.633222

Giblin, J. D. (2014). Post-conflict heritage: Symbolic healing and cultural renewal. *International Journal of Heritage Studies*, *20*(5), 500–518. doi:10.1080/13527258.2013.772912

Korstanje, M. (2016). Inglaterra y el Turismo Oscuro: Los orígenes de la thanaptosis. *RITUR-Revista Iberoamericana de Turismo*, *6*(2), 183–194.

Korstanje, M. E., & Clayton, A. (2012). Tourism and terrorism: Conflicts and commonalities. *Worldwide Hospitality and Tourism Themes*, *4*(1), 8–25. doi:10.1108/17554211211198552

Lesur, G., Kunz, M. W., & Fromang, S. (2014). Thanatology in protoplanetary discs-The combined influence of Ohmic, Hall, and ambipolar diffusion on dead zones. *Astronomy & Astrophysics*, *566*, A56. doi:10.1051/0004-6361/201423660

Logan, W., & Reeves, K. (Eds.). (2008). *Places of pain and shame: dealing with'difficult heritage*. Routledge.

Meschkank, J. (2011). Investigations into slum tourism in Mumbai: Poverty tourism and the tensions between different constructions of reality. *GeoJournal*, *76*(1), 47–62. doi:10.1007/s10708-010-9401-7

Middleton, V. T., Fyall, A., Morgan, M., & Ranchhod, A. (2009). *Marketing in travel and tourism*. London: Routledge.

Sheller, M., & Urry, J. (2004). *Tourism mobilities: places to play, places in play*. Abingdon: Routledge.

Traille, K. (2007). 'You should be proud about your history. They made me feel ashamed:'teaching history hurts. *Teaching History*, (127): 31.

Uzzell, D., & Ballantyne, R. (1998). Heritage that hurts: interpretation in a postmodern world. *Contemporary issues in heritage and environmental interpretation*, 152-171.

Velásquez, C. G., Van Broeck, A. M., & Posada, L. F. (2014). El pasado polémico de los años ochenta como atractivo turístico en Medellín, Colombia. *Turismo y Sociedad*, *15*, 101–114. doi:10.18601/01207555.n15.06

Verma, S., & Jain, R. (2013). Exploiting Tragedy for Tourism. *Research on Humanities and Social Sciences*, *3*(8), 9–13.

Weaver, D., & Oppermann, M. (2000). *Tourism management*. New York: John Wiley and Sons.

Williams, S., & Lew, A. A. (2014). *Tourism geography: critical understandings of place, space and experience*. Abingdon: Routledge.

Zerva, K. (2010). Turismo oscuro y destinos: En búsqueda de una experiencia auténtica. *Investigación en Ciencia Regional*, *1*(1), 63–72.

KEY TERMS AND DEFINITIONS

Capitalism: Signals to an economic system centered not only in private ownership, but also in the circulation and capital exchange. The main assets of capitalism include capital accumulation, profits, voluntary exchange, and private property which lead to a price system.

Globalization: It refers to a much deeper process that connects disperse cultures, nations and economies, into the same platform where the exchange of worldviews, products or ideas is integrated.

Mobilities: This represents an academic paradigm born from social sciences that explores the socio-economic background that facilitates the peoples´ movements.

Risk Society: A term formulated by Ulrich Beck to explain modernity after Chernobyl. Instead of industrial society which was based on class formation, risk society put all classes in egalitarian conditions before the risk.

Thana Capitalism: Neologism coined by Maximiliano Korstanje to denote a new state of capitalism, which replace the risk society. In thana-capitalism the others´ death is the main commodity to trade off.

Chapter 9
Animal Sexual Abuse and the Darkness of Touristic Immorality

Thomas R. Panko
The University of Southern Mississippi, USA

Babu P. George
Fort Hays State University, USA

ABSTRACT

Simply put, tourism is about travel and its associated services. Yet, beyond its glittery appearance, at least sometimes, these services contain elements of domination and control of fellow humans, nature, and culture. Even innocent animals are not spared in the pursuit to making money. The extant literature on "dark tourism" barely addresses the darkness of tourist behavior derived from the nexus between human avarice and animal suffering. Sexual relations with animals has been documented for many centuries; yet, this exploitation as a touristic pursuit is relatively new. In this paper, conditions for the growth of this phenomenon and international regulatory responses are described and the structure and dynamics of the underground animal sex tourism industry are explored.

INTRODUCTION

Globalization of sex tourism implies not only the proliferation of sex tourism into more regions of the world but also its varied forms of development (Jeffreys, 2010). Animal Sex Tourism (AST) is a touristic phenomenon that has developed around

DOI: 10.4018/978-1-5225-2750-3.ch009

the practice of sexual acts with animals. It undoubtedly encompasses one of the most extreme taboos and rarest of paraphilias associated with tourism, zoophilia. DSM-5 (APA, 2013) categorizes zoophilia as a "recurrent and intense sexual arousal involving animals." While often touted as simply a degenerative byproduct of Western capitalism, post-humanists like Bakke (2009), aver that commonalities between humans and animals have far reaching consequences. These commonalities include a variety of sexual forms and calls for a conceptual shift from bestiality to open exploratory zoosexuality. With such a shift, the prevailing anthropocentric world view would be replaced with pan-speciesism.

Aggrawal (2011) classified ten kinds of bestiality related behaviors on a continuum from least harmful to most harmful. At one extreme, the animal is an object of the human's need for sexual gratification; at the other extreme, the animal is an equal partner. The latter extreme is an expression of the emancipation of the human soul from the boundaries of the culturally conditioned human form (Bakke, 2009). From an atheistic perspective, Singer (2001) opines that the behavioral boundaries between humans and animals are arbitrary. Bestiality, then, is the behavioral choice of the individual; morality is a religious construct to which they are not obligated to conform. Beirne (1997) offers a typology of interspecies sexual assault including sexual fixation, commodification, adolescent sexual experimentation, and aggravated cruelty. He posits that most 'interspecies sexual assault' behaviors can be best understood by following a moderated view somewhere between the extremes of anthropocentrism and 'pseudo-liberal tolerance'.

To promote sexual tolerance and understanding toward people who may have engaged in unnatural sexual activities, Timpf (2013) reported on a "sensitivity training" workshop hosted on the Yale University campus. Among the many responses to survey questions regarding various types of sexual behavior in which attendees may have participated (including "consensual pain during sex"), three percent of the attendees said they had engaged in bestiality. *Zoophiles Engagement fur Toleranz und Aufklarung* (Zoophiles for the Ethical Treatment of Animals) is arguably the most well-known zoophillic organization (ZETA, 2014). ZETA's principles were originally forged by zoophiles in the U.S. and adopted by their counterparts in Germany in the 1990's. ZETA's principles are featured on its organizational website (ZETA, 2014). The principles emphasize kind treatment of animals, valuing the animal's well-being before one's desires for sexual satisfaction, discouraging bestiality in the presence of others, and censuring those who engage in and promote animal sexual abuse. ZETA publicly declared its position on these principles by conducting the world's first march for zoophile rights in Berlin on February 1, 2013. Their website also advertises "Animal Passions", a documentary about a man who discovers his zoophilia early in life, faces and solves a myriad of problems, and finally achieves inner peace when he marries his mare (ZETA, 2014).

ZETA's arguments are deeply contentious. It contends that, since interspecies intercourse is not defined as sexual abuse, why must it be so when a human participates? Further, while they lack the ability to speak the language of humans it is erroneous to assert they cannot convey their dissent. After all, through sounds, body language, facial expressions, etc. humans can interpret when animals are hungry, thirsty, anxious about certain situations, want attention, or to be walked. Why, then is it impossible for them to communicate when it's about sexuality? ZETA believes in the possibility of a mutually beneficial relationship between humans and animals since they assert that sexual advances often are initiated by the animal. The organization's followers add that masturbation and penetration are commonly employed professional breeding practices. These views are countered by a large body of scholarly research. Interspecies coupling is deeply harmful to the animals according to these studies (Ascione, 2008; Beetz & Podberscek, 2005; De Giorgio, Polacco, Rossi, Lodise, & Rainio, 2009).

Human-animal sexual interaction has been commercialized in a novel way by Zeta Paws, a West Virginia company that has been producing and selling silicone zoophilic adult "toys" in the shapes of a range of animal penises (categories include canines: dingo, fox, hyena, timber wolf; equines: horse; mythical animals: dragon, gryphon, werewolf, as well as humans) since 2001 (Zoofur.com, 2014). So, even if a person is adamantly opposed to interspecies coital activity, it is possible to vicariously experience "animal-like" sex via these adult "toys" (Zoofur.com, 2014). Eror (2012) reports that Michael Kiok, a ZETA member who has taken a vocal stand on a proposed change in German law that would outlaw bestiality, has ranked male dogs as the sexiest animals followed by female dogs, male horses, and then all other animals. Whether sales of Zeta Paws items parallel Kiok's rankings is undetermined. In contrast to this liberal perspective, bestiality is opposed on many grounds. Many view these practices as unhealthy, immoral, illegal, and dangerous, a form of animal abuse as well as an assault upon generally held ethical principles.

Cultures around the world have shown a mixed bag of responses, from extreme veneration to mindless abuse, when it comes to attitude towards animals Fennell (2011). Elephants are exploited by making them carry unbearable amounts of forest wood while the elephant figures are worshipped in the Hindu temples as incarnation of divinity. While societies have been relatively tolerant of the exploitation of animals for physical labor, there is a significant level of disgust about when using them as objects of carnal pleasures (Markwell, 2015). Here, the moral position is that animal cruelty in any form is unacceptable and AST is abdominal and should not be allowed to flourish under the label of tourism in the 21st century. However, both sides of the issue herein will be presented objectively and without bias.

AN OVERVIEW OF BESTIALITY

Sexual relations with animals are an ages-old practice and far more commonplace than is generally held. Human-animal sexual behavior allegedly occurred in ancient Egypt, Greece, Rome and other regions. Nadeau (2012) reports that anthropologists have discovered prehistoric depictions of bestiality including a cave painting in northern Italy around 8000 BC that depicts a man with full erection standing behind a female deer. Further, Dekkers (Singer, 2001) contends that "love for animals" is shown in ways far beyond a pat or hug. In his book *Dearest Pet: On Bestiality*, Dekkers (2000) provides many examples of human-animal sexual activities including: a Bronze Age Swedish rock drawing of a man having sexual intercourse with an large unidentified quadruped; a 17th century Indian miniature of a deer mounting a woman; an 18th century European engraving of a nun coupling with a donkey while other amused nuns spectate; and a 19th century Japanese drawing of a woman coupling with a giant octopus who seemingly is performing oral sex on her while simultaneously caressing her with its many limbs.

The Christian Bible admonished bestiality as a perversion. In multiple places in the Old Testament, such behavior was punishable by death (Leviticus 18:23; Leviticus 18:29; Leviticus 20: 15-16; Deuteronomy 27:21; and Exodus 22:19, New International Version). During medieval times, men were often burned to death for having sex with animals. There is no specific mention of it in the Qur'an, even though clear rulings on the morality of homosexuality, rape, polygamy, and pedophilia are proscribed.

However, there are some regional cultural features within Islam that appear to advocate bestiality. Sex with animals is a common practice in rural Pakistan and obligatory in rural Morocco Muslim boys as part of their sexual apprenticeship as part of their transitional rite of passage from adolescence to manhood (WikiIslam, n.d.). Masters reports a popular Arab saying that "the pilgrimage to Mecca is not complete without copulating with the camel" (Masters, 1966).

Bolliger and Goetschel (2005) point out that the Age of Enlightenment led to more rational views and relatively open discussions on this topic not marinated by prejudices and emotional overtones. More recently, they assert that religious prescriptions have given way to ethical precepts and regulations based on 'the dignity of the animal's life'. In *The Scotsman* newspaper, Stephen and Hall (2005) reported that recently discovered secret document revealed that in the 1920s, Soviet dictator Joseph Stalin was fascinated with the idea of developing super warriors to rebuild his Red Army. These invincible troops would be insensitive to pain and devoid of many weaknesses inherent in humans. To that end, he dispatched one of his foremost scientists to conduct experiments in Africa featuring the artificial insemination of apes as well as the reverse process of using monkey sperm to impregnate humans. These experiments were total failures but do provide an interesting historical insight into the interface between human-animal sexuality.

Another sensational story, involving human-animal pornography, put this behavior in the limelight. Bodil Joensen, a Danish zooporn star, was featured in many pornographic films in the bestiality sub-genre. She garnered a cult-like following from her live performances with swine and was the focal point of the 2006 British documentary *The Dark Side of Porn: The Search For Animal Farm*, which featured a collage of scenes from her many bestiality films (Wikipedia, n.d.). Joensen also owned a farm near Copenhagen which she financed by allowing animal sex tourists to visit and make their own personal films with her animals. Stevenson (2000), a rare films collector and exhibitor, proclaims Joensen as erotic cinema's most exploited figure. In the literary realm, authors such as the Marquis de Sade have featured bestiality in their writings. Matthews (1994) and others have even eulogized zoophilia.

Although the popular consensus holds that bestiality is an aberrant behavior, experts are divided (Beetz & Podberscek, 2005). In the literature, zoosadism (the pleasure derived from cruelty to animals, including sexual pleasure) is distinguished from zoophilia (sensual and sexual but not violent behaviors). Studies have indicated that zoosadists are significantly more likely to become violent towards their fellow human beings (Schlesinger, 2004). However, the relationship could be bi-directional). Duffield, Hassiotis, and Vizard (1998) found indications of zoophilia among young sexual abusers in general. Feelings of guilt associated with human-animal behaviors are capable of producing severe states of anxiety (London & Caprio, 1950).

Interspecies sexual orientations involving humans and animals mimic modes of human sexual orientations. Affectional orientation, sexual fantasy orientation, and erotic orientation are observed in human-animal relationships, too (Miletski, 2005a). This being the case, most reports about bestiality are about abuse because popular media outlets frequently obtain their information about this behavior from criminological reports that are indicative of violence and psychiatric disorders (Beetz, 2004).

Zoophilia is a behavioral condition that can be identified via stringent diagnostic procedures.

Arousal behavioral patterns, measured phallometrically, can provide clues to potential affinity for particular animals, too (Earls & Lalumiere, 2002). Emotional or physical absence of a father figure during childhood may be a nascent factor in the development of animal cruelty practice observes Felthous (1980). In some instances, zoophilia becomes violent concurrently with cycles of depression (Bhatia, Srivastava, & Sharma, 2005). In one study, psychiatric patients were found to exhibit a significantly higher rate of bestiality (Alvarez & Freinhar, 1991). White (2007) discusses the relationship of offenders with multiple paraphilias and the commission of sexual crimes (even serial murder). He asserts that criminals with paraphilia(s), intentionally or unintentionally, leave behind salient information related to their paraphilia(s) at crime scenes. This type of evidentiary exchange "*a la Locard*" could be of crucial importance to investigators.

Is there a relationship between zoophilia and pornography? Certainly there is a plethora of printed and visual material available on this relationship. In general, in places where zoophilic activity and the creation of pornography are legal, it is also legal to produce animal pornography. According to the New York Daily Sun (2013), zoophilic pornography is only legal in Brazil, Denmark, and Sweden. The United States has no federal laws prohibiting sex between humans and animals. However, the U.S. Supreme Court developed the "Roth Test" in 1957 to define "obscenity" (18 USC 1461). The ruling prohibits mailing obscene books, and was further strengthened by *U.S. v. Miller* (1972) (455 F.2d 899) to include books describing bestiality between women and a dog as "unmailable". Since that time there have been additional revisions which now make it illegal to mail, import, transport, broadcast, sell, transfer, or distribute obscene material via cable or subscription television. Further, if there is any direct or circumstantial evidence that the material was made outside the country, the courts will assume it was transported and in violation of USC 1462.

Legal Frameworks

The legal-ethical framework by which human-animal coital coupling is treated varies from country to country and even within the same country. A wide spectrum of sanctions affiliated with zoophilia includes fines, whippings, incarceration (up to life certain), and executions. Laws and sanctions are dynamic and are modified over time. In the UK, bestiality was punishable by a life sentence. However, today England and Wales have laws which clearly and specifically prohibit penetration of a human being by the penis of an animal and penetration of an animal by a human's penis. However, the same practices are legal in some countries (e.g., Denmark) as long as the animal is not harmed.

By contrast, many countries and U.S. states are less precise about the scope of law in that they outlaw sex with animals without defining what constitutes sex. Even if bestiality is not explicitly prohibited, there are often other laws which can be used to effectively prosecute cases. For example, most countries have animal cruelty laws and 'crimes against nature' and a prosecutor in these circumstances will argue that all zoophilic activity is animal abuse. In the U.S., such behaviors are treated as misdemeanors or felonies.

According to the New York Daily Sun (2013), zoophilia is legal in the following countries: Belgium, Brazil, Cambodia, Denmark, Finland, Germany, Hungary, Italy, Japan, Mexico, the Philippines, Poland, Portugal, Russia, Sweden, and Thailand. Since then, many countries have passed legislation against bestiality. For instance, zoophilia was outlawed in Norway in 2008, The Netherlands (2010), and Australia (2011). Some of the new legislation addressed the fact that bestiality laws were not on the books or that existing laws required greater specificity. Anecdotally, bestiality is considered child abuse in some societies; in some U.S. states it still constitutes a legal ground for divorce. In the United States, bestiality was specifically banned in Pennsylvania in 1999; Iowa (2001); Illinois and Maryland (2002); Washington and Arizona (2006); Indiana, Tennessee, and Colorado (2007), Alaska (2010), and Florida (2011) (Wikipedia, n.d.). On another front, Winn (2011) reported that the U.S. Senate repealed the military bans on sodomy and sex with animals contained in Article 125 of the Uniform Code of Military Justice (UCMJ).

Zoophilia as a Tourism Product

As mentioned elsewhere, while zoophilia is age-old, its transformation as a touristic pursuit is relatively new. Researchers have studied zoophilia from a variety of disciplinary backgrounds and tourism researchers have studied facets of human-animal interactions. Yet, most of this research has understated how tourist interactions negatively and positively impact wildlife. Some of the impacts are immediate (ex. hunting) while some require longer periods of time (ex. feeding wild animals).

There is scant research on animal sex tourism. The prevalence of a combination of social taboos, religious proscriptions, and legal bans make zoophilic behavior at home problematic. Thus, zoophiles seek alternatives. This search serves as a primary "push" factor behind animal sex tourism. AST occurs when zoophiles leave their regular places of residence for short periods of time motivated by the desire to engage in sexual encounters with animals.

In many parts of the world, especially where laws are favorable or implementation is lax, animal bordellos and animal brothels have been developed to cater to the demand for AST. Wild (2011) cited a report in the German magazine, *Bunte*, that near Moca in the Dominican Republic, Jose Maria Martinez has opened "The Big Surprise Farm" where according to anecdotes, animal sex tourists can arrange a one-week package tour. Included in the package is the opportunity to engage in "barnyard petting" with a range of animals (chickens, horses, etc.). Tourists are lodged in luxury barns with air conditioning, plasma television, and an around the clock supply of bestiality films (an erotic art form for many people).

Libertine Denmark and Norway have been receptive to peoples' rights to express their sexuality in virtually any manner including with animals provided they are not harmed. Danish animal owners have openly advertised the services of their animals on the internet and through a variety of promotional venues. This has attracted tourists (primarily from Norway, Sweden, Holland, and Germany) and constitutes a profitable business venture. Due to the clandestine nature of much animal sex tourism it is difficult, if not impossible, to determine its annual economic value. However, one bit of financial information was reported in the Danish newspaper

24timer (IceNews, 2008). According to that account, animal owners typically charged their customers between 85 and 170 United States dollars.

Opposition to this kind of financial venture asserts that the animals are heavily stressed, suffer from pain and physical injuries and have earned Denmark the sobriquet "animal whorehouse". PETA (People for the Ethical Treatment of Animals) spokesman, Martin Mersereau, asserts there is a well-established link between cruelty to animals and cruelty to humans and notes that a recent study found that 96 percent of those who engaged in bestiality also admitted to sexual assaults on people (Wnd.com, 2006). Numerous groups have organized and circulated petitions to address the injuries and suffering associated with bestiality (Snider, 2012).

In the United States, Exitpoint Stallions in the state of Washington served as a bestiality farm and tourist destination. *Seattle Times* newspaper (Sullivan, 2005) ran coverage of the activities that had taken place on the farm in a series of reports. When raided by police, hundreds of hours of videotapes were confiscated. The tapes contained scenes of men engaging in sex acts with animals. Animals found at Exitpoint Stallions farm, and asserted to have been sexually exploited, included horses, chickens, goats, sheep, dogs, and mice (lubricated with Vaseline and with their tails cut off). Through internet chat rooms and word of mouth, the farm was known to be a tourist destination for animal sex lovers who, in addition to satisfying their sexual proclivities, could also make personal videos. With the aid of a friend, one tourist had his sexual activity with a horse videotaped. Unfortunately, however, as a result of that anal sex he died due to perforation of his colon (Spokesman-Review, 2010). As another example of animal sex tourism, Swedish news website *The Local* (2008) exposed a network of approximately thirty zoophiles who met regularly around the country to have sex with animals. The group filmed their activities and made them available for distribution to other animal sex enthusiasts.

Yet it must be noted that a critical segment of animal sex tourists are not pre-planned "core" animal sex seekers. Rather, they are situational animal sex seekers in their role as tourists and out of curiosity are "just looking for a new experience". These are otherwise mainstream tourists whose primary travel motivation is something else but explore opportunities for animal sex activities that come their way. Klain (1999) observes a similar pattern among child sex tourists.

Whether an urban myth or reality, "Boy's Town" in Tijuana, Mexico, reputedly features sexual performances between a woman and a donkey and has been a planned or opportunistic destination of tourists for many years. More deliberate destinations are the animal brothels in Denmark and Germany. Also, quite contrary to the extremist view that AST invariably involves penetrative sex, many tourists do not wish to have such intensive encounters. They merely want to watch animal to animal sexual acts. Also, some animal sex tourists get attached to particular species and particular animals with whom they come into contact. Reportedly, some tourists have purchased the animals they love from animal brothels.

The Business System of AST

How the role of an individual as "tourist" might initiate or ignite his/her zoophilic tendency is not readily evident. Tourism destination environments and 'servicescapes' are often structured to provide a feeling of liberation and a heightened sense of importance for tourists (Rosenbaum & Wong, 2007). MacCannell (1973) observes that "touristic gaze" is a search for authenticity, a search for pure objects of consumption. In the context of AST, authenticity can mean both the authenticity of the observed tourist object (the 'uncultured' animal) and the authenticity of the tourist's first person experience. Animal sex tourists might be considering satisfaction on both counts. Taking cues from Urry (1990), it could be argued that human sexual encounters in contemporary society have become increasingly artificial. Thus, the superficiality of sexual encounters facilitates experimentation with animals.

Unlike most other forms of touristic development (ex. petting zoos, theme parks, lodging attractions such as the twice daily parade of ducks at The Peabody Hotel in Memphis, Tennessee, and opportunity to hand feed giraffes who poke their heads through the dining room windows at Giraffe Manor Hotel in Nairobi, Kenya, each morning at breakfast time), the AST supply chain is not readily apparent. No well-known organized tour operator is known to market AST-related products or services. Consequently, AST exists and thrives in some locations, as a *sub rosa* economy via an informal network of concerned parties. Generally, when touristic advertisements are promulgated, the key message is subtly embedded. Sometimes, tour packages feature the option of visiting animal farms with the opportunity for animal sex tourism. Given the general illegality of animal sex tourism, these networks could be sharing the infrastructure of drug cartels, pornography purveyors, and crime syndicates.

The private nature of the internet is often criticized as a facilitator of the expansion of animal sex tourism. For the most part, support for AST stems from websites which clandestinely or otherwise, sell services to AST customers. The proliferation of peer to peer networks and the social media has made the exchange of information much easier for practitioners while simultaneously making it more difficult for law enforcement agencies to carry out their responsibilities.

Implications for Tourism Policy

In human-animal interactions, Orams (2002) asserts that humans are clearly a beneficiary; benefits to animals are more problematic. Hughes (2001) opines that, even when sustainable tourism proponents advocate for animal welfare, the rights and welfare of individual animals are rarely considered. In consensual zoophilia, animals supposedly derive equal benefits but it remains unclear what consensus would mean for animals. Regardless of advocating particular value judgments, policy approaches to address AST could range from total prohibition to promotion. Empirical research is needed to produce a greater body of knowledge to support decisions. Unfortunately, this pursuit is handicapped by a paucity of credible primary data sources. Instead, tourism researchers must rely on internet items, anecdotal information, or chat rooms.

An important political question is how to find the path of least resistance among oppositional views on AST. The fact that countries, and cultural groups within countries, have varying ethical-legal postures on zoophilia makes management of trans-border AST even more problematic. Given its global nature, a comprehensive extra-territorial legislative framework is vital to eliminate cruelties associated with animal sex tourism.

National regulatory frameworks should incorporate punishments for perpetrators even when the crimes are committed in a foreign territory not having its own laws to deal with AST related crimes. Increased judicial cooperation among countries is essential in eliminating any legal vacuum that might still exist. Other forms of tourism that involve practices not widely accepted could provide guidelines for decision makers.

CONCLUDING REMARKS

This paper examined the structure and dynamics of animal sex tourism. Progress in this investigation was hampered by the lack of credible primary data sources. However, a sparcity of existing literature was combined with piecemeal information gathered from online sources and chat forums. While reporting the various dimensions of this issue, this discussion has been impartial in the spirit of the scientific method. The direction of the future development of animal sex tourism is unclear. AST is almost certain to continue but changes in consumer behavior, societal values, and how regulatory systems respond to such changes are difficult to predict. In the meantime, continued scholarly research is encouraged.

REFERENCES

Aggrawal, A. (2011). A new classification of zoophilia. *Journal of Forensic and Legal Medicine*, *18*(2), 73–78. doi:10.1016/j.jflm.2011.01.004 PMID:21315301

Alvarez, W. A., & Freinhar, J. P. (1991). A prevalence study of bestiality (zoophilia) in psychiatric in-patients, medical in-patients, and psychiatric staff. *International Journal of Psychosomatics*, *38*(1-4), 45–47. PMID:1778686

American Psychiatric Association (APA). (2013). *Diagnostic and Statistical Manual of Mental Disorders* (5th ed.). Arlington, VA: American Psychiatric Association.

Ascione, F. R. (Ed.). (2008). *The international handbook of animal abuse and cruelty: Theory, research, and application*. Purdue University Press.

Bakke, M. (2009). The predicament of zoopleasures: Human-non-human libidinal relations. In T. Tyler & M. Rossini (Eds.), *Animal Encounters* (pp. 221–242). Leiden, Netherlands: Brill Publishers. doi:10.1163/ej.9789004168671.i-266.58

Beetz, A. M. (2004). Bestiality/Zoophilia: A scarcely investigated phenomenon between crime, paraphilia, and love. *Journal of Forensic Psychology Practice*, *4*(2), 1–36. doi:10.1300/J158v04n02_01

Beetz, A. M., & Podberscek, A. L. (Eds.). (2005). *Bestiality and Zoophilia: Sexual relations with animals*. West Lafayette, IN: Purdue University Press.

Beirne, P. (1997). Rethinking bestiality: Towards a concept of interspecies sexual assault. *Theoretical Criminology*, *1*(3), 317–340. doi:10.1177/1362480697001003003

Bhatia, M. S., Srivastava, S., & Sharma, S. (2005). An uncommon case of zoophilia. *Medicine, Science, and the Law*, *45*(2), 174–175. doi:10.1258/rsmmsl.45.2.174 PMID:15895645

Bolliger, G., & Goetschel, A. F. (2005). Sexual relations with animals (zoophilia): An unrecognized problem in animal welfare legislation. In A. M. Beetz & A. L. Podberscek (Eds.), *Bestiality and Zoophilia: Sexual Relations with Animals* (pp. 23–45). West Lafayette, IN: Purdue University Press.

De Giorgio, F., Polacco, M., Rossi, R., Lodise, M., & Rainio, J. (2009). Fatal blunt injuries possibly resulting from sexual abuse of a calf. *Medicine, Science, and the Law*, *49*(4), 307–310. doi:10.1258/rsmmsl.49.4.307 PMID:20025108

Dekkers, M. (2000). *Dearest pet: On beastiality*. Brooklyn, NY: Verso Books.

Duffield, G., Hassiotis, A., & Vizard, E. (1998). Zoophilia in young sexual abusers. *Journal of Forensic Psychiatry*, *9*(2), 294–304. doi:10.1080/09585189808402198

Earls, C. M., & Lalumiere, M. L. (2002). A case study of preferential bestiality (zoophilia). *Sexual Abuse*, *14*(1), 83–88. PMID:11803597

Eror, A. (2012, December 7). The government wants to stop this guy from boning his dog. *Vice*. Retrieved October 28, 2013, from http://www.vice.com/read/bestiality-is-still-legal-in-germany-but-not-for-long

Felthous, A. R. (1980). Aggression against cats, dogs, and people. *Child Psychiatry and Human Development*, *10*(3), 169–177. doi:10.1007/BF01433629 PMID:7357998

Fennell, D. A. (2011). *Tourism and animal ethics*. Routledge.

Hughes, P. (2001). Animals, values and tourism: Structural shifts in UK dolphin tourism provision. *Tourism Management*, *22*(4), 321–329. doi:10.1016/S0261-5177(00)00070-4

IceNews. (2008, May 20). *Animal brothels legal in Denmark*. Retrieved January 27, 2014, from http://www.icenews.is/2008/05/20/animal-brothels-legal-in-denmark/

Jeffreys, S. (2010). Globalizing sexual exploitation: Sex tourism and the traffic in women. *Leisure Studies*, *18*(3), 179–196. doi:10.1080/026143699374916

Klain, E. J. (1999, April). *Prostitution of children and child sex tourism: An analysis of domestic and international responses*. Alexandria, VA: National Center for Missing and Exploited Children.

Local. (2008, November 11). *Swedish bestiality ring exposed*. Retrieved January 18, 2014, from http://www.thelocal.se/20081111/15610

London, L. S., & Caprio, F. S. (1950). Zoophilia (bestiality). In *Sexual deviations* (pp. 588–596). Washington, DC: Linacre Press. doi:10.1037/11274-013

MacCannell, D. (1973). Staged authenticity: Arrangements of social space in tourist settings. *American Journal of Sociology*, *79*(3), 589–603. doi:10.1086/225585

Markwell, K. (2015). Exploited elephants and pampered pets: Reflecting on tourism–animal relationships. *Animals and Tourism: Understanding Diverse Relationships*, *67*, 288.

Masters, R. E. L. (1966). *Forbidden sexual behavior and morality: An objective re-examination of perverse sex practices in different cultures*. New York: Matrix House.

Matthews, M. (1994). *The horseman*. Amherst, NY: Prometheus Books.

Miletski, H. (2005a). A history of bestiality. In A. M. Beetz & A. L. Podberscek (Eds.), *Bestiality and zoophilia: Sexual relations with animals* (pp. 1–22). West Lafayette, IN: Purdue University Press.

Miletski, H. (2005b). Is zoophilia a sexual orientation? A study. In A. M. Beetz & A. L. Podberscek (Eds.), *Bestiality and zoophilia: Sexual relations with animals* (pp. 82–97). West Lafayette, IN: Purdue University Press.

Nadeau, B. (2012, December 1). Germany weighs bestiality ban amid rise of pet porn, animal brothels. *The Daily Beast.*

New York Daily Sun. (2013, May 31). *Is bestiality legal?* Retrieved October 28, 2013, from http://www.newyorkdailysun.com/is-beastiality-legal/

Orams, M. B. (2002). Feeding wildlife as a tourism attraction: A review of issues and impacts. *Tourism Management, 23*(3), 281–293. doi:10.1016/S0261-5177(01)00080-2

Rosenbaum, M. S., & Wong, I. A. (2007). The darker side of the servicescape: Investigating the Bali Syndrome. *International Journal of Culture, Tourism and Hospitality Research, 1*(2), 161–174.

Schlesinger, L. B. (2004). *Sexual murder: Catathymic and compulsive homicides.* Boca Raton, FL: CRC Press.

Singer, P. (2001, March 12). *Heavy petting.* Retrieved January 25, 2014, from http://www.nerve.com/Opinions/Singer/heavyPetting/main.asp

Snider, B. (2012, February 21). Popularity of animal brothels increasing in Germany. *The Examiner.* Retrieved January 27, 2014, from http://www.examiner.com/article/popularity-of-animal-brothels-increasing-germany-petitions

Spokane Spokesman-Review. (2010, April 18). In brief: Officials allege beastiality at farm. *Spokane Spokeman Review.* Retrieved January 27, 2014, from http://www.spokesman.com/stories/2010/apr/18/in-brief-officials-allege-bestiality-at-farm/

Stephen, C. & Hall, A. (2005, December 20). Stalin's half-man, half-ape-super-warriors. *The Scotsman.*

Stevenson, J. (2000). Dead famous: The life and movies of cinema's most exploited figure, Bodil Joensen. In J. Stevenson (Ed.), *Fleshpot: Cinema's Sexual Myth Makers & Taboo Breakers* (pp. 177–190). Manchester, UK: Headpress.

Sullivan, J. (2005, July 16). Videotapes show bestiality, Enumclaw police say. *Seattle Times.* Retrieved January 27, 2014, from http://seattletimes.com/html/localnews/2002384648_farm16m.html

Timpf, K. (2013, March 5). *Yale hosts workshop teaching sensitivity to bestiality.* Retrieved October 8, 2013, from campusreform.org/blog.

Urry, J. (1990). *The Tourist Gaze*. London, UK: SAGE Publishers.

White, J. H. (2007). Evidence of primary, secondary and collateral paraphilias left at serial murder and sex offender crime scenes. *Journal of Forensic Sciences*, *52*(5), 1194–1201. doi:10.1111/j.1556-4029.2007.00523.x PMID:17681002

WikiIslam.net. (n.d.). *Islam and beastiality*. Retrieved January 27, 2014, from http://www.wikiislam.net/wiki/Islam_and_Beastiality/

Wikipedia. (n.d.a). *Bodil Joensen*. Retrieved December 10, 2013, from http://en.wikipedia.org/wiki/Bodil_Joensen

Wikipedia. (n.d.b). *Zoophilia and the law*. Retrieved January 27, 2014, from http://en.wikipedia.org/wiki/zoophilia_and_the_law

Wild, C. (2011, July 26). Dominican Republic's first animal farm. *News365*.

Winn, P. (2011, December 1). *Senate approves bill that legalizes sodomy and bestiality in U.S. Military*. Retrieved January 27, 2014, from http://cnsnews.com/news/article/senate-approves-bill-legalizes-sodomy-and-bestiality-us-military

Wnd.com. (2006, September 28). *PETA says barnyard brothels 'revolting'*. Retrieved January 27, 2014, from http://www.wnd.com/2006/09/38123/

ZETA. (2014). Retrieved January 27, 2014, from zeta-verein.de/en

Zoofur.com. (2014). Retrieved January 27, 2014, from http://www.zoofur.com/

ADDITIONAL READING

George, B. P., & Panko, T. R. (2011). Child sex tourism: Facilitating conditions, legal remedies, and other interventions. *Vulnerable Children and Youth Studies*, *6*(2), 134–143. doi:10.1080/17450128.2010.521599

Hicks, J. R. (2013). *Tourism and Animal Ethics*. Routledge.

Jiménez-Jiménez, F. J., Sayed, Y., García-Soldevilla, M. A., & Barcenilla, B. (2002). Possible zoophilia associated with dopaminergic therapy in Parkinson disease. *The Annals of Pharmacotherapy*, *36*(7-8), 1178–1179. doi:10.1345/aph.1A412 PMID:12086551

Markwell, K. (2015). Birds, beasts and tourists: human–animal relationships in tourism. In K. Markwell (Ed.), *Animals and tourism: understanding diverse relationships* (pp. 1–25). Toronto: Channel View Publications.

Panko, T. R., & George, B. P. (2012). Child sex tourism: Exploring the issues. *Criminal Justice Studies*, *25*(1), 67–81. doi:10.1080/1478601X.2012.657904

Panko, T. R., George, B. P., & Henthorne, T. L. (2009). Cruise crimes: Economic-legal issues and current debates. *The Amfiteatru Economic Journal*, *11*(26), 585–596.

Wilcox, D. T., Foss, C. M., & Donathy, M. L. (2005). A case study of a male sex offender with zoosexual interests and behaviours. *Journal of Sexual Aggression*, *11*(3), 305–317. doi:10.1080/13552600500333804

Yİğİt, A., & Yaşar, A. (2016). Zoophilia: An evaluation from perspective the holy religions, legislation and ethics. *Eurasian Journal of Veterinary Sciences*, *32*(2), 114–119.

KEY TERMS AND DEFINITIONS

Animal Rights: Rights believed to belong to animals to live free from use in medical research, hunting, and other services to humans.

Animal Sex Tourism: Tourism motivated by the desire to have sexual relation with animals.

Bestiality: Savagely cruel or depraved behavior to animals.

Zoophilia: An erotic fixation on animals that may result in sexual excitement through real or imagined contact.

Zoosadism: Pleasure derived from cruelty to animals, sometimes considered to be a precursor to sociopathic tendencies.

Chapter 10
Banalizing the Alterity:
When Suffering Turns Attractive

Maximiliano E. Korstanje
University of Palermo, Argentina

Lourdes Cisneros Mustelier
Universidad de la Habana, Cuba

ABSTRACT

This chapter discusses the problem of poverty as something finely integrated in dark tourism. Though originally, both concepts sound very distant, no less true is that dark tourism and slum tourism are inextricably intertwined. Throughout this chapter review, we placed a hot debate on the role of globalization as a chief agent oriented to connect dissimilar economies into an all-encompassing system. The question whether tourism should be considered ethical or not still remains open. In days of Thana-Capitalism the suffering pivoted as the main commodity not only that helps structuring social institutions, but the necessary mediator between lay-people and their states.

INTRODUCTION

In the academy, the attention given to themes associated to development, sustainability and problems emerged from real estate speculations has reached a significant facet of maturation (Holden, 2003; Lea 1993; MacBeth, 2005; Kampaxi, 2008). However, over recent years some critical voices questioned to what extent tourism should be considered an ethical activity (Hultsman, 1995; Malloy & Fennell, 1998; Garrod & Fennell, 2004; Fennell, 2015). Starting from the premise that tourists only are in

DOI: 10.4018/978-1-5225-2750-3.ch010

quest of pleasure-maximization, this raises the pungent question, what is the role of otherness in this hedonist behaviour?

Within philosophy, ethics are valorised as a form of enhancement which leads the self to progress. In tourism fields, for some reasons very hard to explain now, ethics was originally associated to the needs of protecting the interests of natives, or vulnerable agents as women, children. Ethics are commonly understood as the system of codes that promotes the correct conduct (Rushworth, 2003). While aboriginals have been historically debarred to live in conditions of poverty during years or occupying marginal position in main economy, no less true was that tourism offers a fertile ground to abandon poverty, slum accelerating the conditions for a fairer wealth distribution (Altman, 1989; Waitt, 1999; Korstanje, 2012).

Beyond European paternalism, which accompanied the inception and evolution of social anthropology, the fragility of local voices subrogates a sentiment of empathy from where tourism is rechanneled. This essay-review explores not only the ebbs and flows of ethics in tourism, but also the effects of neo-capitalism producing poverty worldwide. To be more exact, one of the promises of neoliberalism which is associated to the possibilities poor nations better their situation by embracing liberal trade, development and sustainability remain unchecked. In second terms under the quandary tourism is ethical or not, this chapter-review dissects the role of market and rationality as the main tenets of global consumption. Most likely, the fascination for others` pain derives from European Paternalism that accompanied not only the rise and expansion of colonialism, but also social sciences as well.

THE RATIONALITY OF DEVELOPMENT

At some extent, tourism metaphorically reflects the allegory depicted as a vehicle towards development was originally studied by Emanuel de Kadt who in his book, *Tourism: passport to development?,* dangles the probabilities that culture plays a vital role in explaining why development fails while in others points reaches success. For de Kadt, as well as many theorists of development, the problem of development are not constituted in the content of programs, unless by the fact some cultures are symbolically determined to accept authoritarian values, which impedes the revitalization of democratic institutions. Those countries which kept a past of violence, genocide or slavery have lesser probabilities to embrace development as a main option than other nations which forged an stable democracy. This discourse which was reinforced during neoliberalism not only resonated in tourism fields during 90s but also persisted up to date. The current narratives emulated by academy envisages tourism as a main instrument towards development, which means the revitalization of history, tradition and further profits for community. Since authorities needs to foster stable economies for gaining reelections, no less true was that tourism would alleviate poverty endorsing further legitimacy to politicians. Jose Osmar Fonteles describes how the wonderland of development not only is far from being real, but also sometimes collapses before the principle of liberal consumption. The life of residents is often affected by the arrival of tourists as well as the environmental problems the activity left. Under the dichotomy of rationality, what development exhibits is the lack of any rational basis simply because profits are expatriated to US and Northern Europe (precisely places where investors and tourists come from), while territory and its resources are seriously placed in jeopardy. Fonteles acknowledges that beyond the popularity of sustainable tourism and development, pollution is considerably higher today than other times. In order to prevent real estate speculative policies, governments should directly intervene to protect the interests of all stakeholders.

Initially, John Urry coins the term "tourist-gaze" as an attempt to describe a visual attachment to possess what is being watched. Though he glossed over the fields of ethics, the tourist gaze has three aspects: the re-enchantment of consumption, time-space dimensions, and visualization of performing arts. Therefore, travels re-symbolize spaces at the time they are transformed into commodities. The potential consumers, tourists, are bombarded by images: advertising and visual stimuli channelling them to interpret landscapes in specific ways. The decentralized control of space is accompanied solicitation of credit from international banking apparatuses. Such national policies create dependency of tourist-destination state to global capital. Late modernity deregulates finance, and thereby introduces an uncontrolled flux of capital which re-draws the contours of a globalized world. As J. Urry (2002) puts it, modernity is based on the monopoly to produce signs. Landscapes produce gazes to be visually consumed. He was a pioneer among scholars who thought that we are in conditions to forge a discipline aimed at exploring the paradigm of mobilities. Acknowledging that travels not only generate specific ways of tourist-gazes, but they are classified by a broader cultural matrix that gives meaning to social system, he argues that we move inside the territory we can move, interpreting the events according to the value of our society, by negotiating our identities with others. Any movement, of course, is a type of negotiation, a rite where interaction pivots (Urry, 2002; Lash & Urry, 1994). In the opposite direction, Dean Maccannell interrogates on the Ethics of sightseeing discussing the intersection of modernity, consumption and tourism. Part of the problem stems from the epistemology of capitalism which ponders consumption as something to be valued by all members of society. The social change not only is not an easy task, but sometimes face serious obstacles which should be overcome. At the time, watching represents an hermeneutical interpretation, connecting peoples with landscapes, and experiences, the derived meaning of events are not chaotically organized in social imaginary. There is a meta-discourse which precedes behaviour social scientist should unravel. To what extent the message is correctly deciphered seems to be the key-issue of any social scientist. Unlike other texts, in the Ethics of sightseeing, the debate is posed to the direction of philosophy. The history witnessed how the sacred-life has set the pace to more secular forms. If Toteminsm, as a system of beliefs, is enrooted in primitive mind, tourism plays an analogous role in modern societies. In the MacCannell's conception, West has advanced in the trace of technology imposing to the world a new secular view about relation. The sacred-space that characterized the gaze of aborigines, today, has been replaced by a new one more elaborated, secular and fictional sightseeing: *tourism*. What is important to discuss here, seems to be the connection of tourists with social symbolism that mediates between self and consumption. Money serves a mediator connecting all dispersed consumers. In late modernity, consumption and mobility pave the ways for the advance of alienation and depersonalization. Since tourism commoditizes others by the introduction of sightseeing, Maccannell is not enthusiastic on the fact, tourism would help communities to abandon poverty and alienation (MacCannell, 2011). These worries are in consonance with the seminal book authored by Comaroff and Comaroff, Ethnicity INC. Beyond the promises of the globalized world, per the argument readers will find in this text, there is an underlying logic of commoditization and consequent exploitation by which human beings, their cultures and traditions become in business enterprises. Since anthropology as academic discipline emerged as an extreme concern in founding parents to the disappearance of non-western cultures, this sentiment has taken the opposite direction. In our days, aboriginals appeal to reinforce their own differences to be sold to the international segment of travelers and tourists. In perspective, cultural tourism is one of the most growing industries in the world. Ethnicity, in this vein, set the pace to a new type of cultural consumption fabricated from outside to regulate emotions. The term "empowerment" as it has been formulated by the specialized literature is defined as strategy followed by local actors to improve economic and social conditions by means of the proactive participation and commitment. At the time, aborigines adopt "empowerment" simply because they know something special can be offered to the international western consumer, their culture is recycled as a commodity. This new type of identity, though more flexible, objectifies the native to the extent to its needs are enslaved to a fabricated past. Basically, cultural tourism not only evokes a vibrant past which does not exist, but confers to local communities the legal mechanism for launching to self-representation. The value of aboriginal cultures is conditioned by those features that legitimate the West supremacy. Aboriginals may say something if this discourse can be commercialized. This alludes to a much deeper process of alienation where cultures are disclosed from their original roots.

In doing so, the culture is sold attending only to the interests of consumers. The enthusiasm and leading role of aborigines as cultural managers blurs the conflictive relations of Fourth World and States, but creating new ones. In this discussion, two significant ideas arise. On one hand, tourism disposes from cultural protection to re-draw the geography of the world. On another, native constructs their sentiment of belonging in view of what tourists want to hear and see. The merit of this work consists in reminding that this trend not only blurs the boundaries between past and present but also impose new economies based on ethno-merchandise where the production never ends. The classic rules of economy teach us that the rise of demands entails a decline in the production. Needless to say, this does not happen with ethno-merchandise. The much demand for cultural consumption, the better for production; that way, the destination never declines in extractives. One of the problems of heritage and tourism are expressed in the violence exerted by states when aborigines reject the possibility to be taxed. While development bring some benefits to local communities, no less true is that it triggers situation of political crisis unless duly regulated (Comaroff & Comaroff, 2009).

The rise of demand for the consuming of slum-tourism, which means the attractions for gazing spaces of poverty, misery and pauperization, seems to be conducive to "the logic of social Darwinism" (Korstanje, 2015). However, less attention was given to the fact that over last decades, these practices were stimulated by the proliferation of slum and slum-dwellers worldwide. From colonialism to the liberal discourse of mobility, Zygmunt Bauman (2000) adds, the question of poverty was replicated in order for status quo keeps its hegemony. At time the financial global elite visit the exotic archaeological ruins, thousands of migrants are disciplined in their arrival to Europe. The term disciplined here is employed to denote how over-seas migrant work-force arrived to US in the end of XIXth century was subject to strict patterns of re-education and control. Some cultural values such as self-determination, development and freedom were the conceptual platforms for the expansion of modern capitalism.

The intersection of development and colonial order was brilliantly addressed by P. McMichael in the book *Development and Social Change*. His main thesis is that Europe, by the introduction of "colonialism", established an ideological background for legitimizing their submissions to its overseas colonies. The exploitation of the non-European "Others" had a pervasive nature. Sooner, aborigines realized the double moral standards of colonial order. Cruelty, submission and violence were applied in the colonies, while in the core democracy prevailed as a valid system of government. This opens the doorstep to the process of "decolonization", where thousands of peripheral voices claimed to access the same rights "the democracy of their white lords" declared. Mc-Michael explains that imperial powers alluded to the theory of "development" to maintain the dependency between center and its periphery. The WWII end conjoined to Truman's administration led the United States to implement a wide range credit system to save the world from Communism. This program mushroomed to become in the development theory. As a mega-project, theory of development was coined in 1940 and lasted to 1970. It not only created a food dependency but also accelerated the slum-dwellers and poverty in the peripheral countries. In order for remaking the old division of labor, Imperial Powers induced "Third Word" to accept international loans, which were used to industrialize their economies. At the time, under-developing nations adopted capital-intense methods in agriculture ruining the condition of small-farmers, who migrated to urban areas, the US and Europe exported industrialized products. It was unfortunate the effects development left in Africa. The old boundaries of ethnicities the first colonial powers found were never honored once WWII finalized. Many human groups were forced to live together within fabricated limits of new nation-states. This resulted in a lot of ethnic cleansing, conflicts and warfare that obscured the original ends of financial aid programs issued by IMF or World Bank. Undoubtedly, the inconsistencies of World Bank in administering the development-related programs not only were admitted but also it woke up some nationalist reactions in the non-aligned countries. To restore the order, a new supermarket revolution surfaced: *globalization.*

As previous argument given, McMichael argues convincingly that globalization was success in expanding thanks to the lack of protective barriers of Third world where the capital investors were welcomed. This, in consequence, provoked two alarming situations. An increase in the unemployment and the decline of unionization in the North was accompanied with the arrival of international business corporations seduced by the low-cost of workers in South. The doctrine of "free enterprise" was presented as a superior ladder in the evolutionary process. Each state should adopt a specialized role in a much wider "world factory" where some provide with the raw-materials and others with elaborated products. This trends which characterizes the 90s decade created a new asymmetry between skilled (located in first world) and under-skilled human resources (situated in the periphery). The recession produced by oil-embargo pressed First World to borrow a massive influx of money to Third world, but now it will be carefully selected by two organisms, GATT and WTO. Both curtailed the protective measure of local economies by consolidating of a new model which combined the reduced public capacity with the needs of governance. If Nationalism showed the importance of nation-state to protect the citizen from Market's arbitraries, now neo-liberalism focused on the inefficiency public administration to regulate economy:

In short, the making of a free trade regime reconstructed food security as a market relation, privileging and protecting corporate agriculture and placing small farmers at a comparative disadvantage. Food security would now be governed through the market by corporate, rather than social criteria. (p. 136)

On one hand, World Trade Organization was relentless by charging or applying sanctions over those countries who affected the new system of import-exports. Less interesting in freeing trade than in consolidating their hegemony, main powers prompted the discourse that Third World had not the right towards "self-sufficiency" any more. On another, globalization accelerated the accumulation of profits (beyond the boundaries and control of nation-states) but enlarging the levels of poverty as never before. Per some calculations, UN declared that only 20% of world population is situated within the 20% of richest people, whereas the rest is facing serious economic problems. It is important not to lose the sight that almost 1 billons of peoples are living in slums.

Last but not least, Korstanje explained that the limitation of development theory rests on the logic how language is used and negotiated. While white-elite marks ethnicities to control them, it avoids any type of mark. The term ethno-tourism or cultural tourism is daily conceived to denote visits to aboriginal reservoirs, while we say "we are making tourism" when we visit Chicago. This means that the core of our language contains "a strong paternalism" which surmises Europeaness as superior to other values. The theory of development is not ethic because of two main reasons. The subordinated role of aborigines impedes the necessary platforms to break its dependency respecting to capitalist nation state but secondly, the theory of development introduces European cultural values which are linked to control and rationality, as the best of possible worlds. Given this argument, failure of development to be adopted in peripheral nations is not explained from the incapacity of the theory but as cultural pathologies of natives (Korstanje 2012).

THINKING ETHICS IN TOURISM

Doubtless, there is consensus to confirm hospitality adjoined to mobility is the touchstone of tourism industry. Following this reasoning, a lot of studies have focused on the commercial nature of hospitality (Lashley & Morrison, 2001; Santos Filho, 2008; Gallarza and Gil, 2008; Santana, 2006; Kathchikian, 2000; Alvarez & Korzay, 2008; Nadeau et al, 2008; Castaño, Moreno and Crego, 2006; Coronado, 2008; Lau and Mckercher, 2006; Toribio, Castellá and Serrano, 2005; Lynch, 2005; McNaughton, 2006; Heuman, 2005; Franch et al, 2008; Capriello & Rotherham, 2008; Kastenholz & Lopez de Almeida, 2008) while less attention was given to the ethical dilemma profit-oriented paradigms cover. At a closer look, hospitality may be only ensured when guests have material resources to pay for it. Neither migrants nor any other undesired guest is accepted by nation-state beyond the paradigm of gift-exchange (Korstanje & Olsen 2011; Korstanje 2016). On another hand, the process of touristification leads local communities towards social benefits but compromises some resources when real-estate is uncontrolled.

Preliminary, the research of Franch et al. explores the Global Warming as a threat to Alpine Areas (The Dolomites area) as well as the urgency of innovative strategies in order for managing unexpected effects that accelerate a profound change in way hosts are symbolically interconnected with their landscapes. The Global Warming impinges on destroying not only the environment by means of snow reductions but also the different industries directly or indirectly linked to tourism and hospitality and of course to winter-season exploitation; Franch et al argue that diversification of business and technology are more than needed to overcome these new pitfalls; by analyzing the testimonies of 16 cableway associations in Trentino, the present investigation revealed deficiencies on radical innovation and behavioral adaptation to GW with the exemption of investments in artificial snow-making (Franch et al., 2010). Policy-makers should take attention to the degree of dependency the community developed respecting to tourism. Y. Ohe (2010) sees the performance of rural destinations can alleviate poverty at a short run, but creating a long run dependence when profitability is pondered as the only requisite. Judging ethics according to context, can give answers in some extreme cases, but it is not recommendable for all cases.

SOME CONCERNS FOR FUTURE RESEARCH

An authorative voice in economy, Robert Sugden lecturer at University of East Anglia UK, agrees that society evolves from a spontaneous order early conditioned by previous negotiations, to a state of further stability where individualism should be sacrificed. In fact, the quest of goal-oriented maximization is left behind to ensure shared conventions. Among frights and nightmares citizen face, behavior is oriented to avoid "chaos" and disorder. The society is united because lay-citizens endorse solidarity to their social institutions, where each side commits to respect the rules only under the premise the other does the same (Sugden, 2005). This is the position from where virtue operates in day-to-day contexts. As stated, in some respect, virtue is defined by Nancy Snow as:

enduring character traits incorporated practical reason, appropriate motivation, and affect, and manifested in cross situationally consistent behavior. (Snow 2010: 117)

As the previous argument given, she contends that behaviour takes two different dynamics, habitual and deliberative. While habitual virtuous acts come from any previous deliberation since the act has been routinized, deliberative subtype pressed people to make a decision. Though in philosophy situationists are consistent with their criticism to the theory of traits, they ignore the fact that behaviour is a multifaceted result where motivations, affects and history are organized by the mind. Each person may adjust their own desires hoping to reach a virtuous result. The development of virtue is in sync with the cultivation of ethical decisions. In times of globalization, we place ethics before the world of business but not for ethical purposes, but only to enhance profits. This represents the case described by Slavoj Zizek of MacDonald and other fast food corporations which sell their products enmeshed in charitable project where consumers help to struggle against poverty in Africa, Latin America or Asia (Zizek, 2008). Further attention can be given to the world of slum tourism, which consists in practices overtly aimed at visiting spaces of mass poverty to get "authentic experience" with the others, but in so doing, visitors takes asunder from real ethics. In a recent and seminal work edited by Clare Weeden and Karla Boluk (Managing Ethical Consumption in tourism), there is clear the needs to rethink classic definition of tourism. Many emerging sub-segments defied the connotation of mass-tourism or even sun-and-beach products over recent years. From dark to slum tourism, the notion of beautiness is experiencing substantial changes. For specialists as Weeden and Boluk, ethics cannot be applied in all contexts because what turns out legal in some nations are not in others. Despite the numerous studies focusing how tourism stimulates consumption are far from taking ethics as a serious option. At some extent, tourist destinations, as Weeden and Boluk put it, embrace some ethical values whether they can be commoditized or used to gain further advantages in an ever-changing market. This begs an interesting question, is the commercial nature of tourism divorced from ethics?

One of the aspects that undermined the role of ethics in tourism fields was the belief that responsibility is deemed as an individual stance (optional) to gain some certification schemes. In this vein, we are not legally pressed to adopt ethics in our professional life, unless it entails additional profits. What this book puts in straights is that "responsible tourism" is part of our moral duties as pundits but we are not forced by the law. A second more epistemological reasons lies in the fact, studies in tourism ethics are scattered or published in humanitarian journals more associated to philosophy, sociology or anthropology instead of coordinating all produced knowledge in only one magazine or platform:

What is unique about ethics is that more than any of these other fields of inquiry, it gets to the job of illuminating the tension that exists between what is good and bad, right and wrong, and authentic and inauthentic in tourism. It does this by forcing us to examine the human condition first, knowing something of ourselves, as a way to understanding tourism. (Preface Fennell 2014, XVI)

From a broader sense, Weeden & Boluk remind though sustainability has recently monopolized a great variety of research which focuses on the failure in developmental programs or negative effects of the industry in local communities, tourism-related policies are profit-centered. The questions whether the sphere of ethics is dissociated from consumption explain why tourists are often insensitive to Other's sufferings.

Other interesting points of convergence in this discussion are presented by Bianca Freire Medeiros, and Rodanthi Tzanelli. While the former in her book (Touring poverty) rationalizes tourism as a need to consume something different appealing to escapement, the latter discusses the problem of slum tourism from the angle of colonialism. What tourists consume not only is the others` suffering but in doing so, avoid their responsibilities to be part of a state which played a vital role ransacking the economies of Third World. Freire Medeiros rejects the possibilities slum tourism really helps others to get away from Favelas and slums, even the needs of selling poverty poses a much deeper ethical dilemma; if poverty becomes in the commodity of tourism, it will be never eradicated. Since commoditized to gain attractiveness, poverty idealizes the miserable conditions of exploitation favelados are facing daily. Beyond the ethical discussion to what extent slum-tourism helps residents to face poverty, Freire Medeiros argues convincingly that in the Favelas the nets of interactions lead to reify tourism as a mechanism to improve residents` lives but in doing so, it produces poverty. To understand this better let explain that in classical economy, commodities are the vital part of merchandise production. In Slum-tourism, the infrastructure, transport, restaurants, tour operators, tour-guides, and every service seems to be based on "the pauperization". The poverty plays a crucial role as a main attraction of these types of sites. Rather, Tzanelli`s insight are not provided by fieldwork (as the book presented by Medeiros) but from a visual ethnography on the cinematic representation of slums in movies entertainment industry. Her main outcome exhibits how the chief ideals and narratives of colonialism still operate through the lens of movies. Based on the examination of plots, she considers that tourists who visit slums are not trying to connect with others but reinforces their own romantic supremacy as white first world citizens. The other presents as a commodity used to reinforce democracy and capitalism as the best of the feasible realities. In a recent book, Korstanje dubbed the term "Thana-capitalism" to denote a new stage of production in globalized economies, where the society of risk as it was imagined by cultural sociologists sets the pace to a facet of consumption where death plays a crucial role. News of disasters, novels, realities, and other cultural entertainment programs reveal not only modern citizens developed a strange aversion to death, but they feel happiness from others` suffering because it is the only way to deride from death. In a climate of extreme competition legalized by social Darwinism, individualism prevails through the lens of consumption. As Korstanje adheres, in times of Thana capitalism there is no place for ethics, since the role of empathy is emptied. One of the best example to explain this further is the plot of Hunger Games, where capitol organizes the Games. In these spectacles of death, participants not only do not cooperate with others, they exaggerate their real probabilities to defeat. Only one can be the winner, and of course, the winner takes everything. This suggests that those material asymmetries which ideologically legitimizes the interests of elite are internalized by citizens as a natural-like situation (Korstanje, 2016b). This seems to be the reason why tourism has serious limitations to be an ethical activity.

CONCLUSION

Throughout this chapter review, we placed a hot debate on the role of globalization as a chief agent oriented to connect dissimilar economies into an all-encompassing system. The question whether tourism should be considered ethical or not still remains open. In days of Thana-Capitalism the suffering pivoted as the main commodity not only that helps structuring social institutions, but the necessary mediator between lay-people and their states. Far from being altered the conditions of exploitation inaugurated by neo-globalization after 90s decade has been enlarged. In order for the system not to collapse, the necessary fallouts as violence, riots, poverty and suffering are being emulated as criterion of attraction for tourist-gaze. This is exactly the point we do not stop consuming news containing images that can affect viewers` sensibility, but indeed we are eager to do it. As Maccannell observed, the limitations of ethics to be framed within consumption rests on the belief that there is a long-simmering divorce between what people wish and should to do. Since modern tourism is a profitable industry oriented to satisfy the hedonist drives which lead to a "pleasure-maximization logic", ethical rules only can be externally imposed by state. In times of our grand-parents, holidays represented a sacred space to be enjoyed in paradisiacal landscapes or sunbathing at a named beach. The chief concept to understand these holiday-makers in terms of Krippendorf was not only the needs of escapement, but also the concept of an apollonian sense of beautiness. This world has gone forever, and this gazing sets the pace to new connotation associated to tragedies, mass death, poverty and all types of human miseries. These death-seekers are in quest of others` suffering in order to confirm these privilege position as first world consumers. Although a complete psychological profile needs further explorations, the following scheme will serve to help understanding the psychology of death-seekers:

- They feel prone to witness events that not involve them directly. This type of vicarious empathy in rare occasions can be crystalized in real assistance to others;

- They valorise present times than past because they keep an ethnocentric viewpoint of events;
- Death seekers only embrace heritage to understand this time is the best of the possible realms;
- Dogmatic in their personality, they do not understand reality unless by their earlier cognitive frames;
- Sites of mass-death, disaster or suffering (Thana-Tourism) are often selected as the primary destinations for visiting in holidays;
- Since they are special, death consumers feel they have the right to interact with others well-skilled like them;
- Death seekers support social Darwinism where the survival of strongest is the main cultural value;
- Consuming others suffering they feel special, superior or more important;
- Frightful personalities that think the world is a dangerous place;
- Death seekers entertain witnessing how others struggle. Very open to mythical conflagrations as goodness against evilness, they symbolically associate death to "condemnation". For them, the correct persons should not die;
- Pathological problems to understand death;
- Regardless the political affiliation, they embrace "counterfeit politics", or the theories of conspiracy.

Last but not least, the concept of Thana-capitalism coheres with previous attempts to describe the expansion of Narcissist culture in the works early published by C. Lasch (1991) or the theory of other-oriented typology as it was formulated by David Riesman in his project, *A Lonely Crowd*. Though the concept of narcissism is still present within the current society of consumption, what Lasch and Riesman left behind was the role of death as a perfect symbolizer of the exclusion narcissism generates. Engaged in forms of spectacle, Thana-capitalism recycles the conditions which may be helpful for social change, into reified products audience witnesses through the lens of TV and Media.

REFERENCES

Altman, J. (1989). Tourism dilemmas for aboriginal Australians. *Annals of Tourism Research*, *16*(4), 456–476. doi:10.1016/0160-7383(89)90002-9

Alvarez, M., & Korzay, M. (2008). Influence o politics and media in the perceptions of Turkey as a tourism destination. *Tourism Review.*, *63*(2), 38–46. doi:10.1108/16605370810883932

Bauman, Z. (2000). *Globalization: The human consequences.* New York: Columbia University Press.

Capriello, A., & Rotherham, I. (2008). Farm attraction, networks and destination development: A case study of Sussex, England. *Tourism Review.*, *63*(2), 59–71. doi:10.1108/16605370810883950

Castaño, J. M., Moreno, A., & Crego, A. (2006). Factores psicosociales y formación de imágenes en el turismo urbano: Un estudio de caso sobre Madrid. *Pasos*, *4*(3), 287–299.

Comaroff, J. L., & Comaroff, J. (2009). *Ethnicity, Inc.* Chicago: University of Chicago Press. doi:10.7208/chicago/9780226114736.001.0001

Coronado, G. (2008). Insurgencia y Turismo: Reflexiones sobre el impacto del turista politizado en Chiapas. *Pasos*, *6*(1), 53–68.

Fennell, D. A. (2015). Ethics in Tourism. In *Education for Sustainability in Tourism* (pp. 45–57). Berlin: Springer. doi:10.1007/978-3-662-47470-9_3

Fonteles, J. O. (2004). *Tourism and Socio-enviromental Factors.* Sao Paulo: El Aleph.

Franch, M., Martini, U., Buffa, F., & Parisi, G. (2008). 4l tourism (landscape, leisure, learning and limit): Responding to new motivations and expectations of tourist to improve the competitiveness of alpine destination in a sustainable way. *Tourism Review.*, *63*(1), 4–14. doi:10.1108/16605370810861008

Garrod, B., & Fennell, D. A. (2004). An analysis of whalewatching codes of conduct. *Annals of Tourism Research*, *31*(2), 334–352. doi:10.1016/j.annals.2003.12.003

Heuman, D. (2005). Hospitality and reciprocity working tourist in Dominica. *Annals of Tourism Research*, *32*(2), 407–418. doi:10.1016/j.annals.2004.07.010

Holden, A. (2003). In need of new environmental ethics for Tourism?”-. *Annals of Tourism Research*, *30*(1), 94–108. doi:10.1016/S0160-7383(02)00030-0

Hultsman, J. (1995). Just tourism: An ethical framework. *Annals of Tourism Research*, *22*(3), 553–567. doi:10.1016/0160-7383(95)00011-T

Kadt, E. D. (1979). *Tourism. Passport to development? Perspectives on the social and cultural effects of tourism in developing countries.* Oxford, UK: Oxford University Press.

Kampaxi, O. (2008). Codes of Ethics in Tourism: Practices, theory and sythesis. *Annals of Tourism Research*, *35*(2), 607–608. doi:10.1016/j.annals.2007.09.005

Kastenholz, E., & Lopez de Almeida, A. (2008). Seasonality in Rural tourism – the case of North Portugal. *Tourism Review.*, *63*(2), 5–15. doi:10.1108/16605370810883905

Kidder, R. M. (2003). *How good people make tough choices: Resolving the ethical dilemmas of ethical living*. New York: Simon & Schuster.

Korstanje, M. (2012). Reconsidering cultural tourism: An anthropologists perspective. *Journal of Heritage Tourism*, *7*(2), 179–184. doi:10.1080/1743873X.2011.639883

Korstanje, M. E. (2015). *A Difficult World, examining the roots of capitalism*. New York: Nova Science Pubs.

Korstanje, M. E. (2016a). Pensando la hospitalidad. *Revista de Sociales y Jurídicas*, (11), 208-214.

Korstanje, M. E. (2016b). *The Rise of Thana Capitalism and Tourism*. Abingdon, UK: Routledge.

Korstanje, M. E., & Olsen, D. H. (2011). The discourse of risk in horror movies post 9/11: Hospitality and hostility in perspective. *International Journal of Tourism Anthropology*, *1*(3-4), 304–317. doi:10.1504/IJTA.2011.043712

Lasch, C. (1991). *The culture of narcissism: American life in an age of diminishing expectations*. New York: WW Norton & Company.

Lash, S., & Urry, J. (1994). *Economies of Signs and Space*. London: Theory, Culture & Society.

Lashley, C., & Morrison, A. (2001). *In the search of hospitality*. London: Butterworth Heinmann.

Lau, G., & Mckercher, B. (2006). Understanding tourist movement pattern in a destination: A GIS approach. *Tourism and Hospitality Research.*, *7*(1), 39–49. doi:10.1057/palgrave.thr.6050027

Lea, J. (1993). Tourism Development Ethics in the Third World. *Annals of Tourism Research*, *20*(4), 701–715. doi:10.1016/0160-7383(93)90092-H

Lynch, P. (2005). Sociological impressionism in a hospitality context. *Annals of Tourism Research*, *32*(3), 527–548. doi:10.1016/j.annals.2004.09.005

Mac-Beth, J. (2005). Towards an Ethics Platform in Tourism. *Annals of Tourism Research*, *32*(4), 962–984. doi:10.1016/j.annals.2004.11.005

Maccannell, D. (2011). *The Ethics of Sightseeing. Dean Maccannell*. Los Angeles, CA: University of California Press. doi:10.1525/california/9780520257825.001.0001

Malloy, D. C., & Fennell, D. A. (1998). Codes of ethics and tourism: An exploratory content analysis. *Tourism Management, 19*(5), 453–461. doi:10.1016/S0261-5177(98)00042-9

McMichael, P. (2016). *Development and social change: A global perspective.* Thousand Oaks, CA: Sage Publications.

McNaughton, D. (2006). The host as uninvited guest: Hospitality, violence and tourism. *Annals of Tourism Research, 33*(3), 645–665. doi:10.1016/j.annals.2006.03.015

Medeiros, B. F. (2015). *Touring Poverty*. Abingdon, UK: Routledge.

Nadeau, J., Heslop, L., OReilly, N., & Luk, P. (2008). Destination in a country image context. *Annals of Tourism Research, 35*(1), 84–106. doi:10.1016/j.annals.2007.06.012

Ohe, Y. (2010). Barriers to Change in Rural tourism. In Managing Change in Tourism: Creating opportunities – overcoming obstacles. Academic Press.

Riesman, D. (2001). *The lonely crowd.* New Haven, CT: Yale University Press.

Santana, A. (2006). *Antropología y Turismo*. Barcelona: Ariel.

Santos Filho, J. (n.d.). Hospitalidade no Brasil Imperio: a visao o naturalista George Gardner. *Revista Brasileira de Pesquisa em turismo, 2*(2), 3-19.

Snow, N. E. (2010). *Virtue as social intelligence: An empirically grounded theory*. Abingdon, UK: Routledge.

Sugden, R. (2005). *The Economics of Rights, Cooperation and Welfare*. Hampshire, UK: Palgrave Macmillan. doi:10.1057/9780230536791

Toribio Camargo, A., Castella Cordoba, P., & Serrano Orquin, I. (2005). Determinación de las preferencias de los clientes internacionales para la practica del turismo rural en la Republica de Cuba. *Pasos., 3*(2), 283–295.

Tzanelli, R. (2016). *Thanatourism and Cinematic Representations of Risk*. Abingdon, UK: Routledge.

Urry, J. (2002). *The Tourist Gaze*. London: Sage.

Waitt, G. (1999). Naturalizing the primitive: A critique of marketing Australias indigenous peoples as hunter-gatherers. *Tourism Geographies, 1*(2), 142–163. doi:10.1080/14616689908721306

Weeden, C., & Boluk, C. (2014). *Managing Ethical Consumption in Tourism*. New York: Routledge.

Žižek, S. (2008). *Violence: Six sideways reflections*. London: Verso.

ADDITIONAL READING

Altman, J. (1989). Tourism Dillemas for aboriginal Australians. *Annals of Tourism Research*, *16*(4), 456–476. doi:10.1016/0160-7383(89)90002-9

Augé, M. (1998). *El Viaje Imposible. El turismo y sus imágenes*. Barcelona: Editorial Gedisa.

Azeredo-Grunewald, R. (2002). Tourism and Cultural Revival. *Annals of Tourism Research*, *29*(4), 1004–1021. doi:10.1016/S0160-7383(02)00005-1

Bandyopadhyay, R., & Morais, D. (2005). Representative dissonance: Indias self and western image. *Annals of Tourism Research*, *32*(4), 1006–1021. doi:10.1016/j.annals.2005.02.002

Bauman, Z. (2007). *Consuming life*. Cambridge: Polity Press.

Bauman, Z. (2011). *Collateral damage: Social inequalities in a global age*. Cambridge: Polity Press.

Bauman, Z. (2013). *Consuming life*. New York: John Wiley & Sons.

Bourriaud, N., Schneider, C., & Herman, J. (2002). *Postproduction: culture as screenplay: how art reprograms the world*. New York: Lukas & Sternberg.

Busby, G., Korstanje, M. E., & Mansfield, C. (2011). Madrid: Literary fiction and the imaginary urban destination. *Journal of Tourism Consumption and Practice* Volume, 3(2).

Castel, R. (2010). *El ascenso de las incertidumbres: trabajo, protecciones, estatuto del individuo*. Buenos Aires: Fondo de Cultura Económica.

Castel, R. (2015). *La inseguridad social:¿ Qué es estar protegido?* Barcelona: Ediciones Manantial.

Clark, I. (2010). Colonial Tourism in Victoria, Australia in the 1840s: Georges augustus Robinson as a nascent tourist. *International Journal of Tourism Research*, *12*(5), 561–573.

Collier, S. J., & Ong, A. (2006). Global assemblages. *Theory, Culture & Society*, *23*(2/3), 399–401. doi:10.1177/026327640602300269

Comaroff, J. L., & Comaroff, J. (2009). *Ethnicity, Inc.* Chicago: University of Chicago Press. doi:10.7208/chicago/9780226114736.001.0001

Cuccia, T., & Cellini, R. (2007). Is cultural heritage really important for tourists? A contingent rating study. *Applied Economics, 39*(2), 261–271. doi:10.1080/00036840500427981

Davis, D., & Weiler, B. (1992). Kakadu National Park –Conflicts in a world heritage area. *Tourism Management, 13*(3), 313–320. doi:10.1016/0261-5177(92)90104-F

De Kadt, E. D. (1979). *Tourism. Passport to development? Perspectives on the social and cultural effects of tourism in developing countries.* Oxford: Oxford University Press for World Bank and UNESCO.

Debord, G. (1983). *The society of the spectacle.* Detroit: Black and Red.

Donohue, K. G. (2003). *Freedom from Want.* Baltimore: John Hopkins University.

Du Cros, H. (2001). A new model to assist in planning for sustainable cultural heritage tourism. *International Journal of Tourism Research, 3*(2), 165–170. doi:10.1002/jtr.297

Duman, T. & Kozak M. (2009). "The Turkish Tourism Product: differentiation and Competitiveness". *Anatolia, an international journal of Tourism and Hospitality Research.* 21 (1): 89-106.

Escobar, A. (1988). Power and visibility: Development and the invention and management of the Third World. *Cultural Anthropology, 3*(4), 428–443. doi:10.1525/can.1988.3.4.02a00060

Escobar, A. (1991). Anthropology and the development encounter: The making and marketing of development anthropology. *American Ethnologist, 18*(4), 658–682. doi:10.1525/ae.1991.18.4.02a00020

Escobar, A. (1992). Imagining a post-development era? Critical thought, development and social movements. *Social Text,* (31/32): 20–56. doi:10.2307/466217

Escobar, A. (2011). *Encountering development: The making and unmaking of the Third World.* Princeton University Press.

Korstanje, M. E. (2012). Reconsidering cultural tourism: An anthropologists perspective. *Journal of Heritage Tourism, 7*(2), 179–184. doi:10.1080/1743873X.2011.639883

Korstanje, M. E. (2015). *A Difficult World. Examining the Roots of Capitalism.* New York: Nova Science Publishers.

Korstanje, M. E., & de Escalona, F. M. (2014). How much mobile we are? *Cultural Anthropology, 175*, 185.

Korstanje, M. E., Tzanelli, R., & Clayton, A. (2014). Brazilian World cup 2014: Terrorism, tourism, and social conflict. *Event Management, 18*(4), 487–491. doi:10.3727/152599514X14143427352391

Lasch, C. (1991). *The culture of narcissism: American life in an age of diminishing expectations*. New York: Norton & WW Company.

Lash, S., & Urry, J. (1993). *Economies of signs and space* (Vol. 26). London: Sage.

MacCannell, D. (1973). Staged authenticity: Arrangements of social space in tourist settings. *American Journal of Sociology, 79*(3), 589–603. doi:10.1086/225585

MacCannell, D. (1976). *The tourist: A new theory of the leisure class*. Berkeley: University of California Press.

MacCannell, D. (1984). Reconstructed ethnicity tourism and cultural identity in third world communities. *Annals of Tourism Research, 11*(3), 375–391. doi:10.1016/0160-7383(84)90028-8

MacCannell, D. (1988) "Turismo e Identidad [Tourism & Identity], In Teodorov Tzvetan. Madrid: Juncar Edition.

MacCannell, D. (1992). *Empty meeting grounds: The tourist papers*. London: Routledge. doi:10.4324/9780203412145

MacCannell, D. (2001). Tourist agency. *Tourist Studies, 1*(1), 23–37. doi:10.1177/146879760100100102

Riesman, D. (2001). *The lonely crowd*. Ithaca: Yale University Press.

Rifkin, J. (1995). *The end of work: Technology, jobs, and your future*. New York: Putnam.

Ritzer, G., & Liska, A. (1997). McDisneyization" and "Post-Tourism": complementary perspectives on contemporary tourism. Touring cultures: Transformations of travel and theory, 96-109.

Ryan, C., & Huyton, J. (2002). Tourist and aboriginal people. *Annals of Tourism Research, 29*(3), 631–647. doi:10.1016/S0160-7383(01)00073-1

Sennett, R. (2011). *The corrosion of character: The personal consequences of work in the new capitalism*. New York: WW Norton & Company.

KEY TERMS AND DEFINITIONS

Consumption: In sociology consumption was defined as the touchstone of capitalist system, which consisted in as a central every-day life form of identity or class structuration.

Dark Tourism: This is a subtype of tourism characterized by the consumption of death or the interests for visiting spaces of mass death and disasters.

Death: This is the termination or end of all biological functions. Within philosophy, the concern for death was the epicenter for the rise and expansion of Existentialism.

Globalization: This can be defined as an economic project of social integration among nations.

Ideology: It exhibits the collection of allegories, ideas and beliefs that conform the social ethos. Though ideology took different meanings depending on the sociological wave, Marxists argue that ideology works as a mechanism of social control.

Poverty: Signals to the scarcity of people or some classes which lacks of the necessary resources or material possession to prosper in the life.

Conclusion

DARK TOURISM AND SOCIETY

With the turn of the century, humankind experienced a set of unexpected risks, threats and the rise of a climate of uncertainness that showed how vulnerable West was. In this context, tourism seems not to be an exception. The tourism industry has been hurt by external circumstances which engendered negative trends. Although the theory of risk perception, which was originated by psychology and sociology four decades back, was familiar to tourism researchers, the attack on World Trade Center in New York inaugurated a new era where the notion of risk played a vital role in the popular opinion. Some studies emphasized on the needs of understanding the nature of risks, as well as adopting a classificatory system to handle situations which may very well threaten the organic image of international tourist destinations. Of course, these specialists agree not only terrorism but also other global risks as virus outbreaks, natural disasters or political instability resonates considerably in popular parlance leading tourism to the economic stagnant (Lepp & Gibson, 2003; Larsen, 2007; Larsen et al., 2007; Korstanje, 2011; Korstanje & Clayton, 2012).

As Faulkner (2001) puts it, the turbulent conjuncture prompted after 2001 posed a great challenge for policy makers who was hovering between developing rational programs in the lines of disaster-management or adopting tourism as an instrument of resilience in post-disaster zones. From that moment onwards, specialists and pundits dangled the possibility to adopt rationality in predicting hypothetical realms. By the articulation of different software and mathematical algorithms, the net of experts constructed conceptual models to forecast potential disasters, and in this way, preventing the dark side of risks and their negative effects in the industry. Gradually the theory of risk not only captivated the attention of tourism scholars but paved the ways for the formation of a precautionary principle aimed at protecting tourism from external and extra-systemic dangers (Cooper & Hall, 2008). Even, some critical writers envisaged the end of tourism in the classic forms we know as a reaction to the globalize forces of capitalism, which subordinated local economies to a salient cultural matrix (Gale, 2009; Tribe, 2009; Korstanje 2016; Tzanelli, 2016).

The atmosphere of apocalypticism that the end of millennium started coincided with the urgency of adopting a new paradigm in tourism-management (Becken & Hughey, 2013). With the benefits of hindsight, one of the main limitations of tourism management rests on its abstract and speculative nature around the meaning of risk in itself. The fact is that risks are "abstract dangers", which may concrete in real threats following a line of probabilities. Risks almost always move in the horizon of probabilities and sometimes never take hit in the real world (Korstanje, 2011). This moot point represented a serious epistemological problem for risk perception theory given the successive failures in preventing the succession of the disaster which took room after 2001. Far from situating as an efficient mechanism to prevent future hazard, risk perception theory as it was formulated in tourism research limited to make opinion polls or conducting questionnaires to measure the major risks tourists feel whereas they are traveling abroad. As we shall see in this chapter, in the threshold of time, risk-perception theory sets the pace to *dark-management* as a platform to helps survivors to reconstruct their communities.

Other more radical studies focused on the role of risk perception as a disciplinary mechanism of control. Equally important, the philosophical dichotomy revolving around the creative-destruction, which was one of the touchstones of liberal economy paved the ways for the adoption of economic policies otherwise would be rejected by citizenry (Klein, 2007; Bianchi, 2006; Korstanje, 2011). Through the articulation of fear-factor, governments somehow curb the check-and-balance systems established in democratic societies, to encourage ethnocentric and chauvinist expressions of nationalisms.

The failures of risk theory to prevent the worst was consonant with the needs of new explanations respecting to why rationality should be prioritized as a mainstream cultural value to implement sustainable policies. In consequence, the theory of governance promptly gained further traction in academic circles not only in Europe and the United States but also in Asia, Latin America and Oceania as well (Scott, Raggio & Cooper, 2008; Bramwell & Lane, 2011; Laws, 2011). Basically, the notion of governance not only evoked a rational paradigm, which is based on the western means-and-ends logic, but (following Michael Hall) also it signals to public policy top take the conception of theory as a policy, and in this way, producing a more sustainable form of tourism (Hall, 2011).

As the previous backdrop, it is plain that tourism-related researchers devoted their time in reaching a model of adaptancy that helps tourism to mitigate the negative effects of climate change, as well as the rise and expansion of radicalized cells as ISIS or Al-Qaeda or any other danger which jeopardizes the industry worldwide. All these academic positions confirmed what Cass Sunstein (2003; 2005) dubbed as "precautionary platform", which is intended to stave off disasters or risky situation before they occur. Of course, As Sunstein noted, this stance has no few problems at the time of evaluating the potential risks society faces objectively. Here two assumptions should be made. On the one hand, we are emotionally determined by our inner-life, which sometimes leads to making wrong decisions or by neglecting some minor risks while others, which turns of high impact, are ignored. On another, the risk is socially constructed and what is a major problem for one society can be a silly thing for others. This raises the question to what extent dark tourism offers the solution to escape the precautionary platform´s promises. Since the future remains inexpugnable, as some studies emphasized, for rational logic, the best course of action corresponds to ipso-facto actions followed after the disaster.

Over the recent decades, the consuming of dark sites was aimed to fulfill the gap the theory of governance and risk perception left. As we have enumerated and defined in several times in this book, dark tourism should be understood as an activity which consists in visiting spaces of death, mourning or mass-suffering in post-disaster or any other contexts. While academicians have not reached consensus in regards to a shared definition of the issue, no less true is that some policy makers saw in dark tourism an efficient instrument to accelerate the times in the recovery process after disasters (Gotham, 2007; Korstanje, 2011). At a first instance, tourism was defined as an instrument of resiliency contributing to effaced communities to overcome from their adversities (Kang et al, 2012; Korstanje & Ivanov, 2012). But this begs a more than intriguing question, what is dark tourism?

What Is Dark Tourism?

Broadly speaking, dark tourism should be considered as the prone to visit macabre spaces of consumption where mass death and suffering prevail. These types of sites oscillate from sites memorizing disasters, genocides or any other cruel act that vulnerated the ontological security of humankind towards historical battles or haunted houses. The vast ranges of activities the term dark tourism encompass seems to be one of the main problems to unify a shared methodology at the time of field-working (Stone, 2011). For the sake of clarity, proponents of dark tourism acknowledge that there is interesting historical evidence that suggests similarly-minded practices existed in ancient times or Medieval Age (Stone, 2012). For Phillip Stone, one of the authoritative voices in dark tourism fields, the phenomenon should be interpreted as an anthropological attempt to domesticate death not only imagining the proper finitude but also experimenting with sensations that reproduce a long-lasting climate of empathy with the alterity (Stone, 2011; Stone, 2012; Stone & Sharpley, 2008).

As the previous argument given, Stone pivots in the doorstep of a new paradigm to understand this slippery matter, which combines heritage with psychological drives to theorize on death and traumatic event. Though much should be written on dark tourism, which as a discipline remains in its infancy, two contrasting academic waves collide. While some scholars concentrate efforts to see dark tourism as an anthropological attempt to discipline death, or being in contact with other´s death (Stone, 2012; Stone & Sharpley, 2008; Stone 2011; Hartmann, 2014; Lennon & Foley, 2000), others voices, more oriented to cultural management paradigm, frame dark tourism as an inherent side of heritage (Strange & Kempa, 2003; Timothy & Boyd, 2006; Kang et al, 2006; Cohen 2011). For the latter, dark tourism should be understood as a fertile ground for affected communities to gain further investors and capital intended to accelerate the recovery process time. At some extent, the understanding of traumatic experiences is re-channeled by circuits of consumption that enhance not only the solidarity among survivors or affected community but also social cohesion (Jamal & Lelo, 2011).

In a seminal book, prefaced by Kai Erikson, Covenry, Corsane & David (2014) bring reflection on the possibility to define dark tourism as a "displaced heritage", which means that while heritage still is at risk in post-disaster contexts no less true is that memorizing trauma is a valid source to produce a new (displaced) heritage. Editors go on to say that:

Disasters can also make us better informed about the heritage we have lost, or are losing, leading to attempts to better preserve what remains by creating new mechanisms to recognize and protect natural and cultural heritage resources. (Covenry, Corsane, & David 2014, p. 2)

As stated in the above citation, they remind that we are being constructed all the time socially, negotiating the border of our own identity with others, and the context. Heritage does not seem to be an exemption because it is formed by everyday objects, elements, and customs entirely-patched to offer a resilient answer to trauma. Therefore, one might speculate that disasters and heritage are inextricably intertwined. In earlier approaches, Erik H Cohen called the attention to the benefits of dark tourism as a pedagogic platform, which would be helpful for survivors to understand the lesson left by disaster (Cohen, 2011) while Biran, Poria and Oren (2011) focused on Auschwitz-Birkenau concentration camp as an intersection between symbolic meaning articulated in a space with personal experiences, motivation and visitors interpretation. In this vein, some specialists, following their applied research outcomes, indicate that dark tourism should be framed as a heritage-experience instead of a form of experimenting with future death.

Though all these studies, in a greater or lesser extent, shed light on the philosophical nature of dark tourism, over recent years some critiques were oriented to point out that there would be some conceptual caveats in adopting dark tourism as heritage simply because the memorized disaster can be repeated. To put this slightly in other terms, the specialized literature starts from the premise that ancient forms of dark tourism have been found in the past, as well as in other cultures. This proofs, without qualms, that the needs of mediating with death are a universal phenomenon. Secondly, dark tourism not only allows the organization of territory, helping or allocating victims of disasters in better households but also gives to the community a lesson in order for the next disaster to be eluded.

Last but not least, the theory of Dark-Tourism-as-heritage over-valorizes the psychological experience as the only valid source for information derived from applied research. The concept of empirical investigation associates erroneously to what tourists say or state. As a side of heritage, dark tourism engages the self with the commoditization of space while bringing further profits for locals and survivors. Hence the phenomena may be instrumentalised as a mechanism of recovery in post-disaster environments.

Most certainly, this reasoning mentioned above shows some conceptual limitations which merit to be discussed. A first glimpse suggests that the concept of authenticity, which is enrooted in the definition of heritage, is very hard to grasp. As Dean McConnell observed, while visitors are in quest of consuming authenticity what they get is the opposite. The evolution of staged-authentic corresponds with the emotional world of tourists. This creates a paradox because people consuming heritage is far from being cognizant what they gaze is a commoditized product. With this concern in mind, it is safe to say that a whole portion of publications appeals to the use and abuse of open-ended questionnaires or interviews to gather information, which later is tabulated at the cabinet. The formulation of questions, though objectively expressed, are intended to know what tourists feel or think respecting to the visited sites. The main problem with the employment of this instrument rests on the fact interviewees lie or simply are not familiar with their psychological emotions. Although many of the produced knowledge aims to outline that visitors are in search of heritage consumption, likely this was only the peak of the iceberg. Secondly and likely most important, there is a misunderstanding whether we take the medieval pilgrims as an evidence medieval travelers visited the site of dark tourism in other times. In fact, the specialized literature in ancient history reveals that pilgrims to Saint's tombs have nothing to do with modern dark tourism because of two main reasons. First of all, ancient travelers were moved by personal sickness, promises, and any other reasons which were enrooted in the individual sacrifice. Rather, modern tourism is based on the spirit of curiosity or pleasure maximization. All these issues have been tackled off in a new emergent book, which is recently published by a high-impact publisher, Routledge.

In the next section, we shall place the book *Dark Tourism, practice and interpretation* under the critical lens of scrutiny. In this review, we conclude that dark tourism evokes a much wider social change, which involves not only leisure practices, but also other social institutions. We are passing to a new stage of capitalism, which we have dubbed as *Thana Capitalism* (for further details see Korstanje, 2016a).

Theory and Practice

The fourteen chapters gathered by editors in this book confront with the different uses and interpretations of dark tourism within specialized literature. It continues the tradition of dark tourism as heritage, which was started by Senior Researchers Phillip Stone and Richard Sharply among others highly-esteemed specialists.

In this book, Hooper and Lennon attempt to reconcile theoretically what in their insights are two contrasting terms, the *darkness,* and *tourism.* In spite of the proliferation of published books, papers and conferences in this problematic, this question remains open to date. This suggests that it is time to reconsider the nature of tourism as the selfish industry, which is aimed at maximizing consumers' pleasure, commodities the alterity. This happens not only because the patterns of consumption today were radically changed towards more sustainable forms, but also because the modern tourists seem to be committed to noble causes. Here a more than pungent question surfaces, what are the real motivation of dark tourists?

Dark tourism should be defined as a recently-born tendency where tourists visit spaces of mass-death, suffering or mourning, in order to be in contact with human vulnerability. The existential fragility of others reminds how the proper life should be reinterpreted, and of course this is one of the main aspects that molds the epistemological borders of dark tourism. Such a tendency created a diversification of sites, which spans from the classic Auschwitz to new emergent zones as Ground Zero in New York. In this respect, researchers have faced serious problems to coordinate their results towards unified models that help to obtain a better understanding of this slippery matter. Editors emphasize that dark tourism always existed not matter the times or cultures, this represents an anthropological drive. Hopper & Lennon successfully set forward an interesting philosophical discussion about the ethics of dark tourism and dark tourism as a consumed heritage. What in modern times happens was that the curiosity for death was commoditized according to new lifestyles and frames. Here two important clarifications should be done. Editors lament how the attention given media and journalism for the theme exhibits not only the rise of applied research, which is captivating the attention of an ever-increasing volume of policy-makers and practitioners but also its Aquila's tendon. In fact, the knowledge production was dispersed according to an economic-centric viewpoint, which is more interested in promoting dark tourism sites instead of understanding the reasons behind. The needs for enhancing profits should be morally reconciled by the needs of memorizing death or at least to what extent the spectacles offered by these sites represents the real facts, or the background earlier than the disaster hits the community. Though these points are not being clearly answered throughout the text, it is evident that both, practices which signal to how dark tourism is managed or performed and interpretation, which reveals tourists' motivations and expectancies, should be ingrained into an all-encompassing model. Methodologically speaking, the investigations selected painstakingly by Hooper and Lennon have been done in basis with interviews, or self-ethnographies conducted in the fieldwork.

Equally important, the chapters which conform this reviewed project can be separately read, but they can be grouped in three main relevant subthemes, *epistemology*, which is based on much deeper interrogations of dark tourism as a new sub-discipline, *visitors' motivation or expectancies*, wherein there are some interesting chapters originally concerned by site conservation issues, and finally, the *commodification of death,* which results in the convergence of politics with the needs to prevent a similar disaster in the years to come.

The first chapter (elegantly written by Ashworth & Tunbridge) evaluates the different definitions objecting that there are a lot of like-minded terms which are used in the fieldwork, such as danger-tourism, battlefield tourism, and disaster-tourism. Secondly, Ria Dunkley brilliantly revolves around the needs of thermalizing death as the symbolical epicenter of dark tourism. In third, Sharpley and Friedrich acknowledge that the wider diffusion of the issue has created some discrepancies at the time of defining what dark tourism means but these obstacles can be overcome when the site connects with educators, policymakers, and other stakeholders. From fourth fifth to seventh chapters, exerts a radical criticism to dark tourism as heritage industry, where the other's suffering is spectacular iced. Eight and nine chapters, instead, emphasize on the intersection of horror and macabre, which creates a spectacle of cruelty.

After further reading, Hopper and Lennon dissect the commoditization of death, articulating interesting source of consumption, not to mention the economic support to affected communities, but at the same time, discussing the visitor's experience as the centerpiece of applied research. For the sake of clarity, we like to delve into the last chapter, authored by Glenn Hooper, who presents a provoking study-case based in Rio de Janeiro Brazil. We say provoking because of this study case, far from being a typical museum, refers to favela tours which assume that slumming and dark consumption are part of the same phenomenon. One of the risks of dark tourism consists in the spectacle of disasters, which enthralls some events or reasons while others are covered.

Though we have been benevolent with this review on the basis of the high-quality found in the book, no less true is that two important caveats should be stressed. First and most important, there is no archeological evidence that proof dark tourism was a timeless drive, which was practiced by other cultures. Though the curiosity for death is enrooted in humankind, dark tourism surfaces in the postmodernity as a result of substantial changes in how the otherness is constructed. Secondly, as we widely criticized in my recently-published book *The Rise of Thana Capitalism and Tourism* (Korstanje 2016a; 2016b), there is methodological myopia to take what tourists think as the only source towards the truth. Sometimes, interviewees lie or simply are emotionally incognizant of their inner-life. To our end, *dark tourism* not only interrogates on the changes towards new lifestyles, which agree with other institutions within society but also expresses the upsurge of a new capitalism where the curiosity for death is the main commodity to be exchanged, *Thana-Capitalism*. Far from being emphatic with other's suffering, it reinforces a sacred aura, which situates Spector-ship as a special privilege class. Though news-containing-death disturbs the sensibility of a global audience, paradoxically they cannot stop consuming them. Scholarship should continue such a heated discussion in the years to come.

Death, Society, and Heritage

The question whether dark tourism captivates the attention of countless scholars remains open, but as M Buda critically discussed, cultural studies in general and psychoanalysis, in particular, have much to say in this respect. Most likely, by its complexity, or technical jargonism, tourism scholars remain unfamiliar with the advances of psychoanalysis worldwide. Precisely, it is unfortunate that this discipline fails to be taken into consideration by Academia when touring and tourism are indistinctively based on the much deeper emotional basis. Given this, Buda reflections on the possibility to define dark tourism within the frame of *affective tourism*. Per her viewpoint, the sentiment of fear or anger not only engage with special borders, but activates personal traumas which are channeled through death drive. At some extent, the influence of language, culture and the biography of self-delineate the contours of experience, leading us to the correct decision. When we choose to visit a tourist destination, glossing over other options, our emotional inner-world bespeaks on behalf of us. Therefore, applied research in dark tourism should abandon the macro-structural approaches that are intrusive or even obscure more than they clarify. Instead, researchers should adopt a minimalist stance reconstructing a valid instrument to expand the current understanding of such a deep-seated issue (Buda, 2015).

In several parts of this concluding chapter, we have evidenced our discontent for the theory of heritage finely-ingrained in dark tourism studies. Nonetheless, further studies reveal that we are in the correct direction. R. Tzanelli (2013) argues convincingly that state poses heritage as a disciplinary mechanism of control, which legitimates the good-exchange. Starting from the premise that heritage organizes the modern consumption, Tzanelli contends that disperse elements as crafts, lore, and customs are organized in an all-encompassing platform to be consumed by first world tourists on the site. For Tzanelli, Weber was right at the time of anticipating "the disenchantment of world" which is today orchestrated by the imposition of cinema and other visual landscapes (Tzanelli 2013). Of course, following her viewpoint, dark tourism seems not to be an exception. In dialogue with Lancaster School and

J. Urry, Tzanelli offers an interesting cultural explanation of dark tourism which merits to be heard. Though we must accept the interests for others´ death coincides with a global lifestyle of consumption, no less true is that it stems from the colonial past. Surfaced over the recent decades as one of the postmodern trends of leisure consumption, dark tourism announces a turning point the distance between sightseers and natives is being blurred. At the time, creativity permits the destruction of obsolete structures, in the same way, Tzanelli adds, disaster takes hit communities. In the public opinion, dark tourism alludes to a climate of human insensibility which was replaced by media consumption. Not only this suggests that the culture of disasters (encouraged by dark tourism) allows the introduction of economic policies in any other way would be rejected by society, but it constructs a global landscape, which set up in first-world nations, resonates the lifestyle of tourism-receiving countries. At some extent, capitalism successfully recycled itself through the disasters and misery it generated in the past, but avoiding its ethical responsibilities for that. While Colonial rule subdued many of the poor countries during nineteen century following the logic of avarice and greed, now those tourists who come from these colonial states avoid their moral responsibilities for what their states have done.

In some concerns, Joy Sather-Wagstaff agrees with Tzanelli, but in others, her diagnosis is based on the political uses of heritage, in imposing a partial truth of the traumatic event. Sather-Wagstaff insists in considering heritage as a "commoditized story" of facts which may be politically tergiversated for status quo to prevent social change. In its alienation nature, hence heritage needs from an externally-designed discourse, which is oriented to ossify the critical consciousness of lay citizens. With strong cases in the sites of dark tourism, Sather-Wagstaff collects her experience of personal ethnographies (for example in Ground-zero). The problem of authenticity as it was put by MacCannell is a futile discussion. Per her outcomes, while the psychological trauma tends to equal human beings inegalitarian conditions before the disaster, heritage leads them to "ethnocentrism". Any attempt to rememorize the tragedy, which entails a loss, activates spirituality to cause an atmosphere of cohesion among survivors, but once time elapsed, there are serious risks such a gap would be fulfilled by allegorical discourses confirmed by politicians and officialdom. Sather-Wagstaff says that:

Sites of historical and cultural importance that represent violent events are particularly prone to a social misunderstanding about their emergence; it is believed that they have come into existence only through the events that take place at particular location: war results in battlefields, genocides produce mass graves, the assassination site of a political leader delineates a national sacred place. However, historical commemorative places are not made as important sites simply because of the events that may physically mark them as distinct places through bloodshed or the destruction of building or landscapes. These places are made through ongoing human practices in time, and I argue, across multiple spaces and places. (Sather-Wagstaff, 2011, p. 47)

However, Sather-Wagstaff surmises the importance of dark tourism as a bridge between emotionality and empathy with the other´s pain. All we, as humans, are equals before death, and therefore, we weave nets of solidarity to understand the feelings of alterity. Given the problem in these terms, she, as good ethnographer, captivates the interests at play in the formation of Ground-Zero, which was rememorized as a founding event for New York City. Dark tourism, after all, seems to be a social construal aimed at serving as a catalyst for the self to mediate successfully with memory and future. Her biography was in some senses affected by what happen in New York in September of 2001. For that reason, Sather-Wagstaff interrogates for their genuine feelings and to what extent marketing and advertising can commoditize them. It is truthful that many disasters which span from Hiroshima to New Orleans, are sold and exchanged as commodities for offering entertainment to a globalized spectatorship. However, there are some exceptional events as 9/11 which inaugurated new experiences. While politicians attempt to impose a biased image of the traumatizing event, which is crystallized by the heritage, dark tourism takes many shapes to overcome the obstacle of American ethnocentrism. In this respect, in post-disaster context, the monopoly of heritage should be disputed, negotiated and agreed among all involved stakeholders, because each one provides its meaning of the event. In her study case, Sather-Wagstaff adds, which is associated to ground-zero, each part imposed a contrasting position respecting to the possibility to reconstruct the space where World Trade Center laid. Such a discrepancy was withered away when the government imposed its one-sided vision. The contributions left by Tzanelli and Sather-Wagstaff are of paramount importance to the present final chapter. First and foremost, we are emotionally conditioned to idealize events, situations in the context of an emergency. Not surprisingly, almost all our beliefs, memories and stereotypes are founded and molded by the fantasy. Though dark tourism has proved to be an efficient platform towards recovery, no less true is that once heritage situated as the only explanation of facts, the probabilities the same disaster repeats are higher. Secondly, the emergence of a new post-disaster marketing, which is oriented to assist others emotionally, and not to enhance the investors' profits is more than necessary.

The Emergence of Post-Disaster Marketing

Over the recent decades, marketing-led efforts were adopted to tourism not only to boost the competition among destinations but also following social purposes (Hall 2014). At a closer look, the history of marketing reveals not only it derives from the warfare tactics developed after WWII. In fact, marketing as it was framed within tourism-related studies contributed to poverty relief and the advance of many under-developed economies worldwide (Aboutadeli, 2016). It is important not to lose the sight tourism, and hospitality are motors of a big services industry which contribute considerably to the creation of jobs, as well as revitalizing local and peripheral economies. In the preface of their book, *Strategic Tools and Methods for Promoting Hospitality and Tourism Services,* Nedelea, Korstanje, and George valorize not only the potentiality of marketing in giving secure information in a context of uncertainness, which will be helpful in the decision making process, but creating a symbolic bridge of empathy with the others' suffering. In this vein, one of the paradoxes of "rational planning" consists of getting unexpected outcomes, but the collateral damages induced by bad marketing. We need the rise of a more ethical marketing to boost local forms of production and peripheral economies.

In his book *Ethics of Sightseeing,* Dean MacCannell wrote that subdued in the roots of instrumentality, taking the others as a factor of pleasure-maximization, the guest and host encounter is emptied unless ethics to be introduced there as a mediator between tourists and what they watch. Beyond the precepts of Marketing, Maccannell initiates a hot debate by discussing the intersection of global modernity with tourism critically. His main goals are associated to forge a more "ethnic tourist", in the same line of Sather-Wagstaff or Tzanelli. Rather, MacCannell acknowledges unless we overcome the vicious circles of culturalism, we would be unable to change the current epistemologies around the otherness. In fact, what is more important, the existent epistemological view of the other should be considerably revisited. Though the science has advanced so much in the recent centuries, humanism has undermined. Equally important once a new technique is discovered, we must interrogate on the sense it gives to human acts.

As the previous argument given, Maccannell adheres to the thesis that tourism opens a double dialogical frame where we see others at the same time these others are watching us. In global capitalism, lay-people are framed and symbolically connected to a hermeneutical interpretation that is subordinated to a much deeper cultural matrix that precedes behavior. Since we effort to behave individually, we are more pressed off our cultural background. More interesting in the philosophy of tourism than in consumption-related issues, in the *Ethics of Sightseeing* Maccannell abrogates for new ways of connecting with the alterity. Following his classic theory, where he claims tourism serves in the same way totem sorts the tribal life, he retains some concerns respecting the gap left by the end of religion would be filled by fictional allegories as tourism and leisure. Tourism not only follows an alienation nature for workers but also enables a cathartic experience between the (repressed) self and the otherness. Citing the advance of psychoanalysis, where we move by an internal social consciousness, which is constrained (repressed) by the imposed rule,

MacCannell is convinced tourists see in others what remains inexpugnable in them. This explains at least his original concerns about staged authenticity and modern consumption, but at the same time lay the foundations for a new ethics in tourism fields. In so doing, Maccannell is interested in developing the ethic of sightseeing, not tourism. "Please note this is an ethics of sightseeing, not of tourism, a much broader topic that includes sightseeing. I anticipate it will be misread as implying more". This begs an interesting question which is not formulated explicitly, does it mean tourism follows an unethical logic?

Toying with the belief that Baudrillard was partially right, he introduces a more than innovating thesis. The monopoly of the market on hands of private sector appears to be changing the geographies of cultures, accelerating not only sense of spaces but individual behavior. In consequence, lay citizens undergo an ever increasing state of fragmentation which engenders some cleavages between the rule and ethics. The tourist experience appears to be impossible without the presence of the other. If excluded, the sense of reality turns in a *pseudo-reality.* Today's tourists, unfortunately, are moved by selfish motives, not only motivated by the consumption of fictional experiences but meeting their cultural dreams of being in contact with the non-western other. Recently, modernity has blurred the borders between evil and good since altruist projects as Eco-risk policies are intended to amass further profits and wealth -instead of protecting the planet. Confronting with Dark Tourism, Maccannell observes that the spectacle of others' suffering become in the touchstone of capitalism, where the alterity is subordinated to maximize my pleasure. The sensibility is the only way to put oneself in the place of others. This provides an exchange between actors that gives origin to solidarity. As Freudian analysts agreed, psychoanalysis amply showed how dreams as souvenirs represent an illusory aspect of reality, which depends on the value given to the object. Fetishism, to cut a long story short, mediates between the self and its fantasy, at the time, the principle of reality fades away. While we are touring in fictional landscapes, tourism exploits the others´ biographies sublimating them as part of a culture of entertainment. Therefore, a more ethnic sightseeing should replace modern standardized tourism. Nonetheless, the problem seems to be that the human sensibility set the pace to the utopia of consumption. As we have discussed the advance of MacCannell for a more ethnic sightseeing, what are opportunities and challenges of dark tourism in the years to come?

CONCLUSION

After further discussion, this corollary theoretically validates two significant assumptions. On the one hand, the expansion of capitalism, which paved the conditions of exploitation to agrarian cultures, adjoined to the current economic problems has made this world an insecure place to live. We are bombarded daily with news that portrays landscapes of trauma, violence and course disasters. Following this, it is important to not the patterns of holiday-making seems to be changing towards more macabre forms. If our grandparents enjoyed from a pharisaical island in the Caribe, now new more morbid forms of consumption are surfaced. To the dark tourism, which was our common theme in this book other macabre trends as slum-tourism, bottom-tourism or even war-tourism are offered to citizens who live in first world cities. Is this a sign of sadism, which was historically repressed in Western capitalism, or simply a form of understanding death in a secularized society?

In the mid of this mayhem, many policy makers interrogated on the needs of adopting a post-disaster marketing model to ameliorate the effects of unseen risks. If the current theoretical framework well established earlier than 90s decade appealed to *precautionary principle* as a valid conduit to protect tourism industry, now it is looming a grim future. Not only climate change has ceased to be a futurist threat to be part of our day-to-day life, but policies in tourism industries are posted to recycle, not to prevent. Post-disaster marketing seems to be oriented to help, (not to protect) residents from the fury of nature as well as taking advantages of the strengths that trigger the process of resilience. In this vein, since dark tourism, which is a new form of thematized misfortune or the run-a-away capitalism, accelerates the timeframe and conditions of recovery, further questions emerge respecting how ethical the process is. Besides, while any disaster opens the doors for new opportunities to embrace social change, no less true is that elite devotes their resorts to prevent such a force. As Tzanelli, MacCannell and Sather-Wagstaff painstakingly addressed, this is the reason why constrained forms of consumption as heritage alludes to rememorize a partial explanation of the event. The abuse of heritage covers partially the responsibilities of those who keep the symbolical and cultural means to monopolize the truth. Given that, the probabilities the same event repeats in the near future seems to be a question of time. We do thank not only IGI Global for the opportunity to publish this book with them, but also all involving international scholars who contributed a chapter. Last but not least, as stated in *The Rise of Thana Capitalism and Tourism* (Korstanje, 2016), it is important to reconsider the recently-laden changes in tourism industry reflects wider alterations in the lifestyle and the forms of consumption. Dark tourism expresses the upsurge of a new capitalism where the other's death is the main commodity to be exchanged, *Thana-Capitalism*. Far from being emphatic with other's suffering, it reinforces a sacred aura, which situates Spector-ship as a special privileged class. Though news-containing-death disturbs the sensibility of a global audience, paradoxically they cannot stop consuming them. Scholarship should continue such a heated discussion in future layouts.

Maximiliano E. Korstanje
University of Palermo, Argentina

Babu P. George
Fort Hays State University, USA

REFERENCES

Aboutalebi, R. (2016). Failure avoidance in the implementation of tourism and hospitalities strategies. In M. Korstanje & B. George (Eds.), *Strategic Tools and methods for promoting hospitality and tourism services* (p. 90). Hershey, PA: IGI Global. doi:10.4018/978-1-4666-9761-4.ch005

Becken, S., & Hughey, K. F. (2013). Linking tourism into emergency management structures to enhance disaster risk reduction. *Tourism Management*, *36*, 77–85. doi:10.1016/j.tourman.2012.11.006

Bianchi, R. (2006). Tourism and the globalization of fear: Analysing the politics of risk and (in) security in global travel. *Tourism and Hospitality Research*, *7*(1), 64–74. doi:10.1057/palgrave.thr.6050028

Biran, A., Poria, Y., & Oren, G. (2011). Sought experiences at (dark) heritage sites. *Annals of Tourism Research*, *38*(3), 820–841. doi:10.1016/j.annals.2010.12.001

Bramwell, B., & Lane, B. (2011). Critical research on the governance of tourism and sustainability. *Journal of Sustainable Tourism*, *19*(4-5), 411–421. doi:10.1080/09669582.2011.580586

Buda, D. (2015). *Affective Tourism: dark routes in conflict.K.* Abingdon, UK: Routledge.

Cohen, E. H. (2011). Educational dark tourism at an in popular site: The Holocaust Museum in Jerusalem. *Annals of Tourism Research*, *38*(1), 193–209. doi:10.1016/j.annals.2010.08.003

Convery, I., Corsane, G., & Davis, P. (Eds.). (n.d.). Displaced Heritage: Dealing with Disaster and Suffering. Boydell & Brewer.

Cooper, C., & Hall, C. M. (2008). *Contemporary tourism: an international approach*. Abingdon, UK: Routledge.

Faulkner, B. (2001). Towards a framework for tourism disaster management. *Tourism Management*, *22*(2), 135–147. doi:10.1016/S0261-5177(00)00048-0

Gale, T. (2009). Urban beaches, virtual worlds and the end of tourism. *Mobilities*, *4*(1), 119–138. doi:10.1080/17450100802657996

Gotham, K. F. (2007). (Re) branding the big easy tourism rebuilding in post-Katrina New Orleans. *Urban Affairs Review*, *42*(6), 823–850. doi:10.1177/1078087407300222

Hall, C. M. (2011). A typology of governance and its implications for tourism policy analysis. *Journal of Sustainable Tourism*, *19*(4-5), 437–457. doi:10.1080/09669582.2011.570346

Hall, C. M. (2014). *Tourism and social marketing*. Abingdon, UK: Routledge.

Hartmann, R. (2014). Dark tourism, thanatourism, and dissonance in heritage tourism management: New directions in contemporary tourism research. *Journal of Heritage Tourism*, *9*(2), 166–182. doi:10.1080/1743873X.2013.807266

Hooper, G., & Lennon, J. (2017). *Dark Tourism, practice and interpretation*. Abingdon, UK: Routledge.

Jamal, T., & Lelo, L. (2011). Exploring the conceptual and analytical framing of dark tourism: From darkness to intentionality. In *Tourist experience: Contemporary perspectives* (pp. 29–42). Abingdon, UK: Routledge.

Kang, E. J., Scott, N., Lee, T. J., & Ballantyne, R. (2012). Benefits of visiting a 'dark tourismsite: The case of the Jeju April 3rd Peace Park, Korea. *Tourism Management*, *33*(2), 257–265. doi:10.1016/j.tourman.2011.03.004

Klein, N. (2007). *The shock doctrine: The rise of disaster capitalism*. New York: Macmillan.

Korstanje, M. (2009). Re-visiting risk perception theory in the context of travel. *E-Review of Tourism Research*, *7*(4), 68–81.

Korstanje, M. (2016a). *The Rise of Thana Capitalism and Tourism*. Abingdon, UK: Routledge.

Korstanje, M. E. (2011). Detaching the elementary forms of dark-tourism. *Anatolia*, *22*(3), 424–427. doi:10.1080/13032917.2011.620800

Korstanje, M. E. (2016b). Risk, Terrorism, and Tourism Consumption: The End of Tourism. In P. Vasant & M. Kalaivanthan (Eds.), Handbook of Research on Holistic Optimization Techniques in the Hospitality, Tourism, and Travel Industry. Hershey, PA: IGI Global.

Korstanje, M. E., & Clayton, A. (2012). Tourism and terrorism: Conflicts and commonalities. *Worldwide Hospitality and Tourism Themes*, *4*(1), 8–25. doi:10.1108/17554211211198552

Korstanje, M. E., & Ivanov, S. H. (2012). Tourism as a form of new psychological resilience: The inception of dark tourism. *Cultur, revista de Turismo e cultura, 6*(4), 56-71.

Larsen, S. (2007). Aspects of a psychology of the tourist experience. *Scandinavian Journal of Hospitality and Tourism*, *7*(1), 7–18. doi:10.1080/15022250701226014

Larsen, S., Brun, W., Øgaard, T., & Selstad, L. (2007). Subjective food-risk judgements in tourists. *Tourism Management*, *28*(6), 1555–1559. doi:10.1016/j.tourman.2007.02.016

Laws, E. (2011). *Tourist destination governance: Practice, theory and issues*. Wallingford: Cabi. doi:10.1079/9781845937942.0000

Lennon, J. J., & Foley, M. (2000). *Dark tourism*. London: Cengage Learning EMEA.

Lepp, A., & Gibson, H. (2003). Tourist roles, perceived risk and international tourism. *Annals of Tourism Research*, *30*(3), 606–624. doi:10.1016/S0160-7383(03)00024-0

MacCannell, D. (1976). *The tourist: A new theory of the leisure class*. Los Angeles, CA: University of California Press.

MacCannell, D. (2011). *The Ethics of Sightseeing*. Berkeley, CA: University of California Press. doi:10.1525/california/9780520257825.001.0001

Nedelea, A., Korstanje, M., & George, B. (2016). Preface. In M. Korstanje & B. George (Eds.), *Strategic Tools and methods for promoting hospitality and tourism services*. Hershey, PA: IGI global. doi:10.4018/978-1-4666-9761-4

Sather-Wagstaff, J. (2011). *Heritage that hurts, tourists in the memory-scapes of Septembre 11*. Left Coat Press.

Scott, N., Baggio, R., & Cooper, C. (2008). *Network analysis and tourism: From theory to practice* (Vol. 35). Bristol, UK: Channel View Publications.

Stone, P., & Sharpley, R. (2008). Consuming dark tourism: A thanatological perspective. *Annals of Tourism Research, 35*(2), 574–595. doi:10.1016/j.annals.2008.02.003

Stone, P. R. (2011). Dark tourism: Towards a new post-disciplinary research agenda. *International Journal of Tourism Anthropology, 1*(3-4), 318–332. doi:10.1504/IJTA.2011.043713

Stone, P. R. (2012). Dark tourism and significant other death: Towards a model of mortality mediation. *Annals of Tourism Research, 39*(3), 1565–1587. doi:10.1016/j.annals.2012.04.007

Sunstein, C. R. (2003). Beyond the precautionary principle. *University of Pennsylvania Law Review, 151*(3), 1003–1058. doi:10.2307/3312884

Sunstein, C. R. (2005). *Laws of fear: Beyond the precautionary principle* (Vol. 6). Cambridge, UK: Cambridge University Press. doi:10.1017/CBO9780511790850

Timothy, D. J., & Boyd, S. W. (2006). Heritage tourism in the 21st century: Valued traditions and new perspectives. *Journal of Heritage Tourism, 1*(1), 1-16.

Tribe, J. (2009). *Philosophical issues in tourism.* Bristol, UK: Channel View Publications.

Tzanelli, R. (2016). *Thana Tourism and the Cinematic Representation of Risk.* Abingdon, UK: Routledge.

Compilation of References

Afanasiev, O., & Afanasieva, A. (2015). The functional significance and place of tourist legends in creating attractive destination properties. *Universities for Tourism and Service Association Bulletin*, *9*(1), 52–59. doi:10.12737/7943

Aggrawal, A. (2011). A new classification of zoophilia. *Journal of Forensic and Legal Medicine*, *18*(2), 73–78. doi:10.1016/j.jflm.2011.01.004 PMID:21315301

Alaeddinoğlu, F., & Aliağaoğlu, A. (2007). Savaş alanları turizmine tipik bir örnek: Büyük Taarruz ve Başkomutan Tarihî Milli Parkı. *Anatolia: Turizm Araştırmaları Dergisi*, *18*(2), 215–225.

Alderman, D. H. (2010). Surrogation and the politics of remembering slavery in Savannah, Georgia (USA). *Journal of Historical Geography*, *36*(1), 90–101. doi:10.1016/j.jhg.2009.08.001

Alexander, E. (2016). *Dark tourism of the Bosnian screen*. Retrieved September 04, 2016, from http://www.worldcat.org/title/dark-tourism-of-the-bosnian-screen/oclc/948964947

Aliağaoğlu, A. (2004). Sosyo-kültürel miras turizmi ve Türkiye açısından örnekler. *Coğrafi Bilimler Dergisi*, *2*, 50–64.

Altman, J. (1989). Tourism dilemmas for aboriginal Australians. *Annals of Tourism Research*, *16*(4), 456–476. doi:10.1016/0160-7383(89)90002-9

Alvarez, M., & Korzay, M. (2008). Influence o politics and media in the perceptions of Turkey as a tourism destination. *Tourism Review.*, *63*(2), 38–46. doi:10.1108/16605370810883932

Alvarez, W. A., & Freinhar, J. P. (1991). A prevalence study of bestiality (zoophilia) in psychiatric in-patients, medical in-patients, and psychiatric staff. *International Journal of Psychosomatics*, *38*(1-4), 45–47. PMID:1778686

American Psychiatric Association (APA). (2013). *Diagnostic and Statistical Manual of Mental Disorders* (5th ed.). Arlington, VA: American Psychiatric Association.

Anderman, J., & Simine, A. (2012). Memory, community and the new museum. *Theory, Culture & Society*, *29*(1), 3–13. doi:10.1177/0263276411423041

Anderson, B. (1983). *Imagined communities: Reflections on the origin and spread of nationalism*. London, UK: Verso.

Anholt, S. (2007). *Competitive Identity: The New Brand Management for Nations, Cities and Regions*. New York: Palgrave Macmillan. doi:10.1057/9780230627727

Argyris, C. (1976). Single loop and double loop models in research on decision making. *Administrative Science Quarterly*, *21*(3), 363–375. doi:10.2307/2391848

Armon-Jones, C. (1986). The social functions of emotion. In R. Harré (Ed.), *The social construction of emotions* (pp. 57–82). Oxford, UK: Basil Blackwell.

Ascione, F. R. (Ed.). (2008). *The international handbook of animal abuse and cruelty: Theory, research, and application*. Purdue University Press.

Ashworth, G. J., & Isaac, R. K. (2015). Have we illuminated the dark? Shifting perspectives on dark tourism. *Tourism Recreation Research*, *40*(3), 316–325. doi:10.1080/02508281.2015.1075726

Ashworth, G., & Hartmann, R. (2005). *Horror and human tragedy revisited: The management of sites of atrocities for tourism*. Elmsford, NY: Cognizant Communication Corporation.

Ashworth, G., & Tunbridge, J. E. (1996). *Dissonant heritage*. New York, NY: Wiley.

Baker, B. (2016, April 27). What Does Wayfinding Add to City Branding? *Small City Branding Around the World*. Retrieved 27 April 2016, from http://citybranding.typepad.com/city-branding/2016/04/what-does-wayfinding-add-to-city-branding.html

Bakke, M. (2009). The predicament of zoopleasures: Human-non-human libidinal relations. In T. Tyler & M. Rossini (Eds.), *Animal Encounters* (pp. 221–242). Leiden, Netherlands: Brill Publishers. doi:10.1163/ej.9789004168671.i-266.58

Baldwin, F., & Sharpley, R. (2009). Battlefield tourism: Bringing organized violence back to life. In R. Sharpley & P. R. Stone (Eds.), *The darker side of travel: The theory and practice of dark tourism* (pp. 186–206). Bristol, UK: Channel View Publications.

Banyai, M. (2009). The image of tourism destinations: A case of Dracula tourism. University of Waterloo.

Barr, P. S., Stimpert, J. L., & Huff, A. S. (1992). Cognitive change, strategic action, and organizational renewal. *Strategic Management Journal*, *13*(1), 15–36. doi:10.1002/smj.4250131004

Bar-Tal, D. (2001). Why does fear override hope in societies engulfed by intractable conflict, as it does in the Israeli society? *Political Psychology*, *22*(3), 601–627. doi:10.1111/0162-895X.00255

Baudrillard, J. (1994). *Simulacra and simulation*. Michigan, MI: University of Michigan Press.

Baudrillard, J. (1996). *The perfect crime*. London: Verso.

Bauman, Z. (1992). *Mortality, immortality, and other life strategies*. Stanford, CA: Stanford University Press.

Bauman, Z. (2000). *Globalization: The human consequences*. New York: Columbia University Press.

Bauman, Z. (2003). *Liquid love: On the frailty of human bonds*. Cambridge, UK: Polity Press.

Bauman, Z. (2005). *Liquid life*. Cambridge, UK: Polity Press.

Bauman, Z. (2007). *Consuming Life*. Cambridge, UK: Polity Press.

Beck, U. (1992). Risk society: Towards a new modernity (Vol. 17). Thousand Oaks, CA: Sage.

Beck, U. (1992). *Risk society: Towards a new modernity*. New Delhi: Sage.

Beetz, A. M. (2004). Bestiality/Zoophilia: A scarcely investigated phenomenon between crime, paraphilia, and love. *Journal of Forensic Psychology Practice*, *4*(2), 1–36. doi:10.1300/J158v04n02_01

Beetz, A. M., & Podberscek, A. L. (Eds.). (2005). *Bestiality and Zoophilia: Sexual relations with animals*. West Lafayette, IN: Purdue University Press.

Beirne, P. (1997). Rethinking bestiality: Towards a concept of interspecies sexual assault. *Theoretical Criminology*, *1*(3), 317–340. doi:10.1177/1362480697001003003

Bellah, R. (2005). Civil religion in America. *Daedalus*, *134*(4), 40–55. doi:10.1162/001152605774431464

Berlin, I. (2013). *Karl Marx*. Princeton, NJ: Princeton University Press.

Berridge, K. (2001). *Vigor mortis: the end of the death taboo*. London: Profile Books.

Bhatia, M. S., Srivastava, S., & Sharma, S. (2005). An uncommon case of zoophilia. *Medicine, Science, and the Law*, *45*(2), 174–175. doi:10.1258/rsmmsl.45.2.174 PMID:15895645

Biran, A., & Hyde, K. F. (2013). New perspectives on dark tourism. *International Journal of Culture. Tourism and Hospitality Research*, *7*(3), 191–198.

Biran, A., Poria, Y., & Oren, G. (2011). Sought experiences at (dark) heritage sites. *Annals of Tourism Research*, *38*(3), 820–841. doi:10.1016/j.annals.2010.12.001

Birdir, K., Dalgıç, A., Güler, A., & Kayaalp, Y. (2015). Hüzün turizmi: Gelibolu yarımadası tarihi milli parkını ziyaret eden yabancı turistlerin deneyimleri. *Journal of Tourism and Gastronomy Studies*, *3*, 12–23.

Blakeley, K. (2007). *Leadership blind spots and what to do about them*. Chichester, UK: Wiley.

Blom, T. (2007). Morbid Tourism: The Case of Diana, Princess of Wales and Althorp House. *Royal tourism: Excursions around monarchy*, 142-158.

Blom, T. (2000). Morbid tourism: A postmodern market niche with an example from Althorp. *Norwegian Journal of Geography*, *54*, 29–36.

Blom, T. (2000). Morbid tourism-a postmodern market niche with an example from Althorp. *Norsk Geografisk Tidsskrift*, *54*(1), 29–36. doi:10.1080/002919500423564

Bolliger, G., & Goetschel, A. F. (2005). Sexual relations with animals (zoophilia): An unrecognized problem in animal welfare legislation. In A. M. Beetz & A. L. Podberscek (Eds.), *Bestiality and Zoophilia: Sexual Relations with Animals* (pp. 23–45). West Lafayette, IN: Purdue University Press.

Botti, L., & Peypoch, N. (2013). Multi-criteria ELECTRE method and destination competitiveness. *Tourism Management Perspectives*, *6*, 108–113. doi:10.1016/j.tmp.2013.01.001

Bowman, M. S., & Pezzullo, P. C. (2009). Whats so darkabout dark tourism?: Death, tours, and performance. *Tourist Studies*, *9*(3), 187–202. doi:10.1177/1468797610382699

Boyd, S. W. (2000). 'HeritageTourism in Northern Ireland: Opportunity Under Peace. *Current Issues in Tourism*, *3*(2), 150–174. doi:10.1080/13683500008667871

Boz, M. (2016). Turizm destinasyonu olarak Gelibolu. *Karadeniz*, *31*, 63–74.

Brisset, W. (n.d.). Bibliographical essay on fear. *Hedgehog Review*, *3*, 115-123. Retrieved from: http://www.iasc-culture.org/THR/archives/Fear/5.3JBrissett.pdf

Buda, D. M., & McIntosh, A. J. (2013). Dark tourism and voyeurism: Tourist arrested for "spying" in Iran. *International Journal of Culture. Tourism and Hospitality Research*, *7*(3), 214–226.

Burawoy, M. (1984). Karl Marx and the satanic mills: Factory politics under early capitalism in England, the United States, and Russia. *American Journal of Sociology*, *90*(2), 247–282. doi:10.1086/228079

Bush, G. H. W., & Scowcroft, B. (1998). *A world transformed.* New York, NY: Vintage Books.

Cantallops, A. S., & Cardona, J. R. (2015). Holiday destinations: The myth of the lost paradise? *Annals of Tourism Research*, *55*, 171–173. doi:10.1016/j.annals.2015.10.002

Capriello, A., & Rotherham, I. (2008). Farm attraction, networks and destination development: A case study of Sussex, England. *Tourism Review.*, *63*(2), 59–71. doi:10.1108/16605370810883950

Carrigan, A. (2014). Dark tourism and postcolonial studies: Critical intersections. *Postcolonial Studies*, *17*(3), 236–250. doi:10.1080/13688790.2014.993425

Castaño, J. M., Moreno, A., & Crego, A. (2006). Factores psicosociales y formación de imágenes en el turismo urbano: Un estudio de caso sobre Madrid. *Pasos*, *4*(3), 287–299.

Çetinsöz, B. C., & Temiz, G. (2016). *Alternatif bir turizm türü olarak Türkiye'nin karanlık (dark) turizm potansiyeli.* Paper presented at International Multidisciplinary Congress of Eurasia. Retrieved From: https://www.researchgate.net/publication/309591517_Alternatif_Bir_Turizm_Turu_Olarak_Turkiye'nin_Karanlik_Dark_Turizm_Potansiyeli

Chang, C. W., Tseng, T. H., & Woodside, A. G. (2013). Configural algorithms of patient satisfaction, participation in diagnostics, and treatment decisions influences on hospital loyalty. *Journal of Services Marketing*, *27*(2), 91–103. doi:10.1108/08876041311309225

Chauhan, V. & Khanna, S. (2009). Tourism: a tool for crafting peace process in Kashmir, J&K, India. *Tourismos: An International Multidisciplinary Journal of Tourism, 4*(2), 69-89.

Chronis, A. (2012). Between place and story: Gettysburg as tourism imaginary. *Annals of Tourism Research*, *39*(4), 1797–1816. doi:10.1016/j.annals.2012.05.028

Clarke, J. N. (2005). Death under control: The portrayal of death in mass print English language magazines in Canada. *Omega*, *52*(2), 153–167.

Clarke, L. (2006). *Worst cases: terror and catastrophe in the popular imagination*. Chicago: University of Chicago Press.

Clarke, R., Dutton, J., & Johnston, A. (2014). Shadow zones: Dark travel and postcolonial cultures. *Postcolonial Studies*, *17*(3), 221–235. doi:10.1080/13688790.2014.993426

Clemmons, D. (2011). *Voluntourism*. Retrieved 1 September 2016, from http://www.Voluntourism.org/contact.html

Cohen, E. (1988). Authenticity and commodization in tourism. *Annals of Tourism Research*, *15*(3), 371–386. doi:10.1016/0160-7383(88)90028-X

Cohen, E. H. (2011). Educational dark tourism at an in populo site: The Holocaust Museum in Jerusalem. *Annals of Tourism Research*, *38*(1), 193–209. doi:10.1016/j.annals.2010.08.003

Cole, S. (2007). Beyond authenticity and commodification. *Annals of Tourism Research*, *34*(4), 943–960. doi:10.1016/j.annals.2007.05.004

Collins-Kreiner, N. (2010). Researching pilgrimage: Continuity and transformations. *Annals of Tourism Research*, *37*(2), 440–456. doi:10.1016/j.annals.2009.10.016

Collins-Kreiner, N. (2015). Dark tourism as/is pilgrimage. *Current Issues in Tourism*, 1–5.

Comaroff, J. L., & Comaroff, J. (2009). *Ethnicity, Inc*. Chicago: University of Chicago Press. doi:10.7208/chicago/9780226114736.001.0001

Cooper, J. M. (1984). Plato's theory of human motivation. *History of Philosophy Quarterly*, *1*(1), 3–21.

Coronado, G. (2008). Insurgencia y Turismo: Reflexiones sobre el impacto del turista politizado en Chiapas. *Pasos*, *6*(1), 53–68.

Crapanzano, V. (2004). *Imaginative Horizons: literary-philosophical anthropology*. Chicago: University of Chicago Press.

Crozier, J. (2013). *The Dark Tourism Lecture JC v2*. Retrieved 1 September 2016, from https://www.youtube.com/watch?v=E52W8GA4DKA

Dalton, D. (2014). *Dark tourism and crime* (Vol. 34). Abingdon, UK: Routledge.

Dalton, D. (2014). *Dark Tourism and Crime*. Florence, Italy: Taylor and Francis.

Damoison, D., & Dalembert, L. P. (2003). *Vodou. Un tambour pour les anges*. Paris: Editions Autrement.

Dann, G. (1994). Tourism: The nostalgia industry of the future. In W. Theobald (Ed.), *Global tourism: The next decade* (pp. 55–67). Oxford, UK: Butterworth-Heinemann.

Dann, G. (1998). *The dark side of tourism. Etudes et rapports, se'rie L*. Aix-en-Provence: Centre International de Recherches et d'Etudes Touristiques.

Dann, G. M., & Seaton, A. V. (2001). Slavery, contested heritage and thanatourism. *International Journal of Hospitality & Tourism Administration*, *2*(3-4), 1–29. doi:10.1300/J149v02n03_01

Darwling-Carter, G. (2010). Quand on parle de tourisme. *Antilla*, *1415*, 38–40.

De Giorgio, F., Polacco, M., Rossi, R., Lodise, M., & Rainio, J. (2009). Fatal blunt injuries possibly resulting from sexual abuse of a calf. *Medicine, Science, and the Law*, *49*(4), 307–310. doi:10.1258/rsmmsl.49.4.307 PMID:20025108

Debord, G. (1994). *Society of the spectacle*. New York, NY: Zone Books.

Debrix, F., & Barder, A. (2009). Nothing to fear but fear: Governmentality and the biopolitical production of terror. *International Political Sociology*, *3*(4), 398–413. doi:10.1111/j.1749-5687.2009.00083.x

Debrix, F., & Barder, A. (2012). *Beyond biopolitics: Theory, violence and horror in world politics*. New York, NY: Routledge.

Dekkers, M. (2000). *Dearest pet: On beastiality*. Brooklyn, NY: Verso Books.

Depremin acısı anı defterinde ölümsüzleşiyor. (2016). Retrieved from: http://aa.com.tr/tr/turkiye/depremin-acisi-ani-defterinde-olumsuzlesiyor/629373

Diyarbakır Askeri Cezaevi Gerçekleri Araştırma ve Adalet Komisyonu Raporu. (2012). Retrieved From: http://bianet.org/files/doc_files/000/000/370/original/111203-DC-Sempozyum_Sunum_%C3%96zetleri.pdf

Document: New world order: George Bush's speech, 6 Mar 1999. (n.d.). Retrieved from: http://al-bab.com/albab-orig/albab/arab/docs/pal/pal10.htm

Duffield, G., Hassiotis, A., & Vizard, E. (1998). Zoophilia in young sexual abusers. *Journal of Forensic Psychiatry*, *9*(2), 294–304. doi:10.1080/09585189808402198

Duncan, S. (1978). The Social construction of unreality: an interactionists approach to the Tourist's cognition of Environment. In D. Led & M. Samuels (Eds.), *Humanistic Geography* (pp. 262–282). Abingdon, UK: Routledge.

Dunkley, R. A. (2007). Re-peopling tourism: A 'hot approach' to studying thanatourist experiences. *The critical turn in tourism studies: Innovative research methodologies*, 371-385.

Dunkley, R. (2015). Beyond temporal reflections in thanatourism. *Annals of Tourism Research*, *52*, 172–179. doi:10.1016/j.annals.2015.03.007

Dunkley, R., Morgan, N., & Westwood, S. (2011). Visiting the trenches: Exploring meanings and motivations in battlefield tourism. *Tourism Management, 32*(4), 860–868. doi:10.1016/j.tourman.2010.07.011

Dupont, L. (2009). Cointegration et causalité entre développement touristique, croissance économique et réduction de la pauvreté: Cas de Haïti. *Etudes Caribéennes*. Available from: http://etudescaribeennes.revues.org/3780

Earls, C. M., & Lalumiere, M. L. (2002). A case study of preferential bestiality (zoophilia). *Sexual Abuse, 14*(1), 83–88. PMID:11803597

Edgell, D. L. Sr, & Swanson, J. R. (2013). *Tourism policy and planning. Yesterday, today, and tomorrow*. Abingdon, UK: Routledge.

Eichstedt, J., & Small, S. (2002). *Representations of slavery: Race and ideology in southern plantation museums*. Washington, DC: Smithsonian Books.

Ekman, P., & Davidson, R. J. (1994). Afterword. In P. Ekman & R. Davidson (Eds.), *The nature of emotion* (pp. 176–178). New York, NY: Oxford University Press.

Elias, N. (1985). *The loneliness of the dying*. Oxford, UK: Blackwell.

Ellis, R. (2009). *Experiencing "dark tourism": The real Auschwitz?* (Unpublished undergraduate thesis). University of Bristol, UK. Retrieved from: http://www.bristol.ac.uk/history/media/docs/ug-dissertations/2009ellis.pdf

Eror, A. (2012, December 7). The government wants to stop this guy from boning his dog. *Vice*. Retrieved October 28, 2013, from http://www.vice.com/read/bestiality-is-still-legal-in-germany-but-not-for-long

Faimberg, H. (2005). *The Telescoping Generations: listening to the narcissistic links between generations*. East Sussex, UK: Routledge.

Faucher, L., & Tappolet, C. (2006). *Introduction: modularity and the nature of emotions* (L. Faucher & C. Tappolet, Eds.). Alberta, Canada: University of Calgary Press.

Fellow, P. & Hilmi, M. (2011). *Selling street and snack foods*. FAO diversification booklet 18.

Felthous, A. R. (1980). Aggression against cats, dogs, and people. *Child Psychiatry and Human Development, 10*(3), 169–177. doi:10.1007/BF01433629 PMID:7357998

Fennell, D. A. (2011). *Tourism and animal ethics*. Routledge.

Fennell, D. A. (2015). Ethics in Tourism. In *Education for Sustainability in Tourism* (pp. 45–57). Berlin: Springer. doi:10.1007/978-3-662-47470-9_3

Ferraro, K. (1995). *Fear of crime. Interpreting victimization risk*. New York, NY: Sunny Press.

Festinger, L. (1957). *A theory of cognitive dissonance*. Palo Alto, CA: Stanford University.

Fife, W. (2004). Penetrating Types: Conflating Modernist and Postmodernist Tourism on the Great Northern Peninsula of Newfoundland. *Journal of American Folklore*, *117*(464), 147–167. doi:10.1353/jaf.2004.0036

Fillipi, A. (1988). *Instituciones e Ideologías en la Independencia Hispano-americana*. Buenos Aires: Alianza Editorial.

Flaxman, G., & Rogerson, B. (2010). The economy of fear. *Symploke*, *18*(1-2), 333–336.

Foley, M., & Lennon, J. J. (1996). JFK and dark tourism: A fascination with assassination. *International Journal of Heritage Studies*, *2*(4), 198–211. doi:10.1080/13527259608722175

Fonteles, J. O. (2004). *Tourism and Socio-enviromental Factors*. Sao Paulo: El Aleph.

Foucault, M. (1984). *Of other spaces. Architecture /Mouvement/ Continuité*. Retrieved From: http://web.mit.edu/allanmc/www/foucault1.pdf

Foucault, M. (1975). *Discipline and punish. The birth of the prison*. New York, NY: Vintage Books.

Foucault, M. (1976). The history of the sexuality: Vol. 1. *An introduction*. London: Allen Lane.

Foucault, M. (1980). *Power and knowledge: Selected interviews and other writings 1972-1977* (C. Gordon, Ed.). New York, NY: Pantheon.

Foucault, M. (1982). The subject and power. *Critical Inquiry*, *8*(4), 777–795. doi:10.1086/448181

Foucault, M. (1990). The history of sexuality: Vol. 3. *The care of the self*. London: Penguin Books.

Foucault, M. (1992). The history of sexuality: Vol. 2. *The use of pleasure*. London: Penguin Books.

Foucault, M. (2003). *Society Must Be Defended* (D. Macey, Trans.). New York, NY: Picador.

Foucault, M. (2003). *Society must be defended: lectures at the Collège de France, 1975-76*. New York, NY: Picador.

Fox, D., Gouthro, M. B., Morakabati, Y., & Brackstone, J. (2014). *Doing events research from theory to practice*. Abingdon, UK: Routledge.

Franch, M., Martini, U., Buffa, F., & Parisi, G. (2008). 4l tourism (landscape, leisure, learning and limit): Responding to new motivations and expectations of tourist to improve the competitiveness of alpine destination in a sustainable way. *Tourism Review.*, *63*(1), 4–14. doi:10.1108/16605370810861008

Frank, R., & Cook, P. (2010). *The Winner-take-All Society: why the few at the top get so much more than the rest of us*. New York: Virgin Books.

Friedrich, M., & Johnston, T. (2013). Beauty versus tragedy: Thanatourism and the memorialisation of the 1994 Rwandan Genocide. *Journal of Tourism and Cultural Change*, *11*(4), 302–320. doi:10.1080/14766825.2013.852565

Furedi, F. (1997). *Culture of fear: Risk-taking and the morality of low expectation*. New York, NY: Continuum.

Garcia, B. R. (2012). Management Issues in dark tourism attractions: The case of ghost tours in Edinburgh and Toledo. *Journal of Unconventional Parks Tourism and Recreation Research*, *4*(1), 14–19.

Garrod, B., & Fennell, D. A. (2004). An analysis of whalewatching codes of conduct. *Annals of Tourism Research*, *31*(2), 334–352. doi:10.1016/j.annals.2003.12.003

Geertz, C. (1994). Thick description: Toward an interpretive theory of culture. In M. Martin & C. McIntyre (Eds.), Readings in the philosophy of social science. Cambridge, MA: MIT Press.

Geertz, C. (1982). The way we think now: Toward an ethnography of modern thought. *Bulletin - American Academy of Arts and Sciences. American Academy of Arts and Sciences*, *35*(5), 14–34. doi:10.2307/3823993

Gentry, G. W. (2007). Walking with the Dead: The Place of Ghost Walk Tourism in Savannah, Georgia. *Southeastern Geographer*, *47*(2), 222–238. doi:10.1353/sgo.2007.0023

Giddens, A. (1971). *Capitalism and modern social theory: An analysis of the writings of Marx, Durkheim and Max Weber*. Cambridge University Press. doi:10.1017/CBO9780511803109

Giddens, A. (1990). *The Consequences of Modernity*. Cambridge, UK: Polity Press.

Giddens, A. (1991). *Modernity and self-identity. Self and society in the late modern age*. Cambridge, UK: Polity.

Glassner, B. (1999). *The culture of fear: Why Americans are afraid of the wrong things*. New York, NY: Basic Books.

Global Forum on Food Security and Nutrition. (2014). *Street food and urban and periurban agriculture and horticulture: perspectives for a strategic coalition towards food security*. Discussion No. 110 from 17 November to 12 December. Author.

Gnoth, J., & Matteucci, X. (2014). A phenomenological view of the behavioural tourism research literature. *International Journal of Culture, Tourism and Hospitality Research*, *8*(1), 3-21.

Godfrey, J., Wearing, S., & Schulenkorf, N. (2015). Medical volunteer tourism as an alternative to backpacking in Peru. *Tourism Planning & Development*, *12*(1), 111–122. doi:10.1080/21568316.2014.960602

Goudie, S. C., Khan, F., & Kilian, D. (1999). Transforming tourism: Black empowerment, heritage and identity beyond apartheid. *The South African Geographical Journal*, *81*(1), 22–31. doi:10.1080/03736245.1999.9713658

Gretzel, U. (2016). *Smart Tourism*. Retrieved 28 Dec 2016, from https://www.youtube.com/watch?v=tlGvJgTqtmo

Guidotti-Hernández, N. M. (2011). *Unspeakable violence: Remapping US and Mexican national imaginaries*. Durham, NC: Duke University Press. doi:10.1215/9780822394495

Hally, M. B. (2009). *A guide for international nursing students in Australia and New Zealand*. Sydney, Australia: Elsevier.

Hammond, M., & Wellington, J. (2013). *Research Methods. The Key Concepts*. London: Routledge.

Handayani, B., Ivanov, S., & Korstanje, M. E. (2017). Smart Tourism for Dark Sites: The Sacred Site of the Dead, Trunyan Cemetery. In M. E. Korstanje & B. Handayani (Eds.), *Gazing at Death: Dark Tourism as an Emergent Horizon of Research* (pp. 15–42). New York: Nova Publishers.

Harding, S. G. (1986). *The science question in feminism*. Ithaca, NY: Cornell University Press.

Harré, R., & Parrot, W. G. (1996). *The emotions: Social, cultural and biological dimensions*. London, UK: Sage.

Hartmann, R. (2014). Dark tourism, Thana-Tourism, and dissonance in heritage tourism management: New directions in contemporary tourism research. *Journal of Heritage Tourism*, *9*(2), 166–182. doi:10.1080/1743873X.2013.807266

Harvey, D. (1989). *The condition of postmodernity* (Vol. 14). Oxford, UK: Blackwell.

Harvey, D. (1990). *The condition of postmodernity: An enquiry into the origins of cultural change*. Cambridge, MA: Blackwell.

Hayano, A. (2011). Suicide Forest in Japan. *VICE News*. Retrieved 15 August 2016, from https://www.youtube.com/watch?v=4FDSdg09df8

Heron, B. (2011). *Voluntourism: Helping or Hurting? The Agenda with Steve Paikin*. Retrieved 1 September 2016, from https://www.youtube.com/watch?v=uzeM3DqEzXw

Heron, B. A. (1999). *Desire for development, the education of white women as development workers* (Doctoral dissertation). National Library of Canada, Bibliothèque nationale du Canada.

Heron, B. (2007). *Desire for development: Whiteness, gender, and the helping imperative*. Wilfrid Laurier Univ. Press.

Heuermann, K., & Chhabra, D. (2014). The Darker Side of Dark Tourism: An Authenticity Perspective. *Tourism Analysis*, *19*(2), 213–225. doi:10.3727/108354214X13963557455766

Heuman, D. (2005). Hospitality and reciprocity working tourist in Dominica. *Annals of Tourism Research*, *32*(2), 407–418. doi:10.1016/j.annals.2004.07.010

Hewison, R. (1987). *The heritage industry*. London, UK: Methuen.

Hjalger, A. M., & Richards, G. (2002). *Tourism and gastronomy*. London: Routledge.

Hofstadter, R. (1992). *Social Darwinism in American Thoughts*. Boston: Beacon Press.

Holden, A., & Novelli, M. (2011). *The Changing Paradigms of Tourism in International Development: Placing the Poor First—Trojan Horse or Real Hope?*. Academic Press.

Holden, A. (2003). In need of new environmental ethics for Tourism?"-. *Annals of Tourism Research, 30*(1), 94–108. doi:10.1016/S0160-7383(02)00030-0

Holden, A. (2013). *Tourism, poverty and development*. Abingdon, UK: Routledge.

Holdenrid, C. (2013). *Dark Tourism*. Retrieved 1 September 2016, from https://www.youtube.com/watch?v=ZWO5U1dtfqE

Holloway, J. (2010). Legend-tripping in spooky spaces: Ghost tourism and infrastructures of enchantment. *Environment and Planning D: Society and Space Environ. Plann. D, 28*(4), 618–637. doi:10.1068/d9909

Holmes, K., Smith, K. A., Lockstone-Binney, L., & Baum, T. (2010). Developing the dimensions of tourism volunteering. *Leisure Sciences, 32*(3), 255–269. doi:10.1080/01490401003712689

Howie, L. (2010). *Terror on the Screen: Witnesses and the Re-animation of 9/11 as Image-event, Popular Culture*. Washington, DC: New Academia Publishing, LLC.

Hughes, P. (2001). Animals, values and tourism: Structural shifts in UK dolphin tourism provision. *Tourism Management, 22*(4), 321–329. doi:10.1016/S0261-5177(00)00070-4

Hultsman, J. (1995). Just tourism: An ethical framework. *Annals of Tourism Research, 22*(3), 553–567. doi:10.1016/0160-7383(95)00011-T

Hyde, K. F., & Harman, S. (2011). Motives for a secular pilgrimage to the Gallipoli battlefields. *Tourism Management, 32*(6), 1343–1351. doi:10.1016/j.tourman.2011.01.008

Hyman, R. (1975). *Industrial Relations: a Marxist introduction*. London: The Macmillan Press. doi:10.1007/978-1-349-15623-8

IceNews. (2008, May 20). *Animal brothels legal in Denmark*. Retrieved January 27, 2014, from http://www.icenews.is/2008/05/20/animal-brothels-legal-in-denmark/

Ide, A. (2014). Dark tourism and information technology. Information Processing Society of Japan research report. *Computers and the Humanities Research Group report, 2014*(4), 1-6. Retrieved 13 June 2016, from https://ipsj.ixsq.nii.ac.jp/ej/?action=pages_view_main&active_action=repository_view_main_item_detail&item_id=101443&item_no=1&page_id=13&block_id=8

Ilgar, R. (2015). Mabetleşen bir mekân: Gelibolu yarımadası tarihi savaş alanları turizmi. *Çanakkale Araştırmaları Türk Yıllığı, 13*(19), 1-20.

Illeris, K. (2009). A comprehensive understanding of human learning. In K. Illeris (Ed.), *Contemporary Theories of Learning – Learning theorists…in their own words*. Abingdon, UK: Routledge.

Illouz, E. (2008). *Saving the modern soul: Therapy, emotions, and the culture of self-help*. Berkeley, CA: University of California Press.

Inglis, D., & Holmes, M. (2003). Highland and other haunts. *Annals of Tourism Research*, *30*(1), 50–63. doi:10.1016/S0160-7383(02)00031-2

Ira Byock, M. D. (2002). The meaning and value of death. *Journal of Palliative Medicine*, *5*(2), 279–288. doi:10.1089/10966210275364l278 PMID:12006230

Is Voluntourism, W. (2013). *Storm Warriors International*. Retrieved 29 August 2016, from https://www.youtube.com/watch?v=MyR1nZbAWH0

Isaac, R., & Ashworth, G. (2012). Moving from the pilgrimage to dark tourism: Leveraging tourism in Palestine. *Tourism. Culture & Communication*, *11*, 149–164.

Izard, C. E. (1991). *Psychology of emotions*. New York, NY: Plenum. doi:10.1007/978-1-4899-0615-1

Jamal, T., & Lelo, L. (2011). Exploring the conceptual and analytical framing of dark tourism: From darkness to intentionality. *Tourist Experience: Contemporary Perspectives*, 29-42.

Jeffreys, S. (2010). Globalizing sexual exploitation: Sex tourism and the traffic in women. *Leisure Studies*, *18*(3), 179–196. doi:10.1080/026143699374916

Jenkins, O. (2003). Photography and travel brochures: The circle of representation. *Tourism Geographies*, *5*(3), 305–328. doi:10.1080/14616680309715

Johnston, T. (2013). Mark Twain and The Innocents Abroad: Illuminating the tourist gaze on death. *International Journal of Culture, Tourism and Hospitality Research*, *7*(3), 199–213.

Jones, K. (2006). Chapter In L. Faucher & C. Tappolet (Eds.), Quick and Smart? Modularity and the Proemotion (pp. 3–28). Alberta, Canada: University of Calgary Press.

Kadt, E. D. (1979). *Tourism. Passport to development? Perspectives on the social and cultural effects of tourism in developing countries*. Oxford, UK: Oxford University Press.

Kampaxi, O. (2008). Codes of Ethics in Tourism: Practices, theory and sythesis. *Annals of Tourism Research*, *35*(2), 607–608. doi:10.1016/j.annals.2007.09.005

Kan, A. K. S., Adegbite, E., El Omari, S., & Abdellatif, M. (2016). On the use of qualitative comparative analysis in management. *Journal of Business Research*, *69*(4), 1458–1463. doi:10.1016/j.jbusres.2015.10.125

Kang, E. J., Scott, N., Lee, T. J., & Ballantyne, R. (2012). Benefits of visiting a 'dark tourismsite: The case of the Jeju April 3rd peace park, Korea. *Tourism Management*, *33*(2), 257–265. doi:10.1016/j.tourman.2011.03.004

Kastenholz, E., & Lopez de Almeida, A. (2008). Seasonality in Rural tourism – the case of North Portugal. *Tourism Review.*, *63*(2), 5–15. doi:10.1108/16605370810883905

Kidder, R. M. (2003). *How good people make tough choices: Resolving the ethical dilemmas of ethical living*. New York: Simon & Schuster.

Kızılırmak, İ., Alrawadieh, Z., Küçükali, S., & Atsız, O. (2015). *Çanakkale'de düzenlenen Anzak tur programlarına yönelik bir içerik analizi.* Research Paper. Retrieved from: https://www.researchgate.net/publication/299599754_Canakkale%27de_Duzenlenen_Anzak_Tur_Programlarina_Yonelik_Bir_Icerik_Analizi

Klain, E. J. (1999, April). *Prostitution of children and child sex tourism: An analysis of domestic and international responses*. Alexandria, VA: National Center for Missing and Exploited Children.

Klein, N. (2007). *The shock doctrine: The rise of disaster capitalism*. New York: Macmillan.

Knudsen, B. T. (2011). Thana-tourism: Witnessing difficult pasts. *Tourist Studies*, *11*(1), 55–72. doi:10.1177/1468797611412064

Koch, A. (2005). Cyber citizen or cyborg citizen: Baudrillard, political agency, and the commons in virtual politics. *Journal of Mass Media Ethics*, *20*(2-3), 159–175. doi:10.1080/08900523.2005.9679706

Korstanje, M. (2014). *Conceptual discussion of dark tourism: suffering, egoism and the depersonalization of death*. Conference, GOA University India. 02-03 May 2014. "Globalization of tourism, opportunities and challenges".

Korstanje, M. (2015). *The anthropology of dark tourism, exploring the contradictions of capitalism.* Centre for Ethnicity & Racism Studies. Retrieved from: http://cers.leeds.ac.uk/files/2015/02/Korstanje_CERS_15.pdf

Korstanje, M. (2015a). *The anthropology of dark tourism, exploring the contradictions of capitalism.* Centre for Ethnicity & Racism Studies. Retrieved from: http://cers.leeds.ac.uk/files/2015/02/Korstanje_CERS_15.pdf

Korstanje, M. E. (2016a). Pensando la hospitalidad. *Revista de Sociales y Jurídicas*, (11), 208-214.

Korstanje, M. E., & Ivanov, S. H. (2012). Tourism as a form of new psychological resilience: The inception of dark tourism. *Cultur – revista de cultura e turismo, 6*(4), 56-71.

Korstanje, M. E., & Ivanov, S. H. (2012). Tourism as a form of new psychological resilience: The inception of dark tourism. *Cultur-Revista de Cultura e Turismo, 6*(4), 56-71.

Korstanje, M. (2010). Profiling modern risks. An appraisal of the works of Bauman, Beck, Castel, Giddens, and Baudrillard. *Journal of Anthropology*, *6*(2), 161–172.

Korstanje, M. (2012). Reconsidering cultural tourism: An anthropologists perspective. *Journal of Heritage Tourism*, *7*(2), 179–184. doi:10.1080/1743873X.2011.639883

Korstanje, M. (2015b). The spirit of terrorism: Tourism, unionization and terrorism. *PASOS. Revista de Turismo y Patrimonio Cultural*, *13*(1), 239–250.

Korstanje, M. (2015c). *A difficult world: Examining the roots of capitalism.* New York, NY: Nova Science Publication.

Korstanje, M. E. (2011). Detaching the elementary forms of dark-tourism. *Anatolia, 22*(3), 424–427. doi:10.1080/13032917.2011.620800

Korstanje, M. E. (2011). Influence of history in the encounter of guests and hosts. *Anatolia, 22*(2), 282–285. doi:10.1080/13032917.2011.597991

Korstanje, M. E. (2014). Chile helps Chile: Exploring the effects of earthquake Chile 2010. *International Journal of Disaster Resilience in the Built Environment, 5*(4), 380–390. doi:10.1108/IJDRBE-01-2012-0002

Korstanje, M. E. (2015). *A Difficult World, examining the roots of capitalism.* New York: Nova Science Pubs.

Korstanje, M. E. (2016). *The Rise of Thana Capitalism and Tourism.* Abingdon, UK: Routledge.

Korstanje, M. E. (2016). *The Rise of Thana-Capitalism and Tourism.* Abingdon, UK: Routledge.

Korstanje, M. E., & George, B. (2015). Dark Tourism: Revisiting Some Philosophical Issues. *E-review of Tourism Research, 12*(1-2), 127–136.

Korstanje, M. E., & George, B. P. (2015b). The media or the message? An examination of myths as resources to understand the tourism phenomenon. *International Journal of Tourism Anthropology, 4*(2), 122–141. doi:10.1504/IJTA.2015.070055

Korstanje, M. E., & Handayani, B. (2017). *Gazing at death, New-York.* Nova Science Publishers, Inc.

Korstanje, M. E., & Ivanov, S. (2012). Tourism as a Form of New Psychological Resilience: The Inception of Dark Tourism. *Cultur: Revista de Cultura e Turismo, 6*(4), 56–71.

Korstanje, M. E., & Ivanov, S. H. (2012). Tourism as a form of new psychological resilience: The inception of dark tourism. *Cultur-Revista de Cultura e Turismo, 6*(4), 56–71.

Korstanje, M. E., Mustelier, L. C., & Herrera, S. (2016). Understanding the Indiscipline of Tourism: A Radical Critique to the Current. In *Global Dynamics in Travel, Tourism, and Hospitality* (pp. 208–221). Hershey, PA: IGI-Global. doi:10.4018/978-1-5225-0201-2.ch012

Korstanje, M. E., & Olsen, D. H. (2011). The discourse of risk in horror movies post 9/11: Hospitality and hostility in perspective. *International Journal of Tourism Anthropology, 1*(3-4), 304–317. doi:10.1504/IJTA.2011.043712

Korstanje, M., & Busby, G. (2010). Understanding the Bible as the roots of physical displacement: The origin of tourism. *E-Review of Tourism Research, 8*(3), 95–111.

Korstanje, M., & Handayani, B. (2016). *Gazing at Death: dark tourism as an emergent horizon of research.* New York: Nova Science Pubs.

Korstanje, M., & Ivanov, S. (2012). Tourism as a form of new psychological resilience: The inception of dark tourism. *Cultur*, *6*(4), 56–71.

Kowalczyk, A. (2014). *From street food to food districts – Gastronomy services and culinary tourism in an urban space*. Retrieved from www.turystykakulturowa.org

Krentzman, A. R. (2013). *What Is Spirituality?* Retrieved 15 July 2015, from University of Minnesota, Center for Spirituality and Healing and Charlson Meadows website: http://www.takingcharge.csh.umn.edu/enhance-your-wellbeing/purpose/spirituality/what-spirituality

Lang, B. (1999). *The future of the Holocaust: Between history and memory*. Ithaca, NY: Cornell University Press.

Lasch, C. (1991). *The culture of narcissism: American life in an age of diminishing expectations*. New York: WW Norton & Company.

Lashley, C., & Morrison, A. (2001). *In the search of hospitality*. London: Butterworth Heinmann.

Lash, S., & Urry, J. (1994). *Economies of Signs and Space*. London: Theory, Culture & Society.

Lau, G., & Mckercher, B. (2006). Understanding tourist movement pattern in a destination: A GIS approach. *Tourism and Hospitality Research.*, *7*(1), 39–49. doi:10.1057/palgrave.thr.6050027

Lea, J. (1993). Tourism Development Ethics in the Third World. *Annals of Tourism Research*, *20*(4), 701–715. doi:10.1016/0160-7383(93)90092-H

Lennon, J. J., & Foley, M. (1999). Interpretation of the unimaginable: The US Holocaust Memorial Museum, Washington, DC, and dark tourism. *Journal of Travel Research*, *38*(1), 46–50. doi:10.1177/004728759903800110

Lennon, J. J., & Foley, M. (2000). *Dark tourism*. Cornwall, UK: Cengage Learning EMEA.

Lennon, J. J., & Foley, M. (2009). *Dark tourism: The attraction of death and disaster*. London: South Western Cengage Learning.

Lennon, J., & Foley, M. (2000). *Dark Tourism – The Attraction of Death and Disaster*. London: Thomson.

Levin, D. M. (1999). *The philosopher's gaze: Modernity in the shadows of enlightenment*. Berkeley, CA: University of California Press.

Levitt, L. (2010). Death on display: reifying stardom through Hollywood's dark tourism. *The Velvet Light Trap*, (65), 62-70.

Light, D. (2007). Dracula tourism in Romania Cultural identity and the state. *Annals of Tourism Research*, *34*(3), 746–765. doi:10.1016/j.annals.2007.03.004

List of Phobias. (n.d.). Retrieved From: http://phobialist.com/

Loane, S., Bell, J., & McNaughton, R. (2006). Employing information communication technologies to enhance qualitative international marketing enquiry. *International Marketing Review*, *23*(4), 438–455. doi:10.1108/02651330610678994

Local. (2008, November 11). *Swedish bestiality ring exposed.* Retrieved January 18, 2014, from http://www.thelocal.se/20081111/15610

Lockstone-Binney, L., Holmes, K., Smith, K., & Baum, T. (2010). Volunteers and volunteering in leisure: Social science perspectives. *Leisure Studies*, *29*(4), 435–455. doi:10.1080/02614367.2010.527357

Lockstone, L., Smith, K., & Baum, T. (2010). Volunteering flexibility across the tourism sector. *Managing Leisure*, *15*(1-2), 111–127. doi:10.1080/13606710903448202

London, L. S., & Caprio, F. S. (1950). Zoophilia (bestiality). In *Sexual deviations* (pp. 588–596). Washington, DC: Linacre Press. doi:10.1037/11274-013

Longino, H. E. (1990). *Science as social knowledge: Values and objectivity in scientific inquiry.* Princeton, NJ: Princeton University Press.

Losev, A. F. (2001). *Dialectics of Myth.* Moscow: Mysl'. (in Russian)

Lovelock, B. (2003). A comparative study of environmental NGOSperspectives of the tourism industry and modes of action in the South and South-East Asia and Oceania regions. *Asia Pacific Journal of Tourism Research*, *8*(1), 1–14. doi:10.1080/10941660308725451

Lovelock, B., & Lovelock, K. (2013). *The ethics of tourism: Critical and applied perspectives.* Routledge.

Lowith, K. (2002). *Max Weber and Karl Marx.* London: Routledge.

Lynch, P. (2005). Sociological impressionism in a hospitality context. *Annals of Tourism Research*, *32*(3), 527–548. doi:10.1016/j.annals.2004.09.005

Lyons, K. D., & Wearing, S. (2008). Volunteer tourism as alternative tourism: Journeys beyond otherness. *Journeys of discovery in volunteer tourism: International case study perspectives*, 3-11.

Mac-Beth, J. (2005). Towards an Ethics Platform in Tourism. *Annals of Tourism Research*, *32*(4), 962–984. doi:10.1016/j.annals.2004.11.005

MacCannell, D. (1973). Staged authenticity: Arrangements of social space in tourist settings. *American Journal of Sociology*, *79*(3), 589–603. doi:10.1086/225585

MacCannell, D. (1976). *The tourist: A new theory of the leisure class.* Berkeley, CA: University of California Press.

MacCannell, D. (1976). The Tourist: A New Theory of the Leisure Class. New York: Schocken. 1984 Reconstructed Ethnicity: Tourism and Cultural Identity in Third World Communities. *Annals of Tourism Research*, *11*(3), 375–391. doi:10.1016/0160-7383(84)90028-8

MacCannell, D. (1992). *Empty meeting grounds: The tourist papers*. London: Routledge. doi:10.4324/9780203412145

MacCannell, D. (2001). Tourist agency. *Tourist Studies*, *1*(1), 23–37. doi:10.1177/146879760100100102

Maccannell, D. (2011). *The Ethics of Sightseeing. Dean Maccannell.* Los Angeles, CA: University of California Press. doi:10.1525/california/9780520257825.001.0001

Maguire, R. (2014). The limits of Haitian so sovereignty: Haiti through clear eyes. *The Journal Haitian Studies*, *20*(2), 165–177. doi:10.1353/jhs.2014.0027

Malloy, D. C., & Fennell, D. A. (1998). Codes of ethics and tourism: An exploratory content analysis. *Tourism Management*, *19*(5), 453–461. doi:10.1016/S0261-5177(98)00042-9

Markwell, K. (2015). Exploited elephants and pampered pets: Reflecting on tourism–animal relationships. *Animals and Tourism: Understanding Diverse Relationships*, *67*, 288.

Marschall, S. (2014). Tourism and remembrance: The journey into the self and its past. *Journal of Tourism and Cultural Change*, *12*(4), 335–348. doi:10.1080/14766825.2014.890208

Marx, K. (1967). Capital Volume 1: the process of capitalist production. New York: International Publishers.

Marx, K. (1973). *Grundriss. Foundations of the Critique of Political Economy*. Harmondsworth, UK: Penguin Books.

Marx, K., & Engels, F. (1902). *Wage-labor and capital*. New York: Labor News Company.

Marx, K., & Engels, F. (1959). *The communist manifesto* (Vol. 6008). New York Labor News Company.

Massey, D. (2005). *For space*. London, UK: Sage.

Masters, R. E. L. (1966). *Forbidden sexual behavior and morality: An objective re-examination of perverse sex practices in different cultures*. New York: Matrix House.

Matthews, M. (1994). *The horseman*. Amherst, NY: Prometheus Books.

McGehee, N. G., & Santos, C. A. (2005). Social change, discourse and volunteer tourism. *Annals of Tourism Research*, *32*(3), 760–779. doi:10.1016/j.annals.2004.12.002

McGehee, N., & Norman, W. (2002). Alternative Tourism as Impetus for Consciousness-Raising. *Tourism Analysis*, *6*, 239–251.

McLennan, S. (2014). Networks for Development: Volunteer Tourism, Information and Communications Technology, and the Paradoxes of Alternative Development. *PoLAR: Political and Legal Anthropology Review*, *37*(1), 48–68. doi:10.1111/plar.12050

McMichael, P. (2016). *Development and social change: A global perspective*. Thousand Oaks, CA: Sage Publications.

McNaughton, D. (2006). The host as uninvited guest: Hospitality, violence and tourism. *Annals of Tourism Research*, *33*(3), 645–665. doi:10.1016/j.annals.2006.03.015

Mead, G. H. (2009). *Mind, self, and society: From the standpoint of a social behaviourist* (Vol. 1). Chicago, IL: University of Chicago press.

Medeiros, B. F. (2015). *Touring Poverty*. Abingdon, UK: Routledge.

Meethan, K. (2001). *Place, Culture, Consumption*. Basingstoke, UK: Palgrave. doi:10.1007/978-1-349-87747-8_8

Mellor, A. P., & Shilling, C. (1993). Modernity, self-identity and the sequestration of death. *Sociology*, *27*(3), 411–431. doi:10.1177/0038038593027003005

Merleau-Ponty, M. (1996). *Phenomenology of perception*. New Dehli: Motilal Banarsidass Publisher.

Meschkank, J. (2011). Investigations into slum tourism in Mumbai: Poverty tourism and the tensions between different constructions of reality. *GeoJournal*, *76*(1), 47–62. doi:10.1007/s10708-010-9401-7

Metraux, A. (1958). *Le vodou haitien*. Paris: Gallimard.

Mezirow, J. et al. (1990). *Fostering critical reflection in adulthood: A guide to transformative and emancipatory learning*. San Francisco, CA: Jossey Bass.

Miles, S. (2014). Battlefield sites as dark tourism attractions: An analysis of experience. *Journal of Heritage Tourism*, *9*(2), 134–147. doi:10.1080/1743873X.2013.871017

Miles, W. F. (2002). Auschwitz: Museum interpretation and darker tourism. *Annals of Tourism Research*, *29*(4), 1175–1178. doi:10.1016/S0160-7383(02)00054-3

Miletski, H. (2005a). A history of bestiality. In A. M. Beetz & A. L. Podberscek (Eds.), *Bestiality and zoophilia: Sexual relations with animals* (pp. 1–22). West Lafayette, IN: Purdue University Press.

Miletski, H. (2005b). Is zoophilia a sexual orientation? A study. In A. M. Beetz & A. L. Podberscek (Eds.), *Bestiality and zoophilia: Sexual relations with animals* (pp. 82–97). West Lafayette, IN: Purdue University Press.

Minic, N. (2012). Development of dark tourism in contemporary society. *J. Geogr. Institute Cvijic*, *62*(3), 81–103. doi:10.2298/IJGI1203081M

Mitin, I. I. (2006). Tourist myths and complex characteristics of the territory in human geography. *Turizm i kul'turnoe nasledie*, *3*, 103–110.

Moeller, M. (2005). *Battlefield tourism in South Africa with special reference to Isandwlana and Rorke's drift KwaZulu-Natal* (Unpublished MPhil Thesis). Faculty of Economic and Management Sciences, University of Pretoria.

Moscardo, G. (2010). The Shaping of tourist experience: the importance of stories and themes. In M. Morgan, P. Lugosi, & J. R. Ritchie (Eds.), *The tourism and leisure experience: Consumer and managerial perspectives* (pp. 43–58). Bristol: Channel View Publications.

Mowatt, R. A. (2011). Visiting death and life: Dark tourism and slave castles. *Annals of Tourism Research, 38*(4), 1410–1434.

Mowforth, M., & Munt, I. (2015). *Tourism and sustainability: Development, globalisation and new tourism in the third world.* Routledge.

Mugnano, S., & Carnelli, F. (2017). A "New Normality" for Residents and Tourists: How Can a Disaster Become a Tourist Resource? In Tourism in the City (pp. 321-332). Berlin: Springer Int. Publ.

Nadeau, B. (2012, December 1). Germany weighs bestiality ban amid rise of pet porn, animal brothels. *The Daily Beast.*

Nadeau, J., Heslop, L., OReilly, N., & Luk, P. (2008). Destination in a country image context. *Annals of Tourism Research, 35*(1), 84–106. doi:10.1016/j.annals.2007.06.012

Nekljudov, S. (n.d.). *FAQ: Mythology in the culture: 7 facts about the role of myth in the history of culture and myth-making in the modern world.* Retrieved September 4, 2016, from http://postnauka.ru/faq/6599

Neumann, F. (1966). *The democratic and the authoritarian state: Essays in political and legal theory.* New York, NY: Free Press.

New York Daily Sun. (2013, May 31). *Is bestiality legal?* Retrieved October 28, 2013, from http://www.newyorkdailysun.com/is-beastiality-legal/

Niemelä, T. (2010). *Motivation Factors in Dark Tourism - Case: House of Terror.* Available from: http://www.theseus.fi/bitstream/handle/10024/14984/Niemela_Titta.pdf

Norridge, Z. (2009). Finding a home in Hackney? Re-imagining narratives of slavery through a multicultural community museum space. *African and Black Diaspora: International Journal (Toronto, Ont.), 2*(2), 167–179.

Novelli, M. (2007). *Niche Tourism: contemporary issues, trends and cases.* London: Routledge.

O'Toole, W. (2011). *Events Feasibility and Development.* Oxford, UK: Elsevier.

Ohe, Y. (2010). Barriers to Change in Rural tourism. In Managing Change in Tourism: Creating opportunities – overcoming obstacles. Academic Press.

Olsen, K. (2002). Authenticity as a Concept in Tourism Research. *Tourist Studies, 2*(2), 159–182. doi:10.1177/146879702761936644

Ong, F., Lockstone-Binney, L., King, B., & Smith, K. A. (2014). The Future of Volunteer Tourism in the Asia-Pacific Region Alternative Prospects. *Journal of Travel Research, 53*(6), 680–692. doi:10.1177/0047287514532365

Ong, F., Pearlman, M., & Lockstone-Binney, L. (2011). An examination of not-for-profit volunteer tourism sending organisations guiding considerations that influence volunteer tourism programmes. *World Leisure Journal*, *53*(4), 296–311. doi:10.1080/04419057.2011.630787

Orams, M. B. (2002). Feeding wildlife as a tourism attraction: A review of issues and impacts. *Tourism Management*, *23*(3), 281–293. doi:10.1016/S0261-5177(01)00080-2

Ordanini, A., Parasuraman, A., & Rubera, G. (2013). Service innovation viewed through a service-dominant logic lens: A conceptual framework and empirical analysis. *Journal of Service Research*, *14*(1), 3–23. doi:10.1177/1094670510385332

Page, S. J. (2013). *Tourism management. An introduction* (4th ed.). Abingdon, UK: Routledge.

Panakera, C. S. (2007). World War II and tourism development in Solomon Islands. In C. Ryan (Ed.), *Battlefield tourism: History, place and interpretation* (pp. 125–141). The Netherlands: Elsevier. doi:10.1016/B978-0-08-045362-0.50017-8

Park, Y. P. (2014). *Heritage Tourism*. Abingdon, UK: Routledge.

Pilato, M., Bellia, C., & Séraphin, H. (2016). *Street food and food safety: A driver for tourism?* PEEC2016 International Conference, Bucharest University of Economic Studies, Bucharest, Romania.

Podoshen, J. S. (2013). Dark tourism motivations: Simulation, emotional contagion and topographic comparison. *Tourism Management*, *35*, 263–271. doi:10.1016/j.tourman.2012.08.002

Podoshen, J. S., Venkatesh, V., Wallin, J., Andrzejewski, S. A., & Jin, Z. (2015). Dystopian dark tourism: An exploratory examination. *Tourism Management*, *51*, 316–328. doi:10.1016/j.tourman.2015.05.002

Pollock, G. (2003). Holocaust tourism: being there, looking back and the ethics of spatial memory. In D. Crouch & N. Lübbren (Eds.), *Visual culture and tourism* (pp. 175–190). Oxford.

Popper, K. (1993). *Unended Quest: An Intellectual Autobiography, Karl Popper*. London: Routledge.

Popper, K. (2013). *Realism and the aim of science: From the postscript to the logic of scientific discovery*. Abingdon, UK: Routledge.

Popper, K. R. (1968). Epistemology without a knowing subject. *Studies in Logic and the Foundations of Mathematics*, *52*, 333–373. doi:10.1016/S0049-237X(08)71204-7

Poria, Y. (2007). Establishing cooperation between Israel and Poland to save Auschwitz Concentration Camp: Globalising the responsibility for the Massacre. *International Journal of Tourism Policy*, *1*(1), 45–57. doi:10.1504/IJTP.2007.013897

Poria, Y., Reichel, A., & Biran, A. (2006). Heritage site management: Motivations and expectations. *Annals of Tourism Research*, *33*(1), 162–178. doi:10.1016/j.annals.2005.08.001

Potts, T. J. (2012). Dark tourismand the kitschificationof 9/11. *Tourist Studies*, *12*(3), 232–249. doi:10.1177/1468797612461083

Powell, R., & Iankova, K. (2016). Dark London: Dimensions and characteristics of dark tourism supply in the UK capital. *Anatolia, 27*(3), 339–351. doi:10.1080/13032917.2016.1191764

Raine, R. (2013). A dark tourist spectrum. *International Journal of Culture, Tourism and Hospitality Research, 7*(3), 242-256.

Rapson, J. (2012). Emotional memory formation at former Nazi concentration camp sites. In M. Robinson & D. Picard (Eds.), *Emotion in motion: Tourism, affect and transformation* (pp. 161–178). London, UK: Routledge.

Reed, K. (2009). The social construction of volunteer non-governmental organization worker identities: Preliminary analysis of effects and implications for information behaviors. *Proceedings of the American Society for Information Science and Technology, 46*(1), 1–4. doi:10.1002/meet.2009.1450460336

Reijnders, S. (2009). Watching the detectives inside the guilty landscapes of Inspector Morse, Baantjer and Wallander. *European Journal of Communication, 24*(2), 165–181. doi:10.1177/0267323108101830

Riesman, D. (2001). *The lonely crowd.* New Haven, CT: Yale University Press.

Robb, E. M. (2009). Violence and recreation: Vacationing in the realm of dark tourism. *Anthropology and Humanism, 34*(1), 51–60. doi:10.1111/j.1548-1409.2009.01023.x

Robertson, R. (1995). Glocalization: Time-space and homogeneity-heterogeneity. In M. Featherstone, L. Scott, & R. Robertson (Eds.), *Global modernities*. London, UK: Sage. doi:10.4135/9781446250563.n2

Rojek, C. (1997). Indexing, dragging and the social construction of tourist sights. In C. Rojek & J. Urry (Eds.), Touring cultures: Transformations of travel and theory (pp. 52–74). London, UK: Routledge.

Rojek, C. (1993). *Ways of escape*. Basingstoke, UK: Macmillan. doi:10.1057/9780230373402

Rojek, C. (1997). Indexing, dragging and the social construction of tourist sights. In C. Rojek & J. Urry (Eds.), *Touring cultures: Transformations of travel and theory* (pp. 52–74). London, UK: Routledge. doi:10.4324/9780203427736

Roochnik, D. (2008). *Beautiful city: the dialectical character of Plato's" Republic*. Ithaca: Cornell University Press.

Rosenbaum, M. S., & Wong, I. A. (2007). The darker side of the servicescape: Investigating the Bali Syndrome. *International Journal of Culture, Tourism and Hospitality Research, 1*(2), 161–174.

Ross, J. I. (2012). Touring imprisonment: A descriptive statistical analysis of prison museums. *Tourism Management Perspectives, 4*, 113–118. doi:10.1016/j.tmp.2012.07.001

Ryan, C. (2005). Dark tourism–an introduction. *Taking Tourism to the limits: issues, conceptys and managerial perspectives*, 187-190.

Ryan, C., & Kohli, R. (2006). The Buried village, New Zealand–An example of dark tourism? *Asia Pacific Journal of Tourism Research, 11*(3), 211–226. doi:10.1080/10941660600753240

Santana, A. (2006). *Antropología y Turismo*. Barcelona: Ariel.

Santos Filho, J. (n.d.). Hospitalidade no Brasil Imperio: a visao o naturalista George Gardner. *Revista Brasileira de Pesquisa em turismo, 2*(2), 3-19.

Sather-Wagstaff, J. (2011). Heritage that hurts: Tourists in the memoryscapes of September 11 (Vol. 4). Left Coast Press.

Sather-Wagstaff, J. (2016). *Heritage that hurts: Tourists in the memoryscapes of September 11*. Abingdon, UK: Routledge.

Schlesinger, L. B. (2004). *Sexual murder: Catathymic and compulsive homicides*. Boca Raton, FL: CRC Press.

Schneider, M. R., Schulze-Bentrop, C., & Paunescu, M. (2010). Mapping the Institutional Capital of High-Tech Firms: A Fuzzy-Set Analysis of Capitalist Variety and Export Performance. *Journal of International Business Studies, 41*(2), 246–266. doi:10.1057/jibs.2009.36

Schön, D. A. (1983). *The reflective practitioner: how professionals think in action*. London: Temple-Smith.

Schroeder, T. (2006). Chapter. In L. Faucher & C. Tappolet (Eds.), An unexpected pleasure (pp. 255–272). Alberta, Canada: University of Calgary Press.

Scruton, D. (1986). *Sociophobics: The anthropology of fear*. Boulder, Colo.: Westview Press.

Seaton, A. (2011). *Social affiliations and emergent motivations in thanatourism behaviour at Lansdown Tower and Cemetery*. Paper presented at Tourism Imaginaries, Berkeley University of California, Berkeley, CA. Retrieved From: http://www.tourismstudies.org/tourismimaginariesAuthors.htm

Seaton, A. V. (1996). Guided by the dark: From thanatopsis to thanatourism. *International Journal of Heritage Studies, 2*(4), 234–244. doi:10.1080/13527259608722178

Seaton, A. V. (1999). War and thana-tourism: Waterloo 1815–1914. *Annals of Tourism Research, 26*(1), 130–158. doi:10.1016/S0160-7383(98)00057-7

Seaton, A. V. (2000). Another Weekend Away Looking for Dead Bodies…: Battlefield Tourism on the Somme and in Flanders. *Tourism Recreation Research, 25*(3), 63–77. doi:10.1080/02508281.2000.11014926

Seaton, A., & Lennon, J. (2004). Thanatourism in the early 21st century: Moral panics, ulterior motives and alterior desires. In T. V. Singh (Ed.), *New horizons in tourism: Strange experiences and stranger practices* (pp. 63–82). Wallingford, UK: Cabi. doi:10.1079/9780851998633.0063

Seaton, T. (2009a). Thanatourism and its discontents. An appraisal of a decade's work with some future issues and directions. In J. Tazim & M. Robinson (Eds.), *The sage book of tourism studies* (pp. 521–542). London, UK: Sage. doi:10.4135/9780857021076.n29

Seaton, T. (2009b). Purposeful otherness: Management implications. In R. Sharpley & P. R. Stone (Eds.), *The darker side of travel: The theory and practice of dark tourism* (pp. 75–109). Bristol, UK: Channel View Publications.

Selwyn, T. (1996). Introduction. In T. Selwyn (Ed.), In the Tourist Image. Myths and Myth Making in Tourism (pp. 1–32). Chichester, UK: Wiley.

Séraphin, H., & Nolan, E. (2014). Voodoo in Haiti: A Religious Ceremony at the Service of the 'Houngan' Called 'Tourism'. In Rituals and traditional events in the modern world. New-York: Routledge.

Séraphin, H., Butcher, J. & Konstanje, M. (2016). Challenging the negative images of Haiti at a pre-visit stage using Visual Online Learning Materials. *Journal of Policy Research in Tourism, Leisure and Events*. doi: 10.1080/19407963.2016.1261146

Séraphin, H., Gowreesunkar, V. & Ambaye, M. (2016). The Blakeley Model applied to improving a tourist destination: The case of Haiti. *Journal of Destination Marketing Management.* doi: 10.1016/j.jdmm.2016.07.004

Séraphin, H. (2017). Assessing dark tourism as a sustainable economic activity for emerging destinations using a multi criteria approach. In M. E. Korstanje & B. Handayani (Eds.), *Gazing at death*. Nova Science Publishers, Inc.

Shackley, M. (2001). *The legend of Robin Hood: myth, inauthenticity, and tourism development in Nottingham, England. In Hosts and guests revisited: Tourism issues of the 21st century* (pp. 315–322). Cognizant Communication.

Sharpley, R. (2005). Travels to the edge of darkness: towards a typology of dark tourism. *Taking tourism to the limits: Issues, concepts and managerial perspectives*, 217-228.

Sharpley, R. (2009a). Shedding light on dark tourism: An introduction. In R. Sharpley & P. R. Stone (Eds.), *The darker side of travel: The theory and practice of dark tourism* (pp. 3–22). Bristol, UK: Channel View Publications.

Sharpley, R. (2009b). Dark tourism and political ideology: Towards a governance model. In R. Sharpley & P. R. Stone (Eds.), *The darker side of travel: The theory and practice of dark tourism* (pp. 145–166). Bristol, UK: Channel View Publications.

Sharpley, R., & Stone, P. (2009a). Representing the macabre: Interpretation, kitschification and authenticity. In R. Sharpley & P. R. Stone (Eds.), *The darker side of travel: The theory and practice of dark tourism* (pp. 109–128). Bristol, UK: Channel View Publications.

Sharpley, R., & Stone, P. (2009b). Life, death and dark tourism: Future research directions and concluding comments. In R. Sharpley & P. R. Stone (Eds.), *The darker side of travel: The theory and practice of dark tourism* (pp. 247–251). Bristol, UK: Channel View Publications.

Sharpley, R., & Sundaram, P. (2005). Tourism: A sacred journey? The case of ashram tourism, India. *International Journal of Tourism Research*, *7*(3), 161–171. doi:10.1002/jtr.522

Shondell Miller, D., & Gonzalez, C. (2013). When death is the destination: The business of death tourism–despite legal and social implications. *International Journal of Culture, Tourism and Hospitality Research*, *7*(3), 293–306.

Singer, P. (2001, March 12). *Heavy petting*. Retrieved January 25, 2014, from http://www.nerve.com/Opinions/Singer/heavyPetting/main.asp

Skinner, J. (2012). *Writing the dark side of Travel*. New York: Berghan Books.

Skoll, G. (2014). *Dialectics in Social Thought: The Present Crisis*. New York: Palgrave Macmillan. doi:10.1057/9781137387066

Slade, P. (2003). Gallipoli thanatourism: The meaning of ANZAC. *Annals of Tourism Research*, *30*(4), 779–794. doi:10.1016/S0160-7383(03)00025-2

Slyusareva, N. A. *(2015)*. The conflict of myth's interpretations in the modern museum practice. *Cennosti i smysly*, *6*(40), 138-146. (in Russian)

Smith, V. L., & Font, X. (2014). Volunteer tourism, greenwashing and understanding responsible marketing using market signalling theory. *Journal of Sustainable Tourism*, *22*(6), 942–963. doi:10.1080/09669582.2013.871021

Snider, B. (2012, February 21). Popularity of animal brothels increasing in Germany. *The Examiner*. Retrieved January 27, 2014, from http://www.examiner.com/article/popularity-of-animal-brothels-increasing-germany-petitions

Snow, N. E. (2010). *Virtue as social intelligence: An empirically grounded theory*. Abingdon, UK: Routledge.

Solomon, A. (2015). Authenticity and simulation in post tourism. *Synergy*, *11*(1), 41–53.

Solomon, R. (2008). *True to our feelings: What our emotions are really telling us*. New York, NY: Oxford University Press. doi:10.1093/acprof:oso/9780195368536.001.0001

Spokane Spokesman-Review. (2010, April 18). In brief: Officials allege beastiality at farm. *Spokane Spokeman Review*. Retrieved January 27, 2014, from http://www.spokesman.com/stories/2010/apr/18/in-brief-officials-allege-bestiality-at-farm/

Stephen, C. & Hall, A. (2005, December 20). Stalin's half-man, half-ape-super-warriors. *The Scotsman*.

Stevenson, J. (2000). Dead famous: The life and movies of cinema's most exploited figure, Bodil Joensen. In J. Stevenson (Ed.), *Fleshpot: Cinema's Sexual Myth Makers & Taboo Breakers* (pp. 177–190). Manchester, UK: Headpress.

Stocker, M., & Hageman, E. (1996). *Valuing Emotions*. Cambridge, UK: Cambridge University Press.

Stokes, R. (2015). *Can dark tourism ever be a good thing?*. Available from: http://newint.org/features/web-exclusive/2013/01/21/dark-tourism/

Stokke, O. S. (2007). Qualitative comparative analysis, shaming, and international regime effectiveness. *Journal of Business Research*, *60*(5), 501–511. doi:10.1016/j.jbusres.2007.01.003

Stone, P. (2005). *Review: Dark tourism –cashing in on tragedy?* Paper presented at the Tourism Society Seminar Event, London, UK. Retrieved from: www.dark-tourism.org.uk

Stone, P. (2007). *Dark tourism: the ethics of exploiting tragedy*. Available from: http://works.bepress.com/cgi/viewcontent.cgi?article=1020&context=philip_stone

Stone, P. (2010). *Death, dying and dark tourism in contemporary society: A theoretical and empirical analysis* (Unpublished doctoral dissertation). University of Central Lancashire, UK. Retrieved from: http://clok.uclan.ac.uk/1870/

Stone, P. (2010). *Death, Dying and Dark Tourism in Contemporary Society: A Theoretical and Empirical Analysis*. Available from: http://clok.uclan.ac.uk/1870/1/StonePPhD_thesis_final.pdf

Stone, P. (n.d.). Enlightening the "dark" in dark tourism. *AHI*, 22-24.

Stone, P. R. (2010). *Death, Dying and Dark Tourism in contemporary society: the theoretical and empirical analysis* (Doctoral Thesis). University of Central Lancashire. Available at https://core.ac.uk/download/pdf/6677.pdf

Stone, P., & Sharpley, R. (2008). *Consuming Dark Tourism: A Thanatological Perspective*. Academic Press.

Stone, P. (2006). A dark tourism spectrum: Towards a typology of death and macabre related tourist sites, attractions and exhibitions. *Tourism: An Interdisciplinary International Journal (Toronto, Ont.)*, *54*(2).

Stone, P. (2006). A dark tourism spectrum: Towards a typology of death and macabre related tourist sites, attractions and exhibitions. *Tourism: An Interdisciplinary International Journal*, *54*(2), 145–160.

Stone, P. (2009). "It's bloody guide" - Fun, fear and a lighter side of dark tourism at the dungeon visitor attractions, UK. In R. Sharpley & P. Stone (Eds.), *The darker side of travel: The theory and practice of dark tourism* (pp. 167–185). Bristol, UK: Channel View Publications.

Stone, P. (2009a). Dark tourism: Morality and new moral spaces. In R. Sharpley & P. R. Stone (Eds.), *The darker side of travel: The theory and practice of dark tourism* (pp. 56–72). Bristol, UK: Channel View Publications.

Stone, P. (2009b). "It's a bloody guide": Fun, fear and a lighter side of dark tourism at the dungeon visitor attractions, UK. In R. Sharpley & P. R. Stone (Eds.), *The darker side of travel: The theory and practice of dark tourism* (pp. 167–185). Bristol, UK: Channel View Publications.

Stone, P. (2013). Dark tourism scholarship: A critical review. *International Journal of Culture, Tourism and Hospitality Research*, *7*(3), 307–318. doi:10.1108/IJCTHR-06-2013-0039

Stone, P. (2013). Dark tourism scholarship: A critical review. *International Journal of Culture. Tourism and Hospitality Research*, *7*(3), 307–318.

Stone, P. R. (2011). Dark tourism: Towards a new post-disciplinary research agenda. *International Journal of Tourism Anthropology*, *1*(3-4), 318–332. doi:10.1504/IJTA.2011.043713

Stone, P. R. (2012). Dark tourism and significant other death: Towards a model of mortality mediation. *Annals of Tourism Research*, *39*(3), 1565–1587. doi:10.1016/j.annals.2012.04.007

Stone, P., & Sharpley, R. (2008). Consuming dark tourism: A thanatological perspective. *Annals of Tourism Research*, *35*(2), 574–595. doi:10.1016/j.annals.2008.02.003

Stone, P., & Sharpley, R. (2009). *Darker Side of Travel: The Theory and Practice of Dark Tourism (Aspects of tourism)*. Channel View Publications.

Strange, C., & Kempa, M. (2003). Shades of dark tourism: Alcatraz and Robben Island. *Annals of Tourism Research*, *30*(2), 386–405. doi:10.1016/S0160-7383(02)00102-0

Sugden, R. (2005). *The Economics of Rights, Cooperation and Welfare*. Hampshire, UK: Palgrave Macmillan. doi:10.1057/9780230536791

Sullivan, J. (2005, July 16). Videotapes show bestiality, Enumclaw police say. *Seattle Times*. Retrieved January 27, 2014, from http://seattletimes.com/html/localnews/2002384648_farm16m.html

Svendsen, L. (2008). *A philosophy of fear*. Chicago: Reaktion Books.

Takahashi, Y. (1988). Aokigahara-jukai: Suicide and Amnesia in Mt. Fujis Black Forest. *Suicide & Life-Threatening Behavior*, *18*(2), 164–175. doi:10.1111/j.1943-278X.1988.tb00150.x PMID:3420643

Tanaś, S. (2014). Tourism 'Death Space' and Thanatourism in Poland. *Current Issues of Tourism Research*, *3*(1), 22–27.

Tarlow, P. E. (2005). Dark tourism. Niche Tourism, 47. In Niche tourism: contemporary issues, trends and cases. London, Routledge.

Tarlow, P. (2005). Dark tourism: The appealing "dark" side of tourism and more. In M. Novelli (Ed.), *Niche tourism: Contemporary issues, trends and cases* (pp. 47–57). Oxford, UK: Elsevier. doi:10.1016/B978-0-7506-6133-1.50012-3

Tarlow, P. E. (2007). Dark tourism: the appealing dark side of tourism and more. In M. Novelli (Ed.), *Niche tourism* (pp. 47–58). London: Routledge.

Taş, İ. (2016). Türkiye'nin hüzün turizmi profili. *The Journal of Academic Social Science Studies International Journal of Social Science*, *48*, 183–198.

Thirkettle, A., & Korstanje, M. E. (2013). Creating a new epistemiology for tourism and hospitality disciplines. *International Journal of Qualitative Research in Services*, *1*(1), 13–34. doi:10.1504/IJQRS.2013.054342

Thomson, I. (2004). *Bonjour blanc, a journey through Haiti*. London: Vintage.

Timothy, D. J., & Boyd, S. W. (2006). Heritage tourism in the 21st century: Valued traditions and new perspectives. *Journal of Heritage Tourism, 1*(1), 1-16.

Timpf, K. (2013, March 5). *Yale hosts workshop teaching sensitivity to bestiality*. Retrieved October 8, 2013, from campusreform.org/blog.

Tinker, I. (1997). *Street Foods: Urban Food and Employment in Developing Countries*. New York: Oxford University Press.

Tinson, J., Saren, M. A. J., & Roth, B. E. (2015). Exploring the role of dark tourism in the creation of national identity of young Americans. *Journal of Marketing Management*, *31*(7-8), 856–880. doi:10.1080/0267257X.2014.995207

Toribio Camargo, A., Castella Cordoba, P., & Serrano Orquin, I. (2005). Determinación de las preferencias de los clientes internacionales para la practica del turismo rural en la Republica de Cuba. *Pasos.*, *3*(2), 283–295.

Tribe, J. (2010). Tribes, territories and networks in the tourism academy. *Annals of Tourism Research*, *37*(1), 7–33. doi:10.1016/j.annals.2009.05.001

Tucker, H. (2016). Empathy and tourism: Limits and possibilities. *Annals of Tourism Research*, *57*, 31–43. doi:10.1016/j.annals.2015.12.001

Türkiye Diyarbakır Askeri Cezaevi İle yüzleşiyor. Diyarbakır Askeri Cezaevi Gerçekleri Araştırma ve Adalet Komisyonu Raporu. (n.d.). Retrieved From: http://bianet.org/files/doc_files/000/000/370/original/111203-DC-Sempozyum_Sunum_%C3%96zetleri.pdf

Tzanelli, R. (2016). *Thana Tourism and the cinematic representation of risk*. Abingdon, UK: Routledge.

Tzanelli, R. (2016). *Thana tourism and the representation of risk*. Abingdon, UK: Routledge.

Tzanelli, R. (2016). *Thanatourism and Cinematic Representations of Risk*. Abingdon, UK: Routledge.

Tzanelli, R. (2016). *Thana-Tourism and Cinematic Representations of Risk: Screening the End of Tourism*. Abingdon, UK: Routledge.

Uriely, N. (2005). The tourist experience: Conceptual developments. *Annals of Tourism Research*, *32*(1), 199–216. doi:10.1016/j.annals.2004.07.008

Urry, J. (1990). *The Tourist Gaze*. London, UK: SAGE Publishers.

Urry, J. (2002). *The tourist gaze*. London: Sage.

Urry, J., & Larsen, J. (2011). *The tourist gaze 3.0*. London: Sage. doi:10.4135/9781446251904

Verma, S., & Jain, R. (2013). Exploiting Tragedy for Tourism. *Research on Humanities and Social Sciences, 3*(8), 9–13.

Virilio, P. (2010). *University of disaster*. Cambridge, UK: Polity Press.

Vis, B., Woldendorp, J., & Keman, H. (2007). Do miracles exist? Analyzing economic performance comparatively. *Journal of Business Research, 60*(5), 531–538. doi:10.1016/j.jbusres.2007.01.006

Wagner, L. R. (2015). *Hold tight, don't let go*. New York: Amulet Books.

Waitt, G. (1999). Naturalizing the primitive: A critique of marketing Australias indigenous peoples as hunter-gatherers. *Tourism Geographies, 1*(2), 142–163. doi:10.1080/14616689908721306

Wallace, W (1972). *Causality and Scientific explanation*. Ann Arbor, MI: The University of Michigan Press.

Walter, T. (2009a). Dark tourism: Mediating between the dead and the living. In R. Sharpley & P. R. Stone (Eds.), *The darker side of travel: The theory and practice of dark tourism* (pp. 39–55). Bristol, UK: Channel View Publications.

Walter, T. (2009b). Disaster, modernity, and the media. In K. Garces-Foley (Ed.), *Death and religion in a changing world* (pp. 265–282). Armonk, NY: Sharpe.

Wang, N. (1999). Rethinking Authenticity in Tourism Experience. *Annals of Tourism Research, 26*(2), 349–370. doi:10.1016/S0160-7383(98)00103-0

Wearing, S. (2005). *Voluntourism - Can It Influence Mass Tourism?* Retrieved 1 September 2016, from http://www.Voluntourism.org/news-studyandresearch1105.htm

Wearing, S., & McGehee, N. G. (2013a). Volunteer tourism: A review. *Tourism Management, 38*, 120–130. doi:10.1016/j.tourman.2013.03.002

Wearing, S., & McGehee, N. G. (Eds.). (2013b). *International volunteer tourism: Integrating travellers and communities*. CABI. doi:10.1079/9781845936969.0000

Weeden, C., & Boluk, C. (2014). *Managing Ethical Consumption in Tourism*. New York: Routledge.

West, B. (2010). Dialogical memorialization, international travel and the public sphere: A cultural sociology of commemoration and tourism at the First World War Gallipoli battlefields. *Tourist Studies, 10*(3), 209–225. doi:10.1177/1468797611407756

White, G. M. (2015). Is Paris burning? Touring Americas good war in France. *History & Memory, 27*(2), 74–103. doi:10.2979/histmemo.27.2.74

White, J. H. (2007). Evidence of primary, secondary and collateral paraphilias left at serial murder and sex offender crime scenes. *Journal of Forensic Sciences, 52*(5), 1194–1201. doi:10.1111/j.1556-4029.2007.00523.x PMID:17681002

White, L., & Frew, E. (2013). *Dark tourism and place identity: managing and interpreting dark places* (Vol. 37). London: Routledge.

White, L., & Frew, E. (2013). *Dark Tourism: place and identity: managing and interpreting dark places*. London: Routledge.

Wight, A. C. (2006). Philosophical and methodological praxes in dark tourism: Controversy, contention and the evolving paradigm. *Journal of Vacation Marketing*, *12*(2), 119–129. doi:10.1177/1356766706062151

WikiIslam.net. (n.d.). *Islam and beastiality.* Retrieved January 27, 2014, from http://www.wikiislam.net/wiki/Islam_and_Beastiality/

Wikipedia. (n.d.a). *Bodil Joensen.* Retrieved December 10, 2013, from http://en.wikipedia.org/wiki/Bodil_Joensen

Wikipedia. (n.d.b). *Zoophilia and the law.* Retrieved January 27, 2014, from http://en.wikipedia.org/wiki/zoophilia_and_the_law

Wilbert, C., & Hansen, R. (2009). *Walks in spectral space: East London crime scene tourism. In Strange spaces: Explorations into mediated obscurity* (pp. 187–203). Farnham, UK: Ashgate Pub.

Wild, C. (2011, July 26). Dominican Republic's first animal farm. *News365.*

Wilkinson, P. F. (2010). *Review of* "The darker side of travel: The theory and practice of dark tourism", by Sharpley and Stone. *e-Review of Tourism Research, 8*(1).

Willson, G. B., McIntosh, A. J., & Zahra, A. L. (2013). Tourism and spirituality: A phenomenological analysis. *Annals of Tourism Research*, *42*, 150–168. doi:10.1016/j.annals.2013.01.016

Wilson, J. (2011). Australian prison tourism: A question of narrative integrity. *History Compass*, *9*(8), 562–571. doi:10.1111/j.1478-0542.2011.00789.x

Wilson, J. Z. (2004). Dark tourism and the celebrity prisoner: Front and back regions in representations of an Australian historical prison. *Journal of Australian Studies*, *28*(82), 1–13. doi:10.1080/14443050409387951

Wilson, J. Z. (2008). *Prison: Cultural memory and dark tourism.* New York: Peter Lang.

Winn, P. (2011, December 1). *Senate approves bill that legalizes sodomy and bestiality in U.S. Military.* Retrieved January 27, 2014, from http://cnsnews.com/news/article/senate-approves-bill-legalizes-sodomy-and-bestiality-us-military

Winter, C. (2009). Tourism, social memory and the Great War. *Annals of Tourism Research*, *36*(4), 607–626. doi:10.1016/j.annals.2009.05.002

Wise, N. A. (2011). Post-war tourism and the imaginative geographies of Bosnia and Herzegovina and Croatia. *European Journal of Tourism Research*, *4*(1), 5.

Wnd.com. (2006, September 28). *PETA says barnyard brothels 'revolting'*. Retrieved January 27, 2014, from http://www.wnd.com/2006/09/38123/

Woodside, A. G., & Baxter, R. (2013). Achieving accuracy, generalization-to-contexts, and complexity in theories of business-to-business decision processes. *Industrial Marketing Management*, *42*(3), 382–393. doi:10.1016/j.indmarman.2013.02.004

Yalçınkaya, A. (2011). Hafıza savaşlarından sahiplenilmiş şehitliğe: Madımak katliamı örnek olayı. *Mülkiye*, *66*(3), 333–394.

Yamaç, Z. (2015). Sakarya destinasyonunun imaj algısına yönelik bir araştırma. *İşletme Bilimi Dergisi, 3*(2), 85-61.

Yankovska, G., & Hannam, K. (2014). Dark and toxic tourism in the Chernobyl exclusion zone. *Current Issues in Tourism*, *17*(10), 929–939. doi:10.1080/13683500.2013.820260

Yeoman, I. S., & Beeton, S. (2014). The State of Tourism Futures Research: An Asian Pacific Ontological Perspective. *Journal of Travel Research*, *53*(6), 675–679. doi:10.1177/0047287514551054

Yeşildağ, B. (2010). *Savaş alanları turizmi ve Gelibolu Yarımadası Tarihi Milli Parkı örneği* (Unpublished MA Thesis). Çanakkale 18 Mart University, Social Sciences Institute. Retrieved from: http://acikerisim.lib.comu.edu.tr:8080/xmlui/bitstream/handle/COMU/668/Baris_Yesildag_Tez.pdf?sequence=1

Yıldız, Z., Yıldız, S., & Aytemiz, L. (2015). Kara turizm, terör turizmi ve Türkiye potansiyeli. *İnsan ve Toplum bilimleri Araştırmaları Dergisi, 4*(2), 390-407.

Yoshida, K., Bui, H. T., & Lee, T. J. (2016). Does tourism illuminate the darkness of Hiroshima and Nagasaki? *Journal of Destination Marketing & Management*, *5*(4), 333–340. doi:10.1016/j.jdmm.2016.06.003

Young, C., & Light, D. (2016). Interrogating spaces of and for the dead as alternative space: Cemeteries, corpses and sites of dark tourism. *International Review of Social Research*, *6*(2), 61–72. doi:10.1515/irsr-2016-0009

Yuill, S. M. (2003). *Understanding visitor motivation at sites of death and disaster* (Unpublished MA Thesis). Office of Graduate Studies of Texas A&M University. Retrieved from: http://oaktrust.library.tamu.edu/bitstream/handle/1969.1/89/etd-tamu-2003C-RPTS-Yuill-1.pdf?sequence=1&isAllowed=y

Zainal, A. (2012). *Current issues in hospitality and tourism research and innovations: Proceedings of the International Hospitality and Tourism Conference, IHTC 2012*. Boca Raton: CRC Press.

Zamyatin, D. (2013). Geo-cultural branding of territories: the conceptual grounds. *Labirint. Zhurnal social'no-gumanitarnyh issledovanij*, *5*, 11-23. (in Russian)

ZETA. (2014). Retrieved January 27, 2014, from zeta-verein.de/en

Žižek, S. (2003). *The puppet and the dwarf: The perverse core of Christianity*. Cambridge, MA: MIT Press.

Žižek, S. (2008). *Violence: Six sideways reflections*. London: Verso.

Zoofur.com. (2014). Retrieved January 27, 2014, from http://www.zoofur.com/

Zotic, V., Alexandru, D. E., & Dezsi, Ş. (2014). Debate on tourism in postmodernism and beyond. *Turističko poslovanje*, (13), 79-93.

About the Contributors

Maximiliano E. Korstanje is editor in chief of International *Journal of Safety and Security in Tourism* (UP Argentina) and *International Journal of Cyber Warfare and Terrorism* (IGI-Global USA). Besides being Senior Researchers in the Department of Economics at University of Palermo, Argentina, he is a global affiliate of Tourism Crisis Management Institute (University of Florida USA), Centre for Ethnicity and Racism Studies (University of Leeds UK), The Forge (University of Lancaster and University of Leeds UK) and The International Society for Philosopher, hosted in Sheffield UK. With more than 700 published papers and 25 books, Korstanje was awarded as Outstanding Reviewer 2012. International Journal of Disaster Resilience in the Built Environment. University of Salford, UK, Outstanding Reviewer 2013. Journal of Place Management and Development. Institute of Place, Manchester Metropolitan University, UK and Reviewer Certificate of Acknowledgement 2014. International Journal of Contemporary Hospitality Management (IJCHM), University of Central Florida, US. Now he co-edits almost 10 specialized journals in such themes as human rights, mobility, tourism and terrorism. Korstanje is subject to biographical records for Marquis Who's Who in the World since 2009. He had nominated to 5 honorary doctorates for his contribution in the study of the effects of terrorism in tourism. In 2015 he was awarded as Visiting Research Fellow at School of Sociology and Social Policy, University of Leeds, UK and the University of La Habana Cuba. In 2017 is elected as Foreign Faculty Member of AMIT, Mexican Academy in the study of Tourism, which is the most prominent institution dedicated to tourism research in Mexico.

Babu P. George (PhD) in Philosophy in Management Studies. Besides serving as Associate professor at Fort Hays State University Kansas USA, Babu P. George has more than fifteen years of advanced business research, university teaching, and administrative service experience, in the US and internationally. Before joining Fort Hays State University in 2015, Dr. George has worked for Swiss Management Center University, University of Liverpool, University of Nevada Las Vegas, Alaska Pacific University, and the University of Southern Mississippi, among others. He is a visiting professor at various higher education institutions around the world. He is the editor of *International Journal of Qualitative Research in Services*. Until recently, he was the managing editor of *Journal of Tourism*. He has more than a hundred peer-reviewed and well-cited research publications to his credit. He has authored or edited more than seven books. He is a passionate observer of the complex dynamics of creative destruction that makes idea innovations possible. In his free time, he offers free consulting for the budding grassroots level entrepreneurs.

* * *

Oleg Afanasiev, PhD (Dr.Sc.) in Geography, Professor. An expert in regional and domestic tourism, tourist design technology, information technology in tourism, tourism infographic, toponymic territorial systems, theory and practice of regional nature use, pedagogical technologies in the field of tourism. Total scientific publications – more than 200, including 1 monograph, 8 study guides and textbooks, articles in scientific journals.

Lourdes Cisneros Mustelier is dean of tourism at the University of La Habana, Cuba. As key note speakers she has served in many proceedings and conferences worldwide. In her field of experience, she was visiting professor of various prestigious educational establishment as University of Andalucia, Spain; University of Valencia, Spain; University of Xian, China, University of California at Fullerton US and University of Cartagena de Indias, Colombia. Lourdes Cisneros Mustelier is member of Consejo Ampliado del Ministerio de Turismo de Cuba, and holds her doctorate in Economics, University of la Habana, Cuba.

Funda Çoban is an assistant professor at University of Aksaray/Turkey and gives lectures on sociological theory and contemporary political philosophy as well as social movements and gender issues. She did her BA and MA in International relations at Gazi University, and got her PhD in Political Science at Ankara University. She published many articles in distinguished Turkish journals and wrote some book chapters. Her PhD thesis was published under the name of A Quest in Context of the Everyday Constitution of Political: Street Politics in 2015.

Bintang Handayani's work scrutinises personification and impression management of a nation and its market offerings in consumer cultures. It tackles nation-brand images (NBI), service evaluation and international public behaviour in various contexts, including tourism and hospitality attributes, dark sites phenomenon, nation's positioning, place attachment, place identity, meanings of place from socio-cultural, authenticity, and post-modern perspectives, coupled with communication theories and media studies.

Thomas R. Panko is a Visiting Professor in the School of Criminal Justice of the University of Southern Mississippi.

Hugues Séraphin holds a PhD from the Université de Perpignan Via Domitia (France). He is also a fellow of the HEA. He joined The University of Winchester (Business School) in 2012. Dr Hugues Séraphin has been teaching for over 10 years. He started his career as a lecturer in French at Golden Hillock School (Birmingham, UK), and then taught Travel and Tourism at Kingston College (London, UK) for 6 years. He also used to be a visiting lecturer at Normandy Business School (France), Sup de Co Larochelle (France), ESC Pau (France) and Université de Perpignan Via Domitia (France). His teaching and research interests include Event Management and Tourism Management.

Index

G

H

I

L

M

N

O

P

Q

R

S

T

www.ingramcontent.com/pod-product-compliance
Lightning Source LLC
LaVergne TN
LVHW081326300926
849161LV00008B/1891